Retail Wheeling:

A Guide for End-Users

Second Edition

Retail Wheeling:

A Guide for End-Users

Second Edition

by

Peter C. Christensen, P.E., J.D.
Strategic Energy Ltd.

PennWell Books
PennWell Publishing Company
Tulsa, Oklahoma

This Book Is Not Intended To Provide Specific Legal Advice
Please note that this book is not intended to provide the reader with specific legal advice. For solutions to legal matters, please consult your attorney. The author is solely responsible for the contents of this book. Any opinions expressed are those of the author only and do not necessarily reflect those held by Strategic Energy Ltd., its employees, or its clients.

PennWell Publishing Company
1421 South Sheridan/P.O. Box 1260
Tulsa, Oklahoma 74101

Library of Congress Cataloging-in-Publication Data
Christensen, Peter C.
Retail wheeling : a guide for end-users / Peter C. Christensen.
-- 2nd ed.
p. cm.
Includes bibliographical references (p.) and index.
ISBN 0-87814-651-2
1. Electric utilities. 2. Interconnected electric utility systems. I. Title.
HD9685.A2C48 1996
333.79'32--dc20 96-9920
CIP

Printed in the United States of America

1 2 3 4 5 00 00 99 98 97

Dedication

To my Mom. 'Nuf said.

Contents

Figures

Preface to Second Edition

About one year has passed since I wrote the preface to the first edition of this book, and at that time I would have doubted that a second edition would have been required only a year later. But movement in the industry toward retail wheeling has continued to accelerate, and even the optimistic among us are continually surprised at the pace of implementation of retail electricity competition in the United States.

Some developments were anticipated. No book on a subject as dynamic as this could be expected to remain completely timely for years. The first edition of *Retail Wheeling: A Guide for End-Users* was written shortly after the Federal Energy Regulatory Commission (FERC) issued its Notice of Proposed Rulemaking on open access transmission tariffs (the "giga-NOPR"). The final rule on these tariffs was expected in the Spring of 1996, and was, in fact, issued on April 24, 1996, two years to the day after California issued its famed "Bluebook" on restructuring the industry in that state. FERC's Order 888 (so named for the street address of FERC's new offices in Washington) was very consistent with the giga-NOPR, but FERC at the same time issued a new NOPR that would already change transmission capacity reservation rules. This NOPR, along with FERC's Order 889 on transmission information, issued the same day, necessitated the need for a second edition.

The developments that were not anticipated at this point, but which also require updated analysis, are the state retail wheeling pilot programs that are in place at the time of this writing. Although Illinois was the first state in which end-users were allowed to directly and openly access competitive suppliers of electricity, the nature of that state's programs limits the value of the experience. On the other hand, the retail wheeling pilot program in New Hampshire, which was mandated by the state rather than volunteered by the utilities, offers a more focused glimpse at what may be in store for retail end-users. Therefore, these initiatives also warrant a second edition.

Even with these developments, the decision of whether to tackle another writing project at this time was a serious one. The consulting firm for which I work, and which has offered unwavering support, Strategic Energy Ltd. (SEL), is actively involved in state retail wheeling programs throughout the country. There is a temptation to spend all our time knocking on every door that may open to opportunity, but sometimes a longer view is required. For this reason, the decision has been made to spend the time to update this book and to share the lessons learned in the past year. As ever, SEL's best customer is an educated one, and this book furthers that goal.

Fortunately, most parts of this book remain applicable. The keys to taking advantage of a competitive electricity market continue to be rebundling, aggregation, and optimization of multiple suppliers. The basic principles of understanding transmission to ensure reliability and of shopping for each component of electricity service separately have been borne out by recent experiences in retail and wholesale markets. Therefore, this edition is more of a refinement than a rewrite of the first edition. It is, or course, also an update, including a revised update on state retail wheeling initiatives. As with the first edition, sections such as the state retail wheeling update (Appendix E) will also be outdated by the time this edition is published.

Some things never change. The term "retail wheeling" still evokes an emotional response in some quarters, but it will still be used herein generically to refer to retail competition as a concept. Stranded investment recovery remains the primary source of contention among stakeholders, since this comprises most of the potential cost savings to end-users and lost revenues to producers. And true to American tradition that dates back to the Constitutional Convention, the battle over state vs. Federal jurisdiction continues to be fought. The focus of these issues may evolve, but Americans seem to prefer conflict over resolution, which may be why taking on the traditional structure of the electricity industry engages the interest of so many people.

The purpose of this book is to provide electricity end-users and their suppliers with a handbook on retail wheeling. As the industry evolves and issues are resolved, this handbook will continue to be modified. Moreover, as the lessons from the new retail wheeling pilot programs are learned, and as the industry's experience with competition grows, this book will attempt to pass on those lessons and experiences.

A mentor of mine from my utility days once warned me to be careful of what I ask for, since I just might get it. I think a few players in the retail wheeling game are beginning to learn this lesson the hard way. Retail wheeling is here, and it is at least as complicated as we feared. But given the potential benefits of true competition, a prepared and knowledgeable end-user should only fear the fear itself.

P.C. Christensen

Preface to First Edition

Not only is the electricity industry undergoing fundamental changes, the *rate* of change has been escalating in recent years. While change was certainly expected, this increased pace of change may be a surprise to many people. Not because change is not needed, but simply because one would think that the sheer momentum of decades of strictly regulated monopolism and the billions of dollars involved would tend to prevent rapid change. But the forces of competition are even greater, and the cracked door to an open electricity market will never be closed.

Any fundamental shift in structure brings uncertainty, confusion, and fear. While these reactions certainly exist among the investor-owned utilities and their employees, the major customers of those utilities are equally concerned about the future of the electricity industry and the impact it will have on their costs. A good portion of my firm's consulting business is merely informing our industrial end-user clients about what is happening, how the system works now and how it will work in the future, and what they need to know to purchase power in an open market.

Therefore, the purpose of this book is to shed light on what retail wheeling is, what it means to end-users, how it will work, and what an end-user needs to know to take advantage of it. Our consulting practice has identified a large gap in knowledge between the electric utilities and their large customers, i.e., few end-users really understand what exactly it is they are buying. Therefore, when confronted with the prospect of taking control of electricity purchases, end-users are naturally apprehensive.

But end-users are not reluctant to implement retail wheeling. The potential for substantial cost reductions is so great that very few large users, or even smaller users, can afford not to push for direct retail access or some sort of competitive sourcing even if some uncertainty exists. Therefore, the intended audience for this book is those end-users that will take advantage of retail wheeling but need to know more about it.

There are a multitude of books, articles, and conferences that provide endless discussion over the issues and theories involved in a competitive electricity market. This book, on the contrary, attempts to take a more "nuts and bolts" approach to the issue. That is, it is time to discuss not whether retail wheeling can be implemented, or how certain legal, regulatory, or economic issues should be resolved, but rather how it will work. Retail wheeling is not only inevitable in most if not all states, but it is also imminent in some states, so end-users are anxious to acquire the knowledge they will need to optimize power costs in the new market.

Of course, one of the major pitfalls in writing a book about retail wheeling at this stage is that things will continue to change. While subsequent editions can be written, the rate of change far exceeds the time lag in publishing treatises such as this. Therefore, the reader is cautioned that some aspects of this book may either be rendered moot or even inaccurate as retail wheeling develops. To minimize this problem, aspects of retail wheeling that are most subject to change and uncertainty are discussed generically or from multiple perspectives. I apologize for any misleading information that may result from the inherent inability to entirely predict all aspects of a fundamentally changed industry.

Another issue worth raising at this point is the problem many people have with the term "retail wheeling." The words themselves seem to raise the emotional level of the industry restructuring debate. In a roundtable discussion recently held in Iowa, at least one panel moderator refused to allow the term "retail wheeling" to be uttered, instead preferring the more politically correct "retail competition." In California, the Public Utility Commission has adopted the term "direct access" as a less offensive euphemism for retail wheeling. Actually, Iowa is correct; what is really at stake here is the introduction of competition on the retail level, whether that involves "wheeling" or not. But since labels tend to stick, regardless of accuracy, I will often use the term "retail wheeling" when referring to any sort of retail competition.

This book is divided into two sections: (i) a background of the industry and the development of retail wheeling, including a discussion of alternatives to retail wheeling as a means to lower electricity costs, and (ii) the "nuts and bolts" of how to buy electricity in an unbundled, competitive electricity market. The appendix includes some discussion of stranded investment and federal vs. state jurisdiction, which are important albeit transitory issues facing the restructuring effort.

As the industry is restructured, I intend for this book to evolve into a handbook for retail wheeling, i.e., a true guide for end-users. If this helps resolve some of the uncertainty that results from the impending fundamental changes, then my goal will have been realized. With apologies to Hunter S. Thompson, there is no room for fear and loathing in the electricity industry.

P. C. Christensen

Acknowledgments

This book was written on a very fast track due to the timeliness of the subject matter. As a result, I required more from those who supported me in this effort than what I am sure they bargained for. Among those who I must thank, the first and foremost are my wife, Cindy, and my son, Paul. The level of support I received was matched only by the level of neglect I returned during the months I was involved in this project.

Second only to my family on the list of contributors is the consulting firm for which I work, Strategic Energy Ltd. (SEL), and its employees and clients. I am indebted to Rick Zomnir, President of SEL, not only for the opportunity to write this book but for the opportunity to enjoy my work so much. Others at SEL who particularly deserve my gratitude are Dana Buchanan, my principal assistant in the assembly of this book; Pat Purdy, for his expertise in the natural gas industry; Steve Schroth and Dan Hu, for the system lambda data; and most of all Scott Faber, Alex Galatic, and again, Dana Buchanan who competed with each other to find the most errors in my manuscript.

For the second edition, additional acknowledgements are due to John Molinda, who keeps all of us at SEL from getting carried away, and Lara Prachar, who patiently proofed this edition.

Part I

Background

Chapter 1

Why Retail Access?

"Retail wheeling" describes the ability of a retail electricity consumer, or end-user, to purchase electricity from the supplier of its choice in a competitive market. Also referred to as "direct access," retail wheeling involves the abandonment of the conventional regulated electric utility structure of vertically integrated monopolies with franchised service territories and guaranteed rates of return on investment. In its place, retail wheeling requires a competitive generation industry that can be accessed by the end-user via the existing transmission and distribution infrastructure.

This raises a mind-boggling array of issues and questions that are technical, economic, or legal in nature. For example, will utilities still have an obligation to serve? Can reliability be maintained if every end-user has access to the transmission grid? Who pays for expensive power plants that cannot compete in an open market? For many years, the seemingly insurmountable mass of unanswered questions kept restructuring to the distant future, but as more of these issues are resolved, the closer retail wheeling is to reality. At this point, retail wheeling is inevitable and imminent, and utilities, regulators, and consumers are forced to surmount the issues in order to shape the restructured industry in their best interest.

Why this seeming sudden interest in restructuring the electricity industry? The existing system of cost-based, regulated monopolies has served this country well during the past half a century, and American electricity consumers have become accustomed to safe, reliable, and readily available power supplies. Until the mid-1970s, the price for this power was relatively low, but this is no longer the case. Quite simply, retail wheeling is here because electricity costs are too high. While electricity costs in the United States are favorable to that in many other industrialized countries, American industry cannot pay more for power than what could be paid if prices were market based rather than cost based.

American industry faces stiff competition from overseas. Foreign manufacturers and suppliers can often take advantage of national subsidies not available to domestic companies. American industry has successfully competed in world markets without government help because of high productivity and superior quality. But when even a small difference in price can make or break a product line, or when every dollar in operating costs directly affects a company's bottom line, electricity costs can no longer be ignored, especially for electricity-intensive industries.

The frustration experienced by industrial electricity consumers primarily stems from electricity remaining the last of the large commodity industries that still does not respond to the same competitive pressures that all other industries must face. When a manufacturer approaches each of its suppliers for the lowest cost product that meets its needs, it cannot help but to sense exasperation as it faces its electric utility without any competitive choices to leverage an optimum price. This frustration is magnified as it finds itself in a competitive market with higher costs than its competitors simply because its manufacturing facilities are located in regions with high-cost electric utilities.

This phenomenon, called price disparity, exists uniquely in the electricity industry. The variation in price that often exists between two adjoining electric utilities is the equivalent of a gas station with $2 per gallon gas across the corner from one with $1 gas. This situation would never exist in a truly competitive market, especially with a product as inherently fungible as electricity. Yet there are many areas of the country where neighboring utilities have rates as disparate as in the gas station example.

The answer is to inject competition in the industry. Competition has been proven in many industries to result in lower costs and higher quality. In the first ten years of the restructured telecommunications industry, prices for long distance telephone service dropped by 66%, while prices for regulated local telephone service rose 13% during the same time frame. Today long distance companies keep offering lower prices, new products and services are introduced, and quality of service has become a marketing tool.

Similarly, in the natural gas industry, prices for industrial gas users dropped 52% since the industry was restructured during the 1980s, and even residential rates dropped 10%, although most residential customers continue to buy gas from regulated local distribution companies. As for quality of service, industrial end-users have more flexibility and control over their gas purchases than ever before and are now responsible for how firm their service is, which is usually a function of how much the user is willing to pay. The natural gas experience shows that all gas customers benefit from the introduction of competition to otherwise monopolistic energy industries.

Furthermore, no one can argue that deregulation of the airlines industry has not made air travel more accessible to non-business travelers. When the Federal Aviation Administration regulated routes and fares, the airline industry operated efficiently with high load factors, i.e., full airplanes, but costs were prohibitive for much of the public. When competition replaced the regulated route system with the hub and spoke system, airline load factors dropped, but so did fares for many classes of customers, and air travel was newly available to broader sectors of the public. The airline example shows that competition can also be ruinous. While many new regional carriers have flourished, only one major airline formed as a result of deregulation has survived, and unemployment in this industry has increased while salaries have dropped. There is little doubt that many electric utilities will fail to survive. Yet, lower prices and better service for the end-user are equally assured.

Fundamental economic principles appear to indicate that high electricity prices in the U.S. should not be a surprise. Traditional ratemaking methodologies base utility profits on the level of capital investment so that utilities are encouraged to invest in facilities without any corresponding incentive to minimize costs. The result is a utility infrastructure in the U.S. that is largely overbuilt, including generation and transmission. At this time, and in the foreseeable future, the U.S. is flush with excess generation and transmission capacity because of this incentive to build facilities. In a monopoly environment, excess supply results in higher costs for all ratepayers because the cost of that supply, along with the utility's guaranteed return on investment, is paid for by all ratepayers. On the other hand, in a competitive market, excess supply leads to lower costs because of the traditional relationship between supply and demand. Retail wheeling will naturally lead to lower prices primarily due to fundamental economic principles which are not allowed to apply to the traditional electricity industry.

Some suggest that ensuring a competitive wholesale electricity market will achieve the benefits of competition without incurring the complexity associated with an open retail market. The Energy Policy Act of 1992, which is discussed in Chapter 2, ensures a competitive wholesale market, but as we shall see, there was little wholesale activity that was thwarted by a lack of open access. In the United States, 40% of all generated power is traded on the wholesale market before it is distributed and sold. In contrast, only 5% of power generated in Canada is sold to another utility before it is retailed. In other words, the wholesale market in this country was very active even without mandated access. Furthermore, utilities as wholesale buyers do not have a great incentive to search for and negotiate lower cost power since all wholesale power costs are passed on to the retail customers. Therefore, ensuring a truly competitive wholesale market will not, and has not, ensured a sufficient injection of competitive forces into the electricity industry.

Electricity is a $250 billion dollar per year industry in this country. To open these sales to the lowest cost supplier would provide the competitive force necessary to ensure that costs are minimized and efficiency is maximized. Not all end-users, however, will benefit from widespread retail wheeling. Some end-users, especially those in extremely electricity intensive industries, have necessarily developed special, low-cost contracts with their suppliers that provide the below-market rates necessary for survival. In a very few cases, retail wheeling will equalize rates so that some end-users will be forced to pay higher rates.

If most power is sold on a spot market basis or from a single "poolco," as is done in the United Kingdom, power prices will be truly nondiscriminatory because transparency of prices is a cornerstone of a commoditized market. Of course, one of the tenets of the conventionally regulated market is nondiscriminatory pricing, but many end-users have been able to negotiate special contract rates that result in below-tariff prices. The more probable model for a competitive market, however, will still allow bilateral contracts, i.e., an end-user will be able to negotiate prices directly with suppliers, thus allowing rates independent of the commoditized price in exchange for varying degrees of reliability. Therefore, depending on how the competitive market is structured, retail wheeling may actually further the intent of the traditional regulatory model.

Many argue that because electricity is a product that is critical to the survival of most of the general public, the free market should not be trusted to ensure a reliable and economic supply. While electricity is certainly a necessary component of modern life, there is no reason to believe that the market cannot be trusted to serve every customer at a reasonable price. In fact, one could argue that the existing system of investor-owned, profit making utilities is inconsistent with this social necessity. In other words, if this country decides that electricity is too important to be trusted to private, profit-making companies, then all electricity generation, transmission, and distribution should be owned and operated entirely by the state.

An investor-owned utility that makes money for investors is fundamentally inconsistent with a franchised customer base and fixed rates of return. However, this country is committed to the private ownership of the means of production, so an entirely state-owned infrastructure is not considered an option. Therefore, to be consistent with the fundamental tenets of American free-enterprise, the supply of electricity *must* be trusted to the open market. Indeed, even traditionally socialistic countries, such as England and Norway, have privatized their electricity industries, and many of the former Soviet-bloc countries are rushing to privatize their electric systems as well.

The Federal Energy Regulatory Commission (FERC) has made no secret of its commitment to competitive energy markets. In its Notice of Proposed Rulemaking on open access transmission tariffs, issued on March 29, 1995, FERC stated that its goal is "to encourage lower electricity rates by structuring an orderly transition to competitive bulk power markets." Explaining this policy, FERC said, "Experience has shown that competitive pressures cannot be contained for long without serious distortions." FERC has learned from similar changes in other industries that once cracks appear in a monopoly structure, American commitment to competition cannot be held back.

Beyond this fundamental need for competition in principle, retail wheeling offers pragmatic ratemaking advantages as well. Once considered cutting-edge ratemaking, least cost planning and integrated resource planning have only resulted in additional layers of bureaucratic entanglement in utility operations and expansion of the inefficiencies inherent in monopoly control of a necessary commodity. Retail wheeling will benefit all customers by improving the planning process and eliminating unnecessary and uneconomic investments.

Integrated resource planning (IRP) is a planning methodology that intends to optimize production through the assessment of all available power resources and alternatives, such as new capacity, conservation, independent power production, off-system purchases, etc. The process should take into account system operation, reliability, nonrenewable resource conservation, and environmental concerns while balancing sources of supply and demand at the same time. Basically, the IRP process is a method of optimizing resources and minimizing costs through the creation of a detailed, sophisticated, and exhaustive regulatory process.

However, the goals of IRP are met in other industries simply through market signals. There is no need for a regulatory body to determine whether, when and where to construct a new generation station if the market itself makes that determination. A truly competitive electricity market will dictate the efficient use of available generation and the optimum timing and placement of new resources simply because there will be no room for unnecessary and inefficient resource planning in a competitive market. The advent of retail wheeling will eliminate the need for IRP and the regulatory morass that follows. Certainly veterans of California's BRPU (Biennial Resource Planning Update) process will welcome a better way.

Even least cost planning (LCP), which attempts to minimize utility costs by demanding utilities to consider the least cost method to meeting immediate changes in demand, does not deliver the cost reductions promised by retail wheeling. Today, the utility and the regulator only consider what is the least cost option. However, there is still no incentive to minimize cost overruns, so uncompetitive generation results. Retail wheeling would require a generation company to not only consider the least cost option, but will also require the determination of whether the output of that least cost option could be sold on the open market. Without this additional market signal, overpriced generation cannot be eliminated.

Furthermore, existing ratemaking methodologies, which respond to political pressures rather than market pressures, include subsidizations of certain classes of customers by others. These cross-subsidizations remove an important market signal that further reduces the overall efficiency of today's electricity industry. Most utilities subsidize the cost of servicing their residential customers through revenues from industrial customers. Because residential service costs significantly more than industrial service, regulators and policy makers have found that these subsidies are more politically acceptable than passing on the true cost of service. However, this leads to inefficient use of electricity because of incorrect pricing signals and the unfair placement of the burden of retail service on those industries that are electricity intensive.

Rate class subsidization is one of many types of "social ratemaking" that will have to be eliminated in an open, competitive market. Many regulators pass on the cost of other politically favorable social programs to large industrial electricity customers. While these programs may certainly be desirable and in the public interest, funding them through electricity rates is a form of regressive taxation, because everyone must use electricity, and unfairly punishes those industries that use great quantities of electricity. In other words, why should an aluminum smelter bear the majority of the cost of an electric vehicle research program just because aluminum production requires immense quantities of electricity? Retail wheeling will require that these programs be funded through conventional revenue generation methods rather than through utility bill collections.

One socially beneficial program that is almost entirely funded through utility rates is demand-side management (DSM). Many groups have initially opposed the development of retail wheeling because these utility funded DSM programs could not be similarly funded in a competitive market without unfairly penalizing the native utility. However, it is difficult to imagine a more effective form of DSM than having the price of electricity fluctuate with supply and demand as it should in an open market. As electricity prices rise as demand reaches a peak, many customers will choose to curtail their demand rather than pay the substantially higher rates for peak power. Except for minor differences in on-peak and off-peak power rates, there is little incentive now for most users to change their usage habits in response to supply situations. If all users, including residentials, had real-time pricing information, the corresponding reductions in overall system peak demands would dwarf all present DSM programs.

Some argue that retail wheeling will only benefit large industrial customers at the expense of residential ratepayers. While this has not been the case in natural gas re-regulation, the concern is valid given the subsidization of residential customers by industrial customers in many states. But many residential groups are starting to realize that competition will improve the efficiency of the electric industry so that even they will benefit. In California the residential ratepayer advocacy group TURN (Towards Utility Rate Normalization) has moved from opposing retail wheeling in any form to opposing the schedule that pushes off retail access for residentials in California until 2002. In other words, they recognize the benefits of retail wheeling and want it for their constituents at the same time the industrials get it.

Others argue that retail wheeling will eliminate the traditional obligation to serve and thus leave some customers without electric service. The obligation to serve is the quid pro quo of a utility's guaranteed service area and guaranteed rate of return in the traditional regulatory bargain. Of course, there is no obligation to serve in a competitive market (except for monopoly transmission and distribution services), but there is always an opportunity to make a sale. That is, the market can always be trusted to meet the needs of all customers, even in areas where the service may be expensive or difficult to reach. While a single homeowner on top of a mountain may have to pay more for electricity service than apartment dwellers, there will be no shortage of suppliers willing to provide that service. Once again, the market replaces the need to grant monopoly status in exchange for an obligation to serve.

Groups that have come out opposed to retail wheeling include labor unions and environmental groups. While the former are simply concerned about the loss of utility jobs without considering the benefits to the overall economy, environmentalists are concerned that retail wheeling's demand for the lowest cost generation will preclude the use of more expensive but environmentally favorable generation, such as solar power and wind generation. Some environmental groups, however, realize that retail wheeling will optimize generation planning thus minimizing the use of fossil fuels that are predominately used for electrical generation. Also, as discussed above, the reduction in peak demand that will result from the real-time pricing of power will significantly reduce the need for dirtier, peaking generation. Of course, an open market will not allow costly renewable resource generation to compete against fossil fuel generation, so as with other social programs, those programs will have to receive some sort of subsidization if found to be in the public interest. In other words, if the public wants green power, it will have to be willing to pay for it.

In summary, retail access to the competitive generation market is simply consistent with the American way of doing business. Competition and free market forces have consistently proven to be the most efficient and fair way of providing products for American consumers. While the unique nature of electricity poses some interesting challenges for the introduction of competition, most of the issues that some consider insurmountable are merely transitory problems that should and will be resolved. Electricity users are now merely *ratepayers*, which is frighteningly synonymous with *taxpayers*. Once the growing pains are healed, a competitive market for electricity will benefit all consumers by converting them from *ratepayers* to *customers*.

Chapter 2

Development of Retail Wheeling

While the purpose of this book is to provide a "nuts and bolts" guide to retail wheeling for end-users, a foundation must be laid upon which the end-user's new tools can be used. Because most end-users have had so few alternatives to native utility service for so many years, many industrial energy purchasers do not have an understanding of the electricity industry. Although a detailed technical understanding of the electricity business is not required to buy power in a retail wheeling world, familiarity with the development of the industry will put many issues in perspective.

In addition to its history, an understanding of the existing utility industry structure will provide end-users with the foundation required to build an overall purchasing strategy. Once this structure is understood, the end-user is in a better position to realize the ramifications and opportunities that the introduction of competition has and will bring. Finally, the profile of a restructured, competitive industry is beginning to take shape as the individual states are beginning to experiment with direct retail access.

History of the Industry

Competition is not new to the electricity industry. Not long after Thomas Edison constructed his first generation and distribution system in New York City in 1882, numerous local power systems were built. These new systems were mostly neighborhood affairs that were designed to provide street lighting and power for street cars (traction) and light industry. As with any newly emerging technology, standards were few and regulations were non-existent. The result was a mishmash of multiple, isolated systems feeding only dense population areas.

However, customers in those areas often had multiple suppliers to choose from and true competition existed. In Chicago by 1905, 21 municipal franchises to provide electricity were granted, three of which were city-wide. As late as 1922, there were 3,774 privately owned electric utilities. Some customers could literally choose one of many lines along a single pole from which to take power. Although the relative price of power was priced high enough to remain a luxury for most residential users, this competitive pressure encouraged rapid technological advancement.

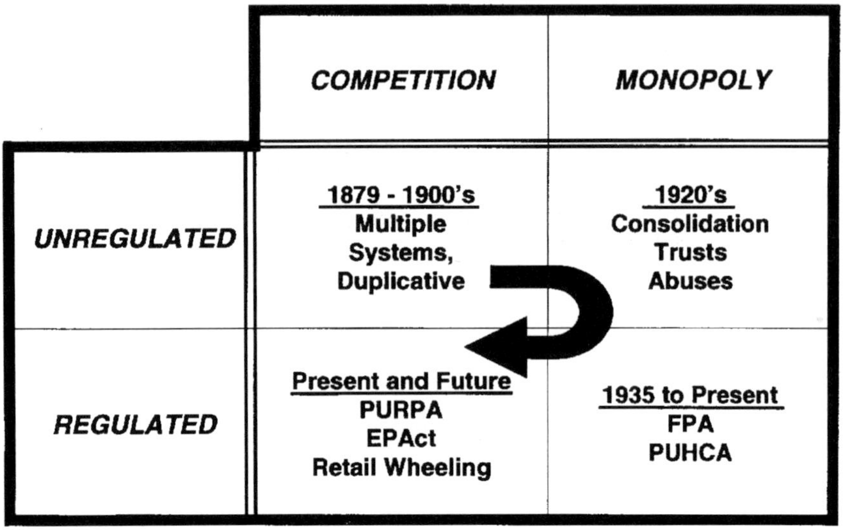

Figure 2-1. Major paradigm shifts in the electric industry involve changes from monopolies to competition and from no regulation to regulation.

The electric industry was competitive but legally, economically, and technically unregulated. As with many other industries, unregulated competition became ruinous, and the first major paradigm shift began to occur, i.e., from unregulated competition to regulated monopoly (see Figure 2-1).

In addition to the technical problems of incompatibility and unreliability of the numerous, isolated systems, the market forces of competition began to apply pressure on these systems, and many were forced out of business. From 1922 to 1927, over 1,600 of these privately owned systems were eliminated. The remaining utilities began to merge and become larger in order to survive in a competitive world.

By this time, the concepts of "natural monopoly" and "economies of scale" began to infiltrate the industry. Given the size of facilities at the time (typical generation stations built in the 1910s were rarely larger than 10 MW), there were actual economies of scale to be realized. Furthermore, the inefficiencies of building multiple distribution systems on the same street were not hard to notice. Acting on its own, the electric utility industry began to capitalize on these concepts to its advantage without respect to the impact on industry structure as a whole.

As technology progressed, greater amounts of power could be transported over longer distances so that larger, centralized generators could feed whole cities. Because larger generators required an expansive transmission system to distribute the power, the newly merged, large utilities became vertically integrated, i.e., a single company owned the means of production, transportation, and distribution. The reluctance of utilities today to break this vertically integrated structure stems from the technical need for vertical integration when the industry was growing.

In 1925, the Pennsylvania state government proposed to develop a series of large generation stations connected by a high voltage transmission system that would feed multiple distribution utilities. The local utility industry initially opposed the centralized scheme claiming that it resembled communism. Eventually, the development of a large hydroelectric project in 1926 forced the development of the first integrated, centrally dispatched power pool in 1927. Centralized power generation grew from 40% of total electricity production at the turn of the century to over 80% by the 1930s.

This movement towards centralized generation combined with transmission was also the origins of today's interconnected transmission grid. In order to provide for reliability during planned and unplanned outages of the generators, the large utilities tied their transmission systems together within their own companies and between other utilities. The use of an interconnected transmission grid also allowed the purchase of off-system power when it was more economical than internal generation. Thus was created the highly interconnected and integrated infrastructure of generation and transmission that is so ingrained in the electric utility industry today.

The human forces of greed and ambition soon replaced efficiency as the principle shaper of the industry as it became more entrenched in the unregulated monopoly quadrant (see Figure 2-1). The majority of electric utility assets fell into the hands of a few monopolists. Most notable among these were Henry Villard's attempt to grow his Edison General Electric Co. into a worldwide trust and Sam Insull's empire that included eight holding companies, five investment companies, two service companies, two securities companies, and 14 operating companies.

By the mid-1920s, 16 holding companies controlled 85% of the nation's electric industry. True trusts were formed out of the numerous and duplicative systems, and the abuses that trusts can bring soon followed. Elaborate holding company structures were developed that were used to sell fictitious services, demand unreasonable prices for real services, transfer assets from overpriced power to paper subsidiaries, and to cheat small investors with watered stock.

In 1928 the U.S. Senate ordered the newly formed Federal Trade Commission to investigate the electricity industry. After many years of debate and an 84-volume report, Congress passed the Federal Power Act of 1935 (FPA) and the Public Utility Holding Company Act of 1935 (PUHCA). The FPA formed the Federal Power Authority, which later was renamed the Federal Energy Regulatory Commission (FERC). The FPA granted federal regulators authority over (i) interstate transmission, which was later determined to be all transmission, and (ii) wholesale power transactions, i.e., sale for resale. PUHCA gave the newly formed Securities and Exchange Commission (SEC) the authority to restructure and regulate the electricity industry through tight control of utility asset acquisition and securities sales. PUHCA also included a "death sentence" clause that broke up the holding companies and eliminated the complicated pyramid holding company structures.

More importantly, the FPA and PUHCA signalled the second major paradigm shift in the industry: from unregulated monopoly to regulated monopoly (see Figure 2-1). One supposes that Congress, if unusually foresighted, could have elected to steer the industry to a regulated competitive structure, but this was not the case. Instead, the FPA and PUHCA established an industry structure that was to serve the country, and serve it well, for more than half a century.

As the post-war country grew, so did the utility industry. For the most part, the growth of an investor-owned utility, which makes money for its shareholders through capital investment, parallels the growth of its load. And between 1920 and 1970, the use of electric energy doubled every 10 years. The period between 1935 and the mid-1970s was the golden age for electric utilities because growth was steady, and prices either grew only with inflation or actually decreased on a nominal basis. Because prices remained low, there was relatively little need for replacing the regulated monopolies with a competitive market.

Of course, investor-owned utilities were not the only supplier of electricity during this development period. Many of the small distribution systems created in the earliest days of electrification were owned and operated by the town government that franchised the service. While many of these municipal electric systems eventually merged with private utilities as the industry grew, a fair number remained independent and publicly owned. In most states, the municipal electric companies even remained independent of the state regulatory bodies that were formed to control the larger private utilities from the potential "abuses" of the private ownership of a monopoly.

The father of public power was U.S. Senator George Norris of Nebraska, who argued against the ownership of the electricity industry by private investors. Instead he advocated federal control and ownership of power generation and transmission and local government control and ownership of distribution facilities. Government control of public services was a popular concept in the era of the "New Deal" of the 1930s and Norris is considered the chief architect of the Tennessee Valley Authority, a large, federally subsidized generation and transmission company. Norris' legacy lives on as Tennessee and Nebraska are the only two states with no investor-owned utilities.

Municipal electric companies continue to thrive, and most states have specific statutes that allow the creation of new municipal electric companies in towns presently served by private utilities. This process of municipalization is an increasingly viable alternative to conventional utility service for some end-users, especially since the passage of the Energy Policy Act of 1992, which is discussed in detail below. The use of municipalization as either a source of leverage against a native utility or as a viable alternative is discussed in detail in Chapter 3.

Many municipal electric companies do not generate power themselves but either purchase shares of other generation facilities or purchase power from other utilities. Because municipal electric companies purchase power for resale to their own customers, they are considered wholesale buyers so that their power purchases are regulated by FERC. Most municipal electric companies have full requirements power purchase contracts with state or regional joint action agencies, or "umbrella" groups, that generate and transmit power for member municipal electric companies. These joint action agencies also often provide operation, engineering and financial services as well. Ironically, the joint action agencies along with their members begin to resemble investor-owned utilities in their manner of operation and structure.

The first electric companies were developed in large cities because the limitations of transmission technology required a concentration of load near generation sources. But even as technology developed, few investor-owned or municipal electric companies were willing to feed rural areas simply because the revenues from sales to these small, dispersed loads could not justify the expenditures necessary to deliver the power. As a result, many rural communities, especially in poor agricultural areas, did not have the modern conveniences brought by the availability of low-cost electricity.

The need to improve the quality of life in these poorer rural areas, and the need to inject investment and bring jobs to rural America, triggered the creation of the Rural Electrification Administration (REA) in the 1930s. The purpose of the REA was to provide funding and low-cost financing to rural electricity customers so that they could construct the necessary generation, transmission, and distribution equipment to electrify the countryside. These REA funded utilities were set up as cooperatives where the customer was also part owner of the utility. Because REA cooperatives were formed and financed under a separate federal government agency, they too largely escaped oversight by state regulators. To a large degree, they are also unregulated by FERC.

Today, cooperatives are divided into generation and transmission cooperatives, or so-called "G&Ts," and distribution cooperatives that are members of the larger G&Ts. The distribution cooperatives are separate companies, but either are part owners of the G&Ts (and thus their generation and transmission assets), or they have full requirement contracts with the G&Ts.

It is unclear as to how municipal electric companies and cooperatives will be affected by the introduction of competition. Many municipal electric companies are opposed to retail competition because they fear the loss of their major industrial customers without their own low-cost generation to offer to other end-users. However, if a municipal electric company is not regulated by the state regulatory agency that implements a retail wheeling program, those customers of the municipal utility may not be able to leave that system unless the local charter is changed. Of course, since larger industrial customers can often wield significant local political pressure due to their effect on the local economy, it is likely that those end-users will also be able to access low-cost power once allowed by state law or state regulatory agencies.

As for cooperatives, their regulatory structure is in transition. At the time of this writing, Congress is debating the future of the REA, now called the Rural Utilities Service (RUS). Federal subsidization of rural distribution facilities may still be required, but the regulatory structure, or lack thereof, appears to be inconsistent with the evolving structure of a competitive electricity industry. Even the future of the TVA is uncertain as it attempts to enter the competitive wholesale market while it exposes its captive customers to low cost suppliers. It appears that in order to allow federally developed power companies to participate in the competitive industry, privatization of these federal programs may be necessary.

Existing Industry Structure

Although there were few major regulatory changes during the utility industry's golden age, technical advancements and economic considerations led to some voluntary organizations and operation mechanisms that define the industry infrastructure now. Although these structures may or may not exist in their present form in a retail wheeling environment, the forces that led to their creation will still exist and will shape the future electricity industry.

Most centralized, investor-owned utilities have numerous choices of supply for meeting their customers load requirements. Although this choice is often driven by certain technical and political requirements, the overriding factor is economics, i.e., which source provides the next megawatt-hour at the lowest cost. Note that this is a question of incremental cost rather than total cost, since fixed costs are recovered regardless of whether or how the asset is used operationally.

The first step of this process, referred to as unit commitment and economic dispatch, is to estimate the system load profile, i.e., the expected demands on the system from the utility's customers. Load profiles are estimated on an annual, monthly, weekly, and daily basis. Some utilities develop elaborate models for determining expected load based on how much load is connected to the system and the type of load that is served, e.g., residential, commercial, and certain types of industries. These models will then use sophisticated probability analysis to determine the most likely demands based on certain key variables, especially weather. Most utilities, however, determine their load profiles on primarily historical data and make adjustments for known or predicted load growth and changes in weather.

Once the expected load profile is determined, certain patterns are developed (see Figure 2-2). First, utility planners will note that there is a certain demand on the system that is always present due in part to demand diversity among various loads (for example, as one refrigerator shuts off, another is turning on), but this steady demand is mostly due to large industrial loads that draw power 24 hours per day. This load is termed base load, and because of its high load factor, it is the easiest and least costly to supply. As other industrial loads come on during the day, and as the bulk of residential and commercial loads make their expected daily swings, a large but anticipated increase in system demand is seen. This daily cycle of demand increases in the morning and decreases at night is termed cycling or intermediate load. This load is also relatively inexpensive to meet because it is anticipated and can be met by throttling major steam-driven turbines.

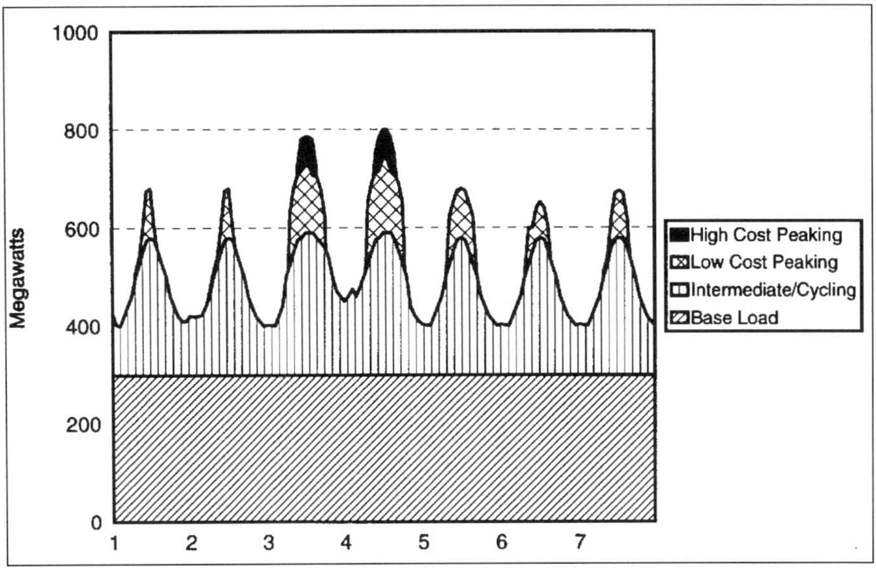

Figure 2-2. Typical weekly electric utility load profile.

The most expensive load to supply is peaking demand. This is the load that either exceeds the daily anticipated cycling load or the load that exceeds the utility's supply of low cost base load and intermediate load generation assets. The utility must have adequate resources to meet this peak load on demand or be able to purchase this supply from off-system sources, even if it occurs only a few hours per year. Also, the utility must be able to meet this peak demand with very short notice of hours or even minutes. Normally the utility will monitor the system load as it climbs during the morning. If the rate of increase in demand is greater than the predicted load profile, or if the demand at a certain time of the day is greater than expected, the utility will begin to make arrangements to procure peaking power.

Given a certain demand profile, the utility will attempt to match its resources to the profile given the economics of each generation unit. For example, nuclear power plants are ideally suited to base load because (i) nuclear power, from an incremental basis, is very low cost and (ii) nuclear units cannot be readily throttled and take days to bring on or off line. On the other hand, gas-fired internal combustion generators are well suited for peaking loads because they can be brought on line very quickly even though they may be more expensive to run. The challenge, therefore, is to constantly match the utility's load with the lowest cost generation resource.

As load changes during the course of the day, week, or month, the utility will attempt to minimize its fuel costs by determining which unit can supply the next megawatt-hour at the lowest cost. To do this, the heat rates of each unit must be determined to calculate an incremental cost of generation for each unit. Note that the fixed costs of these units do not enter into the decision of which unit to run, although we will soon see that other factors will play a part in this process. If the incremental cost of each unit in a utility's system is known, the utility can then choose the lowest cost unit to supply the system's next needed increase in demand.

This system incremental cost value, called "system lambda," gives the cost of producing another megawatt-hour (in dollars per megawatt-hour) given all system resources. A utility will calculate this value on a periodic basis, usually every six minutes. This value will then determine which unit will either be throttled up or turned on to meet new demand. Many utilities will also compare their system lambda to the present wholesale market price to determine whether it would be cheaper to purchase that next megawatt-hour from off-system sources rather than generate it themselves.

This process of constantly determining the most economic combination of power sources is called "economic dispatch." The process, for the most part, is automated through an energy management system or EMS. Once this system decides to increase output from a certain generator, a signal is sent to that generator through an automatic generation control (AGC) system. The AGC system tells the generator to throttle up or down to follow the change in system load. The hardware and software systems to implement economic dispatch and AGC have been developed over the past decades and have become refined, standardized and very sophisticated. But as we shall see, these systems will be replaced and rendered obsolete, at least on an overall system basis, by an open market.

Market, technical and political forces already affect the economic dispatch system, sometimes to such a degree that the system is rendered meaningless already. For example, a nuclear power unit must usually run full time for financial and technical reasons. The only way a utility can pay for the tremendously high fixed costs of a nuclear unit is to operate the unit whenever possible. Therefore, the system lambda of a nuclear generator will often be artificially set to zero so that the EMS will always keep the plant at full output. If the utility's minimum base load is less than the output of the unit, either the power must be sold to the wholesale market, which will usually be a very low clearing price that will lose money for the utility, or some other use for the power must be found. This is why many nuclear utilities have installed pumped storage facilities, which pump water to a reservoir on top of a mountain at night, using excess nuclear generation, and generate power during the day when demand is greater.

Transmission capacities and limitations are another factor that should, but do not always, affect the economic dispatch calculation, and this factor enters into the equation in different ways. Most obviously, lower cost off-system power can only be purchased when there are adequate transmission resources between the involved control areas. (Chapter 7 discusses this determination.) However, even the choice of which generator to run within a control area should also account for transmission capacity. For example, a generator with a low incremental cost may be far enough from the incremental load system to invoke significant losses or may contribute to the overloading of certain transmission lines. Some utilities use sophisticated EMS programs that incorporate a load flow analysis so that generation is optimized with transmission limitations taken into account. This is done by incorporating a penalty factor on the cost of those units that are electrically distant from the associated load center.

Transmission capacity between control areas also affects system operation with respect to instantaneous fluctuations in load. Since no utility can match generation with load on a real-time basis, utilities will depend on transmission resources to deliver and absorb mismatches between scheduled and actual power. This constantly fluctuating mismatch, which is dependant on the type of load on the system, is termed area control error, or ACE. Utilities quantify ACE and regulate these quantities with self-imposed limitations in order to (i) minimize inadvertent interchanges between control areas, (ii) keep the utility's generation and net interchange levels at the desired values, and (iii) minimize dependance on the transmission system. For example, all positive and negative mismatches must balance over a certain time period, and the ACE must fluctuate from positive to negative (i.e., cross the zero axis) a fixed number of times per hour. These limitations can be very difficult for some utilities to meet, such as those with large arc furnace loads, which cause very large and sudden demands on the system. Meeting loads that cause ACE problems require operators to provide sufficient reserves on the system, which necessarily reduces the efficiency and optimization of the system realized through the precise matching of generation and load.

Another example of when economic dispatch does not match political and market realities is the case of independent power generation. As we will see, federal law requires utilities to purchase power generated either by a qualifying small power producer, which is one that uses renewable resources to generate power, or excess power generated in a cogeneration configuration. These units are also considered "must-run" units because of legal and contractual commitments and also require a fixed incremental cost of zero to be input into the system. These are anomalies to the existing economic dispatch system and are increasing in number as control of the electricity industry shifts away from the centralized monopoly utility.

In a purely or even partially competitive market, the existing economic dispatch system will require so many exceptions that it will cease to operate. If an end-user in a retail wheeling world (or a wholesale buyer today) can arrange for its own generation independent of the native utility, this generation must be dispatched by that utility as must run units to meet that customer's contractual requirements. As more of the utility's load has access to the open market through bilateral contracts, only a small amount of load will be dispatched from the economic dispatch model. At some point, certainly when the market is fully competitive, the decision of which generator should run to meet the utility's load will be entirely controlled by market forces rather than by centralized decision making.

When the economic dispatch model was being developed, smaller utilities discovered that their limited assets were not always ideally suited to changing load profiles and that neighboring utilities often were able to supply their needs more economically than their own resources. In most parts of the country, each dispatch center will take advantage of this by merely purchasing power from that neighboring utility through a wholesale, bulk power purchase. But in some areas, most notably the eastern United States, utilities formed voluntary groups that would allow member utilities to "pool" their resources to maximize efficiencies.

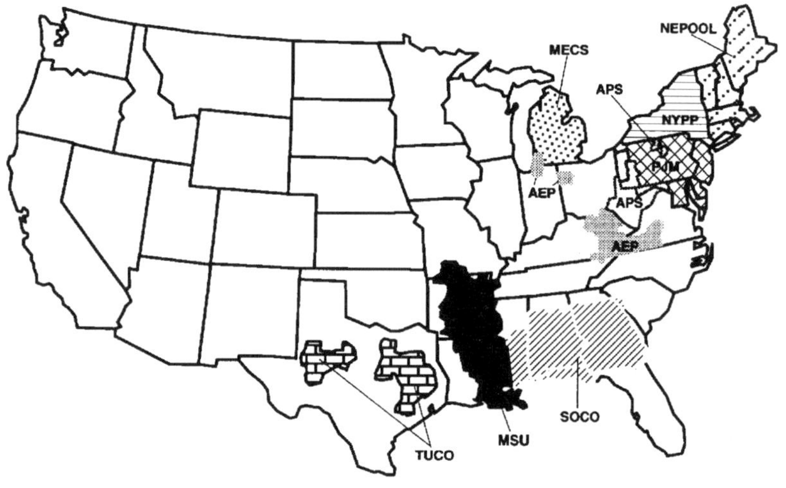

Figure 2-3. "Tight" power pools in the U.S., which are mostly located in the east, have centralized economic dispatching functions.

These power pools can be divided into two types. "Tight" power pools (see Figure 2-3) are those in which the member utilities have actually released the control of their generation units to a centralized pool operation center. For example, all generation units among the utilities in NEPOOL (the New England Power Pool) are dispatched out of a single control center in West Springfield, Massachusetts. Tight power pools such as NEPOOL take advantage of the diversity in resources among the various utilities in the pool. In the west, many utilities have grouped together to facilitate easier bulk power transfers among the member utilities without releasing control to a single control center. These "loose" pools are not true pools, and they will probably become looser as the member utilities begin competing with each other for wholesale and eventually retail loads.

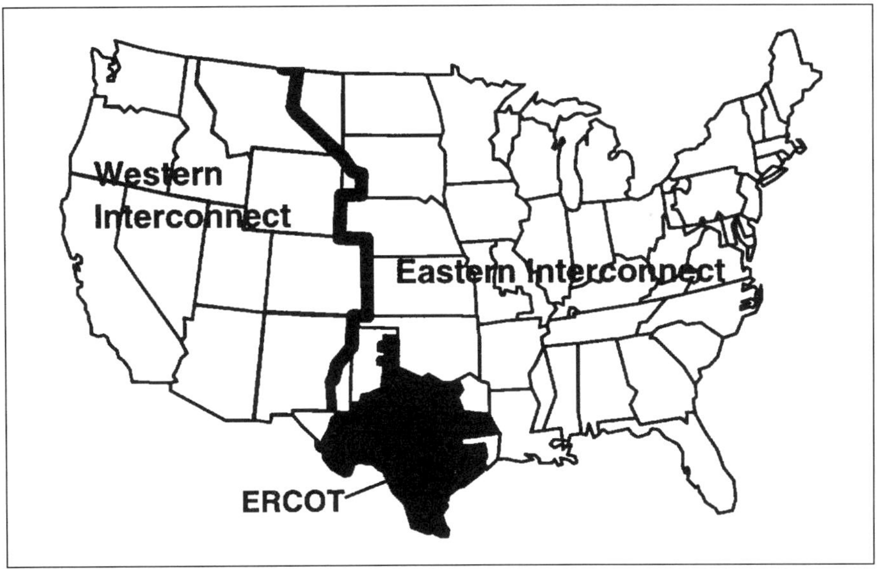

Figure 2-4. The U.S. is divided into three major interconnection areas that are largely isolated from each other.

Beyond the pools, all electric utilities east of the Rocky Mountains are interconnected to form a large, single transmission grid (see Figure 2-4). This means that every generator and synchronous motor are not only spinning at the same speed but are also at the same point in their rotation at any given moment. Transmission lines are little more than wires connecting the components of a single, large machine of continental proportions. Similarly, all utilities west of the Rockies are interconnected, but the two systems are, for all practical purposes, isolated from each other. Finally, for what are surely historical and cultural reasons, most of Texas is in its own isolated interconnected system. For the most part, power cannot be wheeled from one system to another.

Because the North American electric industry is divided among a few large, interconnected systems, a problem in one part of the country can negatively affect millions of customers across a large portion of the country. For example, the sudden loss of a large nuclear plant in Mississippi can shake the entire eastern U.S. electrical system as the grid struggles to reestablish equilibrium after the sudden change in configuration. In some circumstances, this equilibrium may never be reached and the system becomes unstable, as was the case in New York in 1965.

In the infamous 1965 blackout, circuit breakers intended to protect major transmission lines feeding the New York City area tripped due to abnormally high line currents caused by a large interchange of power from Canada. The result was an instantaneous demand for power through remaining weaker ties that quickly overloaded and tripped. As more lines tripped, the entire interconnected system became increasingly unstable until most of the Eastern Seaboard was without electric power. This event dramatically illustrated the need for centralized system transmission and reliability planning. Therefore, utility engineers have developed methodologies for determining the circumstances that lead to system instability and use these studies to establish special operating procedures to avoid recurrences of the 1965 blackout.

These stability and planning studies must be done on a regional basis because of the interconnected nature of the electrical system. Therefore, in the aftermath of the 1965 blackout, utilities formed, on their own, the North American Electric Reliability Council (NERC), which divided most of the U.S. and Canada into nine reliability regions (see Figure 2-5). These reliability councils perform system load and stability studies on a regional basis so as to make decisions regarding transmission and generation installations and operations. Although voluntary, the agreements made among the utilities are pseudo-regulatory in nature, i.e., the actions of the NERC regions are supported by state and federal regulatory agencies in efforts to further system reliability.

Introduction of Competition

In the mid-1970s a number of factors combined to bring an abrupt change to the pattern of growth that utilities became accustomed to in the so-called "golden age." First, inflation rates and then interest rates began to rise. Since utilities are highly capitalized, any increase in interest rates will substantially impact the return for investors. Second, the so-called energy crisis, which was triggered by the Arab oil embargo of 1973, doubled the price of oil that was widely used by utilities for peak and even base-load generation at the time. The perceived natural gas shortage also increased the price of that fuel. Since fuel costs are at least two-thirds the cost of delivering power, these higher fuel costs significantly impacted rates. Third, the nuclear accident at General Public Utilities' Three Mile Island plant in 1979 resulted in massive changes in safety requirements for all nuclear plants. Many utilities were constructing nuclear power plants at the time because of the promise of low-cost power, new design changes and the unexpected political incorrectness of nuclear power made the construction of these plants prohibitively expensive. Furthermore, the cessation of the continued growth in demand seen for decades reduced the need for these high cost facilities.

These and other factors resulted in a five-fold increase in industrial electric rates, on a nominal basis, from 1972 to 1982. These increases, along with a perceived need to increase the energy efficiency of American industry, prompted Congress to pass the Public Utility Regulatory Policies Act of 1978

(PURPA). Although it was not intended to be, PURPA was the first movement in the final paradigm shift from regulated monopoly to regulated competition, the fourth quadrant of Figure 2-1

ECAR
East Central Area Reliability Coordination Agreement

ERCOT
Electric Reliability Council of Texas

MAAC
Mid-Atlantic Area Council

MAIN
Mid-America Interconnected Network

MAPP
Mid-Continent Area Power Pool

NPCC
Northeast Power Coordinating Council

SERC
Southeastern Electric Reliability Council

SPP
Southwest Power Pool

WSCC
Western Systems Coordinating Council

Affiliate

ASCC
Alaska Systems Coordinating Council

Figure 2-5. *North American Electric Reliability Council* (NERC) *regions.*

Public Utility Regulatory Policy Act of 1978.

When electrical technologies were first being developed in the late nineteenth century, industries that recognized the benefit of electrical power could not rely on the few local lighting and traction systems available to meet their needs. As a result, many installed their own generators so that by 1900, 50% of the nation's electricity capacity was generated by non-utility users. As the regulated monopoly industry was formed, however, many state regulatory commissions allowed the interconnected utilities to forbid interconnection to industrial generation for safety and reliability reasons. By the mid-1960s, many states had passed suppliers acts or service territory laws that granted exclusive franchises to the local utilities for the exclusive right to generate and provide electricity to end-users in certain geographic areas. As a result, industrial end-users were forced to purchase power from the native utilities rather than generate it themselves unless the facility could run completely isolated from the power grid.

There are inherent efficiencies in production that are available if the production of electricity is combined with the production of thermal energy, which is commonly referred to as cogeneration, i.e., the simultaneous generation of electricity and thermal energy, which is normally in the form of steam. The overall thermal efficiency of a typical large utility generator is 35% while a smaller industrial steam and electricity generator could easily reach efficiencies of 70%. Recognizing that these efficiencies could ease the nation's dependance on expensive and politically volatile foreign oil, Congress encouraged the development of cogeneration and renewable resource generation, i.e., hydroelectric, solar, or geothermal power, through PURPA.

If an end-user could meet certain efficiency and steam use requirements, PURPA requires the local, native utility to:

(i) interconnect with the end-user's generator so that it runs in parallel with the interconnected system,

(ii) provide backup, supplemental, and maintenance power to the cogenerator at cost-based, tariff rates (backup power is needed to meet the electrical demands of the host facility when the generator experiences an unscheduled outage; supplemental power is the power needed by the facility beyond the capabilities of the cogenerator; maintenance power is replacement power during scheduled outages); and,

(iii) purchase excess energy and capacity from the cogenerator at the utility's avoided cost, which is defined as the cost that the utility would face if it had to generate the power otherwise supplied by the cogenerator.

PURPA left the implementation of many aspects of this program to the states, and many states passed rules and statutes that further encouraged development of non-utility generation (often referred to as NUGs) by granting front end-loaded, avoided cost rates. For example, in New York the Public Service Commission sought to encourage the development of independent and small power production by setting a flat utility purchase rate of 6.0¢ per kilowatt-hour regardless of the cost of producing that power or the utility's avoided cost. Beyond this, California created a number of "standard offer" or SO contracts for NUGs that included a built-in provision for levelizing purchase rates through a front-end loaded calculation. California has, by far, more independent power production than any other state, largely due to these SO contracts, which provide standardized rates, terms, and conditions to encourage independent power development. Front-end loaded rates attempt to average out the avoided costs projected over the course of the NUG's power sales contract to the utility by shifting payments to the early years of the contract (see Figure 2-6). Unfortunately for the utility, the projected increases in avoided costs upon which these contracts were written never materialized. At the time of this writing, the avoided cost of power in California is about 2.8¢ per kilowatt-hour while some of these contracts are paying over 12¢ per kilowatt hour for unneeded energy and capacity. This discrepancy is a major issue in the utility restructuring effort currently underway in California.

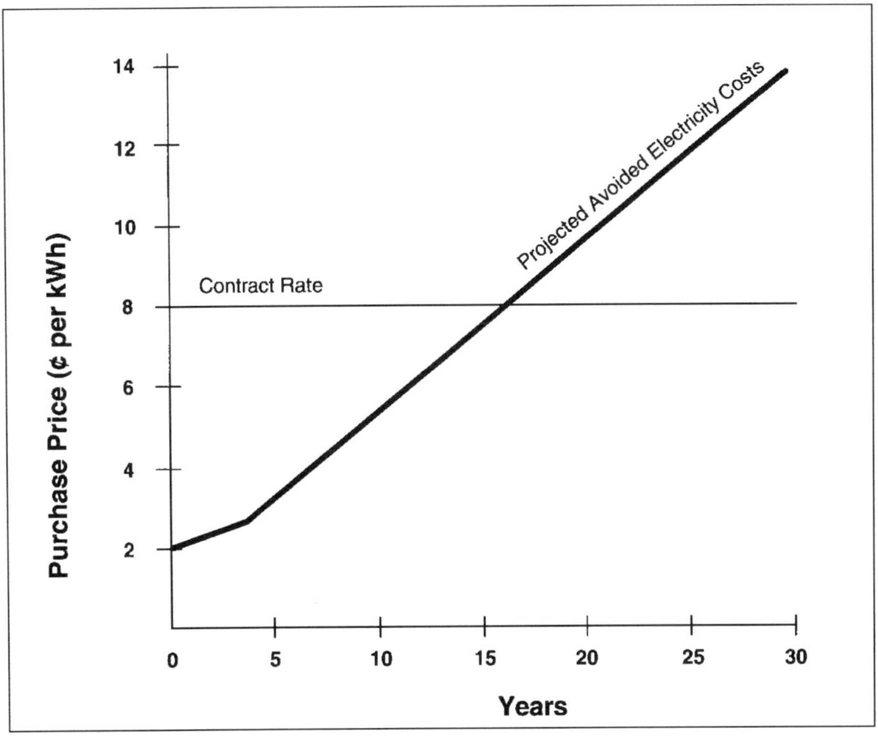

Figure 2-6. Typical front-end loaded rate scheme for purchase of excess cogenerated power.

The response to PURPA, after it was fully implemented in 1982, was far beyond that anticipated by Congress. Rather than just optimize efficiency of industrial energy use, an entire new industry was formed: the independent power industry. Many independent power producers (IPPs) took advantage of the favorable development rates and high utility rates and built projects at virtually all major industrial sites with substantial electrical and steam loads.

The efficiencies of these units and the favorable economics that followed taught the electricity industry a new lesson: the old principal of economies of scale no longer applied. Changes in generation technology and levelized load growth reversed the need for large centralized generation facilities to the point that greater economies were achieved with smaller decentralized units. The electric industry faced a situation in which the incremental price of electricity exceeded the average cost to produce power at the larger plants.

The newly created independent power generation industry was perfectly positioned to capitalize on these fundamental industry changes. In 1989 there were 576 qualified PURPA facilities, but by 1993 there were more than 1,200. The installed capacity of these units almost doubled during this period to nearly 50,000 megawatts, which represented 10% of the total generation capacity in the United States in 1993.

Besides the benefits of greater technical efficiency, competition was reintroduced into the electricity industry for the first time since the early part of the century. Investor-owned, regulated utilities found themselves losing industrial load, which often supply revenues to the utility well above the associated costs to serve the load, to the cogenerators. Even without incentive rates, self-generation became a real alternative to native utility service for many end-users now that PURPA accommodated interconnection. Beyond the economic benefits of cogeneration itself, many industrials soon discovered that a credible threat of cogeneration in an area of excess capacity could be used to leverage the utility into offering below-tariff rates. These "cogeneration deferral" contracts have since become an acceptable alternative to conventional tariff service in many regulatory jurisdictions.

The lesson was clear, competition could be good for the electricity industry, at least with respect to its customers. As the generation component of the industry became more competitive, traditional utilities were unable to adequately respond. Since 1992 and for the projected future, more new generation was and will be provided by IPPs than the utilities. In a survey of utility executives made in 1994, 44% of the respondents said that their utility would never build another generator. In other words, traditional utilities are getting out of the generation business.

As we shall soon see, the Energy Policy Act of 1992 enhanced the opportunity for non-utility generation through the creation of an "Exempt Wholesale Generator." This provision virtually allows anyone to generate electricity (if they can find a wholesale buyer). Therefore, the electricity market with respect to generation is already mostly competitive. However, the Energy Policy Act also addressed one key problem with a competitive generation market in a regulated monopoly industry: how can purchasers of this generation access the market? While the Energy Policy Act may have addressed this issue for wholesale buyers, access to the competitive generation market by retail end-users is what retail wheeling is all about.

The lesson from the success of PURPA was clear: the electricity industry could benefit from the introduction of competition. While this notion was not embraced by utility executives (as late as 1991, only 17% of utility executives believed that wholesale competition was in the public good), those that were involved with natural gas re-regulation realized that the electricity industry could also be unbundled and competitive.

Energy Policy Act of 1992.

While some large industrial end-users have been advocating the restructuring of the American electricity industry for years, a key convert to the religion of competition is FERC. As regulators of all energy markets, FERC commissioners were in a unique position to apply lessons learned in the gas industry to the electricity industry (see below). Because FERC's primary source of jurisdiction in the electricity industry is wholesale transactions and interstate transmission, FERC sought to unbundle transmission from generation, at least with respect to the wholesale market so that electricity would become more commoditized.

As a result, FERC used every opportunity to force open access to transmission. Many of its orders were conditioned on the requirement that the utility offer transmission as a service independent of production. In one of the more notable cases, FERC attempted to require Northeast Utilities to offer unbundled transmission as a prerequisite to its merger with Public Service of New Hampshire. While this requirement was eventually dropped for political reasons, subsequent merger approvals included this and other transmission access provisions.

Some utilities also began requesting the right to sell excess generation at market prices since they would often be able to generate more revenues from open market sales than they would on a cost-plus basis. But since the utility still had monopoly control over transmission, FERC would only allow market based rates if the utility promised to grant transmission access to other wholesale buyers and sellers. FERC was intent on replicating its successes in the gas market by slowly introducing competition to the electricity market.

Congress was not blind to this movement. Electricity was the last of the major industries immune from the forces of free enterprise, and Congress recognized the need for industry reform. While retail wheeling was an elusive and radical concept, Congress was not predisposed against retail competition. Along with many other energy related issues, electricity industry reform was on the agenda for George Bush's long-promised Energy Policy Act.

The lobbying efforts on behalf of investor-owned utilities was intense. Besides claiming technical and legal infeasibility of even wholesale wheeling, the utility industry delivered a parade of horribles in response to the notion of competition in an industry based on natural monopoly and economies of scale. But FERC's successes in natural gas could not be ignored, so a compromise was reached.

The utilities reluctantly agreed to the concept of an open market in wholesale electricity in exchange for a prohibition of retail wheeling. Actually, the utilities did not give up much here. The wholesale market for electricity has been very active in the U.S. for years before the Energy Policy Act debate. Over 40% of all the power generated in the U.S. is traded on the wholesale market before it is sold on the retail market.

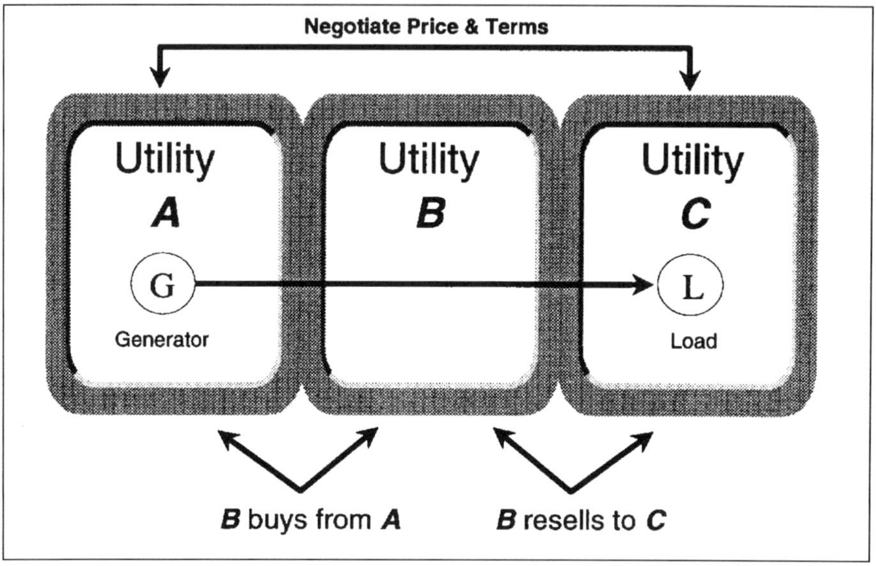

Figure 2-7. Wholesale buy/sell arrangement.

But the wholesale market was a "closed" market. Sales across an intervening utility were and still are done traditionally with a series of "buy/sell" arrangements (see Figure 2-7). For example, if utility B was between Utility A, the seller, and Utility C, the buyer, Utility B would buy from Utility A and resell to Utility C. In some cases, Utility B would even keep the power. Very rarely would Utility B offer the buyer and seller merely transmission service at a price to wheel the power. This closed market led to, or arguably was the result of, an "old boy" network among utility bulk power shoppers.

The Energy Policy Act of 1992 (commonly referred to as EPAct) was intended to open this market. Although limited in scope, as with PURPA, EPAct will probably become the most significant electric utility legislation since the Federal Power Act of 1935. Even though it deals only with wholesale industry, unbundling transmission for wholesale transactions has already triggered interest in unbundling retail transactions. The rules and regulations that will be developed and promulgated for wholesale transmission will be directly applicable to the retail market.

EPAct was signed into law on October 24, 1992, and is a comprehensive national energy policy that includes 30 titles covering many aspects of the energy sector, including energy efficiency, electric cars, global warming, nuclear plant licensing, etc. The part of EPAct that will so greatly change the electricity industry is only one small part of the entire act and is entirely contained in Title VII. The key provisions of EPAct Title VII are as follows:

Transmission access: Under Section 211 of EPAct, any wholesale generator or buyer can petition FERC to mandate wheeling over any "transmission utility's" facilities. The applicant must first request wheeling service from the transmission utility, and the utility has 60 days to respond in writing with (i) any limitations to the requested service due to transmission constraints and (ii) the basis for the proposed wheeling rates. If the utility refuses a "good faith" request to wheel the power at a reasonable rate, the applicant can request a FERC order to mandate wheeling. The FERC will order such wheeling if it is in the public interest and does not "unreasonably impair the continued reliability of the electric systems affected by the order." Interestingly, this rule, and other parts of EPAct, applies to *all* utilities that own transmission facilities, even if they are not regulated by FERC under the Federal Power Act. Therefore, municipal electric companies, cooperatives, and theoretically even independent power producers would be subject to Section 211 requests if they own transmission facilities with voltage levels above 100kV.

The importance of this section is that it requires transmission utilities to, for the first time, "unbundle" transmission from generation, distribution, and other services in order to be able to offer it as a separate service. Since virtually all electric utilities are entirely vertically integrated, a significant question as to how to price this service arises. The equipment costs and operating expenditures that are involved in transmission alone have never been independently calculated. In the past, when a utility agreed or was forced to offer transmission services, a buy/sell arrangement was made and the cost was buried in the margin.

Therefore, EPAct also required FERC to develop a transmission pricing policy to accommodate the wholesale transmission access mandated by Section 211. EPAct requires that wheeling must (i) recover all costs incurred in the transmission service, including embedded costs and expansion costs, (ii) "promote the economically efficient transmission and generation of electricity," and (iii) ensure that costs are "properly" allocated to new and native customers. How transmission pricing will be structured to meet these statutory goals is yet unclear and is a subject of a FERC Notice of Inquiry and subsequent Notices of Proposed Rulemaking.

Many new and interesting issues concerning this newly mandated transmission service quickly arose. For example, could a utility be forced to install new transmission facilities to meet the demands of a shipper if inadequate capacity exists? And if so, does FERC's jurisdiction to enforce EPAct supersede the state's traditional right to regulate transmission facility siting? One of the most interesting new issues raised early on concerned the nature of the transmission service itself. Is all transmission merely a series of contract paths between each generator supply point and each end-user delivery point? Or does providing transmission service incorporate "leasing" out a piece of the entire transmission network's capacity. This debate between offering point-to-point service versus network service was subsequently settled by FERC. These issues are discussed along with other transmission service issues in Chapter 7.

Transmission information: When drafting the Energy Policy Act of 1992, Congress was unusually foresighted when it included a provision that requires all transmitting utilities to provide information to the public on their transmission facilities. EPAct drafters recognized that transmission is the key to accessing low cost generation, and that information must be available to buyers that could indicate whether certain suppliers could physically serve certain loads. Section 213 of EPAct requires:

> the Commission [FERC] shall promulgate a rule requiring that information be submitted annually to the Commission by transmitting utilities which is adequate to inform potential transmission customers, State regulatory authorities, and the public of potentially available transmission capacity and known constraints.

By September of 1993, FERC had promulgated such a rule, which created a new reporting requirement for transmitting utilities called FERC Form 715. This reporting requirement was greatly enhanced in FERC Order 889, issued on April 24, 1996, which defines an internet-based information system that will meet the EPAct requirement on a real-time basis. This system, called OASIS (open access same-time information system) will be discussed in detail in Chapter 7.

Exempt wholesale generators: One of the primary goals of EPAct Title VII was to create an entirely competitive *wholesale* market for electricity. As discussed above, PURPA was the first act of Congress that allowed certain generators to avoid the heavy-handed regulatory requirements of the Federal Power Act and the Public Utility Holding Company Act of 1935. While the exemptions of PURPA only apply to certain classes of generators, EPAct expanded on this idea and exempts virtually all generators from the requirements of PUHCA (although they are still subject to the provisions of the Federal Power Act, which is what EPAct modifies). EPAct created a new class of generator, and another acronym, called an Exempt Wholesale Generator (EWG), which allows virtually anyone to get into the power business and build a generation facility if that power is sold to a wholesale buyer.

An EWG is defined as "any person determined by the [FERC] to be engaged directly, or indirectly through one or more affiliates, ... and exclusively in the business of owning, or both owning and operating, all or a part of one or more eligible facilities and selling electric energy at wholesale." "Eligible facilities" are simply redefined as those that are used for the generation of electric energy exclusively for sale in the wholesale market.

IPP =	Independent Power Producer
NUG =	Non-Utility Generator
APP =	Affiliated Power Producers
QF =	Qualified Facility
SPP =	Small Power Producers
Cogen =	Cogenerators
EWG =	Exempt Wholesale Generator

IPP =	NUG
APP =	IPP with Utility
QF =	IPP/APP under PURPA
EWG =	IPP/APP under EPAct
SPP, Cogen =	Type of QF

Figure 2-8. Types of energy producers and their relationships.

In the alphabet soup of energy acronyms (see Figure 2-8), EWGs include IPPs (Independent Power Producers) and APPs (Affiliated Power Producers), which are those that are owned entirely or in part by traditional rate-based utilities. EPAct allows existing rate-based facilities and hybrid facilities (those with capacity allocated to both the wholesale market and to the regulated utility) to qualify as EWGs. Existing generation facilities can be "spun off" from a traditional utility, leaving that utility's rate base, if allowed by the state regulatory agency. The principle limitation is that no utility can be an affiliate of the EWG of which they are part owners. Furthermore, an electric utility may not enter into a contract to purchase power from an affiliated or associated EWG unless (i) the state regulatory commission can adequately oversee the affiliate transactions to prevent abuse and (ii) the affiliate sale will benefit customers and not provide the EWG with a competitive advantage. Of course, if an EWG has no affiliation with a rate-based utility, these provisions do not apply.

FERC must certify facilities as EWGs, but there are not the efficiency, size, and ownership criteria that face PURPA facilities, so there are few difficult roadblocks to EWG certification. In an early case, a power marketer applied for EWG status without owning any generation facilities. Since there was no "eligible facility," the application was denied. Denial to EWG certification has proven to be rare.

There has been some confusion as to whether a facility should be qualified as a QF (Qualified Facility under PURPA) or an EWG. Certainly if a developer can economically build a facility and has a wholesale buyer for power, he need not worry about steam loads and efficiency requirements and can readily become an EWG. However, there are still benefits to obtaining QF status. For example only a QF can force an interconnected utility to buy excess power. A facility could also become both. If only a portion of a facility's output can be justified based on QF requirements, the remainder can be sold on the open market as an EWG. This is another type of "hybrid" facility allowed by EPAct.

EPAct now gives developers far more opportunity and flexibility than ever before with respect to entering the power market on the generation side. However, an EWG is still only a wholesale supplier and cannot sell power to retail customers and still be exempt from the 1935 Acts and state regulation. Because of the vast amount of excess supply in most parts of the U.S., few developers are finding opportunity to sell power profitably into the wholesale market.

Retail wheeling: In response to intense pressure from investor-owned utilities, and in exchange for allowing open wholesale access, Congress agreed to prevent FERC from conditioning any order on open transmission access for retail customers. Given FERC's interest in introducing competition to the electricity industry, the utilities did not want FERC to begin tacking on retail wheeling mandates to any order that crossed their desks, much as they did with wholesale competition. As a result, EPAct includes the following provision:

> Prohibition on Mandatory Retail Wheeling and Sham Wholesale Transactions. No order issued under this Act shall be conditioned upon or require the transmission of electric energy ...directly to an ultimate consumer.

This prohibition basically prohibits any federally-mandated retail wheeling program unless the Energy Policy Act is revised by Congress. However, a key savings clause was added to prevent a violation of Tenth Amendment issues:

> Nothing in this subsection shall affect any authority of any State of local government under State law concerning the transmission of electric energy directly to an ultimate consumer.

Therefore, FERC cannot issue any order that would limit the right of the individual states to order retail wheeling. Although some utilities that are still fighting competition may disagree, the message to the states is clear: FERC cannot order retail wheeling, but the states can. Later sections of this chapter will cover retail wheeling developments on the state level.

FERC Orders 888 and 889.

On April 24, 1996, FERC ordered the most sweeping and fundamental set of rule changes in the post-EPAct competitive era of the electricity industry. In its Order 888, FERC mandates the functional unbundling of the electricity industry through the implementation of separate, non-discriminatory transmission tariffs that must apply to all wholesale power transactions, including those of the utility that owns the transmission facilities. The order also addresses issues such as stranded investment, jurisdiction, and even the advent of retail wheeling. This rule, along with others issued at the same time (discussed later) not only marks a significant milestone in the road toward a truly competitive electricity market, but also helps pave that road toward retail wheeling.

Order 888 was the result of 20,000 pages of comments and more than a year of consideration by FERC following its landmark Notice of Proposed Rulemaking (NOPR) on open access transmission tariffs issued in March 1995. Commonly called the "giga-NOPR," this set of proposed rules clearly showed that FERC was committed to the introduction of competition to the electricity industry. Although EPAct prohibits FERC from mandating retail wheeling, the giga-NOPR and Order 888 that followed facilitate retail wheeling in that the transmission tariffs mandated by FERC will apply to the transmission component of a retail wheeling transaction. Many states still claim jurisdiction over all aspects of retail electricity sales, including transmission, so a jurisdictional battle may be joined. This jurisdictional issue, which may eventually have to be settled by the U.S. Supreme Court, is discussed in more detail in Appendix A.

In a nutshell, the 800-page Order 888 requires all public utilities (defined below) with transmission assets to offer non-discriminatory, open access transmission and ancillary services to wholesale sellers and purchasers of electric energy in interstate commerce. Each jurisdictional utility has 60 days to file a transmission tariff with certain minimum requirements, although many utilities filed such tariffs based on the rules proposed in the giga-NOPR. Many of the utilities that filed early tariffs will have to re-file to meet the requirements in Order 888. With these tariffs in place, wholesale buyers and sellers will not need to use the EPAct's Section 211 procedure to gain access to transmission since all transmitting utilities will have open access tariffs on file.

FERC found that the use of EPAct Section 211 was an ineffective procedure for gaining transmission access because of the time delay from when service is requested until the wheeling order could be issued. In fact, FERC found that Section 211 "can result in the perpetuation of, rather than the elimination of, undue discrimination and anticompetitive effects," and "is an inadequate procedural substitute for readily available service." Therefore, FERC did not want to rely on EPAct to implement open transmission access that is the key to an unbundled, competitive market.

Instead, FERC turned back to Section 206 of the Federal Power Act of 1935 that gives it jurisdiction over interstate transmission and wholesale transactions. Section 206 is the source of FERC's authority to require transmission tariffs, but it does not apply to all "transmission utilities," as defined in EPAct, that are subject to Section 211. Therefore, Order 888 and its open access tariff requirements only apply to "public utilities," as defined in the

Federal Power Act, which includes investor-owned utilities but not municipal electric utilities, cooperatives, or federal power agencies. FERC does, however, give incentive for these non-jurisdictional utilities to allow open access to their transmission systems by requiring reciprocity, i.e., if a non-jurisdictional utility wants access to a public utility's transmission system via its open access tariffs, it must give that utility access to its transmission system. The non-jurisdictional utility need not file an open access tariff to grant reciprocity, so the issue of how that reciprocal open access is implemented remains. FERC can only encourage the broad use of Section 211 by groups of qualified applicants to gain access to transmission on those utilities outside of Section 206 jurisdiction.

The cornerstone to these open access transmission tariffs is comparability of service. The golden rule of comparability of service requires utilities to offer the same transmission service to all parties, including itself, with non-discriminatory prices and quality of service. Therefore, a wholesale buyer shipping power through an interconnected utility will have the same access to transmission that the utility itself has for its own wholesale transactions. The utility may still give priority to its native retail load. A transmission utility that also provides traditional utility service to retail customers (which is most utilities at this point) can reserve a portion of its transmission capacity for that native load. However, if that utility wants to wheel power in or out of its control area, it must use its own transmission facilities under the same rates, terms, and conditions that it offers to other shippers. Of course, the use of consistent tariffs will facilitate comparable service since all transmission access must conform to the rates, terms, and conditions of the tariff.

In order for a utility to fairly charge itself the same price for transmission service that it charges third-party shippers, the transmission component of the utility's traditional integrated service must be separated from other functions such as generation and distribution. In Order 636 for natural gas (discussed in detail in the next section), FERC mandated corporate separation of gas transportation services in order to effectively "unbundle" that service from other services. In Order 888 for electricity, however, FERC finds only that "functional unbundling" is required. That is, the utilities are not required to spin-off transmission assets to non-affiliated companies, but they must create revenue crediting mechanisms that ensure that the costs and charges for transmission services are independently accounted for to ensure proper ratemaking. This may be difficult for many utilities since transmission was integrated into the overall service of providing electricity to end-user customers.

FERC's new Order 888 requires utilities to offer transmission service as either (i) firm or nonfirm, (ii) network or point-to-point, and (iii) short- or long-term. With respect to firmness, the order specifies priority for both reservation and interruption. Although service must be non-discriminatory, reservation and interruption priority can be based on (i) firm beats non-firm, (ii) network beats point-to-point, (iii) long-term beats short-term, and finally, (iv) price can be used as a tie-breaker. The nature of these services is discussed in more detail in Chapter 7. Order 888 also anticipates an active secondary market for these various services, similar to capacity release allowed in natural gas. That is, if a particular service can be assigned or sold (and some services are more applicable to a secondary market than others), the tariffs must allow the purchaser to do so.

Order 888 requires utilities to offer the many "ancillary" services involved in transmission to transmission users in the tariffs. These ancillary services were defined in the original giga-NOPR (for the first time) as "those services necessary to support the transmission of electric power from seller to purchaser given the obligations of control areas ... to maintain reliable operations of the interconnected transmission system." According to the order, these services include system control and dispatch services, reactive power and voltage support, regulation and frequency response, energy balancing, and operating reserves. Other services necessary for transmission of purchased power such as transmission losses must be purchased by the shipper from some supplier, but the transmission company is not required to offer these services in its open access tariffs. These services and others are discussed in detail in Chapter 8, so further elaboration is not required here.

When FERC was contemplating the mandatory implementation of open access transmission tariffs, the myriad of unresolved issues such as transmission pricing methodologies and parallel path flows threatened to delay the necessary orders by years. Industry experts have argued for years, and continue to argue, the benefits and risks of various ways of pricing and reserving transmission capacity. At first, FERC was challenged to mediate these arguments and select an optimum pricing and reservation methodology that could be applied across the country. Wisely, FERC rejected this challenge and instead opted for rapid implementation over optimization. Included in Order 888 is a "pro forma" tariff that the utilities can use as a model for almost assured approval. The pro forma tariff even has fill-in-the-blank sections for pricing, and it must be filed within 60 days after the order was issued (by June 1996).

The pro forma tariffs included in Order 888 require transmission services to be priced on a postage-stamp basis according to the utility's embedded costs for the transmission facilities. Postage-stamp pricing (so-called because the distance involved is irrelevant) based on embedded costs is the methodology used traditionally by most utilities when transmission services were sold. However, FERC and most industry analysts realize that these methodologies are far from the ideal way to price transmission. Many creative and more realistic methodologies have been proposed, such as megawatt-mile and locational transmission pricing. Nonetheless, rather than rule on these alternative proposals, FERC will require traditional postage-stamp embedded pricing in the pro forma tariffs. Then, if either a shipper or a transmission utility wishes to modify a tariff and incorporate a better pricing scheme, FERC will consider the proposal in a conventional hearing context. While these debates are held, at least the pro forma tariff will be in place, thus ensuring the existence of at least some form of uniform, open access tariff even if that tariff is imperfect.

To ensure that all shippers, including the utility itself, have equal access to transmission resources, FERC is also mandating the creation of an open access same-time information system, or "OASIS," for transmission capacity availability and price information. Learning a lesson from the natural gas industry restructuring, OASIS will parallel the electronic bulletin boards (EBBs) used for gas transportation, except that a common access protocol and information format will be specified. OASIS will provide hourly information on each utility's available transmission capacity and price, and this information will be accessible via the Internet. Furthermore, OASIS will be transactional, i.e., transmission capacity reservations may be made directly on OASIS. This system was the subject of FERC's Order 889, which was issued concurrently with Order 888, and each order references and depends on the other.

Third-party shippers and the transmission utility itself must use OASIS to determine whether transmission capacity exists to implement the transaction desired. This raises some interesting technical issues, because the industry's engineers have struggled with how to quantify incremental transmission capacity on a highly interconnected grid where line loadings constantly change. These issues remained open even as Order 889 was issued, yet OASIS must be operational by November 1996. OASIS and other transmission issues will be discussed in greater detail in Chapter 7.

While the main focus of Order 888 is transmission access issues, it also addresses the thorny issue of stranded investment, at least with respect to wholesale transactions. Not surprisingly, the giga-NOPR's proposed rule allowing full recovery of wholesale stranded costs by utilities was the most contested section of the giga-NOPR. Nonetheless, Order 888 retained most of the language of the giga-NOPR, which requires that all verifiable and justifiable stranded costs be borne by the end-users leaving their native utility. This is contrary to how take-or-pay contracts were dealt with in natural gas, where these transition costs were shared with pipeline shareholders. The discussion in Order 888 includes considerable hand-wringing over the issue of whether stranded costs should be paid by only exiting customers or by all customers. Recognizing valid arguments on both sides, FERC chose to force only those customers leaving to pay for the costs of the transition to competition.

Stranded investment due to the advent of retail wheeling is an issue that FERC is leaving for the states, even though FERC claims concurrent jurisdiction over the issue. However, most states appear to be favoring a broad-base approach to stranded cost recovery. For example, in California, the Public Utility Commission is favoring a "competition transition charge" that will be charged to all end-users regardless of whether they leave their existing supplier. Furthermore, other states are considering some form of sharing of these costs and incentives for utilities to minimize their stranded investments. Regulators in New Hampshire propose a 50/50 sharing of stranded costs between ratepayers and the utilities. Again, this is different than the gas experience where states usually attempted to keep the utilities whole while FERC mandated the sharing of transition costs. The stranded cost issue is perhaps the largest issue facing electricity re-regulation and is discussed in Appendix B.

Besides Order 888 and 889, FERC also issued a new NOPR on April 24, 1996, relating to the reservation of transmission capacity in the form of yet another new acronym, "CRT," or capacity reservation tariff. In its new proposal, FERC is suggesting that all transmission should be point-to-point (as discussed in detail in Chapter 7) and that each path should be separately reserved and priced. This system, according to FERC, would be more consistent with its OASIS model and comparability of service. FERC senses a problem with network service in that it is difficult to quantify its effect on overall transmission capacity, it is impossible to reserve, and it must be priced differently than point-to-point service. The new CRTs would also be very consistent with how transportation was handled in the gas industry, so FERC could borrow many of the pricing methodologies developed there. On the other hand, requiring all transmission to be handled on a point-to-point basis may make aggregation of loads and suppliers very complicated and unwieldy, especially for smaller users. For example, how would an end-user with 20 facilities in a control area arrange for every combination of transmission paths if up to 20 possible suppliers may be used? Perhaps in the third edition of this book this question will be answered and CRT may either fall by the wayside or be the new standard for open access tariffs. In any case, this new NOPR raises awareness of the magnitude of the issue of transmission pricing and reservation.

Although Orders 888 and 889 and the new CRT NOPR can only encourage greater wholesale competition, there is no question that they will facilitate development of retail competition, and this was likely FERC's intent. Because these orders resolve many of the issues that have been slowing the development of retail wheeling, such as federal vs. state jurisdiction and transmission pricing, at least initially, a state will find it much easier to implement a retail wheeling initiative. While some states may delay retail wheeling implementation until other states have succeeded or failed with theirs, many states will be encouraged to implement retail competition now that at least the transmission tariffs are in place. Once state public utility laws are changed or interpreted to allow retail access to competitive generation, there is little regulatory work left to do. Therefore, Orders 888 and 889 are significant developments for retail wheeling even though FERC is not allowed to order retail wheeling.

Federal Legislation.

While retail wheeling has been a state issue since the passage of the Energy Policy Act of 1992 (the last section of this chapter will cover the development of state retail wheeling programs), considerable interest has developed recently in a federally mandated retail wheeling program. Rather than letting a mishmash of fifty different direct access programs develop over time, some advocate the implementation of a single, consistent, nation-wide program that would be implemented by FERC. This would obviously require modifications to EPAct, and such a program has also been tied to the repeal of the Public Utility Holding Company Act of 1935 (PUHCA) and the Public Utility Regulatory Policy Act of 1978 (PURPA), discussed earlier. At the time of this writing, at least three Congressional representatives have introduced restructuring legislation, and the interest in retail wheeling exists on both sides of the aisle. Reaction to these bills has followed expected stakeholder lines. Serious Congressional consideration is not expected until 1997, after the 1996 election year.

Senator J. Bennett Johnston (D-La.) introduced a comprehensive electricity industry restructuring bill on January 25, 1996, that would implement retail wheeling nationwide by 2010. In addition to repealing PUHCA and PURPA, the law would give explicit state authority for implementing retail wheeling. The proposed bill also allows the states to develop their own stranded cost recovery rules; however, if necessary, the federal government would step in to force direct access and address stranded investment in the absence of a state program.

Representative Dan Schaefer (R-Colo.), and Chairman of the House Commerce Energy and Power Subcommittee, has announced plans to introduce legislation that will address retail wheeling and stranded costs. Schaefer has said that he is strongly in favor of competition down to the retail level. Schaefer is unclear as to whether federally mandated retail wheeling is necessary or if federal law is only required to remove the barriers to programs implemented on a state level. In any case, such legislation would be a comprehensive package that would address PUHCA and PURPA as well.

Representative Ed Markey (D-Mass.) has introduced legislation that claims to have bipartisan support, including that from Schaefer. While leaving restructuring details to the states, Markey's "Electric Power Competition Act of 1996" would create federal standards for generation divestiture, unbundling, open-access transmission, and retail direct access. Stranded investment recovery would be allowed under a non-bypassable wires charge that would also fund social programs. Once the states and FERC certify that competition exists, then PUHCA and PURPA would be repealed.

If these three proposed bills are any indication, any federal initiative to introduce retail competition would probably be limited to removing some of the existing barriers to facilitating state development of their own programs. Federal legislation could resolve the jurisdictional issue plus mandate certain FERC interests, such as regional independent system operators. It appears unlikely, however, that Congress is interested in usurping state development of the programs that actually implement retail wheeling. Thus, even if Congress mandates full retail wheeling across the country by a certain date, the "fifty laboratories" theory of implementation will still apply along with the variations and confusion that follow. As for PUHCA and PURPA, repeal seems certain, although it will not occur until competition exists so that the protections that those programs provide are no longer necessary.

Natural Gas Industry Restructuring

Many comparisons have been made between the changes that have occurred in the natural gas industry and those that are occurring in the electricity industry. Both involve the transition of an energy market from a heavily regulated industry to that driven by competitive forces. Many of the lessons learned in gas re-regulation have already been applied to the electricity industry, such as comparability of service for transmission. Indeed, the success of the introduction of competition to the gas industry is one primary driving force behind electricity industry restructuring, and those industry players that lived through natural gas re-regulation are those that are convinced that equal successes are possible with electricity.

There are differences between the natural gas and electricity industries. Yet even FERC commissioners have concluded that the FERC's natural gas experience is relevant to its emerging policies on electricity industry restructuring. FERC Commissioner Donald Santa once admonished, "Avoid superficial parallelism. On the other hand, you would be remiss to ignore the lessons of the natural gas experience."

The natural gas industry, like electricity, has historically been heavily regulated at the federal and state levels. As with the other utility industries, the reason for regulation was to avoid monopoly power, develop economies of scale and to encourage expansion to meet the growing economy. Heavy handed regulation was required in order to guarantee reliability and adequate resources at reasonable prices.

The natural gas industry, however, is somewhat unique in its regulation history since the commodity portion was also regulated through federal price controls. The federal government in the early 1950s controlled the price at the wellhead for all gas sold into the interstate pipeline system. The price of wellhead gas was determined based on a number of factors including geological formations, location and depth of wells and the era in which the well was drilled. With the commodity being controlled along with transportation and distribution costs, few choices were left for purchasers and consumers of natural gas. The result was a fully bundled burnertip gas supply where transportation prices were set by federal agencies on the interstate pipeline systems and by state regulators for local distribution.

This system appeared to work favorably until the late 1960s and early 1970s providing an abundant supply of energy at reasonable prices. As with any heavily regulated industry, however, the production and transportation became inefficient. Additionally, in the early 1970s the U.S. was apparently running out of natural gas due to a perceived threat of scarce resources. During this time domestic oil prices were skyrocketing. It did not make sense for an oil and gas producer to invest in the gas industry where prices were controlled, while oil, an unregulated commodity, was anticipated to go above $40 per barrel. This caused a temporary shortage of natural gas from the lack of investment in production. To complicate matters, gas supplies into the intrastate systems did not have price controls. This allowed producers to sell gas above the controlled prices into intrastate pipelines. Because of these inefficiencies and a lack of incentive to produce, the Natural Gas Policy Act of 1978 was passed by Congress to start unbundling the commodity from transportation and distribution and to clear the way for the price controls to be lifted over a period of time. The immediate result of this Act was that the interstate pipelines were allowed to negotiate individual and unique arrangements. For the most part, these deals tended to be long term (10 to 15 years) with what turned out to be prices significantly above market value.

In the early 1980s, several events occurred that caused some of these changes to backfire on the industry. First, the country faced another recession along with strong foreign competition, which started a redirection of the industrial base. It was apparent that the U.S. economy had to compete in the worldwide markets and could not sustain high energy costs. The need to compete combined with the surging prices caused some facilities to shut down and others to undertake stringent conservation efforts. Additionally, for the first time, residential and commercial customers were addressing more efficient housing and building units. The gas industry experienced a rapid decline in annual consumption within several years from 23 trillion cubic feet down to a little over 16 trillion cubic feet. As one might suspect, this caused an oversupply of the gas commodity.

In 1985, FERC passed its landmark Order 436 which, for the first time, provided open access transportation to the industry. Most industry participants viewed this order as a threat to their monopolistic power. In the discussions prior to the FERC order, the local distribution companies (LDCs) were expected to be the major participant in open access transportation. As it turned out, large industrials sensed an opportunity for the first time to take control of their gas needs and immediately reduce their gas cost. Not only did industrials have access to gas supplies at the wellhead, but they started to peal away at the onion of bundled services provided by the interstate pipelines and LDCs. The industrials also pressured LDCs and state regulators to begin unbundling their systems and offer transportation only services similar to the interstate pipelines.

Order 436 allowed an interstate pipeline to offer firm and interruptible transportation on a non-discriminatory basis. Each pipeline had to establish tariffs and rates with minimum and maximum charges. The order also attempted to provide a transition period that allowed the interstate pipelines and LDCs to start de-contracting their sales obligation over a five-year period. What the order did not address is unbundling and open access to storage or the reformation of the supply agreements between interstate pipelines and producers. This latter issue was covered in Order 500, which addressed take-or-pay obligations that the pipelines incurred and provided a settlement mechanism and a method to pass the cost to downstream customers. During this period, a spot market for gas started to develop. Short-term supplies were selling below $2 per MMBtu while long-term supplies were contracted in many instances above $5 per MMBtu. This price disparity caused a rapid shift in purchasing practices where possible, leaving interstate pipelines with a serious take-or-pay obligation for gas that was not being purchased.

The open access transportation that resulted from FERC Order 436 had an immediate impact on reducing burnertip gas costs. Within a short period, a very competitive commodity market developed which allowed purchasers of natural gas to negotiate directly with the producers and a new industry participant: the gas marketer. Heading into the 1990s, the majority of the gas consumed in our country was through open access transportation. Excess supplies that developed because of over production started to dwindle. This caused extreme volatility in the spot market with unpredictable prices at the wellhead. Also during this time period, natural gas started to be traded on the New York Mercantile Exchange, which led the way to other futures contracts and financial products to be used to establish the price of natural gas.

There were several major areas that left the industry vulnerable. Because FERC Order 436 did not provide for the unbundling of storage service, buyers of gas, primarily LDCs, were not convinced that transportation was as reliable as the bundled citygate sales service that the interstate pipelines still had to provide. As a result, LDCs did not exercise their full rights to convert the former sales service to firm transportation. In fact, five years after the implementation of Order 436, only approximately 25% of the sales service was converted to firm transportation. Interruptible transportation was displacing firm citygate sales service. In the early 1990s, over 50% of the gas consumed was transported on an interruptible basis. This resulted in very low utilization of the interstate pipeline's bundled sales service for which less than 20% of the gas was traded. This left the pipelines between a rock and a hard place since they still had the obligation to serve firm customers even on peak days. On the other hand, interstate pipelines had an advantage on monopolizing the best receipt points, storage and upstream transportation. Many thought this gave the pipelines an unfair advantage over transportation customers.

To address these issues, FERC issued a Notice of Proposed Rulemaking (NOPR) in 1991 to seek comments on further restructuring of the natural gas industry. Comments from this "mega-NOPR" resulted in the landmark FERC Order 636, which completely unbundled intrastate services. No longer could interstate pipelines provide a bundled citygate sales service nor could LDCs depend upon this service. FERC's intent was to level the playing field so that all participants had equal access to supply, transportation and storage. To accomplish this, FERC set up a series of rules that described how access to the services on interstate pipelines would be allocated to former firm citygate sales customers and other shippers. With this allocation, came the obligation of the customers to deal with the stranded investment that would result from the pipelines de-contracting for upstream services. The FERC established a set of rules to deal with these transition costs and prescribed how downstream customers would pay for the restructuring of the natural gas industry. Also, downstream customers had to assume the responsibility of managing their own supply and transportation. Since the pipeline was no longer allowed to make bundled citygate sales, it lost control of most of its storage and transportation assets. Therefore, FERC allowed pipelines to establish a set of operating conditions that, if violated, would result in punitive penalties assessed by the pipelines.

To level the playing field, pipelines were forced to give up access to its competitive gas supply and upstream transportation arrangements. In addition, FERC set up a series of rules that would allow the holders of firm capacity to operate within the pipeline, similar to the way the pipelines conducted their business as bundled citygate sales providers. Issues like no-notice services, secondary receipt and delivery points and the ability to release unused capacity were addressed. Unbundling these services provided aggressive fuel managers the ability to take control of as much of the business as they desired. Many who took the time to understand the unbundling process and the operations of the pipelines, positioned themselves to reduce costs and maintain, or in some instances, increase reliability.

For the most part, the implementation of FERC Order 636 has accomplished the task set out by FERC. Clearly there is competition within all aspects of the natural gas industry except at the distribution level. The playing field has been leveled so that all participants can have equal access to supply, transportation and storage services. The establishment of the electronic bulletin boards, which were mandated by FERC, has made it easier for industry participants to communicate on a frequent basis on issues like operational flow orders, availability of capacity to buy or sell, constraints on the pipeline system and changes to pipeline tariffs. The capacity release market has become robust with most of the deals being done on a short-term basis through pre-arranged negotiations between the releasing and the replacement shipper. FERC anticipated that the electronic bulletin boards would be the primary method to post and bid on excess capacity. As it has turned out, the secondary market has developed its informal system and is operating on pre-arranged deals all within the guidelines of the pipeline tariffs. In the first 18 months of capacity trading, the market clearing price for capacity on most pipelines was about one-third of the maximum tariff rates.

LDCs have yet to completely unbundle their services. Until this is accomplished, many end-users will not realize the full benefit of a completely unbundled natural gas marketplace. In many areas the prices charged for distribution services are not reflective of cost of service rates. That is, there is still some subsidization by the industrial sector to the benefit of the residential commercial customer. If the state regulators and LDCs do not take steps to correct this inequity, industrials will be forced to look at competitive alternatives, such as bypassing the LDC by directly interconnecting with the interstate pipeline.

During the first year and a half of restructured rates and services, the system appears to be working pretty much as FERC had intended. Access to multiple pipelines and supply basins gives natural gas users flexibility to arrange supplies and transportation to meet their needs. A robust capacity release market, although not competitively bid through the pipeline bulletin boards, provides fuel managers the opportunity to craft very creative arrangements. Once LDCs are forced to unbundle their rates and services, then end users will have the opportunity to further manage the risks of supply and transportation.

For the industry to maintain its stability, it will have to have continued access to reliable supplies at reasonable prices. Since open access transportation, the gas industry has truly become a North American marketplace. Access to Canadian supplies, which provide over 10% of the U. S. gas demand, will continue to be a viable option for many end-users. Pipeline expansion projects also will provide additional flexibility to move gas supplies from non traditional supply basins to different parts of the country. There is no major increase in demand expected except in the power generation markets. Experts predict an increase of one and one-half to two and one-half trillion feet a year for new gas fired power generation over the next ten years. These markets will not be developed unless supply costs remain low relative to other energy choices for the power generators. In addition, the industry will have to offer more flexible balancing services and possibly hourly nominations to meet the load profiles of the power generators. The gas industry is poised to meet the challenges of new growth markets. With financial instruments available to manage price risks, open access transportation with flexible services, access to storage and a dynamic capacity release market will provide all of the ingredients for the natural gas industry to meet the needs of its current and future markets.

Comparing natural gas to the power industry, the two share four common characteristics, according to FERC:

- the emergence of competition within the industry,
- public policy has determined that competition is desirable,
- transmission of the commodity remains a regulated monopoly, and
- the focus of regulation has shifted from the entire industry to only the monopoly segment.

From this, FERC has concluded that the lessons of the natural gas industry are applicable to the increasingly competitive electricity industry. A prime example of this is the need for comparability of service in transmission. The need to completely unbundle gas transportation was the missing element of Order 436 and was the principle of Order 636. As we have seen, FERC learned this lesson and is thus requiring functional unbundling of transmission service in its NOPR on open access transmission tariffs. Whenever applicable, this book will compare experiences in gas with developments in power so that the lessons from natural gas reregulation are not lost.

Existing Retail Wheeling Transactions

Retail wheeling is not entirely a new concept. There are many instances of industrial end-users having access to off-system power where the native utility has been forced to wheel the power for a fee. There are also some states that have had some semblance of retail competition on the law books well ahead of recent developments. The key difference between these situations and true retail wheeling is that the end-user does not have the freedom to choose electrical suppliers whenever it wants. Instead, either a specific supplier is involved (usually a government generation project) or the end-user has a one-time choice of suppliers in the case of new load.

A well noted example of an existing retail wheeling transaction is the purchase of low-cost hydroelectric generation from the New York Power Authority (NYPA, formerly the Power Authority of the State of New York, or PASNY). After the collapse of a hydroelectric dam owned by Niagara Mohawk in the late 1950s, the state of New York agreed to fund the reconstruction of the dam in exchange for allowing the state to sell the power at a low cost to new industrial loads as a means to encourage economic development. Pursuant to a state statute dating back to 1961, end-users that have incremental load in New York can purchase this "replacement" power (as in replacement of the dam) or "expansion" power (the program was expanded in later years) for rates as low as 0.6¢ per kilowatt-hour. On top of this, the native utility can add a transmission charge. This program is still available to incremental load in New York.

Unlike true retail wheeling, the customers of NYPA power cannot purchase power alternatively on the open market—although they would not be able to find lower cost power anyway—and the services offered by the native utility are not truly unbundled. However, these arrangements dispel early concerns that placing loads in neighboring control areas is technically infeasible or undesirable.

Similar arrangements exist in the West with low cost hydroelectric power developed by federal agencies, such as the Bonneville Power Administration (BPA) and the Western Area Power Administration (WAPA). As with the NYPA situation, sales from these sources directly to end-users is allowed per specific statutory authority and are not instances of true retail access. WAPA sells hydroelectric power to 148 end-users which are all federal, state, or local government agencies, including hospitals, universities, military bases, and irrigation and water districts. This power is wheeled over 48 transmission companies in 12 Western states. The BPA also has direct end-user contracts, and some of them are industrial consumers buying directly through public utility districts.

There are some examples of off-system access permitted by utilities as part of negotiated deals approved by state regulators. In the early 1980s, Dow Chemical wheeled power from an independent generator that Dow owned in Ontario to a Michigan facility via Ontario Hydro, Detroit Edison, and Consumers Power. More recently, North Star Steel used the promise of jobs and economic growth to extract an arrangement in Arizona that will allow them to truly access the open market. The local utility will provide local control area services and WAPA will provide transmission, but the source of the bulk power will be up to North Star Steel. These types of arrangements are increasingly common as end-users are able to leverage utilities, especially with incremental load.

Retail wheeling in limited forms have been offered by some states for many years. To attract industrial growth, Georgia and Alabama allow new customers to make a one-time choice of supplier as long as it is in-state. However, in these states, there are few choices of suppliers outside the major Southern Company utilities. In Maine, self-service wheeling is allowed, i.e., if a company has multiple facilities in the state and one of them has a self-generation facility, the local utility is required to wheel any excess generation to the other facilities. In New Hampshire, cogenerators can sell power to up to three end-users. However, this has never been done because New Hampshire was one of a few states that sought to encourage independent power production by offering very high, front-end loaded rates for excess power purchases from the local utility. Therefore, a New Hampshire cogenerator can make more money by selling excess power to the utility than by selling on an open retail market.

As further evidence that retail wheeling is technically feasible, municipal electric utility loads, including many that are fed with distribution voltage systems, wheel power today in ways very similar to how retail loads will wheel power in the future. In some cases, the municipal electric company will arrange specific contract paths with its native utility and with neighboring utilities to a specific supplier. In other cases, the municipal will telemeter its load to its supplying utility so that the load is effectively moved from one control area to another. The most common arrangement, however, is for the municipal electric utility to purchase all of its requirements from a joint action agency, or "umbrella group" that provides its member municipal utilities with its bulk power requirements, engineering services, administrative functions, and a host of other services that a small utility could not efficiently do itself. These joint action agencies purchase or generate power much like a large investor-owned utility and then deliver this power to the member municipals via the interconnected, native transmission utility. This power is bought on a short term or long term basis and is nominated to the native utilities. This system functions very similarly to how an industrial end-user will buy power in a retail wheeling environment, which will be explained in detail in Part II. At the time of this writing, as will be discussed in the next section, retail wheeling has begun to occur on a limited basis in at least two states, Illinois and New Hampshire. These states are the first to implement small-scale retail wheeling pilot programs. Given the relatively small amount of load involved in these initiatives, there was little doubt that wheeling would be technically or administratively feasible. While these programs answer many questions and force many issues to be resolved immediately, they are still like the examples given above, i.e., limited examples of retail wheeling. Nonetheless, at this point, suffice it to say, retail wheeling will work because it works already.

State Development of Retail Wheeling Initiatives

As we have seen, retail wheeling must be developed on a state-by-state basis because of the prohibition in the Energy Policy Act against a general FERC mandate for open transmission access. Beyond the retail wheeling transactions described in the previous chapter, retail wheeling interest among the states has exploded since the passage of the Energy Policy Act, which appears to save the development of retail wheeling for the states.

Nevada was the first state with a true retail wheeling statute, which was passed in only three days in response to an interest by North Star Steel in siting a new steel "mini-mill" in the state with large electrical arc furnace loads. This bill was so narrowly drafted, however, that only this particular load for which it was intended could ever hope to meet the bill's requirements. Besides applying only to new load, the end-user must invest over $50 million in capital expenditures in the state, the product manufactured at the new facility must be 50% recyclable, the utility must show that it will not raise residential rates as a result, and the Nevada Public Service Commission must approve every contract for service under the retail wheeling tariff.

Ironically, North Star Steel elected to place the new plant in Arizona after negotiating a special arrangement with Citizens Power—the native utility in the area in which the plant was sited. Under this arrangement, North Star Steel will reportedly have full access to area transmission and will be able to effectively retail wheel, including separate purchase of required ancillary services. This will then be one of the first retail wheeling arrangements in which the end-user is responsible for procuring each unbundled component.

On April 11, 1994, Michigan became, for a very brief period, the leading state in the retail wheeling race with an experimental program sponsored by an industrial users group called ABATE, the Association of Businesses Advocating Tariff Equity. Under this program approved by the Michigan Public Service Commission (MPSC), Detroit Edison and Consumers Power, the state's two largest utilities, are required to offer 90 megawatts and 60 megawatts, respectively, of retail wheeling capacity. The program is designed to commence when either utility requests incremental capacity, so that the direct access load would not invoke a claim of stranded investment by the utilities.

To qualify for this plan, the end-user must have a minimum load of 5 MW and contract for 2 to 10 MW of retail wheeling capacity for a term of five years. Customers would make all arrangements to have power delivered to the host utility and from there the host utility would be responsible for delivering the unbundled service to the customer. All loads dedicated to retail wheeling must be separately metered and capable of being interrupted by the host utility if the customer's supply is inadequate. After the experiment, retail wheeling customers would be permitted to return to the host utility without penalty.

The Michigan retail wheeling experiment is significant because the MPSC based its authority to order the experiment on various provisions of the state's public utility act that grants the MPSC broad authority. In other words, the MPSC found the authority to implement retail wheeling, at least on an experimental basis, without any specific statutory authority to do so.

The Michigan plan is flawed in many ways that will (and did) invite legal challenges sure to delay implementation of the plan or result in its demise. First, the MPSC declared in the order that the FERC could not preempt the Commission's authority to regulate the rates, terms, and conditions of any part of the retail wheeling transaction, including transmission. This appears to be in direct conflict with the FERC's claim of jurisdiction over all interstate transmission. In fact, only one week before the MPSC's order was issued, FERC issued a decision that it had jurisdiction over all interstate transmission services, including those that involve the use of distribution facilities. Therefore, the MPSC order was destined for a court challenge on jurisdiction as soon as it was issued, and Detroit Edison soon challenged the validity of the order on these grounds in federal court.

Second, the MPSC determined that all third-party suppliers involved in the retail wheeling experiment must (i) obtain from the MPSC a certificate of public convenience and necessity to do business as a public utility, (ii) obtain a service franchise from the local municipality, and (iii) obtain from the MPSC approval of the rates, terms, and conditions of each power sales transaction prior to the start of service. These heavy-handed regulatory requirements will certainly discourage participation by many suppliers in the program, which will then skew the results of the experiment. Furthermore, many potential suppliers could never qualify as a "public utility." Therefore, industrial user groups have challenged the order as meaningless given the unrealistic nature of the regulatory requirements.

Since both end-users and utilities oppose the plan on legal and regulatory grounds, the Michigan experimental retail wheeling program appears to be little more than a lawyer's full employment act. However, it is significant in that it indicates an interest by a Commission in the benefits of retail wheeling and the willingness to apply some of its principles.

While this plan certainly created substantial interest in the industry, it was quickly eclipsed by a fully developed retail wheeling implementation plan (not experimental) for California. On April 24, 1994, only 13 days after issuance of the Michigan experimental retail wheeling plan, the California Public Utilities Commission (CPUC) issued its famed "Blue Book"(so-named because of the color of its cover), an order instigating an investigation into restructuring the electricity industry in the state. The Blue Book was the follow up to the CPUC staff's "Yellow Book" which suggested four possible solutions to perceived inadequacies of the existing regulatory structure of the electricity industry in California. The most extreme of those four options was adopted by the CPUC in the Blue Book. This plan, which became the primary focus of state retail wheeling development across the country, proposed the following:

- Direct access would be available to transmission-voltage industrial customers by January, 1996, primary-voltage industrial customers by 1997, secondary-voltage customers by 1998, commercial customers by 1999 and residential customers by 2002.
- Existing economic regulation will be replaced with "the discipline of market forces" for the customer classes that can retail wheel. Until a competitive market is available to all customers, traditional cost-plus ratemaking will be replaced with performance incentives for the utilities. When all customers can retail wheel, the Commission will focus on ensuring non-discriminatory transmission, distribution, and ancillary services that are still natural monopolies.
- Customers can choose whether to be a utility service customer, i.e., continue to take bundled service from the interconnected utility, or be a direct access customer, which can purchase power on the open market and have that power wheeled by the utility.
- The traditional obligation to serve only applies to those customers that choose to remain with their native utility. To return to the utility, a direct access customer must give 12 months notice and pay for any cost actually incurred to supply service.
- A utility can build new generation only for those customers remaining on the system. This unbundled generation from transmission with respect to direct access customers.
- The CPUC promised not to jeopardize the financial integrity of the state's investor-owned utilities and will allow a temporary stranded investment recovery charge as a line item for customers that leave the system.
- The CPUC did *not* claim jurisdiction over the transmission services, and it promised to work with FERC to mitigate existing jurisdictional conflicts. The proposal also fully supports the use of Regional Transmission Groups (RTGs).

- The CPUC encouraged the state legislature to support the plan with appropriate modifications to existing state laws that give the utilities exclusive service territories in exchange for guaranteed rates of return on investment.

Unlike the Michigan experimental retail wheeling plan, the CPUC order recognized the ambiguities in the boundaries between federal and state jurisdiction over transmission. To avoid litigation, the CPUC planned to "build upon and generally support the policies set forth in EPAct, as well as those established by FERC. We do not, therefore, anticipate conflict." Because of the legal challenges to a state's rights to implement retail wheeling that were raised in Michigan, jurisdiction has not been a large issue in California.

But this does not mean that the California plan was without controversy. By the first anniversary of the issuance of the Blue Book in 1995, over 10,000 pages of comments had been filed as various industry players and special interest groups took sides on the debate. Early on, the debate focused on whether retail wheeling was really necessary to inject competition into the industry or whether the wholesale market, if fully competitive, would achieve the same results. This debate evolved in a fundamental difference in opinion over how the electricity industry should be structured in the first place.

Southern California Edison (Edison), the state's second largest utility, advocated competition through the use of a centralized power pool into which all generators would sell and from which all users would buy. This "poolco" model was primarily based on the system developed in Great Britain and is fully described in Chapter 4. To the contrary, the state's largest utility, Pacific Gas & Electric (PG&E), advocated a system of bilateral contracts, i.e., individually negotiated power purchase contracts between buyers and sellers. This would involve the use of a supply coordinator that would act as an interface between these transactions and the transmission grid operator. This model is also fully developed in Chapter 4.

Before long, the entire retail wheeling debate moved from *whether* to *how*. While issues such as jurisdiction, stranded investment, and transmission pricing were still unsettled, the primary discussion focussed on implementation. The CPUC soon found itself embroiled in a debate between poolco and bilateral contracts which it surely never expected when it issued its original order. However, this debate is necessary because it lays the necessary groundwork for retail wheeling. In other words, someone has to break new ground first and address the expected and unexpected thorny issues. This is why most state regulatory commissions found themselves watching developments in California rather than taking on the retail wheeling issue themselves.

The CPUC's original timetable for implementation was quickly rendered optimistic. Edison quickly proclaimed that transition to a retail market should be slow and deliberate. Even PG&E offered to write off a significant portion of its investment in its Diablo Canyon nuclear power plant in exchange for pushing residential retail wheeling to the year 2008. Most significantly, soon after the CPUC plan was unveiled, the California Legislature responded to a perceived threat to its control over a major aspect of the state's economy with its Bill 143, which required involvement by the legislature in the restructuring process. The eventual role of the state legislature is yet unclear, although for now it is serving only an oversight function. If the CPUC either stalls development towards direct retail access or if it oversteps its rulemaking authority beyond the bounds of existing state law, the legislature is sure to become more deeply involved.

As of this writing, California continues its drive toward full retail wheeling for all end-users in all customer classes. On December 20, 1995, the CPUC issued its "final" decision on electricity industry restructuring, which adopted a timetable to implement full retail wheeling over a five-year period beginning in 1998. Rather than phase in retail wheeling by customer class, 1,800 MW of load, shared among all customer classes, would be eligible for direct access no later than January 1, 1998. As proposed in a self-negotiated memorandum of understanding among the major stakeholders in the state, the plan involves both bilateral contracts and a voluntary poolco, which was renamed the Western Power Exchange (WEPEX). While technical issues continue to be ironed out, the principle source of delay in California continues to be stranded cost recovery, especially with respect to the larger nuclear power stations in the state.

During the transition period in California, the WEPEX power pool would be the mandatory source of power for all native load still supplied by the existing investor-owned utilities. For those customers with direct access, which would be all customers by 2003, WEPEX will be a spot market for short-term power requirements. Contrary to earlier models, this power pool will be separate from the operation of the transmission system (which would be included in the original poolco model). California quickly learned that the transmission system must be operated by an independent entity that has no interest in any power transaction, retail or wholesale. As a result, the CPUC suggested the creation of an independent system operator (ISO) that would be separate from the spot market power exchange. A general consensus that such a system is desirable and necessary soon formed, and California was off and running toward building a new electricity system infrastructure. This development continues.

As California became embroiled in its task of creating a centralized operator and power exchange from the ground up, political events in the opposite corner of the country soon propelled another state into the lead of the race to retail wheeling. To fund the buyout of the bankrupt Public Service Company of New Hampshire (PSNH), Northeast Utilities was granted seven years of 5.5% per year rate increases for New Hampshire ratepayers. As a result, PSNH customers have some of the highest rates in the country. In an effort to reduce those rates, Governor Steve Merrill of New Hampshire approved a retail wheeling pilot program that was scheduled to start in May of 1996. Soon after, the legislature passed and the governor signed the nation's first retail wheeling legislation that mandates full retail wheeling for all customers in all classes by 1998. New Hampshire suddenly became the focus of all retail development activity.

The New Hampshire Public Utilities Commission (NHPUC) avoided the poolco/bilateral contracts debate by simply mandating full direct access for all customers in the pilot program. There is one key reason why this was possible without New Hampshire having to go through the process California is going through: the New England Power Pool (NEPOOL). As discussed earlier in this chapter, NEPOOL is a "tight" power pool that incorporates every utility in the six New England states. NEPOOL has developed a very complicated and sophisticated operating system over the past three decades that has been used to facilitate joint economic dispatch and economy energy sales among the New England utilities. Simply put, New England already has a system operator, except that it is not independent.

The downside of implementing retail wheeling in the presence of an entity like NEPOOL is that NEPOOL is simply not structured to offer unbundled transmission services. NEPOOL is so firmly entrenched into the operation of the electricity system in New England, including generation, that introducing competitive suppliers is a difficult task. Other factors that complicate NEPOOL's ability to accommodate an open market are its fundamental dependence on production-cost-based economic dispatch and its requirement that energy and capacity be packaged together. In recognition of these difficulties, FERC Order 888 gives tight power pools such as NEPOOL until the end of 1996 to restructure their organization to accommodate open access transmission (while other utilities must have their open access tariffs operational by June 1996). NEPOOL has, however, gone to great lengths to ensure that the New Hampshire pilot program works, since it needs to benefit from the experiment in order to prepare for retail wheeling like everyone else.

The upside to NEPOOL involvement in the New Hampshire pilot program is that it provides many of the services that an ISO would need to provide, and that infrastructure is already in place, which is not the case in California. As a result, New Hampshire adopted a "top down" approach to retail wheel, at least as far as the pilot is concerned. For the customers selected for the pilot (3% of the state's load, from all customer classes, selected by a random draw of volunteers), rates are developed as follows:

- A 10% "participation incentive credit" is immediately taken off the existing rate.
- The "energy" component of the rate (which actually includes some capacity) was determined to be, after some wrangling among stakeholders, approximately 3.1¢ per kWh This amount is then removed from the existing rate minus the participation incentive credit.

- The remainder is then assessed by the utility as distribution, transmission, and stranded cost recovery.
- The final rate is then the distribution utility assessment plus the new suppliers' "energy cost."

Because of this structure, the savings from the pilot are not great. But the experience gained by participants in preparation for full competition more than makes up for the lack of direct economic benefit. At the time of this writing, a veritable feeding frenzy has erupted in New Hampshire as every active marketer, broker, and utility in the country is fighting for a piece of what would be the first true retail wheeling program in the United States.

Unfortunately for New Hampshire egos, another state took the prize for the first implemented retail wheeling pilot program at the last minute. Two utilities in Illinois with relatively low costs and a desire to succeed with retail wheeling in other service areas submitted voluntary, unilateral retail wheeling pilot programs to the Illinois Commerce Commission (ICC), that state's utility regulatory body. Both plans, from Illinois Power (IP) and Central Illinois Lighting Company (CILCO), offered no stranded cost recovery and open access for selected customers on an experimental basis. The IP plan applied only to industrial end-users and then only to a small portion of their load at 100% load factor, thus limiting the meaningfulness of the program. The CILCO plan, however, involved three small towns in which all customers could participate.

While each plan was expected to be implemented in late 1996, both utilities felt pressure to implement theirs earlier than the other, forcing the ICC to implement both immediately. As a result, on April 22, 1996, at least two end-users, National Steel and LTV Steel, both IP customers, became the first retail customers in the United States to have true access to competitive suppliers. Both reported unexpectedly favorable rates as many utilities and power marketers were anxious to become the first suppliers to a retail wheeling customer. Unlike New Hampshire, the Illinois retail wheeling pilots are "bottom up" programs in that each utility developed retail wheeling tariffs that included specific distribution and ancillary services rates. The suppliers' costs are added to those to make up the total rate.

While Illinois or New Hampshire may appear to be the first states with retail wheeling, enough peculiarities exist with each program so that many issues remain to be resolved. Nonetheless, most state regulatory commissions are closely watching developments in California, Illinois, and New Hampshire to learn from their experiences. Once retail wheeling is effectively implemented in one state, a domino effect is sure to result. No state can afford to subject its industry to electricity rates above those in a retail wheeling state merely because it chooses to stick to the traditional monopoly system. Once the trail has been blazed, other states will soon follow. This has already been seen in the West as Arizona, New Mexico, and Washington have announced retail wheeling initiatives in response to developments in California.

In April of 1994, two states had official retail wheeling initiatives. Two years later, virtually every state is considering retail wheeling in some official capacity, either by the regulatory commission, by the state legislature, or by a major utility. Appendix E is a state-by-state summary of retail wheeling initiatives as of this writing. Given the rapid development of retail wheeling, this list is undoubtedly outdated.

Chapter 3

Alternatives to Native Tariff Service

While retail wheeling appears to be inevitable, it is not now nor will it ever be the only option that industrial end-users of electricity have to lower their cost of electricity. Beyond conventional demand side management tools, industrials still have the option to generate their own electricity; form a new electric utility that can purchase low-cost power on the open wholesale market; negotiate a special, below-tariff rate with their native utility; or explore a variety of unique options that may be particular to their state, industry, or type of load.

It is beyond the scope of this book to fully explore the issues and details involved with each of these options, but end-users should consider purchasing power from a remote supplier through retail wheeling as only one of many options to optimize power costs. Indeed, electricity suppliers in an open market will continue to face competitive pressures from these alternative options.

Self-generation

When the technology of electricity as an energy source was first being developed, many industrial facilities had to generate their own power since there was no reliable network system to supply those needs. By 1900, more than half of the industrial electrical load was self-supplied. While this was not considered "cogeneration" at the time, self-generation is not a concept introduced by PURPA. However, the growth of the interconnected transmission and distribution systems was soon able to provide more reliable and lower cost power than self-generation due to the economies of scale that existed at the time.

By 1965 less than 4% of industrial power requirements were fed from self-generation. Besides the economies of scale, developing state and federal regulatory structures eventually made self-generation contrary to the overall good of the system. By the 1960s many states developed strict "suppliers" acts or service territory laws that gave utilities the exclusive right to feed the load in their geographic service territory. Until PURPA was enacted (see Chapter 2), self-generation was for the most part prohibited.

As discussed on the previous page, PURPA did more than allow industrials to realize the inherent efficiencies of cogeneration and small power production, it spawned the independent power industry. That industry has matured at this stage to the point that most substantial cogeneration opportunities have been developed and the cost of new gas-fired generation is competitive.

Self-generation is not only cogeneration. Many industrial end-users have been able to save overall energy costs through the use of the following installations:

- Peak-shaving: End-users with poor load factors due to predictable process demand spikes can substantially reduce costs through the installation of generators that only serve to reduce demand during those peak load times. This saves money by reducing the utility's demand charge, which is assessed monthly based on the peak demand for that month. Savings are especially significant if the utility has a severe demand ratchet penalty, i.e., the minimum demand for the month is based on some percentage (usually 60% to 80%) of the peak demand over the past 11 months. By reducing the annual or monthly peak with short-term, low cost generation, substantial savings are often possible.
- Back up: Until retail wheeling allows the purchase of low-cost, spot market economy power, many end-users are purchasing interruptible power to lower their costs. Interruptible power is sold from the utility's operating reserves, which must be on-line anyway for reliability reasons, so the cost is often far lower than for firm service. However, to meet certain firm demands, many end-users find that the installation of their own back up generation is cost-justified by the savings that result from the use of interruptible power. Note that this is not the same as diesel back-up generation required for critical power needs, such as for hospitals, but refers to generation required to back up power that can be curtailed by the utility in the event of system capacity shortages.
- Isolated generation: In some cases, cogeneration through parallel operation with the utility, as allowed under PURPA, is not cost-effective because of the backup power costs assessed by the utility. In some cases, an end-user can more effectively provide for its own backup to its self-generation through the use of multiple machines. For example, a small industrial facility may be able to meet all of its electrical requirements with four small internal combustion engines, but may chose to install six in order to provide the same reliability provided by the utility. In such a case, the cost of the additional units justifies complete isolation from the existing utility.

- Excess generation: As discussed above, the Energy Policy Act of 1992 allows virtually anyone to develop a power generation facility *if* that power can be sold on the wholesale market. This provides some flexibility to end-users with self-generation options in that a unit larger than needed to meet the plant's needs can be installed with the expectation that power will be sold to wholesale buyers. However, the wholesale power generation market is so saturated that the price received for this power rarely justifies or even covers the cost of producing this incremental power.

PURPA provides for two types of non-utility owned generation: cogeneration and small power production. These are commonly referred to together as NUGs (non-utility generation) or IPPs (independent power producers). PURPA allows utilities to own no more than 50% of a non-regulated generator, which would be an APP, or affiliated power producer. In the case of a small power producer, PURPA, as implemented by FERC, requires a renewable resource fuel and limits the size to 80 megawatts. This is intended to encourage the development of renewable resource generation, such as hydroelectric and wind-power generation.

Cogeneration refers to the simultaneous production of electricity and useful thermal energy from a single fuel source. It is an attractive alternative to purchasing high priced utility generated power because of its superior energy efficiency. In conventional electric power plants, 35% to 40% of the fuel's energy is directly transformed into electrical energy. By contrast, cogeneration recaptures much of the otherwise wasted thermal energy for reuse as steam or process heat to produce total usable energy efficiencies of 75% or more.

Cogeneration consists of essentially two types of process: "topping cycle," which is defined by FERC as "a cogeneration facility in which the energy input to the facility is first used to produce useful power output, and the reject heat from power production is then used to provide useful thermal energy;" and "bottoming cycle," which is defined as "a cogeneration facility in which the energy input to the system is first applied to a useful thermal energy process, and the reject heat emerging from the process is then used for power production."

In order to qualify as a "qualified facility," or QF, at least 5% of the total energy output of the topping cycle system must be in the form of thermal energy. Also, if a non-renewable fuel is used, the useful power output plus one-half of the useful thermal energy output must be no less than 42.5% of the total energy input. For bottoming cycle plants, power output must be no less than 45% of the energy input.

If a single end-user does not have the steam needs required to build a cogenerator large enough to meet its electrical needs, the end-user may still be able to take advantage of the efficiencies inherent in cogeneration. FERC has allowed arrangements where one facility consumes steam and the other electricity. In such cases, FERC will require joint ownership of the cogeneration facility, close geographic proximity, similar functional characteristics, and the presence of a customer/supplier relationship between the utilities. Therefore, cogeneration can be considered in situations beyond those with obvious application.

Whether cogeneration is an alternative for a business depends upon a number of economic and technical considerations. Some obvious concerns include the present cost of electricity and the incremental cost of fuel for the generator. Less obvious are utility charges for supplementary, backup, and maintenance power, environmental compliance, and local capital improvement property taxes.

When determining whether an end-user should consider the installation of cogeneration, a pro-forma calculation is developed which determines the effective rate of return from the capital expense required for the generation. This analysis must include the cost of financing the project and any desired rate of return. Since the savings from the existing cost of power is a key driver of the economics, the projected cost of that power will then be a significant factor in determining the economic viability of a project. Figure 3-1 is a sample pro-forma model used to account for various economic factors when considering cogeneration.

It is important to carefully consider fuel costs when doing this economic analysis. For economic, technical, and environmental reasons, the fuel of choice for cogeneration has been, and should be for some time, natural gas. As discussed in Chapter 2, the natural gas industry has just been through the reregulation process that electricity is going through now, and competition has resulted in significant opportunities for minimizing gas costs. Some cogeneration developers when doing preliminary economic evaluations of a cogeneration project will use burnertip prices from a local distribution company. Overall economics may be substantially more favorable when gas costs are optimized through aggressive management of transportation, storage, and spot market prices.

As discussed in Chapter 2, PURPA requires utilities to interconnect to qualified facilities, provide those facilities with certain services, and purchase excess power. With respect to interconnection, most utilities will require a potential cogenerator to pay for an interconnection study, which the utility will perform, that will analyze the affect of the new generator on the utility's system. The utility will consider technical issues such as (i) the change in load flow patterns on transmission and distribution lines given either the loss of existing load or the creation of new generation, (ii) the effect of the generator on the utility protection schemes (every generator interconnected with the grid generates current during a system "fault," and this new fault current will impact the operation of devices designed and set to detect those faults), and (iii) how the new generation will be metered. As a result of the interconnection study, the utility may require the installation of certain facilities or equipment to accommodate the cogenerator. While utilities often try to discourage new cogeneration facilities with unreasonable technical requirements, the cost of these requirements is relatively low and regulators often side with utilities in their analysis of technical issues.

COGENERATION ANALYSIS

ASSUMPTIONS

UNIT TYPE	Simple Cycle - LM2500		
UNIT SIZE (kW)	19,000	GROSS MMBTU FUEL/Yr	1,321,264
$/kW INSTALLED	921	FUEL SAVED IN HEAT PROCESS	513,117
TOTAL CAPITAL	17,500,000	NET MMBTU FUEL/Yr	808,147
PERCENT FINANCED BY DEBT	0.0%	MAINTENANCE (FIXED $/kW)	15
COST OF DEBT	12.0%	MAINTENANCE (VARIABLE $/kWh)	0.0024
NPV DISCOUNT RATE	12.0%	MAINTENANCE ESCALATOR	4.0%
TAX RATE (Federal and State)	38.0%	UTILITY STANDBY POWER($/kW-MONTH)	2.50
PROPERTY TAXES	0.66%	BACKUP SERV ESCALATOR	3.0%
HEAT RATE BTU/kWh	10,040	PROJECT LIFE (years)	20
HEAT RECOVERY %	38.8%	TAX LIFE(years)	20
FUEL COST $/MMBtu	2.33	SALVAGE	0%
FUEL COST ESCALATOR	4.0%	INITIAL RATES(¢/kWh)	4.77
CAPACITY FACTOR	94.0%	RATE ESCALATION	3.0%
ENERGY AVAILABLE (kWh/Yr)	156,453,600	ENERGY REQUIRED (kWh/Yr)	140,000,000

Project Year		0	1	2	3	4	5	6	7	8	9
INSTALLED COST		$17,500,000									
OPERATING COST		1st - Yr cost split									
Fuel - Natural Gas	71.7%	1.25	$1,954,469	$2,032,648	$2,113,954	$2,198,512	$2,286,453	$2,377,911	$2,473,027	$2,571,948	$2,674,826
O & M	24.2%	0.42	$660,489	$686,908	$714,385	$742,960	$772,678	$803,585	$835,729	$869,158	$903,924
Property Taxes	4.0%	0.07	$109,725	$103,950	$98,175	$92,400	$86,625	$80,850	$75,075	$69,300	$63,525
Total Operating Costs	100.0%	1.74	$2,724,683	$2,823,506	$2,926,513	$3,033,872	$3,145,756	$3,262,346	$3,383,831	$3,510,406	$3,642,275
¢/kWh Generated			1.74	1.80	1.87	1.94	2.01	2.09	2.16	2.24	2.33
FINANCE COST											
Interest on Debt	0.0%	0.00	$0	$0	$0	$0	$0	$0	$0	$0	$0
Debt Retirement	0.0%	0.00	$0	$0	$0	$0	$0	$0	$0	$0	$0
Total Finance Costs	0.0%	0.00	$0	$0	$0	$0	$0	$0	$0	$0	$0
TOTAL GENERATING COSTS	100.0%	1.74	$2,724,683	$2,823,506	$2,926,513	$3,033,872	$3,145,756	$3,262,346	$3,383,831	$3,510,406	$3,642,275
			1.74	1.80	1.87	1.94	2.01	2.09	2.16	2.24	2.33
UTILITY COST											
Standby Demand			$587,100	$604,713	$622,854	$641,540	$660,786	$680,610	$701,028	$722,059	$743,721
Standby Demand Rate ($/kW-month)			$2.58	$2.65	$2.73	$2.81	$2.90	$2.99	$3.07	$3.17	$3.26
Standby Energy			$52,633	$54,212	$55,838	$57,514	$59,239	$61,016	$62,847	$64,732	$66,674
Standby Energy Rate (¢/kWh)			3.76	3.87	3.99	4.11	4.23	4.36	4.49	4.62	4.76
Total Standby Power			$639,733	$658,925	$678,693	$699,054	$720,025	$741,626	$763,875	$786,791	$810,395
Total Standby Power Rate (¢/kWh)			45.70	47.07	48.48	49.93	51.43	52.97	54.56	56.20	57.89
Maintenance Power			$360,500	$371,315	$382,454	$393,928	$405,746	$417,918	$430,456	$443,370	$456,671
Maintenance Power Rate (¢/kWh)			5.15	5.30	5.46	5.63	5.80	5.97	6.15	6.33	6.52
Total Utility Costs			$1,000,233	$1,030,240	$1,061,147	$1,092,982	$1,125,771	$1,159,544	$1,194,331	$1,230,160	$1,267,065
Total Operating Costs			$3,724,916	$3,853,746	$3,987,661	$4,126,854	$4,271,527	$4,421,890	$4,578,161	$4,740,567	$4,909,341
			2.66	2.75	2.85	2.95	3.05	3.16	3.27	3.39	3.51
AVOIDED UTILITY COST											
Utility Rate(¢/kWh)			4.77	4.97	5.19	5.41	5.63	5.86	6.04	6.22	6.40
Avoided Cost			$6,678,000	$6,964,860	$7,267,680	$7,570,500	$7,887,740	$8,204,980	$8,451,129	$8,704,663	$8,965,803
ANNUAL SAVINGS			$2,953,084	$3,111,114	$3,280,019	$3,443,646	$3,616,213	$3,783,090	$3,872,968	$3,964,097	$4,056,462
PRE-TAX ECONOMICS											
Cash Flow - Nominal $		($17,500,000)	$2,953,084	$3,111,114	$3,280,019	$3,443,646	$3,616,213	$3,783,090	$3,872,968	$3,964,097	$4,056,462
Cumulative Cash Flow - Nominal $		($17,500,000)	($14,546,916)	($11,435,802)	($8,155,783)	($4,712,136)	($1,095,923)	$2,687,166	$6,560,134	$10,524,231	$14,580,694
Cash Flow - 1995 $		($17,500,000)	$2,636,682	$2,480,161	$2,334,653	$2,188,500	$2,051,936	$1,916,631	$1,751,934	$1,601,032	$1,462,801
Cumulative Cash Flow - 1995 $		($17,500,000)	($14,863,318)	($12,383,157)	($10,048,504)	($7,860,004)	($5,808,068)	($3,891,437)	($2,139,503)	($538,471)	$924,330
NPV($;$/kW)		$10,625,812	$559								
IRR		19.9%									
POST-TAX ECONOMICS											
Depreciation -- Tax			$1,148,525	$1,225,000	$1,134,350	$1,049,300	$970,550	$897,750	$830,550	$780,325	$780,325
Savings -- After Tax			$2,267,352	$2,394,391	$2,464,665	$2,533,795	$2,610,861	$2,686,661	$2,716,849	$2,754,263	$2,811,530
Cash Flow - Nominal $		($17,500,000)	$2,267,352	$2,394,391	$2,464,665	$2,533,795	$2,610,861	$2,686,661	$2,716,849	$2,754,263	$2,811,530
Cumulative Cash Flow - Nominal $		($17,500,000)	($15,232,648)	($12,838,258)	($10,373,593)	($7,839,798)	($5,228,937)	($2,542,276)	$174,573	$2,928,836	$5,740,366
Cash Flow - 1995 $		($17,500,000)	$2,024,421	$1,908,793	$1,754,300	$1,610,272	$1,481,473	$1,361,146	$1,228,965	$1,112,401	$1,013,866
Cumulative Cash Flow - 1995 $		($17,500,000)	($15,475,579)	($13,566,785)	($11,812,486)	($10,202,213)	($8,720,740)	($7,359,595)	($6,130,630)	($5,018,229)	($4,004,363)
NPV($;$/kW)		$2,645,527	$139								
IRR		14.2%									

Figure 3-1. Sample pro-forma for evaluating the economic viability of a cogeneration project.

Besides requiring parallel operation with the cogenerator, FERC also requires utilities to provide the following types of services at reasonable costs:

- Backup Power: If an industrial end-user generates its own power, it must ensure that a reliable backup to that power is available to guarantee consistent operation of its processes. Since a refusal on part of a utility to backup self-generation would discourage the installation of efficient cogeneration facilities, FERC requires utilities to provide backup service in the event of an unscheduled loss of the generator. Since the end-user is buying the *capacity* to provide an equivalent level of power, the cogenerator is required to pay a reservation charge in the form of a $ per MW-month assessment. While this charge must be reasonable and set by state regulators based on an allocated share of the utility's embedded costs, this capacity payment can be prohibitive in some cases and thus must be carefully evaluated when doing the economic feasibility evaluations.

- Maintenance Power: Besides allowing for unscheduled outages, the interconnecting utility must also allow for scheduled maintenance outages. If this power was purchased under normal utility tariffs, ratcheted demand charges would be prohibitively expensive. But since maintenance outages can be forecasted and scheduled with the utility, they can be coordinated with the utility's generation maintenance schedule. For this reason, maintenance charges are a relatively minor cost.
- Supplementary Power: Unless the end-user's generation facility produces enough power for the entire plant, the end-user will have to buy additional power from the utility. To prevent utilities from penalizing cogenerators with above-cost rates for this additional power, FERC requires utilities to provide needed power at costs similar to other users. Most utilities place supplementary power under normal tariffs.

PURPA also requires the interconnected utility to purchase excess energy produced by a qualified facility at the utility's "avoided cost." Avoided cost is a heavily litigated concept, but its most common definition is that cost associated with the utility's generating facility that will not be needed by virtue of the purchase from the cogenerator. This avoided cost methodology, referred to as committed unit basis (CUB), includes both investment related fixed costs and all operating costs of the avoided unit. In reality, the CUB defined for cogenerators varies somewhat from the actual avoided cost as used by the utility. This has often been the source of many disputes between utilities and cogenerators.

When PURPA was first implemented, many state regulatory commissions sought to encourage the development of cogeneration by awarding purchase rates above short term avoided costs. These programs have been eliminated for the most part and cogenerators must rely on actual avoided costs. Because these costs are very low given the surplus capacity situation, a developer cannot rely on the sales of excess power to float an otherwise financially marginal project.

An end-user considering the installation of cogeneration facility must consider the impact of retail wheeling in the overall corporate electricity strategic plan. In other words, should an end-user install a cogeneration facility if retail wheeling will provide the same savings or better in a few years? Committing to the installation of self-generation is akin to signing a 15- or 20-year guaranteed service contract with the utility. As suggested below, unless

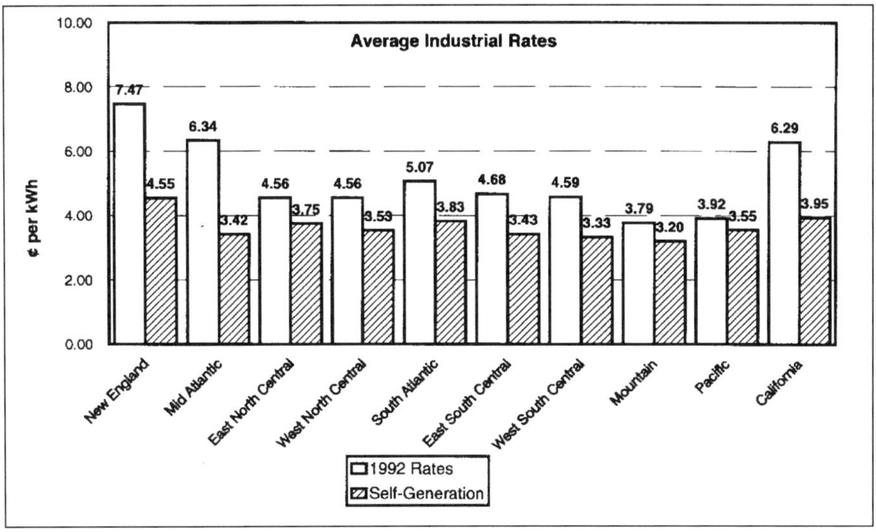

Figure 3-2. Average industrial electric rates compared to average cogeneration costs show generally favorable economics in areas like New England *and* California *and less favorable economics in other* Western *states.*

the rate from such a deal is phenomenally good, the reader is cautioned to carefully consider the rates expected in a restructured electricity market. Figure 3-2 compares the average electricity costs for the various NERC regions with the average cost to develop cogeneration in those areas.

This is not to say that cogeneration will never be more favorable than the price of power with retail wheeling; in some states the eventual retail wheeling price may still be above that of self-generation. Furthermore, substantial synergies may result from the use of excess steam from the cogenerator in the facility's processes, or waste gas can be used to reduce purchased fuel costs. In these cases, the eventual cost of electricity can be well below that of the market price because the inherent efficiencies of cogeneration and the optimization of energy processes in many facilities will surpass the efficiencies obtained by centralized generation facilities built only to generate electricity.

Furthermore, recent developments in the combustion-turbine industry have suddenly made cogeneration a very viable option or source of leverage again. First, combustion-turbine technologies have improved efficiency rates markedly over the past few years. Combining improved efficiency with lower natural gas costs due to that industry's restructuring can lead to very attractive cogeneration economics since fuel costs are usually the largest single cost of a cogeneration facility. Second, the market for combustion turbines, and to a lesser degree other types of generators, has become extremely competitive as manufacturers are struggling to find buyers for their units as retail wheeling nears. As a result, the installed cost of these units has dropped considerably, even in just the past year. Moreover, a very active secondary market for small generators has driven installed prices to unheard of levels. Refurbished used units can be a very attractive alternative for marginally economic projects. Third, in an effort to move more generators, some manufacturers and developers have begun to offer leasing programs that preclude the need for a long-term commitment on part of the end-user. A five-year lease arrangement for a skid-mounted generator set effectively removes the retail wheeling argument that limited the effectiveness of the cogeneration option for many end-users. Finally, cogeneration still offers most end-users an opportunity to bypass the local utility without having to pay a stranded investment charge, although this is being challenged in some states. Once again, cogeneration can be a very viable option for end-users or a very credible threat to existing utility suppliers.

Municipalization

The Energy Policy Act of 1992 gave wholesale buyers of electricity open access to the competitive market for generation by requiring transmission utilities to wheel off-system power to wholesale buyers. This is essentially what retail wheeling will do for end-users, so many industrials ask whether this provision of the Energy Policy Act can be used to get access for end-users.

One easy way to use wholesale access as a means to retail access is to form a paper wholesale company at the end-user's facility. This wholesale company, e.g., the "Widget Power Company," would buy power on the open market then resell it to the facility, which would be the only customer. While this arrangement has been used in the past (and some still exist), this loophole was plugged in the Energy Policy Act for new wholesale companies. Unless a wholesale buyer owns actual transmission or distribution assets, a wholesale company that has only one customer would be considered a "sham" transaction and is specifically disallowed.

So end-users are left with the option of creating their own municipally-owned electric utility in the town in which they are located. The new publicly owned company has full access to the open wholesale electricity market and can thus, in theory, pass on those savings to its industrial customers.

There are over 3,000 municipal electric utilities in the U.S., and because of the benefits of open access, more are being formed. Most states have specific statutes that allow a municipality, or some specifically defined subdivision of local government, to create and operate a publicly-owned electric utility. While some states have shut the door on this process, called "municipalization," most states grant municipal governments the authority to create or purchase an electric distribution company, to operate and maintain an electric system, and to buy and sell power. Furthermore, in many states, these municipal electric companies are unregulated by the state utility regulatory commission (see Figure 3-3).

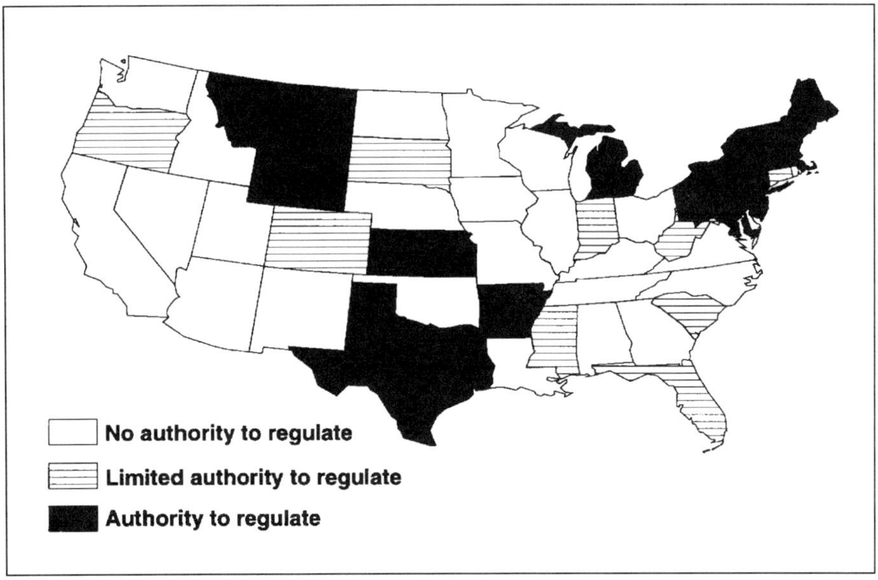

Figure 3-3. States that regulate municipal electric companies.

For an end-user to use this option to its advantage, it must consider a number of factors. First, a thorough review of the applicable state laws is in order. While the majority of states allow municipalization, the process to create a new public utility varies and each state has its own unique differences. For example, in Pennsylvania a municipality may be a city, township, or borough, yet only boroughs have the statutory authority to create a municipal electric utility. Yet other municipalities may municipalize if they are "home rule" cities and have specific authorization to run an electric utility in its home rule charter.

Some states have blocked the creation of new municipal utilities either by specifically disallowing any entity from feeding load in the service territory of an existing utility or by removing the incentive to municipalize. An example of the latter is Arkansas, which requires all new municipal electric companies to ensure that the native utility does not suffer any reduction in revenues as a result of the municipalization. This effectively blocks municipalization because it removes the reason for forming a new utility in the first place.

Most states accommodate the formation of new municipal utilities by providing for the condemnation of utility assets needed for the new company. These state statutes often call for a valuation procedure to determine the cost of the distribution and transmission assets that are to be condemned so as to ensure that the utility is properly compensated. Often, however, the valuation process becomes contentious, as we shall see below. In any case, the first step in the process is to thoroughly review the applicable statutes so that proper procedures are followed.

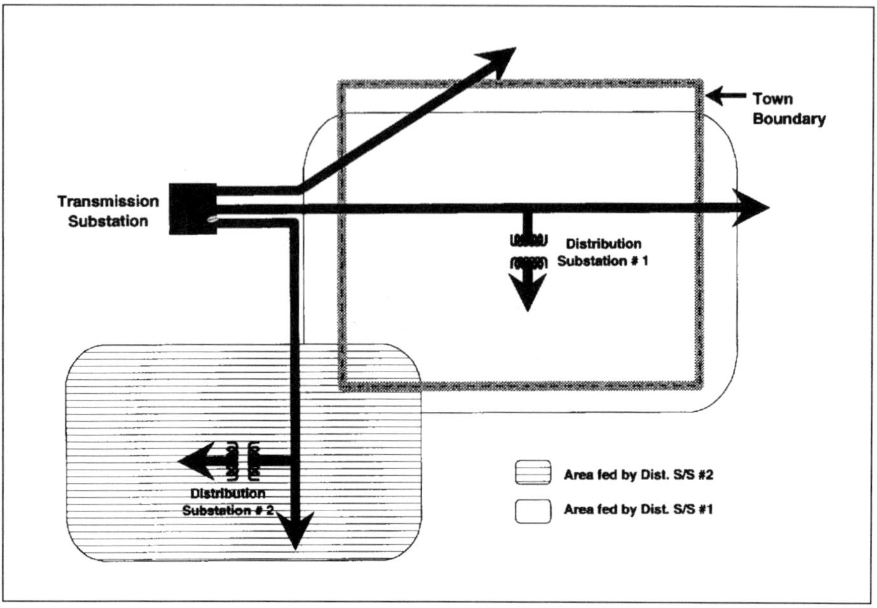

Figure 3-4. The boundaries of a new municipal electric company may overlap town boundaries or may not include all town load.

The next step is to determine the electrical boundaries of the proposed new utility. This is often complicated by the reality that all the residential, commercial, and industrial load within the official city limits does not necessarily correspond to electrical boundaries of load fed by certain substations (see Figure 3-4). In other words, to include all load within town boundaries, part of the load fed by some substations or even some specific distribution circuits would have to be fed by the new municipal and other parts fed by the remaining utility.

This problem can be resolved in one of two ways, depending on state law. Some states allow the boundaries of a new municipal electric company to follow the "natural" boundaries of the electric system. That is, if part of the area served by a certain substation feeds load in neighboring towns, the municipal electric company can own and operate the entire substation and its circuits and thus feed those loads outside of the town's boundaries. This is allowed when it makes economic sense. For those states that don't allow flexible municipal utility boundaries, the new public utility has no choice but to split and separately meter loads off substations and circuits that cross political boundaries.

The new municipal utility need not feed all the load within the town boundaries. As long as the voting electorate in the town agree, only certain circuits need to be municipalized, which could solve the boundary problem. In fact, unless specifically disallowed by state law, even certain voltage levels could be municipalized (such as sub-transmission voltages that feed large industrial users in the town) while lower voltages that feed residential and commercial loads remain part of the native utility's service territory.

Once the boundaries of the new municipal electric company are determined, both electrically and geographically, the end-user should attempt to estimate the cost of condemning and purchasing the necessary transmission and distributing facilities as part of its economic prefeasibility assessment. This is most easily facilitated by reviewing distribution maps (both electrical one-lines and geographic maps) for each circuit within the municipal boundaries. Utilities are under no obligation to provide this information, however, and most will refuse to supply these maps to end-users evaluating their municipalization option.

If this is the case, the end-user can either drive around town and estimate the number and size of all the electrical equipment in the town or an estimation of distribution facility costs can be made based on population. Enough new municipal electric companies have been formed in the recent past that good estimates of facilities costs per residential customer are available. If utility distribution maps are available, they can be used to precisely define what equipment will be included in the purchase.

The issue of how these facilities are valuated must also be resolved. Some state statutes give precise guidelines on facility valuation for condemnation purposes, but most merely require that the utility receive "fair market value" for its equipment. Since there is no active market for installed distribution systems, this is a difficult standard to measure, so some defined and analytical approach must be used. The options usually proposed are original cost less depreciation (OCLD), replacement cost less depreciation (RCLD), or compensation based on loss of revenue or return on investment.

In Indiana, a statute awards the higher of RCLD (called reproduction cost new depreciated, or RCND) or 2.5 times the utility gross sales from the area taken. There is no apparent objective basis for this rule. In Minnesota, the utility must be placed in the same financial position it would have occupied had the acquisition not occurred. This is also arbitrary since the utility now has fewer customers, so its return on investment should not be the same.

These various methodologies were discussed in the case of *City of Sheldon, Iowa v. Iowa Public Service Co.* in 1990. In this case, the City of Sheldon was attempting to form a new municipal electric company, and a dispute arose over how to valuate the distribution assets involved. The Iowa Utilities Board rejected OCLD as inappropriate and found RCLD reasonable. The Board also rejected the utility's suggestion for a flexible approach utilizing OCLD, RCLD, loss of revenue by the utility, and actual revenue paid by the town's residents. This method was found to be so flexible that its credibility and fairness could not be evaluated. However, the Board in *City of Sheldon* did not base the valuation on RCLD alone. Over half of the final cost was to compensate the utility for the investment in its entire generation and transmission system that, theoretically, helps feed the town's loads. This was based on the finding that the utility's system would be underutilitized if the town left the utility. This generation and transmission charge was calculated by multiplying the present value of the utility's projected overall cost of service (as determined in a recent rate case) and multiplying it by the ratio of the town's peak load to the overall system peak.

Since the *City of Sheldon* case was decided in 1990, there has been much discussion of this so-called "stranded investment" argument. It is by no means clear that a utility should be compensated for existing investment in load customers; other industries do not enjoy such protection. A strong argument can be made that the utility can recover its transmission investment through its wheeling rate and its generation investment in competitive sales to other purchasers. Awarding compensation for loss of utilization, as was done in *City of Sheldon*, assumes the excess transmission and generation capacity created by the municipalization will never be used again. This view of stranded cost recovery, i.e., the full recovery of the investment of a utility's entire system, is consistent with FERC's recent Order 888. In that rule, which is part of FERC's new rule ordering open access transmission tariffs, FERC claims jurisdiction over the stranded investment issue with respect to newly formed municipal electric companies that leave the native utility, even if that stranded cost is primarily related to the loss of a retail customer. Unfortunately, FERC allows recovery of all verifiable and legitimate stranded costs due to municipalization. Furthermore, the assessment of that stranded cost is similar to that expressed in the *City of Sheldon* case, i.e., the difference between existing revenues and those that would result due to the loss of the customer. This "revenues lost" test effectively removes the benefits of municipalization by requiring the repayment of all the benefits brought by municipalizing in the first place.

Nonetheless, the issue continues to be debated on the state and federal level. In Maine, for example, the Public Service Commission ruled that a wholesale buyer leaving the native utility's system should share the stranded investment cost with the utility's shareholders. Once the value of the stranded investment associated with the departing municipal load is quantified, which may in itself be a heavily litigated issue, half the cost is allocated to the municipal and half to the utility. The stranded investment issue is discussed in Appendix B.

In the end, the actual value of the condemned facilities is negotiated between the municipality and the utility. In at least one case, however, in Clyde, Ohio, no value could be agreed upon and the municipality decided to build a second, duplicative distribution system for a far lower cost. While this is not always possible given most regulatory commissions' perceived duty to prevent duplicative facilities, this may be an option for a municipality trying to buy a system from a recalcitrant utility.

Besides the cost of purchasing the utility's existing facilities, the end-user must consider other non-bulk power costs such as administrative costs, operating and maintenance costs, and finance costs. These include mundane aspects such as the cost of bucket trucks and billing systems. When averaged on a cost per kilowatt-hour basis, however, these costs are relatively minor. In most cases, all non-bulk power costs, including that for purchasing the utility's assets, do not amount to more than 0.4¢ to 0.6¢ per kilowatt-hour.

The largest cost for a municipal electric utility is, of course, the cost of the wholesale power itself. But before the market can be approached, the buyer must first determine where that power can come from. This involves an analysis of the bulk transmission system that will be used to deliver that power to the wholesale buyer, which requires a determination of the transmission capacity between control areas. For the purposes of this book, this is the same analysis as would be required for an end-user if it was buying power for itself in a retail wheeling environment. Since this is covered in detail in Chapter 7, it will not be reiterated here.

Because the greatest cost of municipalization will be the cost of the wholesale power purchased for the new utility, the most important step in a preliminary prefeasibility analysis is a determination of wholesale power costs. This can be done a number of ways, including market data published in trade journals and bulletin boards or to simply call as many potential suppliers as possible on an informal basis, i.e., there is no need for a formal request-for-proposal at this point.

In order to determine a possible wholesale power price, a supplier will need to know the town's load profile, especially load factor. Depending on the size of the town relative to the end-user's facility, this may be somewhat low, which will raise the price of power. Also, the firmness of the power is important since the residential and commercial users will demand power as reliable as that provided by the native utility. While the end-user may be willing to buy power on the spot wholesale market, which exists today, this may put some of the town's load in jeopardy.

The new municipality should also consider generating its own power, given the availability of low-cost and efficient gas-powered generation technology. Better still, if a large industrial user in the town has or can have a cogeneration facility, the benefits of both cogeneration and municipalization can be combined into a very favorable package.

Finally, municipalization is necessarily a political process. Most state laws require approval by the majority of voters in the municipality through a public referendum. If the end-user is the major employer in the town and it is willing to campaign for lower electric rates as needed for economic health or even viability, most voters are probably willing to help out. Once the public gets involved, however, the end-user is in a difficult position if the native utility decides to cut the end-user a special deal in order to thwart the municipalization effort. Therefore, if municipalization will be used as leverage, the town should only be approached as a last resort. If the end-user agrees to back off once the town is involved, the end-user may be forced to compensate the town in some way for its support.

Another political factor is the need for the end-user to ensure that it retains control of the purchasing policies of the new utility. Most importantly, the new utility cannot use its newly obtained revenue raising authority to raise money for non-electricity needs. The interested reader is advised to contract with the town authorities for a rate that reflects the town's cost of providing that power. Better still, the end-user should play a proactive role in the operation of the municipal electric company, at least with respect to wholesale power purchases.

Competitive Leverage

Both self-generation and municipalization are in many cases viable alternatives for the end-user, but many industrials are skeptical about getting into the power business. Making widgets competitively is hard enough without learning enough about the utility business to make that a success too. But if an end-user has a viable alternative, it can be readily converted into a credible threat that can be effectively used to leverage the native utility into negotiating a special, below-tariff contract.

Until retail wheeling is widely available, end-users are forced to deal with their monopoly supplier. No monopoly will provide meaningful price discounts unless the customer can bring something to the table. In the utility business, this means competitive leverage, i.e., something that can either help or hurt the utility.

The most effective leverage is the threat of losing load and the revenue it brings to the utility. If an end-user can credibly threaten to either curtail production or shut down a certain facility unless power costs are reduced, the end-user has effective leverage. Likewise, losing load to cogeneration or municipalization, if the end-user can convince the utility that it is fully willing and able to take such measures, is equally effective. Sometimes, the end-user is forced to carry out the threat, so the end-user should be prepared to do so if necessary.

Recent developments in the industry have provided another source of leverage, that is retail wheeling itself. This can work two ways. First, if the end-user is located in a state that is seriously considering implementation of retail wheeling, and if the end-user is willing to sign a multiple year agreement with the utility (i.e., three to five years), the end-user can negotiate what is effectively a retail wheeling deferral agreement. That is, by locking in that end-user for a few years, the utility will avoid facing the loss of a customer. Of course, the utility will have to be willing to offer a lower rate in exchange for having a guaranteed customer, but a loss of some revenue is preferable to a loss of all revenue. Many utilities are eager to negotiate special contracts for just this reason.

Second, retail wheeling can serve as a benchmark for the rate that the utility should offer. If the end-user can calculate the price it would probably pay if retail wheeling were in effect, that rate will serve as a reasonable target rate which the utility should offer if it wants to keep that customer. As we shall see below, this rate can be calculated with reasonable accuracy.

Competitive leverage that is unique to a certain industry, facility, or region is also often available. For example, some oil pipelines have the ability to inject a drag reducing agent into the pipeline that substantially reduces the load on the electric-powered pipeline pumps. While more akin to demand side management, the cost of using a drag reducing agent can be calculated on a per-kilowatt-hour basis, i.e., the cost that electricity would have to cost in order to break even with the savings achievable with the demand-side management option. Utilities have been known to negotiate "drag reducing agent deferral contracts" with oil pipeline companies in order to maintain load.

More aggressive leverage options exist, if the end-user is willing to take on a more adversarial posture. One such option is to demand that the utility offer the facility the right to retail wheel, and then file an antitrust claim if they refuse. Since the generation market is competitive and transmission and distribution remain necessary monopolies, for a single utility to require purchase of its generation merely because the end-user is connected to its distribution system constitutes an illegal "tie-in" arrangement. This argument was successful for wholesale buyers (the *Otter Tail* case), but has not been widely used by retail customers because of the "state-action" defense to an antitrust claim. Under the state-action defense, no antitrust violation is found if the state specifically allows the monopoly to exist. While this appears to be the case in most states, the contrary could be argued in any state in which some sort of retail off-system arrangement is allowed or considered. This is effective leverage because the damages awarded in a successful antitrust claim could reach three times the difference between the existing price paid for power and that which would be paid if retail wheeling existed.

In summary, the end-user should carefully review its realistic options for alternative sources of power and any sources of competitive leverage that could be used to negotiate a special contract with the utility. A special contract could be, in many cases, a viable alternative to retail wheeling.

Negotiating a Special Contract

Special, below-tariff contracts between native utilities and their large industrial customers have become commonplace. Any large industrial taking service off tariff rates should consider whether it is paying too much for power. While these may be stop-gap measures by the utility to forestall the demand for retail wheeling, special contracts should be considered a viable alternative to retail wheeling for some end-users.

After the sources of effective competitive leverage have been developed, the end-user should gather as much information about the utility as possible. Information by itself serves as leverage. As with buying a car, the buyer who knows the dealer's cost for that car is in a better position to negotiate. Therefore, the end-user should determine its utility's cost of generation to serve as (i) a benchmark for the price that the utility *could* offer the end-user, and (ii) the basis for the price the end-user would pay if retail wheeling were available.

Fortunately, as of June 1, 1994, this information is available to the public. Among its many reporting requirements for regulated utilities, the Federal Energy Regulatory Agency (FERC) recently amended its rules for reporting information relating to production availability and cost. The purpose of this reporting requirement, called FERC Form 714, is to collect information from electric utility control and planning areas in the United States in order to obtain a broad picture of interconnected control area operations. This information includes comprehensive data concerning area generation, actual and scheduled inter-control area power transfers, control area interconnections and interchanges.

While this information relating to generation capacity and load is valuable for determining overall system reliability and the availability of bulk power, the information that has value to an end-user is production cost data called "system lambda." System lambda is a measure of a utility's incremental cost of generation and is measured in dollars per megawatt-hour. For control areas where demand following is primarily performed by thermal generating units, the system lambda is derived from the economic dispatch function associated with automatic generation control performed at the controlling utility or power pool control center. In other words, it is the value that the utility uses to determine from where it should get its next megawatt-hour. For example, system lambda will be used to determine if it is cheaper to start up an idled generator or to purchase off-system power.

FERC Form 714 requires all utilities to submit this number to the public for every hour of the year. This data can be represented as either a plot of all hourly values from highest to lowest to show an average rate (see Figure 3-5) or as a histogram of average costs (see Figure 3-6). The value of this number for an end-user is that it is an indication of that utility's incremental cost of generation. Some end-users have already used this data to negotiate rates based on the utility's actual cost of production plus a small adder for some contribution to fixed costs. Appendix D contains a table of all 1994 system lambda information as filed to FERC in 1995. Note that many utilities are part of other control areas and thus need not file separately and that not all control areas filed data.

In addition to the utility's cost of incremental generation, the end-user should also attempt to get as much information as possible on the rates paid by other end-users. First, the end-user should make every effort to get the rates paid by its competitors, especially in those industries that are electricity intensive. If the competitor has a special contract, the rate paid can often be gleaned from public documents available from the state public utility commission. In some states, these special contracts are considered public documents, and the actual rate is readily available while in other states, more investigation is required. Some states have no special contracts on file, and the only indication of the rate paid by a competitor is from the tariff.

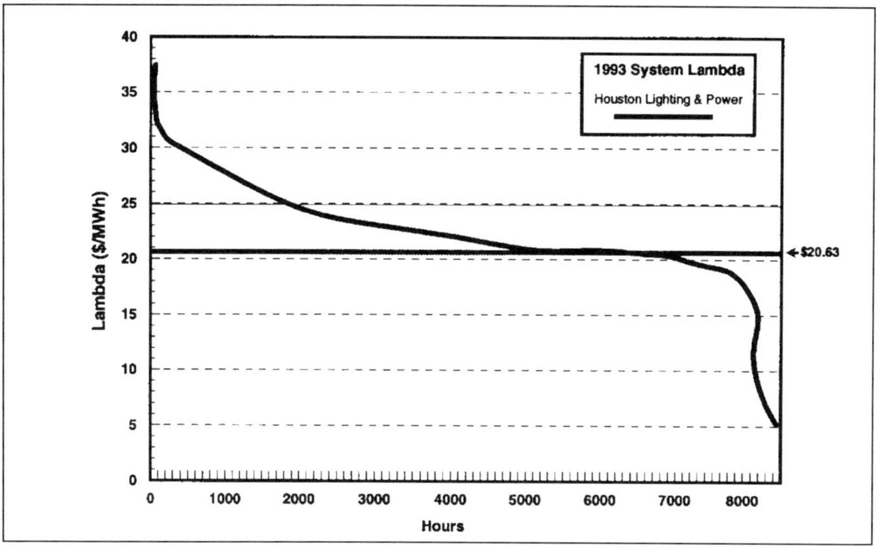

Figure 3-5. System Lambda information arranged from highest to lowest to show average incremental generation rates.

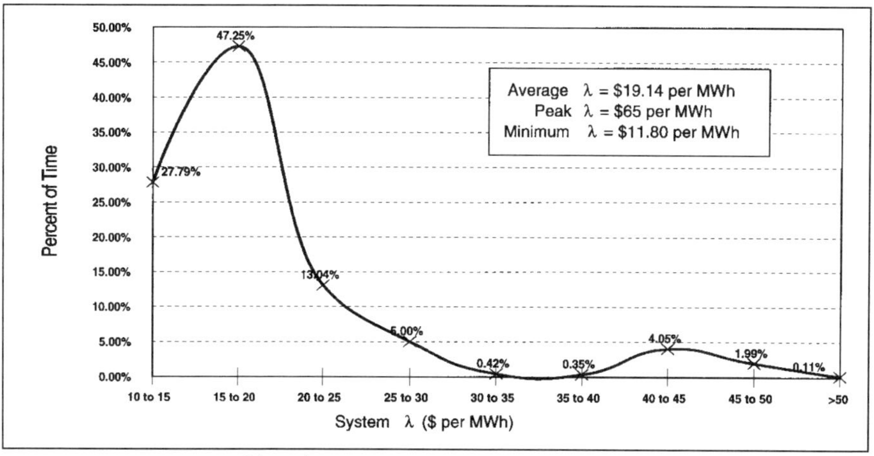

Figure 3-6. System Lambda information arranged as a histogram.

The end-user should also attempt to determine whether any other customers of its utility are receiving special contracts. If so, these may also serve as the benchmarks and perhaps even serve as the highest rate acceptable from the utility, since it was offered before.

Once a utility is sufficiently leveraged so that it is willing or even eager to offer the end-user a rate reduction, the utility may find it difficult to justify to its commission, other rate payers, or its shareholders a blatant below-tariff rate for just one customer. Therefore, the end-user should consider ways to implement a lower rate that is in-line with existing cost-reduction methodologies. These avenues to lower rates can be slight modifications to existing tariffs or creatively worded contracts that result in the desired rate yet are consistent with accepted programs.

For example, an existing interruptible rate tariff could be modified to include a "buy-through" provision that allows the utility to pass on the cost of off-system power purchases made during system capacity shortages as an alternative to calling a curtailment. This would allow the end-user to receive virtually firm service at interruptible rates since the increased cost would only apply a few hours during the year. This may be more palatable to commissions and intervenors because the rates are already approved and only the terms of the service are changed.

Another avenue to a lower rate is the use of real-time pricing, which is an extension of an interruptible buy-through. In a true real-time pricing program, the end-user pays for power at the utility's incremental cost plus a small markup for fixed costs and revenue generation. Since this price fluctuates on an hourly basis, the end-user is given an estimate of the hourly price before the hour as well as daily, weekly, and monthly price forecasts. The end-user then nominates how much power will be purchased that hour based on the price. Over fifteen utilities offer real-time pricing, although most are merely demand-side management tools and not true real-time pricing, so it is a largely accepted ratemaking methodology. The end-user could propose such a scheme, based on an existing program, as an alternative to conventional firm tariff service.

All this information and leverage should be combined into a well-prepared proposal for the utility that includes:

- A well reasoned argument to why the end-user needs lower cost power, e.g., its competitors are paying less, it needs lower cost power to remain competitive, it may have to shut down or shift production if costs remain high.
- A list of options the end-user is considering, e.g., cogeneration, municipalization, etc. These should be presented with enough detail to show that the options are viable economically and technically and to show that the end-user is serious about implementing the alternatives.
- A calculation of benchmark rates that will form the basis of a negotiated rate. These benchmarks could be the cost of power with the alternative, the cost of power with retail wheeling, or the cost of power paid by other utility customer's or the end-user's competitors. These rates should be supportable yet optimistic because they will serve as the opening proposal in the negotiations.

- Possible avenues for implementing a lower rate, such as combined metering, interruptible power, fuel swaps, etc.

At some point in the negotiations, the utility will invariably claim that it would like to help out the industrial customer but that its hands are tied by the state regulatory commission. Equally invariably, this is not true. Most, if not all, state public utility commissions are willing to allow special contracts between utilities and their large industrial customers because (i) it keeps that industrial as a customer of the utility, (ii) it keeps that customer in the state, and (iii) it keeps that industrial from clamoring for retail wheeling. Many commissions are watching developments in those states leading the way with retail wheeling (California, New Hampshire, and Illinois at the time of this writing) so that they do not have to deal with the thorny issues involved.

As with any negotiation, preparation is the key to success, and the end-user is advised to be prepared with a well developed argument for lower rates and credible alternatives to monopoly service. Even if retail wheeling is available, end-users will still need to leverage suppliers to optimize rates. All suppliers will continue to face competition from non-traditional alternatives, and end-users should continue to exploit these options.

Chapter 4

Electric Industry Structure with Retail Wheeling

While it may appear presumptuous to predict the structure of a re-regulated electrical system at this stage of development, it is clear that certain infrastructures will develop. Most of this development has occurred as various state retail wheeling programs are initiated and as FERC continues to introduce competition to the electricity industry where it can. Also, the re-regulated natural gas market provides clear clues as to how the market will respond to competitive opportunities, and many of the structures developed for the gas industry will have parallels in electricity.

Poolco and the British Model

In response to the California Public Utility Commission's Blue Book restructuring proposal, two California utilities, San Diego Gas & Electric and Southern California Edison, proposed the creation of a regional pooling company, or poolco. This model expands upon the tight power pools that already exist in the Eastern United States and is similar to the newly restructured electricity industry in the United Kingdom. Although the various poolco models and proposals vary, they all share the fundamental function of providing centralized generation dispatch and system operation services. Poolco would be an independent entity that would not own any facilities, but would control the operation of most, if not all, generation and transmission facilities in a region.

Under the poolco model and the British system, all generation resources are centrally dispatched on an hourly basis much like they are in the tight power pools that already exist. The difference is that generation resources are dispatched based on a bid price that each generator submits to the pool rather than on the generator's incremental costs. In the U.K. each generator submits its bid on a daily basis, although an hourly or even half-hourly bid has been proposed in the U.S. to ensure more accurate generation dispatch. Once all bids have been received by the poolco, they are prioritized by price. The lowest priced generators are then selected until the level of generation matches the projected load for the period (see Figure 4-1).

The last generator selected to meet projected load, which will be the most expensive, sets the price that will be paid to all other generators. This marginal unit then sets the market clearing price for electricity on the grid, which will be analogous to the system lambda that is used now. Those generators that bid prices lower than the marginal or market clearing price will run (and make a profit if the bid was the actual operating cost) and those with higher bids will not run. In this way, generators compete for the right to generate into the grid based on market signals rather than production costs. For example, nuclear units and other "must-run" units will probably submit daily or hourly price bids of $0.00 per megawatt-hour to ensure that they are always selected. Of course, they will receive the market clearing price for that power rather than their zero bid. During times of light loads, the market clearing price will be very low as generators bid prices below variable costs to avoid having to cycle or shut down a unit. During times of high loads, high-priced peaking units will run, and the bid prices for those units will probably recover substantial fixed costs because the market can bear the price.

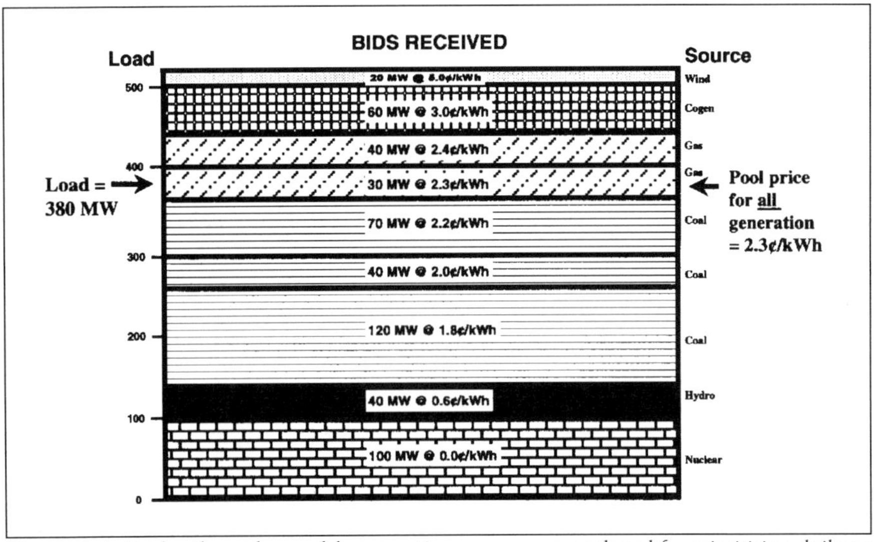

Figure 4-1. Under the poolco model, generation resources are selected by prioritizing daily or hourly price bids compared to projected load.

Buyers off the grid, whether wholesale or retail, then pay this same market clearing price, plus some small adder to pay for poolco services. Under a mandatory poolco system, such as that proposed by the California utilities and the British system, all buyers pay the same price for power, at least on a short-term basis. Although long-term energy and capacity contracts could also be implemented by the pool, the poolco model is best suited for the short-term, spot market for power.

Because the poolco would also be running the transmission system, the poolco models proposed also would account for transmission constraints when determining the market clearing price. The San Diego Gas & Electric proposal suggests multiple spot market centers in various regions to reflect transmission constraints. This would allow a market price that would reflect the ability and cost to move power from low priced areas to high priced areas. This is very similar to how the existing tight power pools operate today, except that the generation dispatch is based on a market price rather than on incremental cost.

Although the poolco model introduces a level of competition to a tightly controlled industry, it is clearly not widely supported as the best way to achieve a competitive market. Many poolco detractors suggest that a mandatory poolco system is not much more than replacing one monopoly system operator for another. That is, if all buyers and sellers must deal with a single entity rather than each other and if the poolco operates the transmission system, there is really no direct access to the competitive generation market. The only way to ensure a truly competitive system is to allow buyers and sellers to directly interact. Some poolco models allow these separate bilateral contracts to simultaneously exist and leave poolco to providing only an optional source of spot market or short-term power. In this case, however, most low cost generation will not enter the spot market, so poolco prices will be rather high.

A source of direct interaction between buyer and seller in a poolco system, and one that exists in the British system, is a contract for differences between the buyer and seller. A contract for differences is basically a hedging agreement where the risk of the volatility of the poolco price is transferred from the buyer to the seller. The buyer and seller agree upon a certain fixed price, which may fluctuate depending on certain market indices, and if the spot poolco price rises above the contract price, the seller pays the difference to the pool. If the poolco price drops below the contract price, the difference is paid to the seller. Therefore, the buyer gets a fixed, predictable price for power and the seller gets a customer. Of course, the transference of risk is a service that no supplier, or independent risk manager, will offer for free. That is, the buyer willing to stomach the volatility of a fluctuating hourly market price will undoubtedly receive a lower overall cost for power than one that requires a fixed price for budgetary reasons. Because of this cost, these contracts for differences will not allow an end-user the market power to negotiate a below-market price for power, as he would be able to under a bilateral contracts model. While contracts for differences provide buying options for some buyers, it is not a substitute for true direct access to the seller.

While the U.K. poolco system has been successfully implemented, by most accounts, it has experienced problems with unexplained elevations in market clearing prices, i.e., price increases not due to loading, weather, or fuel costs. Most likely these increases are due to the fact that during most days of normal system loads, a handful of generators are always those that are setting the market clearing price. Since many low cost and must run generators will always be selected, these incremental units will usually be the system price setters. Even without any illegal corroborative effort, it appears likely that these units could begin to bid higher prices (capped by high-cost peaking units) and still be selected. This phenomenon may explain poolco price elevations of up to 40% in some cases.

Poolco appears to operate best if it is only but one alternative available to buyers and sellers. A centralized market clearing function could serve as a competitive source of short-term, spot market power that many end-users and distributors may wish to turn to. The poolco could be used to supplement long-term, directly negotiated bilateral contracts (see below) or to provide a market to sell unused excess capacity purchased with these long-term contracts. Some end-users may wish to buy all power on the spot market, if prices are low enough, and assume the risk of price fluctuations or hedge the prices with financial instruments.

In summary, poolco can provide a viable source of competitive power as long as it is not another monopoly that merely replaces the existing monopolies. Mandatory pools do not allow true competition nor are they necessary to ensure reliability. In those regions with existing tight power pools, such as New England, poolcos will probably be implemented as a stepping stone to a competitive market since the infrastructure for a centrally-dispatched system is already in place. As long as this is a transitory system, some competition is better than none.

Bilateral Contract Model

While two of California's three large investor-owned utilities argued for a centralized poolco, the other, Pacific Gas & Electric (PG&E), the nation's largest electric utility, advocated a system which allows direct contracts between buyers and sellers. One advantage to the poolco model is that system reliability and operation is easily controlled with today's methods and rules because one entity controls the generation dispatch and the transmission system. Therefore, any alternative system, especially one that allows direct contact between buyers and sellers, must provide for some mechanism to ensure reliability. That is, giving up control of the integrated grid to the market may sacrifice system operation criteria that ensures the reliability that presently exists. PG&E proposes a system that creates a new infrastructure for maintaining reliable system operation while allowing direct access, but it is naturally more complex. This model is called the bilateral contracts proposal. (see Figure 4-2)

Under the bilateral market approach suggested by PG&E, all retail customers would have direct access to the competitive generation market via individually negotiated contracts with the supplier of their choice. A new entity, called a supply coordinator, would act as the interface between the bilateral arrangement and the transmission company, or grid operator. Under PG&E's model, the investor-owned utility would serve as the grid operator and would maintain system reliability, manage emergency responses, and settle imbalances. The grid operator would provide non-discriminatory transmission access under FERC approved tariffs as required by Order 888. The grid operator would also provide those ancillary services that only it can provide, such as scheduling and instantaneous load following. However, the grid operator would not serve as an economic dispatcher of the power entering the system, as it does now or under a centralized poolco model. Rather, the economics of power production would be influenced by the prices established under the numerous bilateral agreements. In this way, generation is truly economically dispatched because the market is deciding which units to operate.

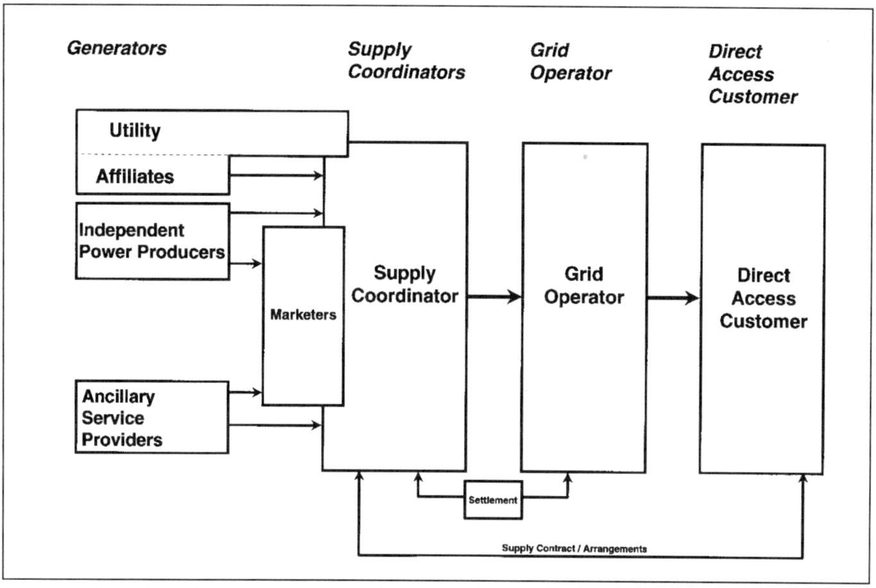

Figure 4-2. Bilateral contracts model using a supply coordinator as the interface between the suppliers, the end-users, and the grid operator.

The supply coordinator would be responsible for supplying its customer's needs on a real-time basis and would ensure that grid operation requirements are met. First, the supply coordinator would have to enroll as such under the grid operator's supply coordinator tariff. The grid operator will be entitled to set a series of requirements and operational parameters to ensure that each supply coordinator has the resources, technology, and expertise to adequately meet its customers' requirements while maintaining system integrity. These grid protocols will ensure that the supply coordinator will not place system reliability or security in jeopardy because it does not have the wherewithal to interface with the grid. These requirements, which will be defined in a supply coordinator tariff approved by the state regulatory body, will be the grid's method to ensure proper operation of the system without assuming all operation itself.

Second, the supply coordinator must be able to arrange to purchase and deliver the energy, capacity, transmission, distribution, and ancillary services as required by its customers. That is, the supply coordinator is responsible for ensuring that it has access to all the unbundled products available on the market to ensure that its customer's demands are always met. If the supply coordinator fails to meet all these requirements, e.g., a supplying generator fails and no backup power was arranged, the customer's demands will have to be supplied by the grid itself. Because the grid will only have adequate supplies to meet system emergencies, failure to arrange for all the customer's needs will result in very expensive penalties to the customer or its supply coordinator.

Third, the supply coordinator must also provide monthly forecasts of the transactions it has arranged to the grid for system planning purposes. Additionally, the supply coordinator must supply the grid with daily schedules of hourly or half-hourly transactions for system scheduling purposes. This is required so that the grid operator will know what to expect of the grid on a real-time basis. The supply coordinator must have a system that will allow scheduling changes up to 20 minutes before the hour (although even last minute changes should be possible) to accommodate sudden changes in demand by its customers. Of course, this scheduling will be automated using uniform formats from which the supply coordinator's data will be downloaded to the grid operator on a daily basis. Scheduling systems like this already exist between some municipal electric utilities and the control center for the control area in which they are located.

Fourth, the supply coordinator must be able to match its customer's loads with the resources arranged either by the end-user directly (using a bilateral contract) or by the supply coordinator. For example, if the end-user opted not to purchase backup power while arranging interruptible, off-system power, the supply coordinator would have to ensure that the end-user is interrupted if the supply is lost. Note that either the end-user or the supply coordinator may purchase some or all of this power from a spot-market system such as a voluntary poolco, as discussed above.

Finally, the supply coordinator will take part in the settlement process. Most likely, the supply coordinator will be responsible for billing the end-user and ensuring that all its suppliers are paid. The supply coordinator will also be responsible for balancing all the power sale and purchase contracts at the end of the day to ensure that no imbalances exist.

End-users will have four options for purchasing power in the bilateral contracts model. First, the end-user could act as its own supply coordinator. This would require the end-user to operate a 24-hour operations center and staff it with qualified personnel. While some larger end-users with multiple facilities may elect to do this, most end-users will not want to make the investment necessary to directly access the grid. Power marketers, as discussed below, will offer supply coordination services so that they can offer a bundled product, much like the utilities do today. Second, power marketers will offer these services in addition to the power that they will sell. Third, the end-user could continue to purchase power from the local distribution company, which will also be a supply coordinator (as it is now, in effect). Finally, the end-user will be able to purchase rebundling services from an independent supply coordinator, i.e., many third parties will offer these services independent of the suppliers of the electricity.

In summary, the existing centralized economic dispatch system has been developed and perfected over a number of years and as been largely successful in optimizing generation costs. However, it does not accommodate competition because a single entity is still controlling the production of electricity from a single point, the control center, and there are no buyer-side signals entering the analysis. The alternative offered by the bilateral contracts model is to let the market decide which generators operate based on either specific contracts with specific buyers—which would be the equivalent of a must run unit—or economic dispatch among the sources secured by a single supply coordinator or power marketer. There is no need for centralized dispatch because the market provides incentive for each supply coordinator or marketer to offer the lowest cost product to its customers. This will force them to only operate the most efficient, low-cost units.

It is clear that some sort of direct access model will eventually be developed for the retail competitive electricity market. While the nomenclature and details provided in PG&E's bilateral contracts model may not be identical to the system that eventually evolves, many of the basic functions will still apply. While implementation of this system may take some time (as it did in gas), competitive forces require a way for buyers to have direct access to sellers. Therefore, this book focuses more on the direct access model rather than the poolco model when discussing how power will be purchased by an end-user in a retail wheeling world.

Hybrid Models

As the states and FERC continue their transition to a competitive retail power industry, the experiences and knowledge gained by one state are soon passed on to others. After a while, a certain consensus builds and certain market structures consistent among all programs begin to take shape. This consensus building has occurred with respect to the poolco vs. bilateral contracts debate. In most states, including California, a hybrid model has become the norm, in which both a poolco function and bilateral contracts are allowed.

In these new hybrid models, direct bilateral contracts between buyer and seller are allowed for those end-users that choose to deal directly with their suppliers. Most regulators assume that bilateral contracts will be limited to industrial and large commercial end-users, although this has not been shown to be the case, as discussed later. To accommodate bilateral contracts, the role of the grid operator, as discussed earlier, is performed by an independent system operator (ISO) that operates the transmission system from a regional basis. ISOs and regional transmission groups (RTGs) are discussed in more detail in the last section of this chapter.

Separate from the ISO is a power exchange that serves as a poolco, but which is entirely voluntary (although in California, the power exchange would be mandatory for native loads served by the existing utilities during the transition period). The power exchange would provide the market with a source of short-term, spot market power (normally on a one-hour basis, but could be as much as one day) and a market clearing price. Generators could always supply power into the exchange, if the price is high enough, and buyers can always buy from the exchange, if the price is low enough. Furthermore, the power exchange provides the market with a daily or even hourly price index that can be used by the financial community for risk hedging.

The power exchange will not, however, be involved in system operation, as envisioned by the poolco concept. The power exchange is only another source of power for the market. In fact, many states are leaving the creation of the power exchange to the private sector since it fills a need demanded by the market rather than by the technical needs of the system or to protect the interests of captive customers. A mandatory power exchange is only needed to act as an interim pool for existing utility generation during the transition period. The market has already responded to the need for an independent power exchange, at least on the wholesale side. The Continental Power Exchange (CPEX), based in Atlanta, is a next-hour market developed as a for-profit enterprise. CPEX provides the mechanism through which member wholesale buyers can sell to or buy hourly power from each other. Private spot markets like CPEX will also be able to serve the retail market and provide end-users with hourly and spot market power without the need for a government-sponsored power exchange to be mandated.

Some regulators predict that the bilateral contract portion of the hybrid system will only supply a small segment of the market while the government-sponsored power exchange will supply the power needs of most consumers through utilities and marketers. However, this has not turned out to be the case in situations where end-users have had the choice. Although the experience has been brief, in both the Illinois and the New Hampshire retail wheeling pilot programs, many end-users, even residential customers, have selected to deal directly with competing suppliers. While many smaller users have simply allowed their loads to be aggregated with others, the level of competition has forced many suppliers to take their products directly to the consumer. While this may mean an additional metering, billing, and administrative burden for the supplier, a direct contract with as many end-users as possible is the only way for competing suppliers to ensure that they serve at least some portion of the market.

Another example of how bilateral contracts are preferred in a hybrid system is Norway. That country restructured its electricity industry in 1991, as part of an overall privatization program, to include the ability for end-users to directly access competing suppliers. Without determining how every service need would be met, leaving that to the forces of the marketplace, direct access was made available to all customers in all classes without a transition period. The result was price decreases for all customers, including a 20% average decrease in residential rates. Norway created a power exchange that would offer spot market power, backup energy, and price transparency to both the retail and wholesale markets. Nonetheless, the power exchange only supplies about 14% of the market while the rest is provided through direct bilateral contracts between supplier and purchaser.

In conclusion, virtually every new retail wheeling proposal offered by regulators or state legislatures includes provisions for a centralized, independent system operator to accommodate direct bilateral contracts, and a power exchange to accommodate a spot market. This hybrid of the original poolco and bilateral contracts models first developed as part of the California debate offers the greatest flexibility and reliability. More importantly, the hybrid model ensures the introduction of competitive forces to the industry while still providing a source of market-priced power to all suppliers and end-users.

Role of Existing Players

While many of today's electricity industry institutions will continue to exist in the future electricity industry, the role they will play will be radically altered in most cases. Even investor-owned utilities will have a place in a competitive marketplace, but the level of that involvement and the success of those companies will depend on how they position themselves. That is, as with any market, each player will have to find its unique niche or a special market in which they can successfully compete. Unlike today, no single company will be able to provide all things to all people. The successful companies will be those that have a vision of the role they can successfully play in a competitive industry and then work towards that vision. Some of the options available to the industry's existing entities is provided below.

Generation companies.

As discussed previously, the independent generation industry has supplanted the investor-owned utilities as the largest source of new generation, although the vast majority of existing generation still is owned by the utilities. In the future, many entities will own generation assets, including those facilities presently owned by utilities. Because the generation industry will be extremely competitive, those investor-owned utilities comfortable with earning guaranteed returns on capital investments in monopoly facilities will divest their generation assets and focus on providing regulated transmission and distribution services. These utilities will auction off their generation assets and collect at least some of the difference between the auction price and their investment cost through mandatory stranded investment transition fees.

Those utilities that choose to remain in the generation business will probably create separate companies for operating their facilities. Although this corporate unbundling or divestiture may never be mandated, it will probably be in the holding company's best interest to have separate business units for competitive services, such as generation, and monopoly services, such as transmission and distribution. The newly formed "gencos" will act just like independent power producers do today, and the difference between them may soon have no relevance. Thus all generation companies will be treated alike, on a regulatory basis, and will participate equally in competitive markets. Some companies will provide base load generation while some will find niche markets in peaking or backup generation. Some may even find that they can be competitive in supplying just load following generation.

Although market pricing will replace economic dispatch on an industry-wide basis, generation companies with multiple facilities will continue to use existing economic dispatch methodologies and automatic generation control to optimize their systems. In order to provide the lowest cost power to the market, a multiple facility operator will dispatch its units much like utilities do today, and the optimum mix of power will set the price that they offer to the market. While the selection of which generation company will provide power to the end-users will be based on market forces, within the suppliers themselves, the economic dispatch models in use today will provide a valuable tool to the generation company of tomorrow.

Transmission and distribution companies.

The regulated monopolies that will own and operate the transmission companies—grid operators, poolcos, or transcos—and the distribution companies—local distribution companies (LDCs) and distcos—will be the remains of the existing investor-owned utilities after the separate generation companies are formed. These utilities will act much as they do today since there is little incentive to optimize costs beyond the regulatory and political forces faced by utilities in the past. Of course, they will operate their systems in an entirely different manner. Transmission companies will operate their systems based on the schedules provided by the supply coordinators (or whatever they will be called), and distribution companies will act much like the LDCs in the gas industry do today. LDCs will probably also offer supply coordinator functions to provide service to those end-users who want no change from the service they get now (but the price will be high).

While FERC will regulate the transcos, state regulators will have jurisdiction over the distcos. Of course, many companies will continue to integrate transmission and distribution services, but the transmission services will have to be at least functionally unbundled from distribution to meet FERC comparability of service requirements. Although transmission companies will still be regulated monopolies, their operation will probably be managed on a more regional basis through regional transmission groups and independent system operators. These new entities will be discussed in the next section of this chapter. Ownership of transmission assets need not change, however, since the fees collected by the RTGs or ISOs will be allocated among the existing transmission companies.

Regulators.

As the industry unbundles, so must the governmental bodies that regulate them. Once the jurisdictional lines are settled (see Appendix A), the functions of most state regulatory bodies will be altered. While some regulatory agencies will be forced to accept major changes in their purview, most will be relatively unaffected. State regulators will continue to have jurisdiction over the siting of generation and transmission facilities although the cost of generation service will be controlled by the marketplace, and the rates, terms, and conditions of transmission service will be controlled by FERC. State regulators will have jurisdiction over distribution facilities and services and their costs.

The amount of regulation will probably increase with retail wheeling and industry restructuring. Retail wheeling as presently being developed is not *deregulation*, it is *re-regulation*. Regulators will still have to ensure that the competitive market remains open and fair to all players and that overall system reliability is maintained. A common analogy is that of airline deregulation. Although the Federal Aviation Administration stopped setting fares and assigning routes, there was still an overriding concern for public safety and airport and air traffic control. As a result, the financial aspect of the airline industry is left to the market, but the system operation is still regulated. Carriers must still follow rules on airport access and air traffic control, and regulators continue to set rules on how air carriers, which are competing for business, can access common facilities. In power, the cost of the power itself will be controlled by the market, but access to the facilities needed to reach that power will still be regulated to ensure system integrity and reliability. Nobody is interested in removing the controls on the transmission infrastructure that control how reliability and stability is maintained, so regulators will still have work to do. If anything, they will have more to do as they must maintain system integrity while dealing with the complexities of a competitive and open marketplace.

North American Electric Reliability Council (NERC).

NERC regions are apparently evolving into regional transmission groups (RTGs), or independant system operators (ISOs), which are discussed below.

Power pools and holding companies.

As discussed in Chapter 2, many utilities today are members of power pools, and in the case of tight power pools, such as those in the Northeast, member utilities even cede the control of their generation and transmission systems to the pool operators. Tight power pools already perform the function of an ISO and a power exchange, but they are not independent from the member utilities and do not conform to the non-discriminatory requirements of FERC. Therefore, the structure and operation of these pools must change.

Most likely, the tight power pools will eventually split into a separate power exchange and an independent system operator, although the change will not be easy. Many of these power pools have developed over decades into very complex structures firmly entrenched into the utility culture. Creating these mechanisms from the ground up in areas where there are no tight power pools is difficult, but tearing down an existing structure to conform to the new marketplace has turned out to be even more difficult. To their credit, it is difficult to change these structures because these pools have been successful in their purpose of optimizing production and transmission in the region. However, the benefits of power system operational efficiencies have been more than negated by the economic inefficiencies of monopoly structures. To introduce the forces of competition as the means to optimize production, while maintaining system integrity and operating the transmission system, requires that these pools be reorganized.

In its Order 888, FERC divides coordination agreements among utilities into four groups:

- Tight power pools, such as those in the Northeast (NEPOOL, PJM), where the pool operates the member utility's generation and transmission facilities for regional optimization.
- Loose power pools, such as the Western Systems Power Pool or the Mid-continent Area Power Pool, in which the sale and movement of power among members is facilitated, but where each member still operates its system independently.
- Holding companies, such as Southern Company, which are like tight power pools in which the members are part of a single holding company.
- Bilateral coordination arrangements, in which two or more utilities have made special agreements to coordinate energy production and purchasing.

In each of these cases, the power pool or the holding company is required to modify the agreements among the members to facilitate the requirements of the open access transmission tariffs before the end of 1996. In the case of the holding companies and the bilateral coordination arrangements, this is not difficult, since these utilities act as a single utility in the marketplace, so the pro forma tariffs are still applicable. Power pools, especially tight pools, have a greater challenge because their members are not accustomed to dealing directly with shippers outside the pool. In fact, the membership agreements in the case of tight power pools effectively do not allow the types of transactions envisioned by FERC. To fully open up the wholesale market to accommodate robust competition, the membership agreements will require substantial modifications.

Again, eventually these power pools will find their own niche in the marketplace. Most likely, this will be as a power exchange and as an independent system operator, although those will have to be implemented separately. Power pools are in a good position to take advantage of the industry structures that appear to be evolving, because they already perform many of the services required in a restructured industry. However, they must remove their affiliation, or at least their conflict of interest, with their member utilities in order to participate.

Municipal electric companies.

Publicly owned power utilities face varied challenges in a restructured, competitive marketplace. On one hand, municipal electric companies have the ability now to actively search the open, competitive wholesale market for low cost power, if they are not bound to existing, long-term full requirements contracts with the native utility or a joint action agency. This ability to shop the market already gives the municipal electric company the ability to provide its retail customers with rates that should be less than that offered by the native utilities to their customers and could even be less than the rates those customers will receive with retail wheeling. The reasons for this are that (i) most municipals do not own generation and thus are not saddled with fixed costs that must be recovered, (ii) municipal electric utilities often have access to low or no interest financing, and (iii) being publicly owned entities, municipals are not required to earn a profit for shareholders. Therefore, the cost of service to feed the load of a municipal electric company should approximate that available in a retail wheeling market. If anything, this cost may be lower, especially for residential loads, since the municipality's load is aggregated.

On the other hand, municipal electric companies see retail wheeling as a threat to their survival. Primarily this is because most municipals are indeed under the obligations of long-term full requirements contracts and thus do not have the option of procuring low-cost, competitively sourced power. Also, in many cases unfortunately, revenue from the sales of power by municipal electric companies is used to fund other municipal obligations, such as road work and fire protection. Therefore, many public utilities will not be able to compete with the open market, so there is little reason for the municipal's customers to remain customers of the public utility. Furthermore, since most municipals do not own their own generation, they have nothing to offer other loads to offset the loss of market share. Therefore, retail wheeling appears to offer only a loss of load to municipal electric companies.

It is not clear, however, whether all municipal electric companies will even be subject to state retail wheeling programs. As seen in Figure 3-3, many state regulatory agencies do not even have jurisdiction over these utilities, and many report only to the town that owns them. But the customers of those utilities, which have ultimate control over the future of the utility itself, will not tolerate above-market prices just because of the legal nature of the utility. Therefore, municipal electric utilities will only survive in a retail wheeling world if they can offer their customers rates that are comparable and even competitive with rates that other customers in the area receive from the open market. In many if not most cases, this should be possible due to the benefits of the municipal structure.

Cooperatives.

The future of the rural electric cooperative is far more uncertain than that of other existing industry players. The source of this uncertainty is the indefinite future of the Rural Utilities Service (RUS), which provides low cost funding for these utilities. If not for this funding, cooperatives would be mostly high-priced local distribution companies fed by high-priced generation and transmission companies. The high price stems from the widely dispersed loads common in rural areas.

As with municipal electric companies, most cooperatives are encumbered with long-term, full requirements contracts with their suppliers, which are the G&Ts in this case. If not for these commitments and the financial obligations to the RUS, cooperatives could perform as well in the open market place as the municipal electric companies in a retail wheeling world for the same reasons as described above. Even though the cost of servicing rural loads is high, those costs will have to be borne by those customers anyway, especially as class cross-subsidization evaporates.

The future of distribution cooperatives and generation and transmission cooperatives appears to be mostly political. Many cooperatives are seeking to replace the low-cost financing from the RUS with market financing because (i) that low cost financing is eroding and (ii) the cooperatives no longer wish to be subject to the regulations that are tied to the RUS financing. Also, as with the municipals, cooperatives are searching for ways to get out from under the long-term supply contracts. Although this book uses a dusty crystal ball to predict the future of the electricity industry, any changes driven by political pressures rather than market pressures is completely cloudy and beyond the power of this or any fortune teller.

Federal power marketing agencies.

Even more so than the future of cooperatives, the future of the federal power marketing agencies (FPMAs) is entirely political. At the time of this writing, political battles in Congress were raging over the future of these entities. Many reformers are looking to sell FPMA assets or privatize them outright in order to generate money to offset the federal deficit. The Western Area Power Administration (WAPA) has already received many bids from investor-owned utilities to purchase transmission assets located in those utility's service areas. On the other hand, many argue that the revenues earned from these sales will never recover the value that the low cost generation owned by these agencies could realize in a competitive market.

The problem with privatization of the FPMAs is what to do with the generation assets that these agencies use to supply governmental loads, wholesale buyers, and in some cases, industrial loads with below-market priced power. Privatization implies the selling of the generation assets which have been funded largely with taxpayer dollars. The benefit of this public investment has flowed to the specific loads that the federal statutes that created the

FPMAs intended to subsidize. These subsidizations, which include some that are valid under prevailing public policy, cannot be sustained in a competitive market without direct payments from the general treasury. On the other hand, competitors in the power supply industry argue that they cannot compete with federally subsidized generation and these agencies should be subject to market forces as are all other suppliers. This is an entirely political debate whose outcome cannot be forecasted.

The Tennessee Valley Authority (TVA), which is like an FMPA but different enough to warrant its own classification, also faces an uncertain future due to political situations. The Energy Policy Act of 1992 carves out a special exemption for the TVA in that its wholesale loads, which include countless municipal electric utilities, cannot access alternative wholesale suppliers, while the TVA cannot feed wholesale loads outside of its traditional service territory. Most utilities would welcome this shield from competition, but the TVA is flush with excess capacity which it sells to many industrials in the area at incremental cost. The TVA could stand to receive substantial revenue increases if it could sell this excess power in the wholesale market outside its borders. However, this would require subjecting its own load to competing suppliers as well.

Like the FPMAs, the TVA's generation assets were largely built with taxpayer-supported funding and thus are not faced with much of the fixed cost burden that investor-owned utilities have. Therefore, the question again arises whether it is fair to allow the TVA, as with the other FPMAs to compete with privately-owned resources with publicly financed resources.

One thing is certain about the political issues surrounding the future of all publicly owned power entities, including the municipal electric utilities, cooperatives, and the FPMAs, which is that eventually they will join the competitive market. Although intense political battles must first be fought, a competitive power market cannot tolerate special subsidies and exceptions for long. The customers of these entities may enjoy special treatment and lower rates now, but at some point those customers will be disadvantaged by being locked into a single supplier. The need to access competitive power will eventually drive public power customers to demand choice like the customers of investor-owned utilities are doing now. It is only a matter of time until the entire power market, including all generation suppliers as well as transmission and distribution suppliers, compete on a level playing field.

Marketers, Brokers, and Supply Coordinators

When the natural gas industry was unbundled and production was deregulated, producers were suddenly faced with the opportunity to sell their products to purchasers other than pipelines. Most producers did not have the expertise nor the personnel to effectively market their product, and dealing with local distribution companies (LDCs) and end-users was vastly different than dealing with the small circle of pipeline companies. Nature abhors a vacuum, so the industry was soon flooded with companies and individuals who were able to provide a new service, that of marketing this gas on the open market.

Because the gas industry was not entirely unbundled after Order 436 and because the market for gas at the wellhead had not matured, huge margins between production costs and sale prices allowed these new marketers to extract enormous profits for a short time. A gold rush ensued and at one point, over 300 marketers had FERC approval to buy and sell gas in the new market. Once the industry matured and became commoditized, the margins were reduced as were the number of marketers. After the margins settled out, many local marketers opened for business to meet smaller industrial and commercial loads while the national marketers continued to feed larger industrial loads. Presently, between 200 and 300 national and local marketers compete to sell gas to LDCs and end-users.

Because many of the changes in the electricity industry were driven by the successes in the gas industry, and because many of the same players are involved, many people see the same opportunity to make profits on the margin in the power industry as was done in gas. One year after the passage of the Energy Policy Act, only four entities had applied to FERC for permission to take title to wholesale power and resell that power on the newly opened market. By early 1996, over 220 marketers had filed similar applications, and the peak number of power marketers is expected to equal that seen in gas.

A power marketer is defined as an entity that purchases and takes title to electric energy before reselling it to wholesale or retail customers. In contrast, power brokers are those that merely put the buyer and seller together and facilitate the sale without taking title to the commodity itself. Power marketers are subject to FERC regulation while power brokers are not. Because FERC regulates the wholesale power industry and interstate transmission, all power marketers must file with FERC for the right to buy and sell power.

In evaluating a power marketing application, FERC is concerned with two potential abuses: (i) self-dealing and (ii) the exercise of market power. Self-dealing occurs when a marketer sells to or buys from an affiliate—usually a regulated utility—on terms that are more favorable that those that would be available to other market participants. The danger is that the regulated affiliate may pass on the difference between the paid price and the market price to captive ratepayers. The other potential for abuse is the exercise of market power due to the monopoly control or ownership of transmission facilities.

To guard against any potential abuses, FERC requires power marketers to:

1) Identify any affiliates. An affiliate is any entity that controls or is controlled by the power marketer. "Control" is defined by any more than a 5% share of either entity by the other, including a share in a certain generation station.

2) Disclose whether the marketer or its affiliate owns or controls any generation or transmission facilities.
3) Disclose whether the marketer or its affiliate holds a franchise service territory for the transmission, distribution, or sale of electric energy.

If any of these factors are present, FERC will still allow the marketer to buy and sell power, but it is now subject to additional regulation as an Affiliated Power Marketer, or APM. An APM must meet five standards beyond that required of non-affiliated power marketers:

1) The marketer must have no market power in generation, i.e., the generation owned or controlled by the marketer's affiliate must be at least 80% committed to long-term supply contracts or to native, captive customers.
2) The affiliate utility must have an open access, comparable service transmission tariff on file. Of course, all public utilities with transmission facilities will soon have to have such tariffs to meet the recent FERC proposed rule on open access transmission (the giga-NOPR).
3) The APM must agree not to sell or buy power from its affiliated public utility unless FERC approves the transaction.
4) Notice must be provided to FERC if the APM buys or sells any power to a utility that has a business relationship with the APM's utility. This can be very broad, since it affects all interconnected utilities, but FERC is primarily concerned that power that would otherwise be bought or sold on behalf of the utility's native customers is not reserved for the marketer.
5) The APM must pay market value for all ancillary services that must be supplied by the utility, such as scheduling and dispatching.

All power marketers must also promptly file with FERC any change in its status (such as new affiliations) and quarterly informational filings that list all transactions made in the quarter, including the type of service, delivery points, and price.

Most power marketers in existence today are either APMs or natural gas marketers. The utilities with APMs are obviously trying to position themselves for a new electricity market by being able to sell power in areas beyond their existing service territories. This type of new business venture makes sense for a utility since it is consistent with their core business, unlike many of the diversified business ventures that utilities entered into in the mid-1980s, such as real estate.

Natural gas marketers are hoping to make margins similar to those enjoyed as the gas industry was being unbundled; however, there are a few key differences in the gas and power industries that will limit the success of power marketers. First, the power industry is much more vertically integrated than the natural gas industry was, so there was always a difference in the price at the wellhead from that at the city-gate. In power, no existing profit margin exists *between* generation and distribution. Second, electricity is becoming commodotized much quicker than natural gas was. Already a futures market has developed for power and many publications, including the *Wall Street Journal*, publish regular market indices. Therefore, power buyers will not tolerate the huge margins that the gas marketers once made. Third, and perhaps most significantly, FERC learned many lessons from the re-regulation of the gas industry and is applying them to electricity. Primarily, FERC has focused on comparability of service with respect to transmission, the key to accessing commoditized generation, so that all players have equal access to the market. This will prevent the post-Order 436 and pre-Order 636 structure where marketers were somewhat isolated from end-users because of the non-comparable service offered by the pipelines.

This is not to say that power marketers will not be successful in the new competitive electric market. First, many power marketers have successfully sold power for traditional investor-owned utilities simply because those utilities do not have the marketing staff or expertise to sell their own power. Second, many marketers are buying low-cost generation assets and then operating them more efficiently so that they can offer power at prices below those offered by utilities, which traditionally had little incentive to be efficient. Third, marketers will be able to offer the bundled product to end-users that is traditionally offered by the utilities.

Those marketers that will be successful will be those that are able to either sell their own low cost generation or are able to combine the many unbundled products and ancillary services and offer a bundled product. However, this rebundling service will also be offered by other third parties as well. Even before retail competition is possible, a few entities have been created to provide the end-user services beyond the energy and capacity itself. These third party suppliers can be classified as buyer's agents, brokers, or supply coordinators. It is important to note that the supply coordinator function described above in Chapter 3 may take on many names, and that supply coordinator is only the name that Pacific Gas & Electric gave to this function in their direct access model proposed to the California Public Utilities Commission.

These third party buyer's agents will provide many of the non-power services that are presently supplied by the utilities except that they will be doing it as a representative of the end-user rather than the seller. The agent will procure the lowest cost energy and capacity on the buyer's behalf without taking title to the power itself. This will ensure objectivity on part of the agent, i.e., a marketer will always have an interest in selling its own power first. The agent will also arrange for transmission, distribution, and ancillary services as well. Finally, the agent will take part in the billing process and make sure all accounts are settled at the end of the day.

The primary advantage for an end-user to buy power through an agent rather than a marketer or broker is that the agent can find the lowest cost power and services on the market rather than have an interest in selling its own assets. Beyond that, agents and supply coordinators will also be successful because many end-users simply will not have the staff or expertise to approach the market as effectively as an agent with experience in the electricity industry. Many companies are down-sizing and are more willing to outsource many functions that are not part of its core business, such as buying electricity. Given the complexity of buying power in an unbundled market (as we shall see below in the next section), many end-users will be better off using an agent rather than trusting a utility, marketer, or broker.

Regional Transmission Groups and Independant System Operators

Under its jurisdiction of wholesale transactions and interstate transmission, FERC must review and approve every wholesale transaction and transmission tariff. As discussed above, there has always been a significant level of wholesale activity, although there was little for FERC to review as most of these transactions were inter-utility buy/sell agreements. When the Energy Policy Act was being developed, FERC thought that an open wholesale market would unleash a pent up demand for wholesale access and that a horde of Section 211 requests would follow. But this never happened because the wholesale market was so active to begin with. Believing that they would not have the resources to handle the number of wholesale transactions and transmission requests, FERC sought to create a new entity that would deal with these issues on a regional basis.

This new entity, called a Regional Transmission Group, or RTG, would be responsible for many of the duties that FERC would otherwise handle. Reportedly, mandated RTGs nearly were to be included in the Energy Policy Act but failed to be included in an eleventh hour final draft. Instead, in 1993 FERC issued a general policy statement encouraging the development of RTGs to facilitate access to transmission services. Even with the requirement that all utilities must file open access transmission tariffs, FERC continues to encourage the development of RTGs as a means to (i) speed the development of competitive markets, (ii) increase the efficiency of the operation of transmission systems, (iii) provide a framework for the coordination of regional planning of the system, and (iv) reduce the administrative burden on the FERC.

Specifically, the functions that FERC envisions an RTG would provide include:

- One-stop access to transmission services, including the handling of technical and procedural issues associated with transmission access. Because the transmission grid is integrated, a single wheeling transaction will usually involve many transmission companies. With an RTG, the shipper needs only to deal with a single entity when arranging the transmission component of a transaction.

- Develop innovative and regionally sensitive transmission pricing mechanisms. FERC has issued a policy statement on transmission pricing that encourages flexibility and promises to give substantial latitude to pricing proposals developed by RTGs.
- Coordinated transmission planning. The functions presently provided by the NERC reliability regions can be performed by the RTGs. These functions, such as system planning for load growth and system stability and reliability studies, should continue to be performed on a regional basis, and an RTG provides the best forum.
- Manage information. FERC is requiring all utilities to submit information on available transmission capacity via real-time information networks (RINs). Just as the NERC regions provide FERC with the transmission information presently required under Form 715 (see Chapter 7), the RTGs will develop the RINs and provide the necessary data.
- Provide dispute resolution. FERC has stated that it is willing to give deference to decisions resolved through RTG dispute resolution procedures. This is a key component to reducing the administrative burden on FERC that a newly competitive market might create.

In the 1993 Policy Statement, FERC listed seven basic requirements that a potential RTG must include in its by-laws or operating agreement, as a minimum:

1) The RTG should provide for broad membership, including non-utility players such as IPPs and power marketers. At a minimum, any entity eligible to apply for, or that is subject to, a mandated transmission order under EPAct must be included.
2) The RTG should provide for a means to adequately deal with state regulatory agencies with respect to facility siting and coordination with functions regulated by the state, such as distribution access.
3) The RTG must impose upon its members an obligation to provide transmission service for other members on a non-discriminatory, open access basis. This requirement is somewhat mooted by the FERC open access tariff requirement, but FERC notes that this does not mean that RTGs are not needed with the advent of open access transmission tariffs.
4) The RTG agreement must require the development of a coordinated transmission plan on a regional basis and the sharing of

transmission information, and this plan must accommodate the transmission needs of non-members. FERC is looking for detailed planning procedures in the RTG bylaws.

5) The RTG agreement must allow fair and non-discriminatory voting procedures and other rules of governance so that utility members do not dominate the RTG. FERC is concerned that RTGs dominated by utility members could discriminate against smaller entities that require transmission services.
6) The RTG must include a dispute resolution procedure that provides an alternative to filing a complaint with FERC. This includes the avoidance of filing a Section 211 request for mandatory transmission in the first place, i.e., such transmission access should be accommodated through the RTG without having to resort to a FERC order.
7) The RTG agreement must include provisions for a member wishing to leave the group.

Before the FERC NOPR on open access transmission tariffs was issued, RTGs seemed to be required in order to ensure access to transmission by non-utility entities. Even with the transmission tariffs, the RTG will still play a key role in providing a forum for buyers and sellers to readily access transmission services and information. Also, the dispute resolution function and the transmission pricing development will relieve FERC of many duties that may be better handled on a regional basis to accommodate regional biases and issues.

The first RTG applications and bylaws have been submitted to FERC, and RTG development is proceeding according to FERC's wishes. The first RTG to receive approval from FERC was the Western Regional Transmission Association (WRTA), which covers the entire Western Interconnect, i.e., all utilities west of the Rocky Mountains. This is the same group, for the most part, that makes up the Western Systems Coordinating Council (WSCC), which is the NERC region for that same area. In other parts of the country, other NERC regions are developing RTG applications as well. This indicates a trend towards the evolution of NERC regions to RTGs. For example, some NERC regions have begun to allow non-utility entities to participate, such as IPPs and power marketers. It makes sense for the NERC regions to become RTGs because the NERC region already performs many of the functions that the RTG must undertake, such as transmission planning and information gathering. Also, most of the transmission utilities required to be in the RTG are already involved in the NERC region.

As RTGs develop for the wholesale market, the role they will play in a retail wheeling market has drawn considerable interest. FERC's RTG application rules will probably have to be revised to accommodate retail wheeling, since many of the early RTG filings specifically disallowed retail wheeling. Also, end-users or their representative groups must also be allowed to join and actively participate in the transmission planning process and the development of transmission pricing methodologies.

For retail wheeling, an RTG will serve many of the same functions that are envisioned for the wholesale market. Most importantly, an RTG will provide a common methodology for accessing and pricing transmission. This will be necessary to ensure non-discriminatory access to available transmission capacity. Furthermore, the RTG's dispute resolution procedures should provide an equitable means to resolving conflicts that may arise when end-users begin to purchase transmission services. For example, disputes are sure to arise over which shipper gets priority when a transmission corridor reaches capacity and some load must be curtailed. The key to the successful use of RTGs in a retail wheeling world is involvement by the end-users or their representatives, which is necessary to protect their interest.

Although FERC is still encouraging the development of RTGs as retail wheeling programs develop across the country, FERC now must also consider how it will supervise the development, and later the regulation, of independent system operators, or ISOs. ISOs were first suggested to take the role of grid operator in the California restructuring model, but they have quickly become a requirement in virtually every proposed state retail wheeling initiative. The perceived need for ISOs by state regulators and legislators is important to FERC, because clearly it is FERC that would regulate them. Therefore, in Order 888 FERC for the first time began to address the role of ISOs in a restructured industry.

The basic function of an ISO is, according to FERC, "to ensure fair and non-discriminatory access to transmission services and ancillary services for all users of the system." The ISO would perform the system operation functions currently provided by the utilities in their control areas, i.e., maintaining system voltage and frequency, monitoring transmission levels, redispatching to ensure system integrity, and coordinating the movement of power throughout the transmission grid. Additionally, in a competitive arena, the ISO would schedule third-party transmission, price and collect transmission costs, and then allocate the revenue to the transmission owners, operate the area's OASIS, as discussed in Chapter 7, and implement the open access transmission tariffs.

Clearly, many of these functions overlap those of the proposed RTGs, yet FERC maintains that there is still a role for each. The key to this difference is in the area covered. Where RTGs will probably evolve from the NERC regions and will focus on broad regional planning issues, the ISOs will evolve from the individual utility control areas. That is, the RTGs will be regional from the start, while ISOs will grow to be regional over time. This process will take time because ISOs will cross state boundaries and multi-state jurisdictional issues will arise. Also, ISOs will require cooperation among existing utility controllers and dispatchers beyond what they are used to now (whereas regional transmission planning is already done to some degree by NERC). The exception to this is in the Northeast where the tight power pools are already acting as a super-ISO (without the "I," of course) in that they are operating generation and transmission systems throughout the region.

In California the initial ISO will incorporate the control areas of the three major utilities in the state, namely Southern California Edison, Pacific Gas & Electric, and San Diego Gas & Electric. Before long, this ISO will certainly extend to other control areas in the state, such as that of the Los Angeles Department of Water and Power. Before similar ISOs develop in other states, the California ISO may extend its area into those neighboring states as more utilities begin to restructure to prepare for retail competition. Then the issues of whether to form a new ISO or to merge with the California ISO will emerge. Given the benefits of joint operation, such as reduced pancaking of rates and regional planning, these ISOs will someday be as regional as the RTGs. At that point, the two entities, both regulated by FERC, will be able to merge in function and in administration.

At the time of this writing, FERC has not mandated the creation of an ISO in any instance, even though it has the authority (and perhaps the desire) to do so. Nonetheless, the development of the California restructuring model is forcing FERC to quickly come to terms with how it will regulate these new entities. In Order 888, FERC for the first time issued a set of guiding principles for the development of ISOs, given their popularity among the states. These principles clearly form the framework of what will be FERC's regulatory scheme for ISOs. The eleven principles for ISOs as issued in FERC's Order 888 are as follows:

1. The ISO's governance should be structured in a fair and non-discriminatory manner. The key to an ISO is its independence. It must not be able to respond any differently to requests for service from a utility feeding native load vs. a marketer feeding an aggressive end-user.
2. An ISO and its employees should have no financial interest in the economic performance of any power market participant. An ISO should adopt and enforce strict conflict-of-interest standards. This means that some utility employees may have to sever all ties to their existing employer once the transmission operation function is moved to the ISO.
3. An ISO should provide open access to the transmission system and all services under its control at non-pancaked rates pursuant to a single, unbundled, grid-wide tariff that applies to all eligible users in a non-discriminatory manner. According to FERC, "the portion of the transmission grid operated by a single ISO should be as large as possible."
4. An ISO should have the primary responsibility in ensuring short-term reliability of grid operations consistent with standards set by NERC. This includes responsibility over such facets of operation as maintenance of the transmission system and reliability planning.

5. An ISO should have control over the operation of interconnected transmission facilities within its region.
6. An ISO should identify constraints on the system and be able to take operation actions to relieve those constraints within established trading rules. In some cases, to maintain system voltage and frequency, the ISO may have to redispatch generation or redirect transmission. However, this must be done in a way consistent with, and in support of, a competitive market.
7. The ISO should have appropriate incentives for efficient management and administration.
8. An ISO's transmission and ancillary services pricing policies should promote the efficient use of and investment in generation, transmission, and consumption. FERC suggests that the ISO and the RTG work together with market participants to find ways to expand the system as necessary when growth is required. This requires the establishment of the proper market signals to which either the ISO or the market participant can respond to meet the need for expansion of the system.
9. An ISO should make transmission system information publicly available on a timely basis via FERC's OASIS requirement, which would be operated by the ISO.
10. An ISO should develop mechanisms to coordinate with neighboring control areas.
11. An ISO should establish an alternative dispute resolution process.

The significance of FERC issuing these guidelines is that it is certainly preparing the industry for retail wheeling. By itself, wholesale wheeling does not require the creation of ISOs, yet they are crucial for the implementation of most state retail wheeling programs. Of course, FERC maintains that it has exclusive jurisdiction over the transmission component of a retail wheeling transaction, and these guidelines are consistent with that jurisdiction. In fact, the open access tariffs required in Order 888 must apply to retail wheeling transactions if allowed by the state. Order 888 and its handling of ISOs is a clear signal that FERC is ready for retail wheeling and willing to assume its regulatory role in the new competitive retail market.

Part II

How to Buy Electricity

Chapter 5

Taking Control of Electricity Purchasing

In a reregulated, unbundled electricity market, end-users will for the first time have the opportunity to take control over the supply of electricity to their facilities. Unless the end-user chooses to continue to take bundled service from the native utility or a power marketer, this will involve an understanding of the numerous individual services and products that go into the bundled service presently provided by the vertically integrated utility. As with natural gas purchases, the end-user that takes control of these opportunities will be the one with the lowest overall energy costs.

When the natural gas market was restructured, end-users for the first time had the opportunity to purchase the unbundled products of gas service separately. These separate products were the gas itself, transportation, storage, local distribution, etc. The same will hold true for end-users of electricity with retail wheeling, except that purchasing power will be far more complex. Besides involving a greater number of unbundled services, the services and products themselves have a greater degree of complexity than those for natural gas or any other product. But where there are challenges, there are opportunities, so the purpose of this section is to bring a comfort level to the end-user when approaching this complex market.

The overall algorithm for purchasing electricity in an open market is fairly straight-forward (see Figure 5-1):

- First the end-user (or his supplier or marketer) must understand the facility's load profile and reliability requirements. Besides quantifying the load profile, an end-user must thoroughly understand the load's interruptibility and predictability.
- Before suppliers for this load can be located, the transmission adequacy feeding the load should be understood and assessed. This will provide the end-user with the knowledge required to access competitive generation. In other words, if electricity becomes commoditized, anyone will be able to find cheap power, but the successful purchaser will be the one that knows how to get it to the load.

- As with any product, the buyer must fully assess exactly which products are necessary to meet the demands of the load. In an unbundled market, the end-user will be able to purchase only those specific products and services required so as to minimize costs. Therefore, a thorough understanding of these unbundled products and how to buy them is necessary.
- Now that the buyer understands the facility's load, which products are needed to meet that load, and how those products will get to his load, the buyer is ready to approach the market. Locating the various sources and suppliers of these products is then the next step.
- The end-user now must determine how these products will be rebundled, billed and actually delivered and controlled. This is an especially difficult issue given the technical requirements and existing infrastructure for delivering electricity. This process will probably be mandated in most states.
- Finally, the end-user must consider many non-power services and products that will soon be available. These are mostly financial services that will help the end-user control the volatility and risk associated with purchasing a market-driven commodity.

Each of these steps will be discussed in detail in the following chapters. However, there is one consideration which the end-user must deal with first, and that is whether he will have access to this process in the first place. Even assuming that retail wheeling has been introduced in their state, not all end-users will be able to access the open market for a number of reasons.

First, the end-user may already have a power service contract that obligates him to purchase power from his native utility for a fixed period of time. This contract may either be a specially negotiated, below-tariff contract as described in Chapter 3, or perhaps a multiple year contract which may be required by the native utility's service tariffs. While the end-user could always try to renegotiate the contract using any available leverage, there would be little incentive for a utility to allow a customer to leave its system.

In some states, mandatory service terms pursuant to tariff provisions will probably be waived once open access is introduced since those terms were not negotiated and they would be inconsistent with any retail wheeling initiative. On the other hand, negotiated contracts will probably be upheld, even if the conditions that led to the deal, e.g., the inability to purchase power from anyone else, are no longer valid. Most states are very serious about protecting the right of a party to enter into a contract and the validity of that contract in order to facilitate free enterprise. In California, for example, high priced cogeneration purchase contracts were upheld even in the face of a radically different power supply situation than that in which the contracts were negotiated.

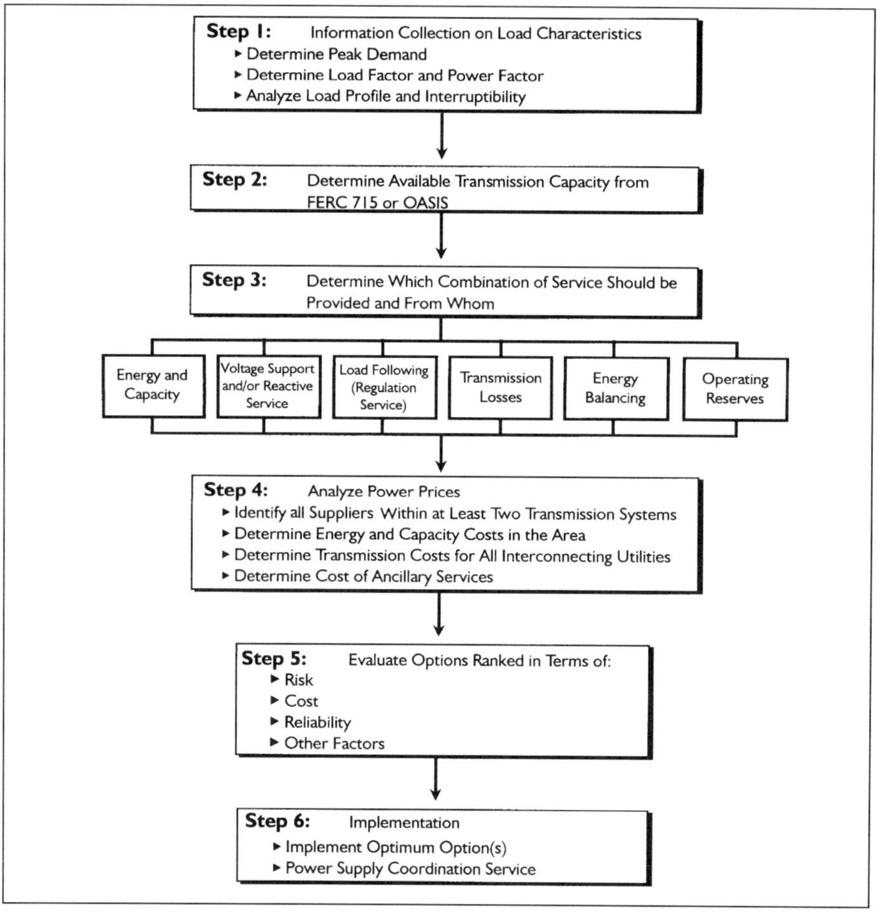

Figure 5-1. Strategy for implementing a retail wheeling transaction.

This does not mean that end-users with long-term service contracts need to stay out of an open retail market. An economic principle of contract law is that, in some cases, a party may wish to break a contract if he is willing to pay the anticipated or agreed-upon damages and those damages are less than the economic benefit of breaking the contract. In other words, an end-user may wish to break a power supply contract if the savings that result from buying in the open market are greater than the cost of breaking the contract. This is obviously a case-by-case situation.

The end-user is also advised to carefully review those contracts to determine whether they can be reasonably interpreted to allow purchases from other sources. This may be especially true if the state regulatory commission has the jurisdiction to interpret those contracts, which is often the case and that commission is actively promoting retail competition in that state's electricity industry. This lesson was learned on the federal level in a wholesale power case before FERC in which a municipal electric company in Virginia sought to purchase power from an investor-owned utility in Indiana using its newly available right to mandate transmission as a wholesale buyer under the Energy Policy Act. The municipal's native utility and existing supplier claimed that its long-term full requirements contract prohibited switching suppliers because only a decrease in the municipal's load was a justification for decreasing the level of purchases. FERC, in its zeal to encourage wholesale competition, decided that the decrease in demand from the native utility that would result from the municipal utility purchasing off-system power was the same as if the demand was reduced due to a loss of load, at least as far as the contract was concerned. This appears to be a somewhat blatant case of FERC busting a power supply contract in order to facilitate wholesale competition. Obviously this case can be used as precedent by retail buyers with apparently full requirements contracts to allow off-system purchases as well.

Another reason an end-user may not have access to a newly competitive retail power market is if that end-user presently takes service from a public power agency, such as a municipal electric company, cooperative, or federal power agency. Since most state regulatory commissions do not have jurisdiction over publicly owned municipal electric companies, it is likely that those commissions could not force those utilities to allow open retail access. On the other hand, retail wheeling in most states will require revisions to existing public utility laws, which is beyond the scope of regulatory commissions. These legislative changes may or may not include introducing competition to the public power sector. There is no reason why they should not since the benefits of competition should apply to all utilities rather than just those that are investor-owned.

Therefore, with respect to municipal electric companies, whether they are subject to a state's retail wheeling initiative depends on whether it is driven by the regulatory commission or the state legislature. However, it appears likely that most municipal electric companies will face the loss of customers to retail wheeling since restructuring will involve rather sweeping changes to state public utility laws in most states.

Cooperatives may be a different story. Since cooperatives are largely unregulated at the state level, an attempt by the state to allow all retail customers access to the open market may lead to interesting state-federal jurisdictional disputes. Already, the lack of jurisdiction by FERC over cooperatives has led to some disputes, and it is unclear how this will play out with respect to retail wheeling. At this time, the largest uncertainty is whether the Rural Electrification Administration will continue to function and exist as it has in the past. There is increasing interest in abolishing, privatizing, or at least reforming the RUS due to federal budget constraints. Most likely, cooperative customers will someday also have access to the open market, although it may not come as quickly as it will for those off state-regulated systems.

Finally, as discussed in Chapter 4, it is also uncertain what will happen to the large, federally-funded power agencies, such as the Tennessee Valley

Authority, Bonneville Power Authority, and the Western Area Power Authority. It is difficult to reconcile the existence of these programs in a competitive market if there is or was any federal subsidization of these utilities, which is certainly the case. In other words, how can a private utility with construction costs still in its rate base compete against generation assets constructed with federal funds? One solution that has been preferred is to auction off those assets to the open market so that (i) cash is generated for the federal treasury, (ii) market forces act on the cost of this power to the open market based on the purchase cost and cost to operate, and (iii) subsidized generation no longer skews the market.

Ironically, it may be in the interest of some end-users to maintain federal control over some of these assets and utilities. Many end-users that built power consuming facilities in response to federally sponsored economic development programs continue to take advantage of the low cost power that resulted from those programs. Purchasing power on the open market may actually cost more because the subsidies buried in the economic development rate would be lost.

A third consideration for end-users approaching the retail market is whether they happen to have any generation facilities, such as cogeneration developed under PURPA. While this may appear to be analogous to a long-term supply contract, this may actually provide greater opportunity for an end-user in an open power market. For example, an oil refinery with a 100 MW load may have installed an 80 MW generator to provide most of its electricity demand by burning by-product fuels. If the fuels used to generate electricity have some market value (that may fluctuate), the end-user should constantly be comparing its cost of generation with the spot market price of power on the open market (the spot market will be covered in detail in subsequent chapters). At many times, the cost of market power, especially during market clearing times, will be less than that of burning even by-product fuels.

Furthermore, an end-user with a cogeneration facility with excess power can use the open retail market to arbitrage its overall energy costs. In some cases, it may be beneficial for that cogenerator to purchase power on the open market to meet internal demand while selling its generation as either some specialty product, such as peaking power, load following, or operating reserve. This is a constantly changing economic decision, but the owner of a cogeneration facility must be aware of the many opportunities to be creative in ways it deals with a retail wheeling market. These options will be explored later.

Finally, companies with multiple facilities, even if dispersed around the country, face a unique set of challenges and opportunities in the retail wheeling world. Many companies have traditionally decentralized those functions which can be easily handled on the local level, and, unfortunately, purchasing electricity has traditionally been no more complicated than signing off on the monthly electric bill before it is passed on to accounts payable. With retail wheeling, corporations with multiple facilities have a strong incentive to finally centralize power purchasing and develop overall corporate strategies to purchasing power.

Primarily, this involves setting up a central purchasing function that buys from the open market for all facilities based on a number of factors. As we will see in later chapters, end-users will be required to meet certain protocols in order to have direct access to a transmission utilities grid (for reliability and operational reasons, as discussed in Chapter 4). While most end-users will probably either contract out for this function or leave it to marketers, those with multiple facilities and/or with significant electricity expenditures will probably find that it is in their best interest to meet these protocols themselves and act as their own "supply coordinator."

Rather than purchase power through a marketer or directly from a utility, an aggressive end-user with multiple facilities may wish to build its own control center in which operators will arrange for large power purchases from the bulk power market and then make arrangements to have that power shipped to the various facilities via transmission arrangements. These same operators will provide for each facilities' backup power needs as well as other unbundled products. If any of the plants have self-generation facilities, this control center can also perform an economic dispatch function that will optimize the use of all of the end-user's generation facilities. Additionally, the incremental cost of the end-user's own generation can be constantly compared to the spot market price of power. There may be many times when it is cheaper for an end-user to back down a cogenerator because replacement power from the open market is less expensive. In other words, the end-user's control center will dispatch not only the company's own generation but also all other market suppliers, such as other utilities, marketers, and IPPs.

The reasons for doing this are simply based on economics. Combining electricity purchasing for all facilities in a single control center will allow the end-user to buy greater quantities of power at lower, bulk rates. Also, the diversity in demand among the various facilities will often allow the end-user to buy lower cost, high load factor power. As discussed above, if any of the facilities have self-generation, the costs of this generation can be part of the decision making process so as to minimize costs by maximizing assets. In reality, the company is now acting as its own utility by dispatching the sources of the lowest cost power—either cogeneration facilities or market supplies—and delivering that power via transmission that it controls to various loads.

This point is made at this stage because these types of end-users must think globally when determining how it will buy power in the retail wheeling world. While the details of doing this are left to the subsequent chapters, readers with responsibility for more than one plant should approach the rest of the issues in this book from the perspective of the entire company rather than for just one plant. While this may be more complex, the resultant synergies and savings from centralized purchasing and power control will justify taking full advantage of the opportunities possible under retail wheeling.

Chapter 6

Understanding Load

Before a shopper can approach any type of market, he or she should understand fully what it is he or she wants. Electricity consists of a number of separate products (see Chapter 8) that are presently supplied as a single, bundled package by the vertically integrated monopoly supplier. In a retail wheeling world, these products will be unbundled and sold separately, and the end-user will have to decide which products to buy. While this may make energy purchasing more complex, the end-user will have the opportunity to save money simply by not being forced to pay for those services and products that are not necessarily needed. For example, an aluminum smelting plant should not require, nor should it pay for, load following services (as discussed in Chapter 8) since its load factor hovers near 100%, i.e., its load is nearly constant. Understanding which products are needed requires complete understanding of the load itself. This is the necessary first step in implementing a retail wheeling transaction.

With retail wheeling, energy buyers for industrial facilities will have to understand their plant's electrical loads better than they ever had to in the past. This understanding is required to determine exactly what power service products are required to meet that load, but more importantly, this understanding is required to ensure the minimum cost to feed the load. With today's market and the obligation to serve, neither the end-user nor the utility had a strong need to understand all aspects of each customer's load. As these customers now access the market individually, such understanding is critical. For this reason, successful marketers and suppliers will also endeavor to understand the nuances of their customer's and potential customer's loads.

This chapter will discuss three critical aspects of the end-user's load: (i) the load profile, (ii) the interruptibility of the load, and (iii) the predictability of the load. The bottom line is, the better each is understood, the lower the cost will be to serve the load in a competitive market.

There are other factors with respect to load that will also affect the price, but to a lesser degree. Most of these are power quality factors, such as power factor, harmonic content, motor starting inrush currents, etc. While the quality of power service is an important aspect of a plant's energy needs, it is somewhat independent of supply side management, i.e., the procurement of bulk power and transmission services. Most power quality issues are plant and load related, and solving power quality problems is considered more of a local demand-side management issue. Except for power factor, which may result in significant reactive power requirements from the grid (and thus discussed as an ancillary service in Chapter 8), power quality correction will not be considered services supplied by off-system suppliers and are thus not dealt with here in detail. It is worth noting though that while most local distribution companies will continue to address power quality issues for their customers, as should any good supplier, some end-users may have to begin to take responsibility for their own power quality problems if they purchase the bare minimum of services from their newly unbundled electricity suppliers.

Load Profile

First, an end-user should have a firm grasp of the facility's load profile, i.e., the amount of electrical demand as a function of time (see Figure 6-1). A plot of demand versus time will also indicate energy use during the period since the area under a demand versus time curve is energy (for those readers with a calculus background, energy is demand integrated over time). Load profiles should be evaluated on an annual, monthly, weekly, daily, hourly, and instantaneous basis since the cost to follow this load shape depends on how it fluctuates over time. Furthermore, this load shape may also influence which unbundled products are required.

The information required to determine a facility's load profile is available from a number of sources. Today, many utilities will provide major industrial end-users with detailed summaries of prior load demands, even on an hourly or sub-hourly basis. The monitoring equipment necessary to gather this data can also be obtained by the end-user at a relatively low cost. For a rough idea of load profile and load factor, electricity bills can be analyzed and summarized. Finally, many trade groups and even utilities are able to supply expected load profile characteristics for certain types of loads in certain types of industries.

The most common quantification of load profile is load factor, which is the ratio of average energy use to peak demand over a certain time period. For example, if a facility uses 10 million kilowatt-hours of energy over the period of one month, its average energy demand is 10,000,000 kilowatt-hours divided by 730 hours per month, which equals 13,700 kilowatts. If the peak measured demand during that same month was 18,000 kilowatts, the facility's monthly load factor is 76.1% (13,700 divided by 18,000). Load factor is a measure of how constant the electrical load is and is also a measure of how efficiently the demand levels set by the load are used. Since traditional utility rate tariffs charge for both peak monthly demand on a dollar per kilowatt basis and for energy on a monthly total cents per kilowatt-hour basis, the lower the load factor, the higher the average cost of electricity.

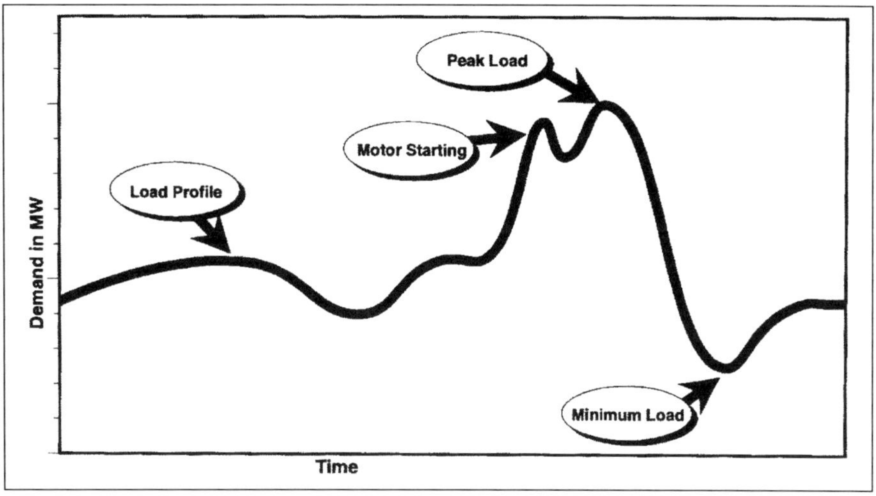

Figure 6-1. A facility's load profile, the electrical demand as a function of time, must be understood as the first step in shopping for power.

A load that is very consistent will have a high load factor (because the peak demand is maintained over a greater period of time) and will cost less on a per kilowatt-hour basis to feed. Therefore, plants with three shift operations pay less for electricity than those with one or two shifts. Also, loads that fluctuate on a weekly, monthly, or annual basis will also pay more for power since the utility is required to deliver the peak demand even during times when less energy is purchased. A load that fluctuates widely on an instantaneous basis, e.g., an arc furnace for a steel "mini-mill," will be far more expensive to feed than a load that fluctuates on an annual basis due to seasonal production changes, see Figure 6-2. Even though they may have the same overall load factor, which can also be calculated as the ratio of maximum demand over average demand, these two loads will face entirely different supply requirements.

Under a traditional utility tariff, load profile and load factor are often the primary determinant in the overall price for power. This may or may not be the case with retail wheeling depending on how the end-user opts to purchase power. If the end-user continues to purchase bundled service from either the existing utility or a marketer, the same influences on the average price of power will result in the same dependance on load factor that exists today. However, if the end-user purchases power on an hourly basis from the spot market (as discussed in Chapter 8), load profile will have less of an effect on overall price. This is because a purchaser of hourly power is not purchasing any capacity, i.e., there is no guarantee that hourly power will be available. Unless the end-user buys backup power separately, there will be no demand component to the end-user's electric bill and thus no dependance on load factor.

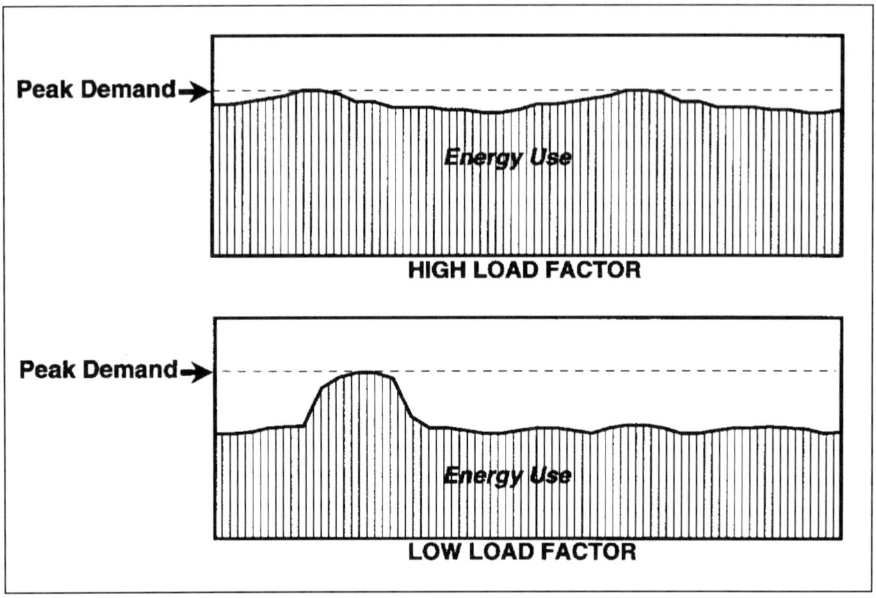

Figure 6-2. Load factor examples.

Interruptibility

A key component of the price for power in an unbundled market will be the firmness of the power purchased. The more reliable the power, the greater the cost. While there is no such thing as absolutely firm power—even firm customers will get curtailed during a "rolling blackout" event—avoiding curtailments during system capacity shortages can be costly. Likewise, the ability to curtail power with varying degrees of notice has varying levels of value to the supplier. Therefore, in order to minimize cost, an end-user should buy power that is only as firm as absolutely necessary.

Traditionally, power is sold as either firm or interruptible, although the terms and conditions of interruptibility vary greatly from one utility to another. Interruptible power service tariffs offered by utilities today offer different notice times, durations, and frequencies of interruption. For example, one utility may interrupt some load with 30 minutes of notice for no longer than eight hours per episode and no more often than five times a year. Others set a maximum number of curtailable hours per year. Many utilities will interrupt non-firm customers whenever the utility's cost to serve that customer is above the interruptible rate while others only interrupt when off-system power must be purchased or only when required to maintain system integrity.

As the number of suppliers increase and the sale of energy and capacity itself is deregulated, a range of new types of services will be available. A broad variety of power products will be marketed (each differentiating themselves from one another to satisfy specific markets), and the level of firmness of these various products will be a continuum rather than a choice of firm or non-firm. The greater the firmness of the supply, the greater the cost. Therefore, it is imperative that the end-user completely understand exactly how firm the supply must be to meet the different types of loads at each plant.

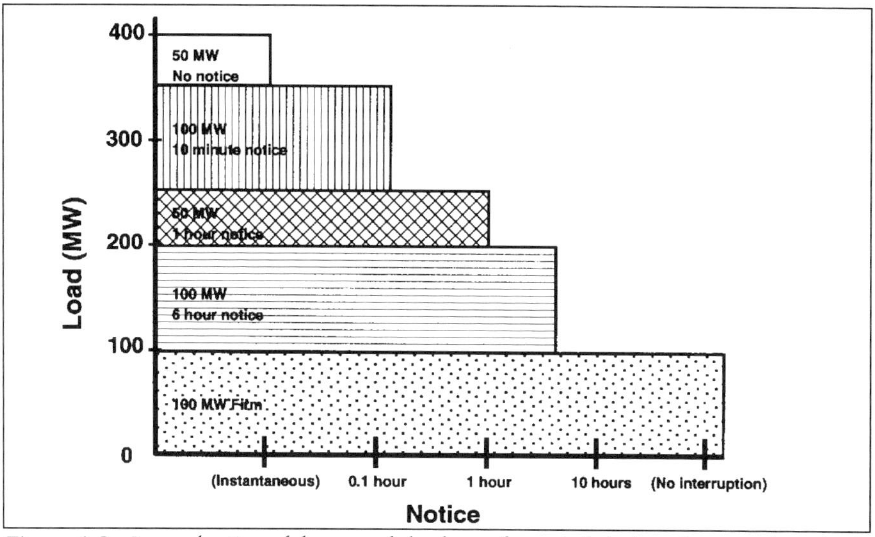

Figure 6-3. An evaluation of how much load can be curtailed given how much notice is required to evaluate the firmness of the power supply required.

Every end-user looking to minimize costs through the use of non-firm power should first complete a detailed assessment of the interruptibility of the load. This should involve an analysis of what level of *demand* can be curtailed, given various levels of notice. The form of this analysis can be a plot of load curtailed versus notice time required, as in Figure 6-3. Included in this analysis is a determination of the cost to curtail the load in lost production and out-of-pocket costs and a similar determination of the cost to restart the load. The evaluation of how much non-firm power to buy and the terms of the interruptibility, combined with a determination of how often the load is expected to be curtailed, should be mostly an economic decision, although some operating and technical issues will also be involved.

The result of this analysis is a determination of whether to purchase backup power and how much. Even firm power can be fed with a combination of interruptible energy and backup capacity. Some end-users have already found that purchasing duplicative interruptible capacity can equal the reliability of more expensive firm capacity. As one end-user phrases it, "three interruptibles make a firm." Of course, this evaluation must include an overall evaluation of the savings generated by purchasing non-firm or spot market power. Putting all this together is the subject of subsequent chapters and would be out of place at this point in the discussion.

Predictability

In the unbundled electricity market of the future, capacity and energy will likely be nominated on an hourly basis, if not more frequently, i.e., an end-user will have to inform its utility or supplier how much power it plans to use in the next hour. Deviations from this schedule, especially if greater, will result in significant penalties and charges. Since the lowest cost power will be that purchased on an hourly basis, the end-user should analyze how predictable its load is.

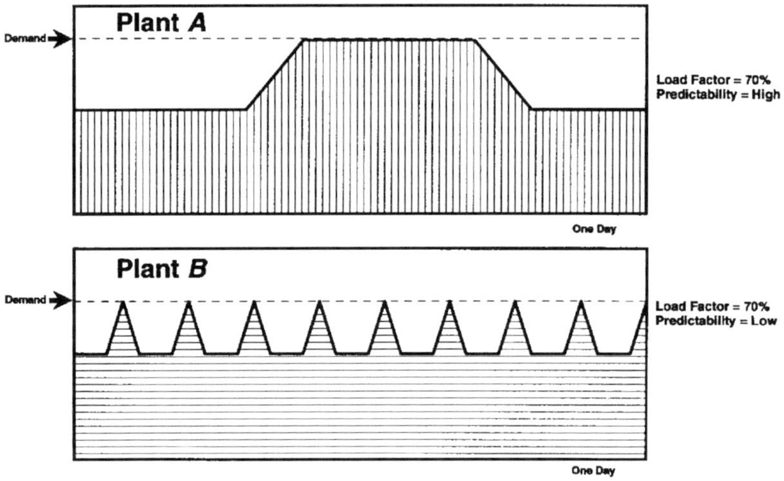

Figure 6-4. Comparison of high and low predictability for loads with identical load factors.

Predictability of load relates to load factor, but load factor does not tell the entire story. In one case, an end-user has a two-shift operation at Plant A, but when the load is on it is very steady. This leads to a load factor of approximately 70%. Another facility, Plant B, is a three-shift operation, but the load constantly spikes to the peak demand, and there is no way to predict or schedule the peaks. See Figure 6-4 for a comparison of these loads. Plant A's load is relatively predictable, even though the load factor is not near 100% because it increases and decreases at the same time every day. The energy buyer at Plant A will be able to accurately nominate the plant's power needs on an hourly or sub-hourly basis to the supplier or coordinator. These nominations can be submitted a day in advance for each hour of the following day. Based on historical load information, the nominated values will very closely track the actual load. Because the deviation from the nominated load to the actual load is minimal, Plant A will pay virtually no penalties for mis-nominations, nor will the plant be required to arrange for any significant capacity outside the nomination level. In summary, the predictability of the Plant A load means that the off-system supplier to which the load is nominated can accurately meet those nominations. Therefore, expensive supplemental and instantaneous load following power is not required. These concepts and ancillary services will be discussed in detail in Chapter 8.

By contrast, the load at Plant B will cost more to serve even if the meterable demand and energy levels for any given month or day are identical to Plant A. In this case, the energy buyer at Plant B cannot accurately predict what the plant's load will be except that it will vary from the peak demand to the base load demand. Even if the spikes could be predicted, the plant's off-system supplier may not be able to accurately follow the load. That is, if the increase in demand is very sudden, the off-system supplier's generators cannot physically keep up with the quickly changing load. Therefore, Plant B must purchase the needed energy and capacity to meet the spikes (or absorb the energy from the off-system supply during non-peak times) from the interconnected native utility or local distribution company. The cost for this service will probably be quite high since many distribution companies will not own their own generation, so transmission capacity must be arranged to supply the peaks. This is the same problem utilities face today with area control error (see Chapter 2).

Because the load for plant B is not predictable, the facility will be forced to buy what FERC calls energy imbalancing and regulation services from the local utility or transmission company. These services are discussed in detail in Chapter 8. For the purposes of this chapter, note that the cost of these services from the local distribution company will be higher priced than the cost to serve the load of Plant A. Therefore, even though the two loads may pay the same price for power under today's regime, the price for power for the two plants will be very different from each other in the future. This change reflects the true cost to feed each load. When shopping for power, though, understanding the predictability of the facility's load will be critical information to have.

Chapter 7

Transmission Evaluation

In a commoditized market, with or without price transparency, access to low cost energy and capacity will be relatively easy to establish. Anyone with a modem or a telephone should be able to find power at prices that are reasonably sure to be near the minimum available. However, whether that power can reach the load is an entirely different matter. The second step of a retail wheeling transaction, after the end-user's load has been thoroughly reviewed and understood, is to analyze the transmission paths from potential suppliers to the facility to be served. For this reason, an end-user will have to have a solid understanding of transmission capacity in and around the facility in order to establish where the lowest cost power can be obtained.

To understand the importance of transmission in a retail wheeling transaction, a simple example may help to illustrate some of the issues. Figure 7-1 shows a simple interconnected transmission system that interconnects three utilities and a 400 MW generator that feeds 400 MW of load among the three utilities. Suppose that the end-user with the 200 MW load on Utility A tires of paying 7¢ per kilowatt-hour to Utility A, and using its newly gained right to access off system power, it negotiates with Utility B to generate 200 MW to feed the load. Getting the lawyers together, they use conventional transmission pricing and come up with the power sale arrangement illustrated in Figure 7-2. Note the 200 MW contract path from Utility A to Utility B. Under traditional transmission pricing methodologies, including those used in the pro forma access tariffs mandated by FERC, the end-user will pay for 200 MW of contract path transmission at postage stamp rates to Utility A.

If the engineers were consulted prior to this deal, they would have first run a load flow study to determine how load is actually moving along the transmission lines. Load flow analysis is a function almost entirely done by transmission utilities in system planning and distribution planning departments to determine whether and where new transmission facilities will someday be required. These studies use sophisticated computer programs that essentially solve thousands of simultaneous equations with thousands of unknowns using complicated algorithms that have been perfected over the years. Load flow software, which is now available for personal computers, will compute how much power flows on each transmission line given the size of each generator and each load and the electrical resistance of each interconnecting transmission line. Figure 7-3 shows the types of load flows expected on the simple interconnected system before the new generator is added to Utility B. Note how the load flows from the 400 MW generator to each load.

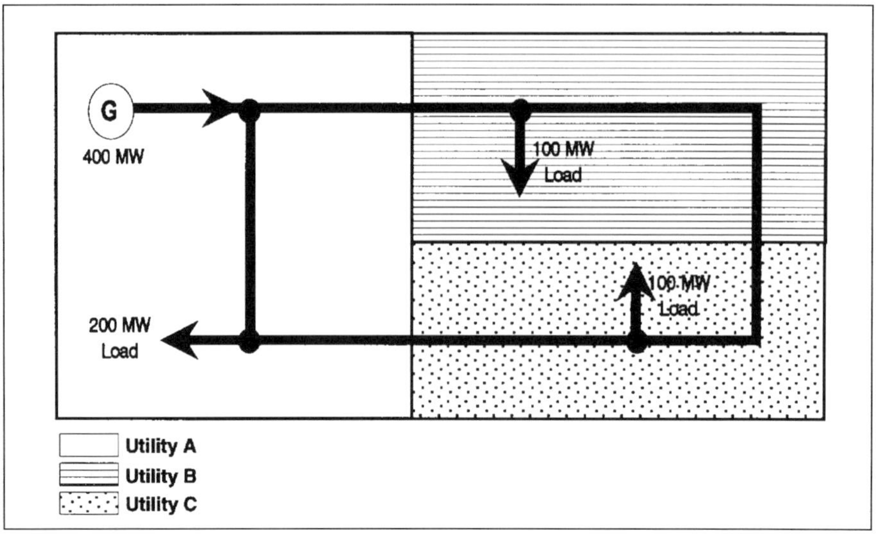

Figure 7-1. A simple interconnected transmission system used to illustrate the importance of understanding transmission in a retail wheeling transaction.

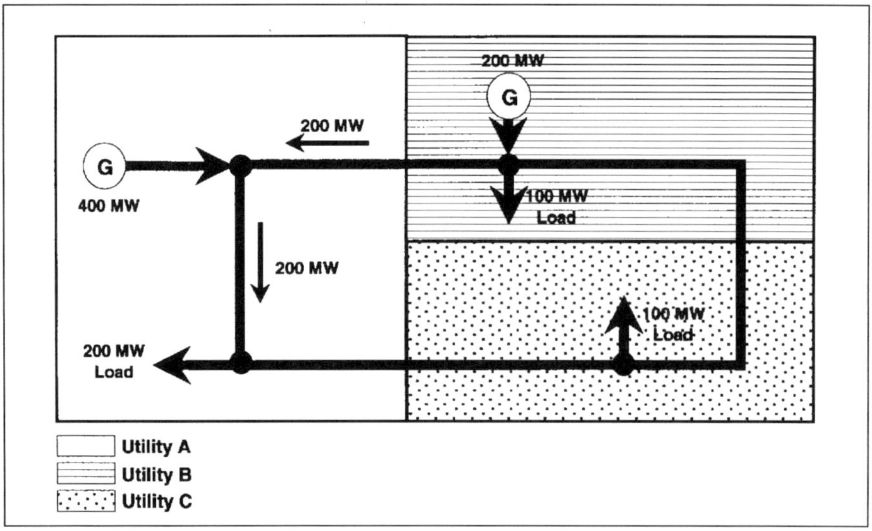

Figure 7-2. A contract path power sale arrangement from Utility B *to the* 200 MW *load.*

Figure 7-4 shows how these load flows change once the new generator on Utility B is added. A first impression is how these flows do not look at all like the contract path model under which transmission services are based today. Rather than 200 MW flowing from Utility B to the load through Utility A, 50 MW is still flowing towards Utility B from Utility A. Rather than placing 200 MW of power on Utility A's transmission line, this retail wheeling transaction is actually *reducing* the amount of power flow on this transmission line!

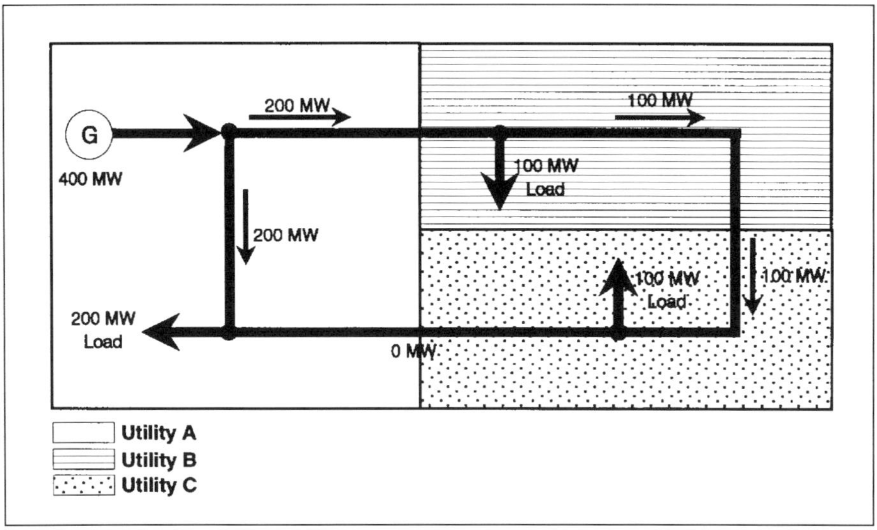

Figure 7-3. Transmission load flows before the new generator is added for the retail wheeling transaction.

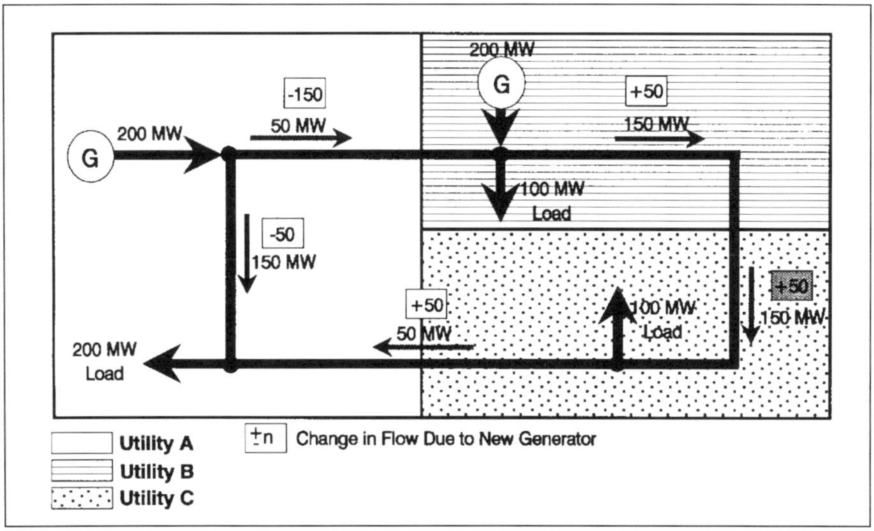

Figure 7-4. Transmission load flows after the new generator is added for the retail wheeling transaction.

Under some proposed transmission pricing methodologies discussed in Chapter 12, the shipper would receive a credit from Utility A for reducing flows on its transmission lines.

On the other hand, consider the load flowing through Utility C's transmission lines. In this case, the amount of power flowing through this line increased by 50 MW. Furthermore, Utility C was not even involved in the contract path agreement illustrated in Figure 7-2. This illustrates how power flows through the transmission lines of an interconnected transmission system based not on the legal arrangements between the various entities who own the facilities, but rather based on the laws of physics. Power flows via the path of least resistance rather than contract paths. Therefore, when shipping power from Utility B to Utility A, some power is bound to flow through Utility C. This phenomenon, called parallel path flows or, incorrectly, loop flows, is a real problem among all interconnected utilities. At this time, the overall effects of parallel path flows are assumed to cancel out among all the transmitting utilities and no compensation is pursued, but in a competitive market, these "gentlemen's agreements" will not last, and every utility involved in shipping power due to a wheeling arrangement will want its share of the compensation.

Besides the parallel path flow issue, this example illustrates a more fundamental point. Suppose that Utility C's transmission line that now carries 150 MW is rated only to carry 120 MW, and the 100 MW carried before the new generator was added approached the capacity of the line. Therefore, as a result of this particular retail wheeling transaction, a transmission line will be overloaded and either trip open or burn to the ground. If there was some way for the buyer and/or seller to know of this transmission constraint, or "bottleneck," an alternative wheeling arrangement would have to be found.

Fortunately, there is a way. As discussed in Chapter 2, the Energy Policy Act of 1992 required FERC to promulgate a rule to require all utilities to provide transmission capacity information to the public. FERC first implemented this requirement in 1993 when it required all transmission utilities with facilities over 100 kilovolts to submit load flow input and output data to the public. This data, supplied under FERC Form 715 reporting requirements, will be discussed in detail later on in this chapter. FERC greatly expanded on this reporting requirement in the open access giga-NOPR by proposing the creation of real-time information networks(RINs) that would provide hourly estimates of available transmission capacity based on FERC Form 715 data. The RIN proposal was then replaced by a new system required in FERC's final order on transmission information, FERC Order 889, issued on April 24, 1996. This order requires transmission utilities to develop an open access same-time information system, or "OASIS." The details of this system are discussed below.

At this point, note that the type of transmission capacity analysis illustrated in the above example is not only possible but is imperative before undertaking any potential retail wheeling transaction. The end-user in a retail wheeling transaction should only pay for the amount of actual transmission capacity that will be used. That is, if 100 MW is to be shipped from one control area to another, 100 MW will not necessarily flow between the interface, so the end-user should not necessarily have to pay for 100 MW of transmission to the transmission company between the control areas. Because power flows are determined by the laws of physics, transmission load flow analysis should be performed for retail wheeling transactions to determine exactly how much transmission capacity is required and where. How transmission capacity is actually arranged and the issues involved in purchasing transmission capacity is the subject of Chapter 8.

FERC Form 715

On September 30, 1993 FERC issued an order that required all transmitting utilities to inform potential transmission customers, state regulatory authorities, and the public of potentially available transmission capacity and known constraints. The new regulation creates a new reporting form, FERC Form 715, Annual Transmission Planning and Evaluation Report. A transmitting utility was defined in the Energy Policy Act, for the first time, as any entity that owns or controls transmission facilities with voltages over 100 kilovolts. While FERC does not normally have jurisdiction over cooperatives, municipal electric utilities, etc., EPAct granted jurisdiction over transmission facilities on these utilities for the purposes of mandating wholesale wheeling. Likewise, these utilities are also subject to the FERC Form 715 reporting requirements.

Form 715 reporting requirements are divided into six parts as follows:

Part 1: Identification and certification - The transmitting utility must submit the name, title, phone number and fax number of the utility contact person who is responsible for the information contained in Form 715. In addition, the utility must provide a certificate of authenticity of the data submitted.

Part 2: Base case power flows - Utilities are required to provide the input data for the load flow cases which detail the transmission system configuration for a specified set of parameters such as the season, year and normal or peak period which can range from the summer 1994 peak assessment through the winter 2004 peak assessment. In addition, utilities are required to provide output files for the above mentioned parameters, which must include solved cases which can be analyzed for comparison purposes.

Part 3: Transmitting utility maps and diagrams - Physical and schematic maps must be provided that detail the interconnection points of utilities, generating plants and substation locations that correspond to the load flow model.

Part 4: Transmission planning reliability criteria - The data provided in this part details the voltage, thermal and stability limits that will be used to determine the availability of potential transmission requests to be allowed by the utilities. This data should be identical to the data used by the utilities themselves to determine the reliability of the system.

Part 5: Transmission planning assessment practices - The procedures used by the utilities to determine transmission adequacy must be provided. The facilities that are out of service for each case must also be listed.

Determination of transmission adequacy requires identification and evaluation of potential system configurations (i.e., contingencies) where facilities are not available. A description of these contingencies must be provided.

Part 6: Evaluation of transmission system performance - The utilities must provide an assessment of the transmission system performance for the present and future. Stability limits and potential problems, if any, must be provided as well as any potential voltage problems.

As with many other regulations and reporting requirements, some utilities meet the barest letter of the FERC Form 715 requirements, although some have submitted very detailed and useful reports. FERC allows NERC reliability regions to submit the load flow data for all utilities within the region, but each individual utility must submit separate reports for the other sections. Most utilities submit basic transmission planning concepts for Part 5 rather than detailed discussions of the particular planning practices of the utility. As for Part 6, which was intended to provide the bottom line incremental capacity data, FERC's new OASIS mandate will provide this information on a same-time basis. The next section describes how the necessary available transmission capacity determination is made.

Transmission Analysis

To adequately evaluate the available transmission capacity for a retail wheeling transaction, the transmission system in and around the end-user's facility should be analyzed to determine (i) how the various control areas are interconnected, (ii) transmission capacities within control areas, and (iii) transmission capacity between the control areas. Control areas are those sections of the interconnected transmission grid that are controlled by a single entity. In most areas of the U.S., control areas correspond to a single utility, although some utilities have more than one control areas (such as Carolina Power & Light). In many parts of the country, especially in the eastern U.S., groups of utilities share a single control area in what is called a tight power pool. A dispatch center in each control area controls all generation and transmission within the control area and power flows between those control areas. Figure 7-5 shows the connections between control areas for the various North American Electric Reliability Regions.

Transmission limitations *within* a control area are determined by running a load flow analysis to determine existing transmission constraints. This load flow analysis is based on information made available through FERC Form 715 data, as described above, which provides to the public the data required to analyze existing and projected power flows on transmission lines. Traditionally, once power is delivered to a control area, the native utility has the responsibility of ensuring that the power can be delivered to the load centers within the control area using the native utility's own transmission or subtransmission system. Since this has always been the responsibility of the native utility, transmission capacities within control centers are very rarely inadequate. However, this may change as more wheeling is done between end-users within control areas.

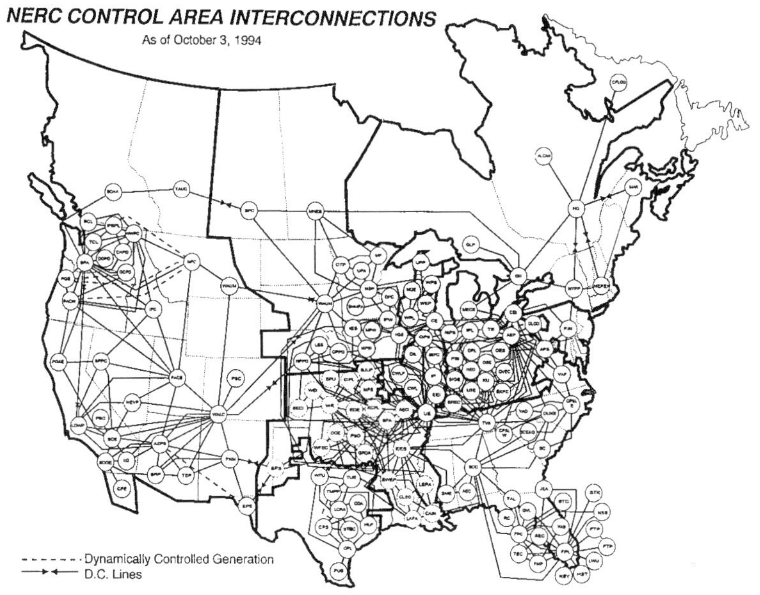

Printed with the permission of CIMMRED Energy Company, ENEREX Inc. Energy Management Services of West Des Moines, Iowa, and the North American Reliability Council.

Figure 7-5: Control area interconnections in the North American Reliability Council Regions.

FERC Form 715 information can also be used to calculate the incremental transmission capacity *between* control areas, which indicates how much *additional* power can be moved between control areas. This information is important to the end-user because it quantifies the ability of the plant to move power in and around the area. Fortunately for end-users, the incremental transmission capacity between control areas will be readily available on OASIS. However, the data used to determine the information supplied on OASIS must still be provided to the public, so that end-users can verify the information, especially in cases in which transmission is denied due to capacity constraints. This background information, which is essentially the requirements of FERC Form 715, will still be of critical importance to the end-user that wants to ensure the most reliable supply of energy and capacity.

The first step in determining the incremental transmission capacity between control areas is to calculate the total transfer limit between control areas. The transfer limit is the total amount of power that can be moved across an interface, which is the sum of all transmission capacity between two control areas, including capacity that flows through facilities in other interconnected control areas. Transmission capacity across an interface is limited by either (i) thermal limits, (ii) voltage limits, or (iii) stability constraints. These three criterion must be evaluated in order to determine the adequacy of electric transmission service. Thermal limits are the transmission line capacity limits that are provided for each line in amperes or megavolt-amperes (MVA). If too much power is forced down a transmission line, the resistance of the wire will heat the line until the line anneals (untwists) or sags below required clearance limits. The amount of power through the line also affects the voltage on either end. To maintain proper voltage on the system, utilities set minimum and maximum fluctuations in voltage of plus or minus 5% or 10% of nominal voltage. Finally, the maximum power allowed to flow through a line is often limited to provide capacity during an emergency condition, such as an instantaneous and unexpected trip of a large generator or transmission line. This emergency capacity is required to prevent an instability situation such as a voltage collapse across the system resulting in a wide area blackout.

These three limits must be defined for every transmission line by the utility and must be provided in FERC Form 715. Utility-grade load flow software is used to convert these limits for each individual line into a total transfer limit between the control areas. While this transfer limit is shown as a single connection between each control area, it often consists of multiple lines between each control area. Most load flow programs can calculate how much capacity exists between control areas by determining how the power splits or is distributed among the various lines and then noting when a certain line is overloaded, i.e., the line's thermal rating or voltage limits are exceeded.

In order to determine the exact transfer limits between control areas, analysis must be performed on the base case that will simulate a retail wheeling transaction. In other words, in determining the exact transfer limit from Utility B to Utility A, the generation in Utility B must be increased by some increment and the generation in Utility A must be decreased by the same increment. The effects on the grid are then examined to determine which transmission line or transformer will overload first. The change in generation required to overload a transmission line or transformer or cause an over or under voltage condition is the transfer limit. The amount of increased load across the various lines across the interface is added and the total transfer limit is expressed in megawatts. Note that the lines or transformers in both Utility A and B are not the only ones monitored. Since power flows affect the entire grid, an overload on a transmission line or transformer in Utility C that is caused by the increased power flow from Utility A to B is also considered in the transfer limit analysis.

Once the transfer limit is determined, the actual power flows across each interface are calculated using the load flow program and the FERC Form 715 information. This assessment is performed for peak load conditions, which is usually the worst case condition for transmission capacity, and includes an evaluation of how capacity varies seasonally and under projected peak load conditions over the next few years. The FERC Form 715 requires that the utilities provide 10 year projections of expected loads, generation, and transmission lines that are in service during that peak season.

Incremental transmission capacity between control areas, which is the value that the potential shipper is most interested in, is calculated from the difference between the transfer limit and the existing power flows determined from the load flow.

Open Access Same-time Information System (OASIS)

On April 24, 1996, the same day that it issued its landmark Order 888 requiring open access transmission tariffs, FERC issued its Order 889 mandating the development of OASIS, the open access same-time information system. OASIS is the system for distributing transmission information to participants of a competitive electricity market. The system will be based on the Internet and must be used by the transmission company for its information on the same basis as used by third-party shippers, which are required to meet the non-discriminatory requirements of Order 888. The progenitor of OASIS is FERC's real-time information system, or RIN, introduced in the giga-NOPR and considered in a separately issued NOPR. Considerable technical analysis was performed to determine what should be included in these information systems (analyzed by a committee FERC creatively called the "what" group) and how that information should be disseminated (analyzed by, of course, the "how" group). The results of the "what" and "how" group analysis lead to the OASIS order, which, if nothing else, recognized that transmission information can be distributed at best on a same-time basis rather than a real-time basis.

Details of the OASIS proposal are provided below, but the key purpose of OASIS is to provide the information on available transmission capacity information that is the subject of this chapter. In Order 889, FERC recognizes the importance of giving market participants, including end-users, access to information on the amount of incremental transmission capacity that exists between control areas. Although FERC took a big step in getting this information to the public with Form 715, it understands the general difficulty that most end-users and electricity buyers have using this data in a meaningful way. FERC's intent was always to have the transmission utility calculate the actual transmission capacity so that end-users would not have to. In Order 889, FERC takes Form 715 data to the next level and requires each utility, as part of its non-discriminatory open access transmission service, to provide the public with its "available transmission capacity" and "total transmission capacity," for which new acronyms were christened, namely ATC and TTC, respectively.

ATC is defined as the capacity that must be available for new firm transmission service requests under the methodology described in Order 889. The information is posted for any path on which service has been denied or curtailed or for which a customer requests information to be posted. The incremental capacity is the technical loading limit of the line (as described above) minus (i) capacity to meet the utility's current and reasonably forecasted retail load, (ii) capacity allocated to network transmission customers, (iii) pending firm transmission contract capacity, and (iv) capacity needed to meet generally acceptable reliability criteria. If there is any room left on the transmission interface, it is defined as available. Note that available capacity includes existing and contractual non-firm requirements. Therefore, it will be important to note that ATC can only be used to determine how much firm capacity is available, although this will provide an indication of how reliable any non-firm service will be, if desired. The specific information that must be posted is described below.

Even after numerous technical sessions, the methodology used to actually calculate incremental transmission capacity for the purposes of OASIS is not yet defined. For now, FERC is requiring all utilities to define the method they use to estimate ATC, although further policy statements on this issue are expected from FERC once the "what" group finalizes its analysis. Utilities are also required to provide to requesting parties (although not to all parties via OASIS) the data and algorithms used to calculate the information posted on OASIS. This allows transmission customers and third parties to duplicate the utility's calculations as a check. As detailed below, ATC must also be provided on an hourly basis, which presents some interesting challenges to the utilities, although existing hardware and software technologies should readily accommodate these requirements once a reasonable and common methodology is approved.

Besides being a source of transmission capacity information, OASIS will also provide a transactional bulletin board for transmission users that can be used to reserve transmission capacity. This will be discussed in more detail in Chapter 8.

FERC Order 889 has three components, each required to ensure that the transmission information system it mandates is consistent with the open access tariff requirements issued in Order 888. The first of these are specific standards or conduct necessary to ensure that transmission access is non-discriminatory and that transmission owning utilities or their affiliates do not gain any advantage in the marketplace because they have control or access to the transmission information. The standards of conduct require strict separation of employees involved in the transmission function of the utility from those involved in wholesale market functions. To be consistent with the functional unbundling requirement of Order 888, marketing employees of the transmission utility must use the same OASIS information that is available to other market participants. If information is provided by the transmission group to the marketing group, it must be immediately posted on OASIS. If the transmission provider offers discounts of transmission rates or ancillary services to affiliates or full-service wholesale customers, those discounts must be offered to all buyers using the same path or any unconstrained transmission path. OASIS becomes, in effect, the tool for assuring a level playing field for all transmission customers and for monitoring transmission owner compliance.

The second component of Order 889 is the posting requirements of OASIS. The following information must be provided to transmission customers on OASIS:

1. Available Transmission Capacity

- OASIS must provide the available transmission capacity (ATC) for transmission interconnections between control areas, as discussed above, and total transmission capacity (TTC), in megawatts and in which direction. This information is required for "posted paths" only, i.e., those interconnections in which transmission service has been denied or curtailed or for those specifically requested by a customer. ATC and TTC need not be continually posted for all transmission paths.
- ATC and TTC must also be given on an hourly, daily, and monthly basis for all constrained paths, i.e., those in which ATC is less than or equal to 25% of the TTC at any time in the previous or following week. ATC and TTC information must be updated when the ATC or TTC changes by more than 10%.
- For unconstrained paths, daily and monthly ATC must be posted and updated whenever ATC changes by more than 20% of the TTC.
- Data and methodologies used to calculate ATC and TTC must be made available upon request for auditing purposes.
- Any system planning studies performed must also be made available.

2. Pricing Information

- Tariff prices for all transmission services, ancillary services, and other related services must be posted and made available for electronic downloading to customers.
- Information on discounts made to non-affiliates must be posted within 24 hours of the transaction.
- Information on discounts made to affiliates must be immediately posted and offered to all other customers using the same path, unconstrained path, or the same ancillary service.
- The resale of transmission capacity or third-party services must be posted in the same location and format as the transmission provider's postings.

3. Specific Service Requests and Responses

- All requests for transmission service must be posted by the date and time received, placed in a queue, and the status provided. The result of the request, whether accepted, withdrawn, or denied, must also be given and the reason for the denial or interruption, if applicable.
- The identity of the party requesting transmission capacity can be masked for up to 30 days.
- Offers to adjust the utility's operation to accommodate a denied request must be posted and offered to other similar parties.

4. Scheduling Information

- Transmission service schedules must be posted and available for electronic downloading within seven days of the start of the requested service.

5. Other Transmission-Related Communications

- A utility's OASIS can also include "want ads" for other desired services, such as transmission loss service.
- The OASIS can also provide a messaging service (E-mail).
- The utility must post employee transfers between the transmission group and any marketing affiliates.

The third component of Order 889 is the standards and communications protocols required to implement OASIS. FERC will ensure that all OASIS nodes follow a common format and technical standards so that users can easily operate all systems. This requirement was the result of FERC's experience in the natural gas industry in which its mandated electronic bulletin boards (EBBs) for transportation information varied significantly in form and content, enough so that considerable confusion in the marketplace resulted. Because Order 889 intends to facilitate information access to all market participants, substantial time and effort will be spent to develop standards and communications protocols to assure universal viability.

Every transmission utility, i.e., those that own or operate transmission facilities with voltages greater than 100 kV, must develop and operate an OASIS. However, many utilities will meet these requirements through NERC regions, power pools, and eventually ISOs and RTGs. FERC estimates that 20 to 35 OASIS nodes will be formed by transmission providers. All OASIS nodes will be developed as Internet World Wide Web sites to assure universal access. Registration and different levels of access will be required for security of the system. The technical specifications of standards and protocols are intended to assure consistency and open access.

Given the data provided by OASIS, the second step of a retail wheeling transaction, determining transmission capacity, should be relatively straight forward. End-users preparing to access the open market for the first time should prepare a general transmission assessment of the entire area within and around the control area in which the facility resides. This general study can be performed using Form 715 data and a utility-grade load flow package and will provide an overall view of where power can be purchased and shipped. If the end-user has a specific supplier or transaction in mind, that particular transaction can be modeled on the load flow model provided by Form 715, and the availability of capacity on the actual transmission paths that the 715 load flow analysis provides can be obtained from the OASIS node for the transmission systems involved.

Once transmission availability is understood, the next step in the power purchasing process is to decide which electricity products will be purchased and transported. The rebundling of the various unbundled products that must be purchased is the subject of the next chapter.

Chapter 8

Unbundled Components

Unbundling Electricity

To describe the future electricity market as being unbundled, two concepts are actually implied. Most commonly, unbundling refers to the separation between generation and transmission, which is a broad-brush approach to differentiating between the competitive and non-competitive aspects of electricity service. However, unbundling also refers to the separation of electric service into many different products and services that comprise the bundled service that end-users traditionally take. The third step of a retail wheeling transaction is the determination of which of these many services must the end-user buy and what are the issues involved in buying them.

Because the electricity industry is presently vertically integrated, the ultimate service provided by an electric utility is not distinguished from the sum of the many services it actually provides. For example, a utility generates power at a generation station then transmits that power along its transmission lines to substations where the power is distributed to the ultimate customers. The transmission component of this transaction can be unbundled from the generation component if those two services can be provided by separate entities.

As we have learned, there are no natural monopolies with respect to generation; that is, electricity can be generated by any number of parties in a competitive environment, assuming they can reach their customers. However, transmission is a natural monopoly, at least with respect to facilities. In order to ensure that generation remains competitive, the company with monopoly transmission facilities cannot tie that service to its competitive generation sales without violating fundamental antitrust principles. Of course, up to now, these violations of antitrust principles were allowed per state law (the "state action" defense), but this will no longer be the case in a competitive market. Therefore, transmission will have to be offered as a separate service from generation and provided and priced on a comparable basis to all customers purchasing equivalent classes of service (e.g., interruptibility). This necessary separation of services is often referred to as "unbundling," and it is the cornerstone to the creation of a competitive electricity market, as it was with the gas market.

Once regulators separate generation from transmission, the market will take care of the rest with respect to unbundling. In a competitive electricity market, suppliers will attempt to distinguish their products and services in order to offer a product that end-users will buy. Since electricity itself is an entirely fungible product, perhaps more so than any other commodity, how that electricity is packaged, marketed and delivered will be critical for the success of some suppliers. Some suppliers will attempt to meet certain niche markets, such as providing backup or load following services. In this respect, the market will further unbundle into a broad spectrum of products and services that presently comprise a single, bundled product.

These unbundled services have been given many names, including ancillary services, local control area services, and regulation services. They will be discussed in detail in subsequent sections of this chapter. This second tier of unbundling, unlike the separation of transmission from generation, will not be entirely mandated as a requirement of competition. Instead, it will be largely the result of a competitive market in that an open market will encourage suppliers to offer products and services distinguishable from those of other suppliers.

Of course, only those services that can be independently procured should be unbundled. That is, if a service is inextricably tied to another, it should not be "unbundled" by that provider and separately priced. For example, protective relaying on a transmission line is a service that is specifically associated with that particular transmission line and cannot be provided by any party other than the transmission line company. On the other hand, transmission losses could be provided by another company, probably far less expensively than by the transmission company. Although losses are specifically associated with the line itself, a third party generation company can be contracted to replace the lost energy and capacity that results from transmission and deliver it to the transmission company.

As for pricing unbundled services, the total price of all the unbundled services should usually be less than the cost of the bundled product, with the only additional cost being that of the entity that "rebundles" the various products for the end-user for a fee. Since each product can be competitively sourced, the forces of competition will act on each service independently. Unless one super-company is able to provide all products at the lowest price, which is hardly ever the case in other industries, the total cost of the unbundled products from the lowest cost provider for each service will necessarily be lower than having all services provided by one supplier. At worst, the cost should be equal.

Determining the cost of the various unbundled services is often very difficult given today's utility industry structure. Even with respect to generation and transmission, a vertically integrated utility will not separate the costs and revenues in its accounting process. Separating these services on an accounting basis is not as easy as merely allocating specific facilities and costs to each function. There are certain services that a generator provides to the transmission system and vice versa. For example, a transmission line may be derated from its thermal limits to accommodate the shift in power flows that will occur when a generator inadvertently trips off line. While derating this line to accommodate this reliability concern may be merely an operating consideration for a vertically integrated utility, imagine if the generator and the transmission lines were owned by separate companies. The transmission company would surely demand compensation for the space on the transmission line reserved for the reliability needs of the generator.

Pricing certain ancillary services, as discussed later, is also made difficult by the fact that many of the distribution or transmission utility's facilities provide more than one service. If these services are considered monopoly services, their cost must be based on the embedded cost of the involved equipment, but how those embedded costs will be allocated among the various services is unclear. Furthermore, some services necessarily overlap and thus further confuse determining the cost for each service. For example, voltage support may involve, to some degree in some circumstances, reactive power supply to the load. If this is the case, the customer should not be billed for both voltage support and reactive power support if they are providing the same service. How these services can be separated to prevent this is equally unclear.

FERC's new Order 888 requiring open access transmission tariffs specifically defines and prices the ancillary services that it determined were necessary. Of course, other services may be further unbundled by the forces of the marketplace, but Order 888 confirms that many of the services presently provided by vertically integrated utilities should and will be separated. The definitions of the ancillary services originally chosen by FERC in the giga-NOPR underwent considerable comment and criticism, and the way they were defined and unbundled may eventually be changed by market forces. However, as the unbundling process matures, FERC's definitions appear to be gaining general acceptance. FERC discusses the following ancillary services in Order 888 (each will be discussed in more detail later in this chapter):

- **Scheduling, System Control, and Dispatch:** While every transmission company must schedule power flows on their system, this is a rather curious ancillary service because it really cannot be separated from the transmission service itself. Therefore, FERC requires that all transmission companies provide this service and that all shippers purchase this service (then why unbundle it?). As for dispatch, this normally refers to dispatching generation, which will now be done by the marketplace. In this case, FERC is referring to the necessary redispatching required to maintain system integrity.
- **Reactive Supply and Voltage Control:** FERC wisely grouped these functions into one to avoid cross billing or double billing by a utility since the facilities required to provide these services are often the same. This is one ancillary service in which the level or quantity purchased may vary from one purchaser to another.

- **Regulation and Frequency Response:** Called "load following" in the giga-NOPR, regulation and frequency response refers to following the instantaneous changes in load of an end-user. This change in definition was required due to the different definitions of load following in the industry.
- **Energy Imbalance Service:** This service balances the difference between the amount of energy scheduled to be delivered by an outside supplier and the energy actually consumed by an end-user. This service will be discussed later as a service ancillary to generation rather than transmission since it is mostly a function of how energy is nominated rather than how it is transported.
- **Operating Reserves:** Order 888 includes both spinning reserve and supplemental reserve in its list of ancillary services. FERC maintains they are two distinct but related ancillary services.
- **Real Power Losses:** Although every shipper must arrange for the replacement of losses due to transmission, FERC is not requiring transmission utilities to provide this service in their open access tariffs since few transmission companies will be in a position to offer this service competitively. Nonetheless, it is an ancillary service that must be considered by the end-user.
- **Dynamic Scheduling:** Dynamic scheduling, sometimes referred to as load following, involves moving a load to another supplier's control area via telemetering. This service is neither required to be offered by transmission providers nor required to be purchased by transmission users. Rather, it is an ancillary service that will be driven by the marketplace when applicable and economic.

End-users must purchase each of the above listed ancillary services, except for dynamic scheduling, although some may be purchased in lesser quantities depending on the nature of the load (for example, the level of reactive power required by an end-user will vary). All services but dynamic scheduling and real power losses must be offered by transmission companies in their open access tariffs, but an end-user is only required to purchase the first two, scheduling, system control and dispatch and reactive supply and voltage control, from the native transmission supplier. All other services, whether required or not, may be purchased from competitive suppliers. For example, rather than purchase the necessary level of operating reserves from the native transmission company, an end-user may wish to competitively procure that service from a neighboring generation company.

The pricing of these ancillary services is another issue temporarily resolved by Order 888, but which will eventually be settled by the marketplace. In the pro forma open access transmission tariffs included in Order 888, these ancillary services are priced together, for the most part, at one mill (one-tenth of one penny) per kilowatt-hour. Although this number is essentially pulled out of the air, it will apply until a transmission company can justify another rate based on actual embedded costs. As discussed above, this is very difficult, but some utilities have tried it, as we shall see in the last section of this chapter.

The remaining sections of this chapter will step through each of the issues associated with the unbundled services and products, which are divided into energy and capacity services, transmission services, and ancillary services. How these individual products and services are procured and rebundled is the subject of Chapter 9.

Energy and Capacity

The basic component of electrical service, and by far the most expensive, is the energy itself. Traditionally, the cost of electricity has been divided into two fundamental components: the cost of the electrical energy and the cost of having the capability to produce and deliver that energy whenever demanded. Therefore, typical electricity bills have a separate energy charge and demand or capacity charge. It is beyond the scope of this book to delve into the principles and practices of ratemaking, but basically, the energy charge should reflect the variable costs of providing electricity, which is primarily the cost of the fuel used in generation, and the demand charge should reflect the fixed costs for the capital investment required to generate, transmit, and distribute the electricity.

In an unbundled electricity market, energy and capacity will take on new meanings and could be purchased independently or together. The traditional distinction between energy and capacity as a function of ratemaking will be lost since rates will be set by the market, not by regulators applying economic principles. End-users will continue to be able to purchase power in the traditional way, although perhaps from a marketer rather than the local distribution company. This will especially be the case for those end-users that will demand traditional firm service or that do not wish to go through the trouble of unbundling their power service. Most larger end-users, however, will probably take advantage of the ability to deal directly with a supplier or group of suppliers and purchase power beyond the control area of the native, interconnected utility or distribution company. In this case, they have a number of options. End-users will have the choice of buying energy only on the spot market and contracting separately for backup capacity, buying varying levels of firm and non-firm power through short and long term contracts, and mixing various types of energy and capacity products to meet the total load requirements of a facility.

Buying on the spot market.

For those end-users that demand the lowest cost power available at all times, some and maybe all of their electrical energy purchases will be made from spot markets, which have already developed to some degree. In the spot market, the buyer only purchases the required energy on an hourly or sub-hourly basis without any promise of reliability, that is, energy only without the capacity component. The spot market price will reflect the ongoing market clearing price for power. In times of low demand and high supply, this price will be very low as many generators will be seeking to dump excess power on the grid instead of having to shut a unit down. During times of high demand and low supply, the spot market price can increase by orders of magnitude as buyers are willing to pay more to keep processes running and suppliers are able to earn a greater return.

A spot market for power already exists in the wholesale market, and systems are being developed to accommodate a more active market through computer trading and information services. Historically, the spot market for wholesale power merely consisted of utilities contacting each other by telephone when they needed power. This is not really an open market because the only information on price is that available from whatever contacts can be made before the transaction must take place. Most utility dispatchers have a small group of other utilities that they regularly call for hourly wholesale purchases. The price is determined informally, usually based on production costs, and relatively small fluctuations occur. As power becomes more commoditized and prices become more transparent, the spot market price for power will more closely reflect a true market price based on supply and demand rather than incremental production costs. The new computerized bulletin boards for spot market power will be discussed in Chapter 9.

When retail wheeling is available, a spot market will also be available through both informal and formal means. If an end-user is willing to stomach the price volatility that is inherent in a spot market, the ultimate average price will certainly be less than if the power was bought through a longer term contract. This is simply because the price certainty of a longer term contract exacts a price. Buyers pay for transferring the risk of price volatility to a supplier when purchasing power at a fixed price. Of course, long term contracts based on spot market prices are available as a means to lock in an end-user to a specific supplier.

In an unbundled electricity market, spot market energy will most likely be purchased on an hourly basis much like natural gas is purchased now on a daily basis. While some suppliers may require more frequent load demand estimates, most suppliers will probably require hourly nominations of energy for each purchaser. These nominations will be made electronically through a communications link to the supplier (or with many suppliers). This communication link via a computer will provide the end-user with hourly pricing forecasts and current spot market prices. The end-user then nominates the amount of kilowatt-hours to be purchased for the next hour at that spot market price. The transaction is then consummated electronically by sending the nomination to the supplier's control center and the transmission or grid operators.

Hourly purchasing exists today with so-called real-time pricing programs, or RTP, and these programs provide a good illustration of how power will be purchased from the spot market in the future (except that multiple suppliers will be available). While many RTP plans are not truly real-time pricing, a good example of an authentic real-time pricing program is the Tennessee Valley Authority's (TVA) Economy Surplus Power (ESP) plan. Under this plan, the end-user pays no demand charge, a relatively small facilities charge (for the computer hardware required to provide hourly price information to the end-user), an energy charge, plus a small percentage margin for revenue. The hourly energy price is based on the TVA's incremental cost for that hour to either produce the energy or purchase it on the open wholesale market. This is an incremental price, not an average price, and thus reflects the cost to generate the additional power required by purchasers under the program. Similarly, in a retail wheeling market, spot market power most often will be based on suppliers' incremental costs since any load sold on the spot market will be incremental sales on top of power sold under longer term contracts. In some cases, the spot market price for energy may fall below a supplier's incremental cost since such a sale may be cheaper for the supplier than shutting down or cycling a unit. In Texas, wholesale market clearing prices for this "dump" energy has dropped below a penny per kilowatt-hour.

Under TVA's ESP program, the end-user is supplied with a computer terminal and communication link to TVA's control center. The TVA supplies pricing forecasts on a monthly, weekly, daily, and hourly basis, with the final price for the next hour determined no earlier than 20 minutes before the hour, although it often changes just minutes before the hour. The end-user, responding to these price signals, nominates hourly energy purchases. The hourly nominations can be made well ahead of time; for example, a plant with a very predictable load can nominate hourly purchases for a week at a time so that new nominations need not be sent in every hour. If prices are changing wildly, the end-user has the option of changing the nomination based on the latest hourly forecast. The timing of the last forecast must be such that nominations can change for the next hour based on the last forecast. In this way, demand is responding to price as it should in a commoditized market.

TVA's real-time pricing plan is structured so that accurate nominations are encouraged. The end-user is only charged for 92% of the power nominated. If the buyer takes between 92% and 100% of what was nominated, any energy above that 92% level is essentially free. If less energy is taken than 92% of the nominated amount, the penalty is built in, i.e., the buyer pays for energy not used. If more power is taken, certain fixed demand and energy penalties are assessed (see below). See Figure 8-1 for an example from an actual TVA customer's data of how a 30,000 kilowatt nomination, reduced to 25,000 kilowatts at 8:00 a.m., was priced. During most of the day, the actual use fell between the scheduled level and the 92% level, except for a one-time demand spike at 5:00 p.m. which resulted in the assessment of tariff demand and energy penalties.

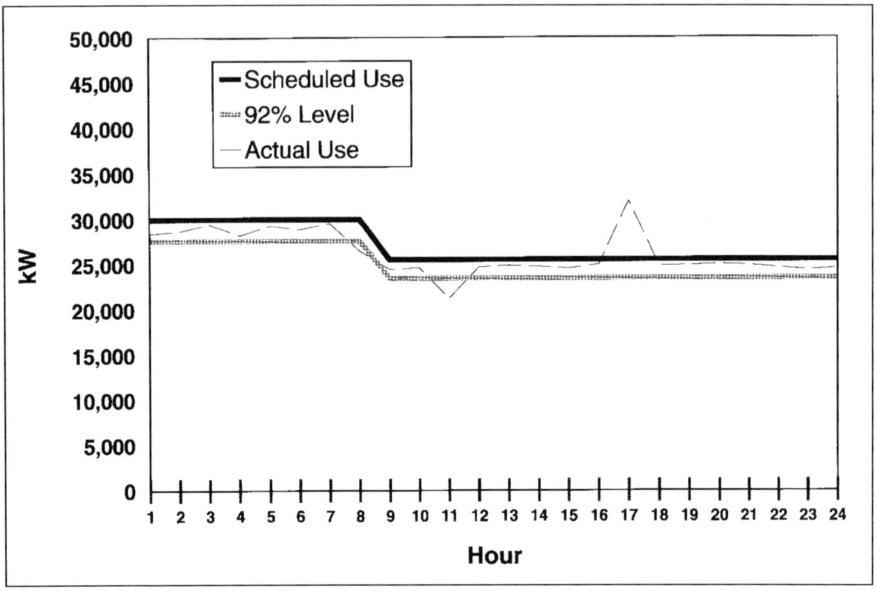

Figure 8-1. Hourly energy scheduling and actual use on TVA's ESP *real-time pricing plan.*

Notice that when energy is purchased on an hourly basis, such as with the TVA ESP plan, the conceptual difference between energy and capacity begin to fade. For any given hour, an ESP customer nominates and pays for some quantity of power, such as the 30,000 kilowatt nomination of Figure 8-1. The customer has just purchased 30,000 kilowatt-hours since the nominated value applies to a one-hour increment. To the end-user and the supplier, there is no difference between energy and capacity since purchasing 30,000 kilowatts for one hour is the same as purchasing 30,000 kilowatt-hours. Therefore the distinction between demand, measured in kilowatts, and energy, measured in kilowatt-hours, is lost in an hourly power market.

Now the reader can understand why TVA has no demand component to the ESP charge. The only thing purchased is energy. ESP power is considered interruptible, but the meaning of this is also lost since as long as power is available at any price, the end-user has the option to buy it. Unless there is a true transmission constraint that prevents the import of power, energy should always be available at some incremental price (and FERC Form 715 data or OASIS will indicate where these transmission bottlenecks are in advance). The beauty of real-time pricing is that the end-user is the one who decides when the price of power is high enough to warrant curtailment.

Except for the fact that the end-user must buy power from TVA, this plan operates much like the market will act in the future. With direct retail access, the end-user will be able to tie into multiple spot market suppliers including other suppliers and even groups of suppliers that form spot markets together, such as the Continental Power Exchange (CPEX). How this is done is the subject of Chapter 9.

Energy imbalances.

Energy imbalance service is an ancillary service defined by FERC as a transmission service that must be provided only by the transmission company, although it is actually an ancillary service associated with the supply of capacity and energy, and it is closely related to buying power on the spot market. FERC defines this service as providing the difference between the hourly amount of energy scheduled by the purchaser and the hourly amount of energy used by the buyer as metered. Since this is an hourly metered quantity, it is not an adjustment for the instantaneous fluctuations in power that virtually all users will see (see load following later on in this chapter). Instead, it is the meterable differences between hourly nominations as discussed above and actual use, similar to the imbalances function in the natural gas industry. It is also analogous to the 8% bandwidth allowed by the TVA when nominating power for its ESP real-time pricing program.

If an end-user uses more or less power than nominated, some other entity must make up the difference to ensure steady voltage on the system. Even if this deficient or excess amount of energy was not consciously made up, the integrated grid would absorb or supply the mis-nominated power automatically. On an instantaneous basis, there is no way for any entity to absolutely track and follow the constantly varying load shape of most end-users. To provide the service of supplying or absorbing energy outside of the nominated value on an instantaneous basis is what some call load following. Accommodating minute-to-minute variations in load is what FERC calls regulation and frequency response service in Order 888. This instantaneous load following must be provided by the local interconnected distribution or transmission company.

The energy imbalance service, however, is required if the amount of metered energy is greater or less than nominated energy, on an hourly or sub-hourly basis (some nominations may occur on a half- or quarter-hour basis). In this case, the imbalance is perceptible and can be supplied a number of different ways. The local distribution or transmission company could provide the extra energy required or absorb the extra energy brought in and charge some fee for this service on a per kilowatt-hour basis. But there is no reason why some other supplier could not supply the transmission or distribution company the mis-nominated power on behalf of the end-user to ensure that, at least on an hourly basis, the transmission or distribution company is kept whole.

For example, if the end-user's load is ramping up in the morning, the supplier may have to start up an additional generator to meet the expected load. Since this unit will come on line with a sudden increase in capacity, there will be an obvious mismatch between the supply and demand as the additional generator comes on line to feed the increasing load. Utilities will let the demand exceed supply by letting the voltage and frequency begin to sag before placing the unit on line, and when the unit is on, the supply will temporarily exceed demand until equilibrium is again reached with the additional unit on the grid. The amount of mismatch before the new unit is added equals the mismatch after so that the total imbalance over the period is zero. This same method of operation will apply to off-system suppliers in a retail wheeling world.

End-users will most likely opt to set up an energy banking service with either their local company, their off-system supplier, or some third party. In this case, all energy brought into the local system through a nominated off-system purchase that is not actually used would be stored in an account (the energy itself would be absorbed by the entity providing the banking service). When nominations fall short of the actual use, energy can be brought out of the account so that the energy need not be supplied by the local utility. As long as the level of the mis-nominations are within a certain bandwidth, this cost of this service should be relatively low and fixed. If the deviations from the nominations are significant, then some sort of penalty may be incurred. This is why predictability of load, as discussed in Chapter 6, has such a big impact on price.

In the FERC's Order 888, a "bandwidth" of 1.5% with a one megawatt floor is suggested for this service. Any deviations less than or equal to 1.5% of the nominated value would be either banked at little or no cost or purchased at 110% of the local utility's incremental cost of production. If the deviations exceed 1.5% of the nominated value, the traditional FERC emergency rate of ten cents per kilowatt-hour would apply. These rates only apply to FERC's pro forma transmission tariffs and most certainly will change as transmission utilities file more sophisticated transmission tariffs to FERC. Because this service could be provided by someone other than the local transmission company, competition for energy imbalance service customers may lower this price.

The reason why this energy balancing service is an unbundled ancillary service is because it can be provided by non-native suppliers and because end-users will require different levels of service. End-users with a ramping load like that described above will have to purchase a "bandwidth" equal to the mismatch metered before and after the supplier's additional machines are brought on-line (or else face daily imbalance penalties). Loads that are widely fluctuating, such as arc-furnaces, will require greater levels of energy balancing service, i.e., a greater bandwidth, while steady loads, such as aluminum smelters, may see very little or no imbalances. These end-users should pay for only the level of service they need, and they should be able to purchase the service from any entity capable of providing it. Varying terms of service, besides price, will also appear in later transmission and distribution tariffs.

Firm vs. non-firm.

Spot market power is considered non-firm energy in that there is no corresponding capacity component to the energy, i.e., the buyer is only buying energy, or one hour of capacity, and not the ability to serve that energy at any time. There are some price and delivery risks associated with buying all spot power, so some end-users desire the security of a guaranteed supply, or firm power. This involves purchasing capacity as well as energy.

Energy is energy, but what exactly is capacity beyond a ratemaking concept? Some argue that capacity, being the ability to serve, is analogous to the firmness of the energy sold, so that a capacity charge will still be used to reflect the firmness of the energy. In a competitive market, however, the price for the energy, as distinguished from transmission and ancillary services, will be market driven, and the firmness of the energy will be reflected in the price. That is, regardless of how the individual supplier sets up its pricing structure, the energy component is still only energy combined with some promises of firmness.

Capacity will then be only meaningful in the terms of backup power. In this respect, capacity is truly the ability to provide power whether the actual energy is ever delivered or not. For example, an end-user that purchases relatively non-firm energy may need to arrange for backup provisions in the event that the energy cannot be delivered. Because this end-user may demand this supply at any time, he must, in fact, pay to reserve part of the facilities that are required to feed the load on demand. Therefore, it does not matter whether any actual energy is ever delivered, that unit must be available to that user at all times. Of course, there is value to having that capacity at hand. This value is then independently procured and priced. But note how, as with energy, the price has nothing to do with fixed versus variable costs, it is instead based on precisely the product or service delivered.

No electrical service is 100% firm. Besides the obvious risks of distribution feeders downed by storms and transformer bushings shorted by unfortunate squirrels, even firm power can be curtailed or interrupted if there are true transmission constraints. For example, while ECAR may be flush with excess generation capacity, if Detroit Edison does not generate a certain level of power within its service territory to support local voltage levels, there will simply not be enough transmission capacity to bring in the power available outside the utility. Therefore, if a utility has internal generation shortages *and* inadequate transmission capacity exists, that utility will have to shed firm load in order to maintain system integrity. To minimize the pain to its firm customers, utilities will rotate the outages so that rolling blackouts result. Additionally, NERC reliability requirements specify automatic load shedding equipment that will dump firm load automatically when frequency drops below a predetermined level.

On the other extreme, a supplier of backup service in an unbundled market may market the energy that could be produced by the unit when the backup customer is not taking service if the price makes it worthwhile. This power would necessarily be interruptible since someone else has the right to the unit's capacity on demand. Depending on the amount of notice involved, this may be an acceptable and inexpensive way to purchase power for some end-users with loads that can be readily curtailed.

In an unbundled, open market, end-users will have their choice of firm-as-firm-can-be, fully interruptible, and every shade of gray in between. The level of firmness will be directly reflected in price, not because of the cost to deliver that level of firmness, but because of supply versus demand. Most importantly, that level of firmness will be based on contractual promises of when that power will be subject to interruption. The parameters will be number of interruptions per period, the length of each interruption, and the amount of notice before an interruption. For example, a supplier may offer energy that will be curtailed no more than twice per year for no more than eight hours at a time, or it may limit curtailments to a total of 16 hours per year. If that power is curtailed beyond the terms of the agreement, then pre-negotiated penalties will apply. These parameters can even be mixed and matched. An end-user may combine two low-cost non-firm supplies to create service that approaches firm.

As with interruptible natural gas contracts, the supplier of some level of firm service will be excused for certain *force majeure* events, which can be negotiated to some degree. Most *force majeure* clauses excuse the supplier for the failure to deliver power during certain acts of God, and natural and man-made catastrophes. However, some suppliers have used these clauses to escape obligations due to certain regulatory changes or economic hardship cases. It is important, therefore, for the end-user to ensure that the *force majeure* clause of a power supply contract does not introduce new degrees of non-firmness to an otherwise firm supply contract.

Putting together this mix of various levels of firm energy and capacity is the reason for evaluating the curtailability of the load as discussed in Chapter 4. Since the cost of power will be directly related to its firmness, any level of non-firmness that can be introduced will reduce power costs. This mix also depends on the cost of backup power, since low-cost non-firm power may be cheap enough to justify the separate purchase of backup power to replace the low cost power in times of curtailment.

Backup power.

Unless the end-user buys all of its power requirements in the form of system service from a local provider, it will have to consider some sort of backup service or allow itself to be interrupted. Because non-firm power will be (and is) priced well below that of firm, many new suppliers are developing backup and peaking power facilities just to feed the new demand for these services.

As discussed above, there is no such thing as absolutely firm power. Even those facilities with multiple transmission level feeds have to plan for the eventuality of a power failure. For critical loads, many end-users install backup diesel generators, and this will still have to be done in a competitive market. But end-users will soon be able to arrange for a broad variety of power backup services to either firm up a non-firm supply or to provide true backup capacity for critical loads.

Backup or standby power is essentially capacity-only power where energy is a small piece of the package. Backup capacity is sold by the megawatt rather than the megawatt-hour. The key to capacity is that it must be available on demand, or else it is not true capacity. Some suppliers will offer to provide the desired level of capacity for a certain number of hours per year or per month on demand, while some will offer the capacity without limit. Some will also charge a certain rate for the actual energy delivered, when and if it is delivered, that is based on the incremental cost of running the unit. This incremental cost is usually not part of the capacity charge since the buyer is only purchasing the ability for that unit to provide power rather than the power itself, i.e., the buyer is paying its share of the fixed cost to install the unit and have it available rather than the cost to actually run the thing.

Backup power capacity supplied for a maximum number of hours per year or month will be the least cost method of buying capacity since that capacity will be sold to numerous buyers. There is no reason why a backup power supplier could not sell the same capacity to more than one buyer if that supplier is willing to either arrange for alternative supplies when more than one customer demands power or that supplier is willing to pay a contractual penalty for failing to provide power. Savvy suppliers of backup power services will install numerous units in areas where weather patterns do not typically coincide so that a high demand in one area could be fed by units in areas without a high demand. For example, consider two 100 MW units each in areas with diverse load patterns. The supplier could theoretically sell 200 MW of backup capacity from *each* unit, if he is willing to risk that both will not be called on at the same time. If 200 MW is demanded in one area, both 100 MW units will then feed that load. Backup capacity could be sold at a very competitive price in this way since the fixed costs are spread over more buyers.

End-users must be cautioned to carefully consider or negotiate any penalties for a backup supplier failing to provide capacity upon demand. While punitive damages are not allowed, the end-user may wish to include a provision in which the backup supplier will compensate the end-user for consequential damages in the event that capacity is not available. Consequential damages can include actual damage to equipment caused by a lack of power, lost production, and even lost profits caused by the lost production. As a minimum, most suppliers will pay for the cost to replace the lost capacity from another supplier, which could be very costly during times of capacity shortages. Unless there is a true transmission constraint between other suppliers where there would be none from the backup supplier, the backup supplier should be able to find alternative supplies and not force an interruption by the end-user.

If the end-user fails to interrupt its load in the event that the primary supplier is not available, and either the backup provider fails to deliver capacity or no backup capacity was arranged, the grid will naturally feed the load anyway. In this case, either all other suppliers will have to contribute to feed this load or voltages will collapse perhaps even causing an unstable condition. Although the grid operator will have emergency capacity to prevent this voltage collapse, which may or may not be available in a system emergency, the price for the grid to supply power to an end-user that fails to interrupt when it has no pre-arranged supply will be extremely expensive. The cost for the grid to back up an end-user's load will be prohibitively high so as to discourage dependance on it and to encourage the end-user to arrange for all of its power needs.

Bilateral contracts.

When retail wheeling becomes fully implemented, end-users will have the ability to execute direct bilateral contracts with suppliers. These contracts can take a number of different forms, and many suppliers will probably offer many creative new packages to differentiate themselves from other suppliers and to lure new customers. End-users will most likely be faced with an onslaught of suppliers offering a myriad of products and services with creative names and descriptions. One need only look at the new forms of packaging long distance telephone service that competition in the telecommunciations industry created. In the end, however, they can all be boiled down to a few key types of products and services.

The majority of the power sales arrangements between suppliers and end-users will be bilateral contracts since most end-users will not want to face the volatility and constant vigilance that buying off the spot market will require. Savvy end-users will combine multiple power supply contracts with spot market options to piece together a tailor-made supply arrangement that will optimize costs.

End-users will be able to purchase power under long and short term contracts, for various levels of firmness, and at various load factors. With respect to term, power supply contracts will be available for any term longer than the hourly service provided by the spot market. While most supply contracts will probably be for a year or more, monthly, weekly, and even daily contracts will be possible. In a fluctuating market, some end-users may want to risk locking in a low price for a month or a year. These longer term contracts will usually cost more than the spot market price, but if the spot market is expected to rise, money could be saved by locking into a longer term contract if the price is right. This is obviously a judgment call on the part of the end-user.

Many end-users will seek longer term power supply contracts in order to guarantee the type of firm service presently offered by native utilities, although these firm supply contracts will probably be available at a lower price from marketers. End-users could also sign long term contracts for non-firm power since many suppliers will be willing to offer a discount in return for a customer commitment. Therefore, while the cost for spot market power may be low, a long-term, non-firm contract might be competitive with the spot market because (i) it offers price certainty for the end-user and (ii) a guaranteed customer for the supplier. These non-firm supply contracts can either be firmed up with other supply contracts, such as backup supply, or require interruptibility by the end-user. Again, the terms of these interruptions and the firmness of the supply are entirely variable and negotiable.

Many end-users will wish to contract with a single supplier for simplicity's sake, but significant power cost savings are possible by arranging for various types of services from many suppliers. Besides buying different levels of firmness, an end-user will be able to efficiently combine high load factor supply with low load factor supply to optimize costs (see Figure 8-2). In a competitive market, suppliers will offer these different types of products in order to find their niche in the marketplace. Many suppliers will be able to generate 100% load factor, base load power at very low incremental costs. For example, a nuclear utility will have to sell base load power at all times, and incremen tal high load factor power may be sold at very low prices at some times. Other suppliers will offer the low load-factor power at competitive prices if they are able to combine many such loads and take advantage of demand diversity among the various customers' loads. If the cost of the base load power is low enough, the cost of the cycling power added to the base load power may be well below the cost to take all power from a single supplier. Most of the low-cost, base load supply contracts will be longer term contracts as well.

Thus the end-user has numerous options for combining short and long term contracts for base load power and cycling power, and each will have various levels of firmness combined with different types of backup capacity reserves. Piecing all these together will be a challenge, but the savings will be worth it.

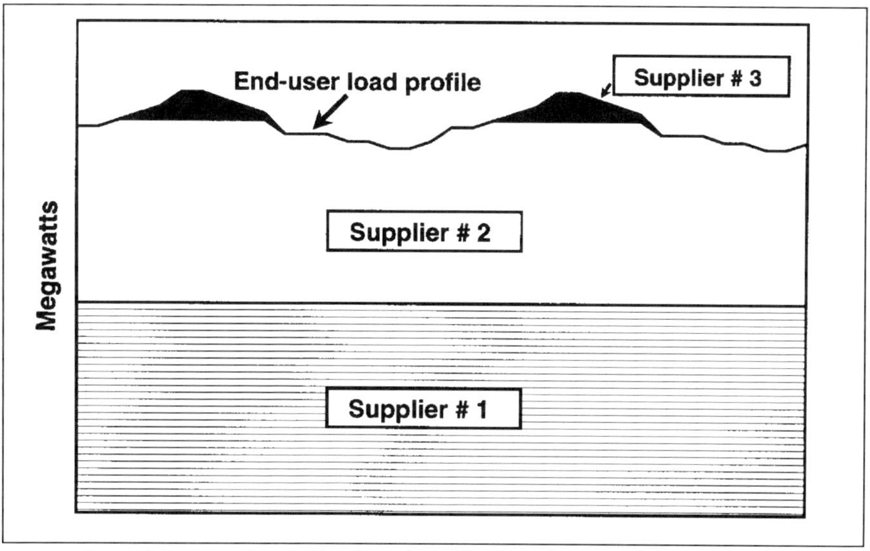

Figure 8-2. An end-user's load can be fed by a combination of high and low load factor supplies.

Transmission

Transmission is the shipment of electrical power from the generator to the end-user. Electricity, as with any other product, must be manufactured, shipped, and retailed (although it must be done on an instantaneous basis), and transmission is the service that brings the power from the seller to the buyer. While energy may be the most significant component of an electrical purchase on a cost basis, transmission is the key to accessing competitive generation by the end-user. In other words, when the electricity market becomes increasingly commoditized, finding low-cost power will be relatively easy, but whether that power can economically be delivered to the end-user's plant will play a large part in determining where that power will be purchased.

Therefore, transmission is not only another unbundled service that the end-user's energy buyer must arrange, it is also the key to accessing the lowest cost energy and capacity, which is the most significant component in the overall energy price. The purpose of this section is to provide an adequate understanding of this most important piece of the electricity puzzle.

Transmission vs. distribution.

In this context, transmission refers to the entire shipping component of the transaction, that is, from the generator all the way to the end-user. However, this component is usually broken down to high-voltage transmission and distribution. As with many products, electricity can be more economically shipped in bulk, and the electrical equivalent of larger shipping containers is increasing voltage. Ohm's law tells us that power is directly proportional to voltage squared. Therefore, doubling the voltage at which power is shipped results in a four-fold increase in transfer capacity.

To illustrate how power is delivered in general, refer to Figure 8-3. Large generators typically produce power at relatively low voltages, e.g., 25,000 Volts. If this voltage is stepped-up with AC transformers to 250,000 Volts, that power can be transmitted to other locations 100 times more economically. This is why high voltage transmission lines are used for bulk power transfers. Typical bulk transmission voltages range from 115 kV to 765 kV. Once bulk power is delivered to a utility's control area, that utility will often use lower voltage lines for moving power within the control area. These sub-transmission voltages range from 34.5 kV to 115 kV. For actual delivery to all but the largest customers, this voltage is stepped down further for economic and safety reasons. Actual power delivery to residential, commercial, and smaller industrial customers is done with a utility's distribution system, which uses voltages ranging from 2.4 kV to 34.5 kV.

Therefore, the term "transmission" really depends on exactly who is shipping to whom. In a retail wheeling world, the end-user will be concerned about bulk transmission, sub-transmission, distribution, or any combination thereof.

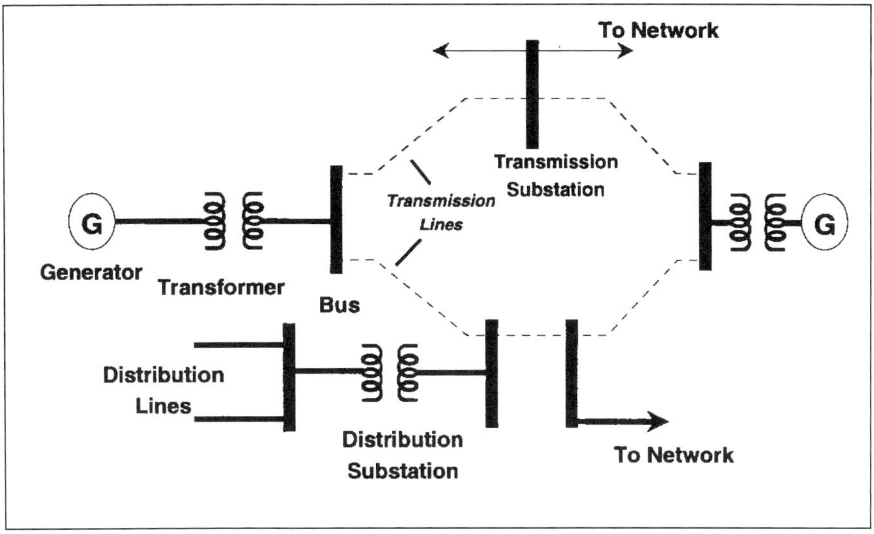

Figure 8-3. Basic electrical power delivery configuration.

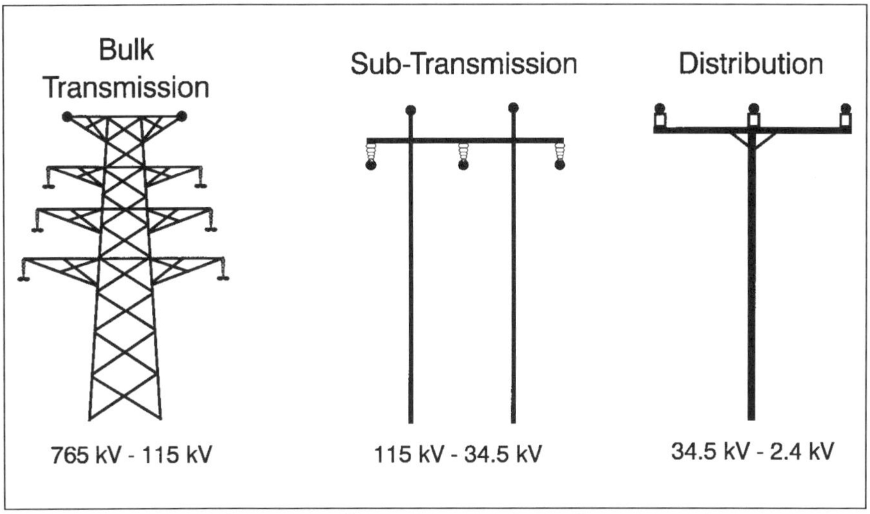

Figure 8-4. Typical configurations of transmission and distribution power lines.

Bulk transmission: If an end-user elects to purchase power from a supplier outside the native utility's control area, which will very often be the case, the end-user must be concerned as to whether adequate transmission capacity exists between those control areas. Because the transmission grid is a highly interconnected web of transmission lines connecting switching stations with multiple links, power will flow from one control area to another over many lines, including those through utilities not associated with the transmission transaction.

To determine the transmission capacity between control areas, which is commonly referred to as the interface between control areas, a load-flow analysis as described in Chapter 7 is required. This analysis, which requires utility-grade load flow software, will provide the transmission capacity, in megawatts, that exists between control areas as though there was a single interconnection since that is what the shipper is generally concerned with rather than the actual flows through each transmission line. As long as none of the actual lines is overloaded, as determined by the loadflow analysis, adequate capacity exists.

In the future, all utilities that supply transmission service will be required to provide this information on available transmission capacity on an hourly basis via a real-time information network. When this system is in place, the end-user will only have to access an electronic bulletin board to determine whether a specific transaction can take place. If the utility reports inadequate transmission capacity, the end-user will have the option of confirming the utility's calculations since the data and the methodology to determine incremental transmission capacity will be available to the public.

Sub-transmission: Once the purchased power has been delivered to the end-user's control area, there may be a concern as to whether that power can be delivered to the end-user's facility. At this stage of industry restructuring, this is less of an issue because the native utility had the obligation to ensure that power could be delivered to those users from various sources within and without the control area. In other words, if the native utility is now providing adequate service, most likely there is adequate sub-transmission facilities within the control area to deliver off-system power, procured by the end-user, within the control area to the end-user.

But as the industry becomes further unbundled, this may not always be the case. At some point, end-users may have to use FERC Form 715 data or OASIS to determine transmission adequacy within a control area. This should not be any more difficult than the analysis required now, and this function will probably be provided on a comparable service basis by the regional transmission group (see Chapter 4).

Distribution: In regulating wholesale transactions, FERC has claimed that transmission service includes delivering power to the purchaser's meter, even if that involves power flows through low-voltage distribution lines. In a retail wheeling world, FERC will regulate distribution to the extent that it is providing transmission service, i.e., the movement of power to the end-user as distinguished from the other ancillary services provided by the local distribution utility. Distribution service will be regulated by state utility commissions.

Because the division between FERC and state jurisdiction appears to be heading towards the difference between transmission and distribution, this distinction has taken on significant importance. This is especially the case for the end-user as retail wheeling develops across the country. If an end-user takes transmission level service, as many large industrial customers do, they should be able to directly access off-system suppliers without involving any distribution services. This would almost entirely release the supply of electricity to that facility from state regulation since no distribution facilities are involved. This may prove to be very beneficial from both an economic and regulatory standpoint. For example, transmission level customers may not be held responsible by the state regulators for any share of the stranded investment costs allocated to distribution customers.

Unfortunately, FERC declared in Order 888 that *all* retail deliveries will involve some distribution facilities. This position was taken to ensure state regulators that they would still have some say in the service to large industrial customers, but it also requires FERC to rule that some high voltage feeds are, as a matter of fact, distribution feeds rather than transmission. Voltage level is but one of eight criteria that FERC will use to decide whether certain facilities are transmission or distribution. Since this decision may have a huge financial impact on the end-user, the attempted bright line between transmission and distribution is sure to get litigated, and the discussion will be very technical. At some point, however, the dividing line between distribution and transmission will be decided for all major distribution companies, and the issue of jurisdiction will be settled once and for all. The end-user will then be clear as to whether services must also be procured from the state-regulated, local distribution company as well as the FERC regulated transmission companies. Jurisdiction between state and federal regulation is discussed in detail in Appendix A.

Network vs. point-to-point service.

As we have seen, transmission was once only provided by a utility to the extent that the transmission utility bought power from the selling utility and resold it to the buying utility. When pure transmission service was sought, utilities attempted to allocate that transmission to certain "contract paths," which are legal fictions that allocate certain transmission transactions to specific lines regardless of actual flows. Contract path transmission agreements assume that power is flowing from one point to another through the grid.

Not long after the Energy Policy Act was passed, in one of the first Section 211 cases, one wholesale buyer discovered that it needed more than mere point-to-point service based on a contract path transaction. In this case, the Florida Municipal Power Agency (FMPA), which purchases wholesale power for member municipal utilities, wished to purchase off-system power and have Florida Power & Light (FP&L) wheel that power through its system. The complicating factor in the case was that there were more than one off-system supplier and more than one delivery point for the power. In a series of landmark decisions, FERC ordered FP&L to provide network service to the FMPA. While no good definition of network service existed at the time, let alone any methodology for pricing it, contract path transactions finally reached the logical limits inherent in the fiction created by traditional transmission service methodologies.

FERC defined "network service" for the first time in the giga-NOPR:

> Network service allows a transmission customer to distribute a given amount of transmission usage between specified resources and specified loads without having to pay multiple charges for each resource-load pairing.

To illustrate this point, a simplification of the FMPA case is in order. Assume that the buyer has multiple delivery points in the native utility's control area. This may be different substations owned by a municipal electric company, as in the case of the FMPA case, or it may be a retail end-user with multiple facilities. For illustrative purposes, assume that each of these delivery points has an 80 MW load. This purchaser finds power for these facilities from a series of separate suppliers, which are each supplying 80 MW of capacity. The purchaser does not want to assign one supplier to each load center, but would rather have all suppliers be able to feed all the loads for reliability and economic reasons. The buyer may wish to dispatch these supplies based on the cost of each supplier and the total load at the time. This will be a very realistic scenario when an end-user with multiple facilities will centralize power purchases either as or through a supply coordinator.

This purchaser must have transmission access from each supplier to each load center. In the FMPA case, FP&L required FMPA to purchase 80 MW of point-to-point transmission capacity for each combination of supplier and load. Therefore, if there were two 80 MW suppliers and two 80 MW loads, FP&L would require FMPA to purchase 320 MW (four times 80 MW) of point-to-point transmission capacity. FMPA claimed that it only needed 160 MW of transmission service because that was the maximum quantity of load being shipped across FP&L's transmission system at any one time.

What the FPMA actually requested is network service, i.e., the use of a portion of the overall transmission *capacity* of the entire transmission rather than only the use of certain facilities that make up the contract path (see Figure 8-5). FERC then ruled that FP&L was required to make available to the FMPA its entire transmission system so that it could move power as it saw fit, within the capacity and reliability parameters of the system. Furthermore, this service must be priced according to the total amount of power shipped on the system as a fraction of the entire system capacity. FERC later required all utilities in their open access transmission tariffs to offer network transmission service as well as point-to-point service, which could be a lower-cost alternative if multiple suppliers or delivery points are not required. In Order 888 FERC requires each public utility to develop tariffs for network and point-to-point service, and the order even includes pro-forma tariffs for each service upon which the utilities had to base their tariffs. Therefore, in a retail wheeling world, the end-user will have total access to its native utility's transmission system, if desired, or only a piece big enough to carry out a specific transaction.

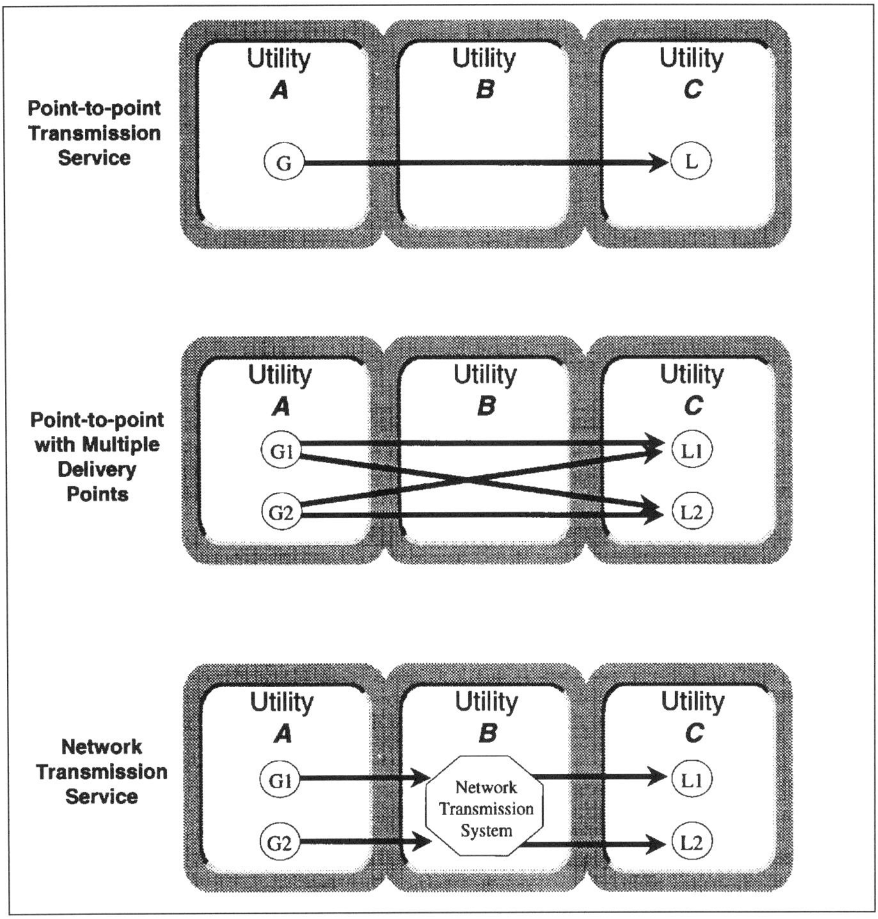

Figure 8-5. A simplified illustration of network vs. point-to-point transmission service.

On the same day it issued Orders 888 and 889, FERC also issued a new Notice of Proposed Rulemaking (NOPR) on new transmission capacity reservation tariffs, or CRTs, that would change the way transmission is reserved. The primary change proposed by FERC is to abolish network service and require all transmission capacity to be reserved on a point-to-point basis. The new CRTs would model electricity transmission reservation and pricing after natural gas transportation reservation. FERC's concern with network service is that it cannot be reserved, it is difficult to quantify its effect on overall transmission capacity, and pricing must be based on total load rather than on the capacity of the transmission path. Under the CRT rules, the customer must specify exact points of delivery and points of receipt. For customers with multiple facilities and multiple suppliers, which will be the case with most end-users, the customer must "set aside sufficient transmission capacity to satisfy its firm reservation needs for any potential combinations of power receipts and deliveries among the designated receipt and delivery points."

Although the CRT change is just a proposal at the time of this writing, the removal of the network service option may have a significant impact on the options an end-user has to purchase transmission capacity. End-users with multiple facilities would probably prefer network service in most cases because it would provide the most flexibility for moving power within and between control areas. Even end-users with single facilities but with multiple suppliers, as will be the case for those end-users that wish to aggressively shop the market, will prefer network service for flexibility and ease of administration. Having to identify, reserve, and purchase every combination of point-to-point transmission service if multiple suppliers and facilities are involved may become unwieldy and actually suppress competitive forces in the industry. However, again, this is only a proposal, and utilities are still required to offer network service at this time. Further details on purchasing transmission capacity under the CRT will be discussed later in this chapter.

Ancillary services and losses.

Transmission service necessarily involves more than shipping power down wires hung up in the sky. However, as discussed above, only those services that can be independently procured, so as to introduce competition, should be separately sold. Those services that meet this qualification are discussed separately in the next section. But some utilities have proposed that some transmission-related services be separately sold even if they cannot be separately procured. For example, a midwest utility once claimed that protective relaying was a service that they provided to their transmission customers, so those customers should pay for it. Of course, protective relaying is inherently related to the specific transmission line that it protects, and there is no way that a group of other companies could install competing facilities on the same line so as to offer competitive service. In other words, protective relaying, in this example, cannot be unbundled from transmission service and therefore should not be considered an ancillary service.

In the recently issued Order 888, FERC specifies certain ancillary services that must be provided along with transmission. Most of these services are not necessarily ancillary to transmission, but instead are ancillary to overall electric service. Therefore, they are discussed below in a separate section. Energy imbalances are really ancillary to energy and capacity sales and as such are discussed above. One service that *is* associated with transmission and that can be independently procured and thus should be unbundled is transmission losses.

In the giga-NOPR that preceded Order 888, FERC listed transmission losses as an ancillary service that must be offered by transmission utilities. In Order 888, however, FERC recognized that transmission loss replacement requires generation resources, and eventually, transmission companies will not be in the best position to offer this service. Therefore, loss replacement service need not be offered by transmission companies in their pro forma open access tariffs, but transmission customers must arrange for transmission loss replacement and inform their transmission company as to the supplier chosen for this service. The inherent complexities with losses on a transmission line make this a very difficult product to quantify, let alone price. Unfortunately, some utilities have taken advantage of this complexity by overcharging for losses. Therefore, some understanding of these issues by the end-user or shipper is warranted.

Losses incurred as a result of shipping electrical power across a transmission line can be broken down into two components: real and reactive power losses. Real power loss is the dissipation of actual energy in the form of heat as electrical current warms the metal in a transmission line. The cause of this heating is the electrical resistance found in all materials, even good conductors such as aluminum. While transmission losses are inadvertent, the conversion of electricity to heat is done on purpose in resistive heat elements in appliances such as toasters, radiant heaters, and electric blankets. Transmission losses can be quantified as either a loss of kilowatt-hours, or reduced capacity on the transmission line in kW.

The difficulty in quantifying transmission losses arises from the physical fact that losses increase as load on the line increases in a squared relationship. These real losses are a function of current on the line, which is abbreviated as "I" and are thus often referred to as I^2R losses (read I-squared R). Because the actual load on a transmission line is constantly in flux, the actual losses on the line vary considerably from one minute to the next. Therefore, it is impossible to accurately meter total losses on a transmission line let alone allocate losses to specific shippers on that line.

Traditionally, FERC has recognized this technical dilemma and has allowed transmission companies to compensate for losses on an average basis. That is, the loading on the line is averaged and the real losses associated with that load can be distributed among all shippers based on their share of the average load. This method is far more favorable to some sort of real-time monitoring given the inherent complexities that really need not be addressed. In most recent cases and in the recently issued FERC Order 888 on open access transmission service, transmission losses have been fixed at 3% of the amount of power transmitted.

The issue then becomes how to compensate the transmission company for these losses. In many transmission agreements, losses are compensated by adding a percentage adder to the transmission rate which reflects the average real losses on an average loaded transmission line (note that losses greatly increase as the line is fully loaded).

In an unbundled market, the real power losses could be replaced by the transmission company, by the supplier of the energy and capacity, or by a third party source on behalf of the shipper. For example, if 100 MW is to be shipped over a transmission line with 3% average losses, the transmission company will require the replacement of 3 MW of power. This could be done by purchasing 103 MW of power from the supplier and have 100 MW delivered (or deliver 97 MW of power for 100 MW purchased). In this case, the end-user is buying transmission losses from the energy and capacity supplier, which may not be the optimum source depending on the nature of the products being purchased. An even less desirable option is to have the supplier generate 100 MW for 100 MW delivered and have the transmission company provide the 3 MW of losses from its own generation facilities. Since transmission companies will eventually no longer be in the generation business, this would probably be very expensive generation.

The end-user or shipper will probably be better off arranging for the delivery of the 3 MW of power—capacity, energy, or both—from an entirely different supplier to the transmission company. In a competitive market, it is likely that some generators will get into the transmission loss supply business, or major suppliers will have a special transmission loss replacement rate. Since the quality of loss compensation power is not critical, this arrangement will probably be far less expensive than the loss replacement rate charged by the transmission company.

The second type of transmission losses is reactive power, which is associated with magnetic and induction losses on the line associated with the alternating current nature of the service. Reactive power losses have a direct impact on the voltage level seen at the receiving bus, so that the replacement of reactive power is often considered analogous to voltage support. In fact, many of the devices used for voltage support also provide reactive power, such as shunt capacitors. Therefore, reactive power loss support is not considered along with real transmission losses, but instead is considered a separate unbundled service along with voltage support (see below).

Purchasing transmission capacity.

Purchasing transmission will not be unlike purchasing the power itself; the end-user will have many choices of firm and non-firm, short and long term capacity, and even the right to resell unused capacity on the secondary market. These choices will be offered through either the open access same-time information system envisioned by FERC, the regional transmission groups discussed in Chapter 4, or from the transmission company directly. With the development of unbundled, non-discriminatory, open access transmission tariffs, purchasing transmission capacity may still be relatively complex, but it will at least be done on an even-handed basis.

An off-system supplier of power will either offer that power delivered to the end-user or at the supplier's system. Since the lowest cost bulk power will be sold at the supplier's busbar (the electrical equivalent of the natural gas burnertip), the end-user will be better off to purchase its own transmission service. If the end-user is served at a transmission voltage (or off a transmission service as defined by FERC), then only transmission service from the interconnected transmission company and any intervening transmission companies is required. If the end-user takes service at a lower voltage or a FERC-defined distribution system, then the end-user will have to purchase distribution services from the local distribution company as well.

The first step for an end-user looking to procure transmission services from a supplier is to decide whether network or point-to-point service is needed, as described above. If the buyer has only one delivery point, i.e., one facility and is buying power from only one supplier, then point-to-point service will be cheaper and more straight-forward. If there are two suppliers or two delivery points, an economic analysis comparing point-to-point against network service may be indicated, although network service will most likely be cheaper. Certainly if there are any more than three possible transmission paths, i.e., more than two delivery or supply points, then network service will be needed. Fortunately, FERC has mandated that all transmission utilities will offer shippers the choice of either type of service (although this may change).

Of course, the end-user must know how much transmission capacity is needed on which transmission systems. This is determined from the load flow analysis described in Chapter 7. This analysis ensures that the end-user only purchases the exact amount of transmission capacity required. Because most end-users will not have load flow calculation capabilities, this determination can be made by the transmission company or the regional transmission group, and the calculations can be checked by the supply coordinator or other independent third party if required.

The next step is to determine whether the transmission capacity exists to implement the transaction desired. In the near future, this will be very easily done by merely accessing the OASIS created by the utility to provide this very type of information. Until this system is available for all transmission companies on a unified format, the end-user may have to perform its own load-flow type analysis to determine whether the transaction can be done without exceeding any transmission capacity limits. The information to do this study is presently available, and the study process is also described in Chapter 7.

Assuming adequate transmission capacity exists, which will often be the case, the end-user must now reserve the capacity. This involves the decision of whether to reserve firm capacity or merely purchase non-firm capacity. Of course, this depends on the type of power purchased, i.e., firm power would be rendered interruptible if it is delivered with non-firm transmission. If a transmission interface is relatively unfilled, there may be little or no risk to purchasing non-firm space, but this judgment will have to be made based on experience and will certainly vary from utility to utility. If firm space is required, a purchase could be made directly through the OASIS or from the transmission utility directly.

Purchasing transmission capacity, even if done through OASIS, must be done under the terms and conditions of the pro forma tariffs regulated by FERC as required in Order 888. These tariffs are somewhat complicated and detailed, and transmission companies will probably revise these tariffs to add more flexibility and options, which will add more complexity. As with purchasing any competitive product, the more the end-user understands that product, and the terms and conditions of its delivery, the greater control over price and reliability it will have. Therefore, the next step for the end-user is to determine the level of service to be purchased as described in the transmission utility's tariffs.

One transmission purchasing issue that is addressed in Order 888 tariffs is priority of reservation and interruption. Once the end-user has decided the degree of firmness of transmission required, given the firmness of the energy or capacity to be shipped, the reservation and interruption priority must be considered. The highest priority for transmission capacity reservation and interruption, at least for now, is the utility's native retail load that is served under a traditional, bundled format. Although FERC considered requiring utilities reserve capacity for native retail load on the same non-discriminatory basis as for all other load, priority was allowed until the transition to a fully competitive market is completed. Once the retail electric industry is completely unbundled, native load will have the same priority as all other transmission customers.

For firm service, priority is given to network customers over point-to-point customers. From there, the term of the service sets the priority. The pro forma transmission tariffs provide that reservations for short-term firm point-to-point service (less than one year) will be conditional for one day for daily service, one week for weekly service, and one month for monthly service. During the conditional period, if transmission capacity is not available because of use by a longer-term customer, the holder of a firm point-to-point reservation would have the right of first refusal to match the term of service of the longer-term customer before being displaced. Beyond term, firm service priority is first-come, first-serve. The tariffs do not require varying levels of firmness, although the transmission company is free to develop such a system. As for non-firm service, network purchases will have priority over non-firm point-to-point service. As with firm service, the length of term will be the next test for priority, and finally, price can be used as a tie-breaker. In summary, (i) firm beats non-firm, (ii) network beats point-to-point, (iii) long-term beats short-term, and finally, (iv) price can be used as a tie-breaker.

The end-user can also consider buying and selling transmission capacity on the secondary market, much like capacity release for natural gas transportation. On one hand, suppose an end-user arranges for 50 MW of firm transmission capacity in a one year contract to bring power from an off-system supplier to a facility. When the facility is down for a three week maintenance outage, the end-user can sell back this capacity on the secondary market for a market price. This transmission service can be interruptible (spot transmission) or firm for three weeks. As with capacity release of natural gas transportation, FERC will cap the price of released transmission at the original tariff rate. On the other hand, an end-user who is experiencing a temporary increase in load can access the secondary market for non-firm transmission during this period. Some aggressive end-users may wish to purchase all of their transmission capacity in the secondary market, since the prices may be lower. In natural gas, the released price of transportation is usually about a third of the tariff rate. This secondary market will be developed as part of the OASIS on available transmission capacity, and it will be regulated by FERC.

FERC envisions much of the transmission purchasing process to be carried out on a regional basis through the regional transmission group or independent system operator. When retail wheeling is prevalent, ISOs and RTGs will allow end-users to access their services as well. While this is still unclear, the RTGs and ISOs will probably be able to provide one-stop shopping for all transmission access services, including the determination of capacity, capacity reservations, and even capacity release. OASIS will probably be set up by the RTGs and ISOs on a regional basis. Furthermore, the end-user will probably pay the RTG or ISO for the transmission service, and the RTG or ISO will allocate those revenues to the utilities involved in the transaction based on the its own pricing formula.

As mentioned earlier, FERC issued a new Notice of Proposed Rulemaking (NOPR) that considers revamping how capacity reservations are made, and that NOPR was issued on the same day that the final open access tariffs were issued. Since this is only a proposed rule, this section will only cover the basic proposal, but if approved, end-users may have to reconsider how they reserve and purchase transmission capacity. The key change suggested in the capacity reservation tariff (CRT) NOPR is the elimination of network service. Under the new CRT, shippers would be required to specify every point of delivery (POD) and point of receipt (POR), and then point-to-point transmission capacity would have to be reserved for every potential combination of POR and POD. While this could result in an unwieldy number of transmission paths for end-users with multiple facilities or multiple suppliers, FERC is interested in eliminating the complications that network service bring to pricing, reservation priority, and OASIS. Under the CRT, all firm transmission service would be reserved, and all reserved service would be firm, leaving non-firm service to minute-by-minute capacity available in the system, and would be offered to the highest bidder. Unlike Order 888's pro forma tariffs, the CRT would apply to all customers, including native retail customers, since they too need firm service. Therefore, all capacity is accounted for in the reservation system since no capacity is reserved for native load or for network service. This will make reservation accounting on OASIS simpler as well.

Another issue with respect to mandated transmission access is whether the transmission company is required to build additional facilities if there is insufficient capacity to meet the shippers needs. Section 211 of EPAct specifically allows shippers to request "any enlargement of transmission capacity necessary to provide [transmission] services." This provision has not, at the time of this writing, been exercised or tested, which is probably due to the general surplus of transmission capacity that exists throughout most of the country. The prospect of mandated transmission construction raises many issues. Of these, pricing may be the most contentious; however, there is a precedent with natural gas transportation. Furthermore, Section 212 of EPAct specifically forbids any new transmission costs that result from a Section 211 request to be allocated to existing customers of the transmitting utility. Another key issue is jurisdiction. State regulatory agencies usually have jurisdiction over transmission facility siting. If FERC can mandate transmission even if it requires new facilities, can FERC preempt the state's existing siting authority? This is a constitutional issue that can only be resolved in the courts.

Transmission and distribution are, and should continue to be, natural monopolies, but only with respect to facilities. That is, no one advocates competition in transmission via duplicative transmission lines. However, there may be competitive transmission ownership through the use of shared ownership of transmission capacity, but this can only work when there is enough capacity to go around. Because transmission facilities are a natural monopoly, if there are capacity limitations, mechanisms must be created to ensure fair access to limited supplies.

Pricing transmission.

The ideal methodology for pricing transmission has been hotly debated for quite some time in the industry, and is still not settled. FERC issued a Notice of Inquiry on the subject in 1993 and issued a rule in 1994 that basically deferred the issue to the RTGs. FERC recognized that no single policy will probably work best in all parts of the country and instead advocated a flexible pricing policy that would allow various pricing methodologies. Of course, this makes determining the price of transmission more difficult for the end-user. While the cost of transmission will only be a small part of an end-users total electricity bill, it may often determine the most economical source of power since many suppliers will be forced to price their energy at prevailing market rates.

As discussed many times so far, FERC is requiring all utilities to provide transmission service at non-discriminatory rates pursuant to unbundled, transmission service tariffs. This makes pricing consistent, if not predictable, depending on how understandable the tariffs are. The tariffs that will be required to be in place at first, the so-called pro forma tariffs, will price transmission on the utility's embedded cost of service using traditional ratemaking methodologies. The price that each customer pays for transmission will be based on a share of the installed cost of the entire transmission system on a per kilowatt basis. While this may not provide the market with accurate pricing signals and may not account for how heavily a line is loaded (such as other proposals do), it is a well-known methodology and is a reasonable starting point. The portion of the total embedded cost that each shipper will pay will be based on the amount of capacity reserved by the shipper as a portion of the overall network capacity of the system. This methodology is not dependant on how far that power is shipped over the system and is thus called a postage stamp rate (since like a letter, it costs the same to ship no matter how far it goes). Elaborate systems to account for distance in transmission rates are being developed, so-called "megawatt-mile" systems, but again, postage stamp rates are a traditional ratemaking methodology and can serve as a reasonable starting point for pro forma tariffs.

Although there are many problems with the current pricing methodology for transmission, one that concerns most end-users is the issue of "pancaking." In the industrial mid-west, there are many small but separate control areas that each have independent transmission services. Moving power a relatively short geographical distance may mean shipping power over two, three, or more utilities. Each utility will add its FERC-approved tariff rate until the cost to move that power can become prohibitive. While a megawatt-mile pricing scheme will remove this problem, end-users will first have to be careful about where they buy power so as not to needlessly increase the price of power by going though too many transmission systems.

This raises a final issue with respect to transmission: is power really being transmitted in a retail wheeling transaction? Even with retail wheeling, most existing generators will still run and most loads will continue to take power as before. Although some generation will be added and some removed, power will continue to move around the grid pretty much as it did before retail wheeling. For example, a large integrated steel mill that uses hundreds of megawatts of power is located adjacent to one of the native utility's large coal-fired plants. The plant was originally built there to feed the needs of the steel mill next door. Unfortunately, the native utility that owns the plant is a very high priced utility, and the end-user is forced to purchase power from an off-system supplier. The coal fired plant still must operate to meet other native load, to provide local voltage support, and to feed loads normally fed by the plants that are now feeding the steel mill. What has changed? Of course, nothing really has. Retail wheeling has sometimes been referred to as wheeling money and not power, which may be the case, but the purpose of retail wheeling is to inject competitive forces in a monopoly industry. Therefore, why should the steel mill pay for transmission (while at the same time the off-system load now fed by the adjacent coal-fired plant also pays for transmission) when no power is really flowing? Even the megawatt-mile concept will still require these phantom payments. There is no good answer for this question, except that transmission charges may have to be considered as one of the costs of competition. It also sends an economic pricing signal in that arranging for power supplies too far away will be discouraged. The transmission system is not designed to have the generators in one part of the country match the loads of another. Transmission charges encourage the use of local generation, so that local load is matched to local resources. In summary, transmission and its pricing mechanisms in a retail wheeling world is but a catalyst for injecting much needed competitive forces into the power generation industry.

Ancillary Services

Beyond the fundamental unbundled services of energy, capacity, transmission, and distribution, a vertically integrated utility provides a number of other services that are necessary for the delivery of reliable electric service. In a competitive market, other suppliers will compete with the local utility to provide many of these services, although some will have to be provided by the local utility because of technical considerations. But when a service can be offered by a third party, market forces will unbundle that service even if regulatory forces do not.

In the unbundled transmission service tariffs required in Order 888, FERC identifies and requires a number of services that it found to be ancillary to transmission service. As discussed above, most of these services are not necessarily tied to just transmission and can be provided by companies other than the local transmission provider. Furthermore, there are other services that have been identified by some providers as ancillary that are in addition to FERC's requirements.

The key to an unbundled service is that it can be provided by more than one party. The only reason to unbundle a service is to make it competitively priced. If it cannot be unbundled, then that service and its cost should be included in the principal service. The end-user will have to carefully decide first which specific services it will require and then which suppliers can provide that service at the lowest price.

Scheduling, System control and dispatch.

According to FERC,

> scheduling is the control room procedure to establish a predetermined (before-the-fact) use of generation resources and transmission facilities to meet anticipated load (including interchange). Dispatching is the control room operation of all generation and transmission facilities on a real-time basis to meet load within the transmission provider's designated service area (or other larger area of coordinated dispatch operation).

These services described by FERC in Order 888 must be distinguished from the economic dispatch function provided by existing vertically integrated utilities and described in Chapter 2. Economic dispatch and unit commitment, often referred to as scheduling, is the selection of the optimum generation resources to meet the utility's load. In a competitive world, the marketplace will perform the economic dispatch (except for suppliers with multiple generation facilities), but the transmission company will still have to operate its system much like it did as a vertically integrated utility. Thus, the scheduling and dispatch required to operate the transmission system to facilitate an open market for the sale of electric energy from the supplier to the end-user is essentially the ancillary service described by FERC. Because this function must be performed by the transmission company, it is not a truly unbundled service, as defined by FERC, and thus is included in the basic transmission service. Indeed, FERC's pro forma tariffs for transmission service includes the cost of this function in the base price.

Scheduling and dispatching of *generation* for an end-user that elects to buy power from many different suppliers either to minimize price or to feed multiple facilities is a service that can be provided by third parties. This is actually a service provided by the supply coordinator described in Chapter 2. This is analogous to the function performed by utilities today in that the supply coordinator is sending each supplier a schedule of its client's power needs. This is in effect dispatching generation units because it is deciding which units run and for how much power. Of course, the market price is the force deciding which generator the supply coordinator schedules and dispatches. From this perspective, the scheduling and dispatch service is part of the "rebundling" fee paid to the supply coordinator, buyer's agent, or marketer.

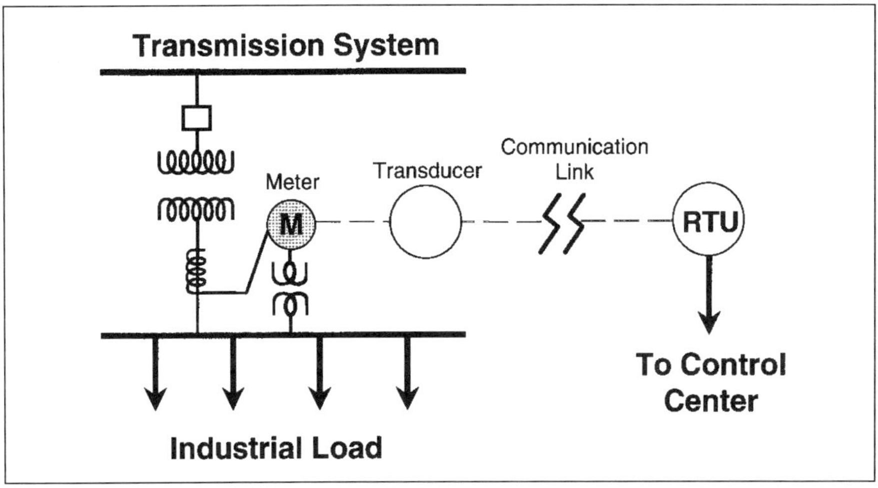

Figure 8-6. Telemetering configuration to transfer an industrial load from one control area to another using dynamic scheduling.

The FERC's Order 888 also discusses dynamic scheduling, which is commonly referred to as load following on a non-instantaneous level. In this situation, the end-user arranges with its supplier to provide all of its demand on a real-time basis through the use of telemetering (see Figure 8-6). As the end-user's metered load increases or decreases, a signal is sent to the dedicated supplier, either a specific generator or a control area, to increase or decrease its output, respectively. In this way, the end-user's load is constantly followed by the supplier so that the end-user's local utility does not feed any part of the load. Essentially, the end-user's load is moved from one control area to another. This type of dynamic scheduling or load following is a service provided by the supplier, but it is actually part of the supplier's product and cannot really be separated from that product. In Order 888, dynamic scheduling is discussed as an ancillary service that need not be offered by a transmission company nor must it be purchased by a transmission customer.

Therefore, in all three definitions, i.e., (i) scheduling and dispatching by the transmission company to operate its system, (ii) scheduling and dispatching by the supply coordinator for the end-user, or (iii) dynamic scheduling or load following, there is no separate, unbundled service that can be provided outside of the base service listed. Therefore, this is not a service that needs to be independently procured or priced by the end-user even though it is often discussed as an unbundled or ancillary service.

Regulation and frequency response.

As we have already seen, the term "load following" can take on many definitions. Many refer to load following as the real-time tracking of an end-user's load by its supplier so that the load is effectively moved from one control area to another. However, in the giga-NOPR that preceded Order 888, FERC described load following as "the continuous balancing of resources," which is a service that the transmission company is "uniquely positioned to provide." In Order 888, FERC renamed this ancillary service as regulation and frequency response service. This service must be offered by every transmission provider in its pro forma tariffs, but transmission customers can acquire this service from third-party competing suppliers at the level required by each individual load.

Regulation and frequency response service refers to the accommodation of moment-to-moment variations in load within a control area so that a constant frequency is maintained. This service involves the instantaneous supply or absorption of energy other than that provided by the end-user's off-system supplier. It is technically impossible, with the exception of fuel cells, for a generator to instantaneously follow a load given the rotational inertia in the generator rotor's mass. However, an end-user's load is constantly fluctuating as loads are turned on and off. This minute-by-minute fluctuation in load has to be provided by some source, and the interconnected grid naturally wants to meet this demand. Although the local transmission company or a third-party supplier can provide this service from an accounting basis, actually, every generator and transmission facility in the entire interconnected grid is contributing to this service.

Every load is different, though, and each has different instantaneous load following requirements. For example, an aluminum smelter has a load that is constant with the only fluctuations coming from auxiliary services such as lighting. On a relative basis, there is virtually no fluctuation. On the other extreme is an arc furnace for metal melting in which huge swings in load occur frequently and very quickly so that they cannot be scheduled. The aluminum smelter can nominate a certain level of load to be purchased from the supplier, and the load taken will be within a fraction of a percent of the nomination. The arc furnace can nominate some average value for demand, but given the cycle that the furnace is in, the load taken will be many megawatts above or below that nomination. The cost of providing load following (under this definition) to the smelter is far smaller than that for the arc furnace, and the smelter should not have to pay for the services provided to the arc furnace (see Figure 8-7).

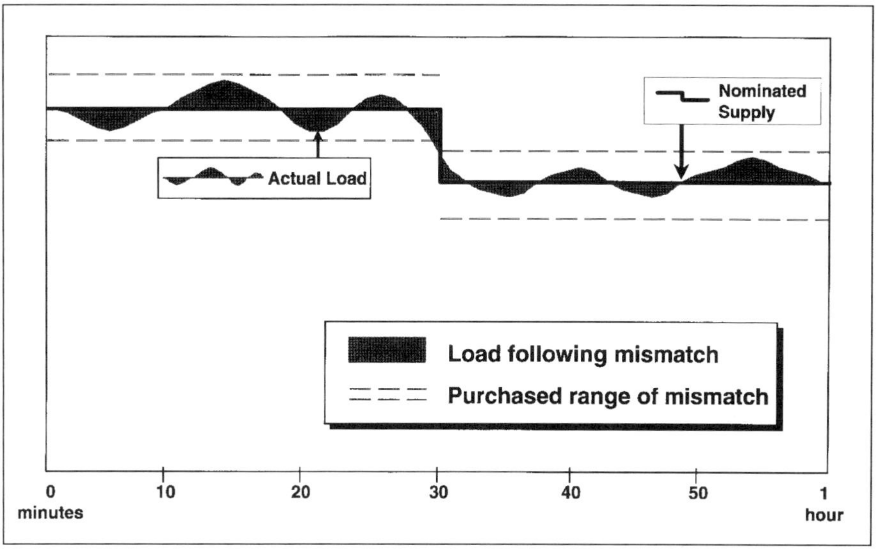

Figure 8-7. Load following is providing for the mismatch between nominated supply and actual load.

Therefore, the native utility will probably structure its tariffs to accommodate the real cost of each load's regulation and frequency control service. This can be done by charging a certain value for each percentage fluctuation off the nominated value. This is similar to the area control error (ACE) function that utilities must monitor now. That is, those loads causing ACE problems will have to pay for the cost of the local utility to feed that load, such as arrange for a certain amount of spinning reserve and excess interface transmission capacity to handle the big swings in load. The fixed and variable costs of these reserves will be passed on in accordance to the fluctuations seen by each load.

In today's market, loads with widely fluctuating demands pay very little difference from more predictable load. An arc furnace that runs all day may have a 70% load factor due to the short time swings in load, where a plant with a very constant load that runs for only two shifts a day may also have a 70% load factor. Each plant will pay the same for its electricity although the cost to feed the arc furnace is much greater because of the problems it causes to the utility's ACE. In one well-known exception, a mid-western utility is charging its arc furnace load an additional 3% load following charge.

Operating reserves.

As discussed in Chapter 2, every utility today must dedicate some amount of generation capacity as operating reserves to protect the reliability of the system. Under current operating rules in most NERC regions, each utility must provide a level of generation equal to 3% of its load in the form of "spinning reserve" and 3% as "quick start" capacity, also called "supplemented reserve,' for a total of 6% operating reserves. Spinning reserve is generation that is on-line but not used. For example a generator with a rated output of 400 MW but only running at 300 MW is contributing 100 MW to the utility's spinning reserve requirements. Of course, one generator can contribute the spinning reserve requirement of many generators that are operating at 100% output. Supplemental or quick start reserve is capacity that is not on-line, but that can be brought on-line within 10 minutes, such as aeroderivative combustion turbines.

Although NERC regions may become RTGs or ISOs, the need for operating reserves will not change in a competitive industry. Instead, the operating reserve requirements to maintain a reliable system will have to be met by the end-users and their suppliers. That is, if an end-user is purchasing 100 MW, at least 6 MW will have to be contributed to the system's operating reserves. In the giga-NOPR, FERC refered to this service as "system protection," which was an unfortunate label since that often refers to the protective relaying schemes used to protect electrical power facilities. In Order 888, FERC corrected this mistake and also seperated spinning reserve and supplemental reserve into two distinct ancillary services.

Operating reserves can be provided to the system by one of three options. First, the supplier could provide the additional capacity. If 100 MW is purchased by the end-user, the end-user may wish to pay that supplier for 106 MW if the supplier has 6 additional megawatts it can place on reserve as spinning or quick-start. Second, a third party could provide this capacity. That same 6 MW could be provided to the system by a third party generator (and for quick start capacity, it need not even be used). This service may be offered by some third parties very inexpensively and will ensure that this service remains priced competitively. Finally, the end-user could contribute to this requirement by promising to curtail its load instantaneously (using transfer-trip relaying tied to a certain contingency) or within 10 minutes to meet quick-start requirements. This is similar to how interruptible service is provided now. Therefore, if the end-user has some interruptible load (only 6% is required), purchasing off-system operating reserves may be unnecessary.

Reactive supply and voltage control.

A hallmark of the American electric system is its reliability, and a key component of reliable service is a constant and predictable service voltage level. All customers require steady voltage, and for some industrial end-users, constant voltage is critical to their manufacturing processes. Supporting and maintaining constant voltage at the customer's busbar is a local function which cannot be provided from a distant supplier. The amount of voltage support a customer needs may vary depending on the type of load, however, and there is no reason that third party suppliers cannot provide some of this function in addition to the services provided by the local utility.

The level of voltage support provided to an end-user is a reflection of the "stiffness" of the electric system feeding a particular load. A stiff system is one that can readily respond to large and quick changes in load, while a weak system will suffer voltage and frequency sags and surges as a result of these changes. A stiff system usually has more value to an end-user than a weak one, and an end-user that has or needs stiff system support should expect to pay more for its power than end-users with less critical needs.

Voltage support is supplied a number of ways. First, the grid itself provides the backbone for supporting the load on the system and the strength of the grid, i.e., the availability of adequate generation and transmission resources for all levels of load directly impacts the ability to maintain constant voltage during fluctuating load cycles. Because an unlimited amount of power cannot be transmitted into a control area, every utility has some level of minimum local generation that must be on-line in order to sustain local voltages. Even if the load in the area is contractually fed from off-system suppliers, these local generators must still run. The operation of these facilities in order to maintain system voltage is a distribution control service that must be provided by the local distribution company or independent generators that it contracts with. The lack of an adequate level of local generation is often the cause for load curtailments, even for firm power. In many of these instances, even the availability of power on the grid would not prevent the rolling blackouts because inadequate transmission resources prevented the ability to move power into the control area.

The need for a certain level of local generation to support voltage has led some to believe that the owners of those generators will be able to take advantage of a competitive marketplace and charge above market rates for operating the unit since it must run for reliability reasons. This concern over locational market power only exists with a poolco system where each generator submits a bid to supply energy to the pool. If that particular unit is the marginal unit (see Chapter 4 for a complete discussion of how poolco works), the generator will be able to bid any price since the unit must run. In a direct access system, the level of generation required for voltage support would be a monopoly ancillary service that is priced on a cost basis. Note that the level of generation that a particular unit must supply as voltage support can fluctuate. The same units that supply this voltage support service on behalf of the local distribution or transmission company will also provide energy for load following and energy balancing services.

As a second source of voltage support, various devices can be installed on the distribution system to change voltage as a function of changing load, such as voltage regulators and load tap changers on transformers. These devices automatically adjust voltages in response to the change in voltages caused by changing loads. These also are normally provided by the local distribution company, but depending on a particular interconnection, an end-user may be able to provide these devices itself for the use at a particular facility.

A third aspect of voltage support is the supply of reactive power. The supply of reactive power is related to voltage support in that an insufficient supply will affect voltage levels, although it is not the only means for voltage support. A full explanation of the physics behind reactive power is beyond the scope of this book, but a brief explanation may help. All power consists of two components: real power and reactive power. Real power is that which delivers energy and does actual work. It is measured in watts (or kilowatts, or kW) and is sold by the hour as kilowatt-hours. Reactive power is measured in volt-amperes-reactive, or VARs, and performs no actual work. The square root of the sums of the squares of real and reactive power is the total power, which is measured in volt-amperes, or VA (commonly expressed as megavolt-amperes, or MVA). This is a triangular relationship, as shown in Figure 8-8.

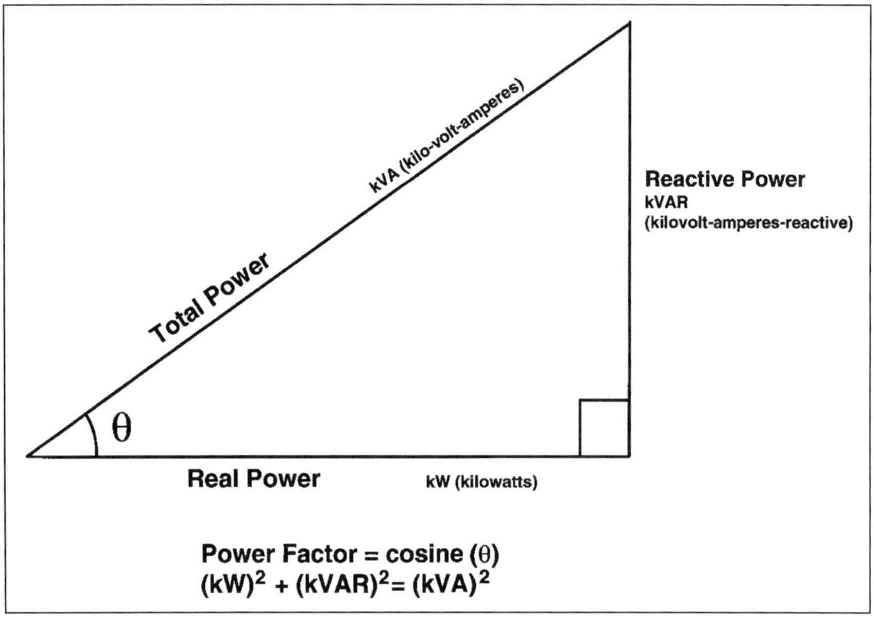

Figure 8-8. The triangular relationship between total, real, and reactive power.

The cosine of the angle formed between the real and reactive power legs of the triangle is the power factor. If the reactive power needs of a load were 20% of that of the real power needs, the power factor would be .787 or 78.7% (the arc-cotangent of 0.2). If a load had no reactive power requirement, the power factor would be one, or unity. Ideally, all loads should have a unity power factor to minimize the reactive power demands on the system. Most utilities charge for supplying reactive power above a certain level to compensate for large reactive power requirements.

Physically, reactive power is related to magnetic losses in the windings in motors, generators, and transformers and in the transmission line wires. Current passing through a wire creates a magnetic field, and some of the energy in the electric current is lost through the magnetic field created. This is in conjunction with real losses, which result from energy lost through the thermal heating of the wire through which current passes.

Reactive power or reactive loss compensation is primarily supplied to the electric grid from synchronous generators that can be operated to create reactive power. The level of reactive power created can be adjusted automatically to meet the reactive power needs of the grid. Unfortunately, reactive power cannot be transmitted over great distances like real power can, so a certain amount of reactive power must be generated locally to meet the reactive power requirements of certain loads. The most common method of doing this is with the installation of capacitor banks, which are static devices that create reactive power. Capacitor banks can be installed near the end-user's busbar or delivery point and sized to correct the load's power factor to unity. This will meet the customer's reactive power requirements without burdening the grid. Of course, installation of properly sized capacitors will often reduce an end-user's electricity bill by removing the charge for reactive power assessed by most utilities. For fluctuating loads with fluctuating reactive power requirements, solid state devices called static var compensators can be installed at a higher cost. These devices can instantaneously change the amount of capacitive compensation to maintain a unity power factor even as load changes.

Voltage support and reactive power devices must be installed by utilities to maintain proper voltages on the system. Since many devices provide both functions, these two services are often combined, as they are in FERC's pro forma transmission tariffs as required in Order 888. Order 888 recognizes that this service can be provided by either the end-user itself (through self-installation of the devices described above), a third party (for example, the installation of a large capacitor bank by a third party to meet the needs of an entire industrial park), or by the transmission company (or local distribution company in the case of retail wheeling). The difficulty lies in pricing these services based on the amount of voltage support required by individual end-users. Perhaps the most straightforward method of monitoring this need will be through a measurement of the reactive power requirements. The amount of voltage support required by an end-user should be proportional to peak demand and perhaps load factor.

Therefore, the end-user's local distribution company or transmission company will probably have two components of the charge for this service. First, reactive power requirements, if not met by the end-user itself or some third party, can be metered and assessed similarly to how reactive power is billed now. Beyond this, distribution and transmission companies will probably be justified in charging a small fee, based on the embedded cost of the voltage support equipment described above, for voltage support services.

These services can only be unbundled to some degree, so they should be included in the base rate for the distribution and transmission service. In the FERC transmission pro forma tariff, the proposed charge for voltage support and reactive power services, combined with load following and operating reserves, is fixed at 0.1¢ per kilowatt-hour. This provides an indication that the charge for this ancillary service should be relatively small.

Other services.

Many utilities have claimed that there are even more ancillary services involved in delivering power to an end-user, and that these services should also be unbundled and separately priced. For example, one mid-western utility suggested that protective relaying, which includes the devices that detect faults such as lightning strikes on transmission lines, should be a separately priced, unbundled ancillary service. But this function cannot be separated from the transmission line itself, and therefore cannot be independently procured. That is, only those services that can be procured by other parties, or that do not need to be purchased at the same level by all customers, should be unbundled. Services offered beyond those described above should be carefully scrutinized to ensure that they are truly an unbundled service and are not already included in the base service offered by the transmission or distribution company.

Although Order 888 identifies and defines certain mandatory ancillary services that each utility must offer, the market may further unbundle some services. For example, some suppliers may provide reactive power compensation and voltage support, based on specific equipment, separately. Because different end-users may have varying needs for each service, this may be competitively priced compared to the combined ancillary service defined in Order 888. If so, market forces will do what FERC does not, but the defined ancillary services set a minimum level of unbundling.

Pricing ancillary services.

While offering a myriad of products and services to end-users is consistent with an open and competitive market, it is inconsistent with the existing electric utility infrastructure. Vertically integrated utilities never had a need to create separate accounts for the various ancillary services, let alone treat generation, transmission and distribution separately. Therefore, the pricing of ancillary services is a difficult issue.

The primary source of difficulty in pricing ancillary services is the lack of an accounting system that tracks the fixed and variable costs associated with the ancillary services. Since many of these services are monopoly services, such as instantaneous load following, the cost of those services should be based on the utility's costs. If there is no accounting system on which those costs are reflected, ratemakers will have a difficult time determining how to allocate total transmission or distribution costs among the various services. For example, a generation facility can provide VAR support for reactive power and operating reserves for system reliability, but how is the total cost of the facility allocated to these functions? It is difficult to determine a percentage of a capital-intensive facility that is allocated to each unbundled product. Furthermore, many facilities and expenses could be allocated to more than one service. This invites the risk of double billing for some services.

As we have already seen, FERC recognizes these pricing problems and is addressing the issue in its mandatory transmission tariffs by fixing the rates, terms, and conditions of many of the ancillary services and then allowing proposals for refined ratemaking once the mandatory pro forma tariffs are in place. FERC recognizes that its required pro forma tariffs are not perfect, but they provide a starting place. Also, as we shall see, unbundled transmission tariffs that have already been filed also provide an indication of the prices involved. The cost of the services identified in Order 888 are as follows (see Figure 8-9 for a summary of these changes):

- Scheduling, System Control, and Dispatch: Because this function, as defined by FERC in Order 888 is a service that must be provided by the transmission company and only by them, it is not a truly unbundled service. FERC recognizes this and thus requires the transmission companies to include this cost in their base rates.
- Energy Imbalances: The service of providing or absorbing energy within 1.5% of what was nominated, to the extent that it can be metered, can be provided by the transmission company at either its incremental cost of energy production or it can create an energy bank. Energy can be deposited or withdrawn from the bank as needed without charge. The cost of this service must be included in the basic transmission charge. If energy beyond the 1.5% bandwidth must be supplied or absorbed, again to the extent that it can be metered, that cost can be as high as the existing FERC emergency rate of ten cents per kilowatt-hour.
- Real-time Supply and Voltage Control, Operation Responses, and Regulations and Frequency Response: These services, which are among the most difficult to quantify with respect to cost, were lumped together by FERC in Order 888 clearly because there was no better methodology to price them individually. In what appears to be a number somewhat pulled out of the air, FERC mandated the price for all three of these services combined to a fixed cost in the pro forma tariffs of 1.0 mills (0.1 cents) per kilowatt hour.
- Real Transmission Losses: As discussed earlier, transmission losses are fixed by FERC at 3%. Although the tariffs allow third parties and off-system suppliers to provide this service, if losses are provided by the transmission company, it cannot charge more than 110% of its incremental cost of production. Obviously, if a transmission company has no generation assets, which will be more the rule than the exception in the future, it cannot provide this service so the production cost rule is not applicable.

Service	Must Buy	Must Buy from Transco	Transco Must Offer	Price
Scheduling, System Control, and Dispatch	✓	✓	✓	Included in Base Rate
Reactive Supply and Voltage Control	✓	✓	✓	1.0 Mill per kWh
Regulation and Frequency Response	✓		✓	1.0 Mill per kWh
Operating Reserves	✓		✓	1.0 Mill per kWh
Energy Imbalance	✓		✓	10¢ per kWh Maximum
Transmission Loss Replacement	✓			3% of Load, Market Price
Dynamic Scheduling				Market Price

Figure 8-9. Summary of ancillary services per FERC *Order* 888.

Open Access Tariff Development

At the time of this writing, about half of the transmission companies that will be required to submit open access transmission tariffs under FERC Order 888 have done so, but many of them filed these tariffs based on the giga-NOPR, so many tariffs will have to be re-filed. As discussed above, the pro forma tariffs required in the order are necessarily generic and less than appropriate for many utilities. Even though all utilities will have filed pro forma tariffs by the time this book is published, these tariffs will be continually modified and perfected as the transition to a competitive marketplace continues.

The key reason for modifying the pro forma tariffs is that these tariffs will apply to retail wheeling transactions when retail wheeling is allowed by the state. Applying the wholesale open access tariffs of Order 888 to the transmission component of a retail wheeling transaction is a change from the giga-NOPR, and it reflects FERC's insistence that it has jurisdiction in this area. This is significant to end-users because it means that the pro forma tariffs will apply to them. It also means that the transmission and ancillary services prices that will apply to end-users will probably not be similar to those in the pro forma tariffs.

To illustrate this point and to provide an indication of what might eventually be included in tariffs driven by a competitive market, this section will discuss transmission tariffs that were designed to be applicable for retail transactions, but which do not conform to the standards of Order 888. These tariffs give the end-user an indication of the magnitude of prices that might be seen in a retail wheeling environment, if they differ from the pro forma tariffs. In Illinois and New Hampshire, where retail wheeling exists on an experimental basis, tariffs have been filed specifically to provide retail wheeling services. Some of those tariffs are included in Appendix C.

Pacific Gas & Electric.

In 1994, Pacific Gas & Electric (PG&E) entered into a transmission services agreement with Destec Power Services, Inc., a power marketer with cogeneration assets in PG&E's service territory. The purpose of this agreement was to enable Destec to market excess cogeneration capacity that they own in California to potential wholesale purchasers. Although probably not necessary merely for the services intended, this agreement detailed and priced many of the unbundled ancillary services that any shipper would need to purchase. It appears that Destec was interested in having a complete transmission service contract in place in the event retail wheeling became possible before mandatory transmission tariffs were in place.

This contract was developed during the same time that PG&E was developing its own, voluntary open access wholesale transmission tariff. Not long after the Destec agreement was filed, the FERC giga-NOPR on open access transmission was issued, but PG&E continued the development of the tariff, at least with respect to ratemaking. PG&E soon thereafter filed its transmission tariff based on the FERC NOPR and the rates determined for the previous tariff and the Destec contract. The Destec contract, which is not a tariff, may provide a good indication of the type of rates that PG&E could justify in an open market.

In this network transmission service agreement, Destec is able to purchase power from a number of suppliers, aggregate them in a Destec controlled pool, and then sell from the pool to Destec's wholesale (at least for now) customers. Destec will buy power in 100% load factor blocks from variable sources on an hourly basis. Likewise, Destec will sell power in scheduled blocks or follow a customer's variable load on a real-time basis. Destec will also purchase a set of control area services from PG&E which are similar to the ancillary services described earlier in this chapter. In addition to these services, PG&E offered network transmission service based on its embedded cost of the entire transmission system. An additional charge would be added for services requiring distribution facilities.

The PG&E/Destec contract is a complex and very lengthy document that will be somewhat replaced by the transmission service tariff that PG&E must file with FERC, although it addresses many specific issues with respect to the sale of specific Destec QF capacity. The contract specified rates for each service on a per kilowatt-month basis so that the load factor of the power for which the service applies will determine the average per kilowatt-hour rate. For network transmission service, PG&E's embedded cost, postage stamp rate specified in this contract is $1.65 per kilowatt-month, which averages 0.226¢ per kilowatt-hour (kWh) at 100% load factor and 0.322¢ per kWh at a 70% load factor. If the load is off the distribution system, the cost is more than double this amount. The ancillary services defined in the contract and their rates are as follows:

- Automatic generation control (AGC) regulation, which is analogous to the scheduling and dispatch service defined in the FERC NOPR except that it also applies to the utility's dispatch function. The allocated cost for this function is $0.156 per kW-month, or 0.21 mills per kWh at 100% load factor.
- Inter-hour load balancing is analogous to regulation and frequency control service defined by FERC, i.e., it covers the non-meterable fluctuations in load that occur on a moment to moment basis. PG&E correctly charges a variable rate for this service, depending on the magnitude of these fluctuations. On average, this cost should be approximately $0.32 per kW-month or 0.43 mills per kWh at 100% load factor and 0.62 mills per kWh at 70% load factor.
- Spinning reserve is the only type of operating reserve identified in the contract, but a 7% margin is required, so the same function is served. The cost for this service is $4.07 per kW-month of power delivered, so the charge to the customer is 7% of this value, or $0.285 per kW-month.
- Energy deviation requirements is the service analogous to energy imbalances as described above. The cost of nominating power within a 1% bandwidth, compared to the 1.5% bandwidth mandated in the FERC tariffs, is included in the base rate.

Figure 8-10 summarizes these rates for both a 100% load factor block of bulk power and a 70% load factor that may apply to a full requirements delivery, each assuming a 730 hour month. Note that no energy imbalances were assumed, i.e., all delivered energy falls within the allowed bandwidth so that no penalties are assessed. Note that the total rate for transmission service can be as low as 3.3 mills per kWh, depending on load factor. This is consistent with the rates for transmission expected using a postage stamp method for a system as large as PG&E's. Note that for some of these services, such as the spinning reserve, Destec has the option to purchase the service from a third party, so some costs may actually be lower once the market becomes more competitive

Northern States Power.

Northern States Power (NSP) filed a general access unbundled transmission tariff with the FERC in October of 1993 in response to an increased level of off-system wheeling through its system. NSP's tariff proposed separate pricing for certain ancillary services, including reactive power, load following, and frequency control and load dispatching. FERC rejected the proposed charges for reactive power, load following and frequency control

Service	$ per kW	¢ per kWh* 70% LF	100% LF
Transmission	$1.65	0.322	0.226
Distribution	($3.37)	(0.659)	(0.461)
Auto. Gen. Control	$0.156	0.030	0.021
Spinning Reserve	$0.285	0.055	0.039
Inter-hour Load Balancing	$0.32 (Average)	0.062	0.043
Total Transmission Rate	$2.39 per kW	0.469¢ per kWh	0.329¢ per kWh
Total Distribution Rate	$4.11 per kW	0.806¢ per kWh	0.564¢ per kWh

* Assumes a 730 hour month.

Figure 8-10. Summary of transmission service rates in the PG&E/*Destec agreement.*

because NSP lacked the proper cost justification support. It did, however, allow a charge for load dispatching. Despite FERC's rejection, the proposed cost can help estimate the price for unbundled products in a competitive market. Prices from this case include:

- Frequency control and load dispatching: Analogous to FERC's definition of "scheduling and dispatch services," NSP was allowed to charge $0.87 per kW-year. For a customer with a 70% load factor, this charge would be 0.014¢ per kilowatt-hour.
- Reactive power: NSP's proposed rate was $3.40 per kVAR per year. For an average load with a 70% load factor and a 90% power factor, this charge would be only 0.03 mills per kWh. While this is not unreasonable compared to existing reactive power charges, it was not fully justified with specific fixed and variable costs required to support the rate from a traditional embedded cost ratemaking methodology, in FERC's opinion.
- Load following: NSP proposed a rate of $1.35 per kW-year, or 0.022¢ per kWh at 70% load factor and 0.015¢ per kWh at 100% load factor. FERC approved this rate.

- Transmission losses: FERC rejected NSP's proposal to charge non-native shippers for transmission losses at its incremental costs and native customers on an average cost basis. This was one of many FERC rulings on comparability of service. FERC now would accept the incremental pricing proposal, but it would be the same for native and non-native customers.
- Transmission: For the transmission service itself, NSP originally only proposed a firm, presumably point-to-point rate of 4.3 mills per kWh. This rate was rejected in favor of a 1.5 mills per kWh non-firm rate, bringing it more in line with expected transmission costs. However, this rate is still not NSP's filed tariff rate.

		¢ per kWh*	
Service	**$ per kW**	**70% LF**	**100% LF**
Firm Transmission	—	0.614 est.	0.430
Non-firm Transmission	—	(0.214 est.)	(0.150)
Frequency Control and Load Dispatching	$0.0725	0.014	0.010
Reactive Power**	$0.283 per kVAR	0.005	0.003
Load Following	$0.1125	0.022	0.015
Total - Firm	—	0.655¢ per kWh	0.458¢ per kWh
Total - Nonfirm		0.255¢ per kWh	0.178¢ per kWh

* Assumes a 730 hour month.
** Assumes a 90% power factor.

Figure 8-11. Proposed Northern States Power transmission tariff rates.

These rates would sum to a firm transmission rate of 0.655¢ per kWh for firm transmission service, which appears to be somewhat high—again, this is not NSP's filed transmission rate, however. The non-firm total rate of 0.255¢ per kWh for a 70% load factor appears to be more reasonable (see Figure 8-11).

Illinois Power.

Illinois Power offered the Illinois Municipal Electric Agency (IMEA), a wholesale customer, an unbundled transmission rate schedule as part of a new interchange agreement. As with the Destec/PG&E agreement, the contract was structured as a tariff that could be used in the event transmission was offered as a separate service. Actually, this schedule was developed in preparation for the experimental retail wheeling program that was implemented in May 1996. Although this was written as a transmission tariff, it was actually only an attachment to a contract between two wholesale entities. Because the rate was only a contract, FERC only had to approve the agreement without performing a detailed analysis of the negotiated rates. Therefore, the rates for the various unbundled services would not necessarily pass FERC's scrutiny, even though FERC approved the contract in January of 1994.

		¢ per kWh*	
Service	**$ per kW**	**70% LF**	**100% LF**
Transmission (Network)	$0.66	0.129	0.090
Reactive Power**	$0.25 per kVAR	0.004	0.003
Voltage Support	$0.26	0.050	0.035
Load Following	$0.12	0.023	0.016
Operating Reserves	$0.23	0.045	0.031
Total	$1.27 per kW	0.251¢ per kWh	0.175¢ per kWh

* Assumes a 730 hour month.
** Assumes a 90% power factor.

Figure 8-12. Transmission services rates from an agreement between Illinois Power and the Illinois Municipal Electric Agency.

The transmission rate schedule in the Illinois Power/IMEA agreement contained various types of transmission and generation services, that is, it is not a transmission only schedule. The schedule offered a broad variety of various transmission services, such as network transmission, short and long term, firm and non-firm, etc. It also differentiates between transmission through Illinois Power's system, as would be purchased by off-system buyers and sellers, and transmission out of or into the utility, as would be required by a customer served by Illinois Power. It is not clear as to whether this differentiation would be allowed under FERC's more recent comparability of service rules. Prices from this agreement are as follows:

- Network transmission service: One of many different transmission rates, network service was priced at only $0.66 per kW-month, which would be 0.9 mills per kWh for bulk, 100% load factor power and 1.29 mills per kWh for 70% load factor power.
- Reactive power: For a load with a 70% load factor and a 90% power factor, IMEA's rate of $0.25 per kVAR-month would be 0.04 mills per kWh.
- Voltage support: This service was not combined with reactive power support as FERC suggested in the NOPR. This separate cost was negotiated to be $0.26 per kW-month, or 0.5 mills per kWh at 70% load factor.
- Load following: IMEA agreed to pay Illinois Power $0.12 per kW-month for this service, which equals 0.23 mills per kWh at 70% load factor.
- Operating reserves: Spinning reserves were separately priced at $0.14 per kW-month while non-spinning reserves (i.e., quick start reserves) were billed at $0.09 per kW-month. Together, Illinois Power's operating reserve supply service would cost 0.45 mills per kWh at a 70% load factor.

Under this tariff, network transmission service will cost 0.251¢ per kWh to ship 70% load factor power. This rate is consistent with expected transmission rates in the area, which is probably a result of a negotiated schedule.

Detroit Edison.

Detroit Edison filed a retail wheeling unbundled transmission pricing proposal with the Michigan Public Utility Commission in June of 1994 in response to the Commission's experimental retail wheeling program. The total cost for transmission and all associated ancillary services, according to this proposal, would be as high as 3.92¢ per kWh! Consumers Power filed a similar tariff showing equally outrageous transmission rates. Obviously, both utilities were, and continue to be, opposed to the experimental retail wheeling program, and were using these rate filings to show that retail wheeling would not provide the economic benefits promised by advocates.

Detroit Edison's premise was that by unbundling and separately pricing the various services that compromise electric service, the sum of the parts would be greater than the total package. The utility offered an analogy of purchasing a car by buying each part and having the customer perform the assembly. Because an individual buyer's cost for each part is higher than the car manufacturer, according to Detroit Edison, buying a car a piece at a time is more costly. Of course, Detroit Edison failed to recognize that truly unbundled services could be supplied by competitive sources, so the price of each service will drop to the price of the supplier that can provide the particular service most efficiently and economically. Therefore, unless Detroit Edison is the most efficient supplier of all services, the total price of the unbundled services supplied separately should be less than the bundled price.

In its proposed transmission tariff, Detroit Edison listed the following ancillary services:

- Reactive power support
- Instantaneous standby
- Long-term standby
- Reliability assurance
- Redundant service
- Voltage control
- Harmonic mitigation
- Billing service
- Relay backup protection
- Technical support

These services are difficult to match with the ancillary services generally recognized to be associated with transmission service. Some of these, such as relay backup protection, do not appear to be truly unbundled services since they cannot be independently procured from a competitive supplier nor do different customers need varying levels of service. Adding each of these services together, including a large stranded investment fee, resulted in the transmission rate that is an order of magnitude higher than expected. This is an example of why unbundling should be driven by either regulators with respect to monopoly services or by the market with respect to competitive services.

Central Illinois Lighting Company.

Appendix C contains sample tariffs (Rates 33 and 34) used for the Central Illinois Lighting Company (CILCO) retail wheeling pilot program. Unlike the New Hampshire retail wheeling program, described below, these tariff are a "bottom-up" design in that the overall rate paid by the end-user is determined by the sum of the individual components, as will be done with true retail wheeling. Rate 33 applies to industrial end-users with loads greater than 10 megawatts (about eight of CILCO's largest customers) while Rate 34 applies to commercial and residential customers participating in the program.

CILCO selected three towns in its service area in which all customers of all classes were eligible to participate.

Under these tariffs, CILCO provides all ancillary services, distribution, and local transmission (within the CILCO control area), but the customer or its agent is free to select the supplier of energy and capacity to meet the load. Because there is no generic retail wheeling provision in Illinois, the supplier will usually be required to provide delivery to the CILCO control area. Note that the end-user can nominate these supplies to CILCO on an hourly, daily, weekly, or monthly basis. This scheduling flexibility allows the participant to chose suppliers in much the same way it will be able to (and should do) in a fully competitive market.

For industrial customers off Rate 33, the total "bottom up" distribution and ancillary services charge is only 3.4 mills per kWh on a 100% load factor basis. The charges negotiated by the end-user for delivered energy and capacity would then be added to this charge (billing is done separately or through CILCO). Many of the ancillary services, including energy imbalances, were priced according to FERC's Order 888. There is no stranded cost component; therefore, the total rate is the sum of the Rate 33 charges and the competitive energy rate.

For residential customers (Rate 34), the CILCO charge is almost 2.5¢ per kWh, upon which the cost of energy and capacity delivered to CILCO must be added. Some might say that the 2.5¢ charge includes some stranded cost component, but the rate is designed to reflect the utility's added distribution costs required to serve small residential customers. Compared to similar charges from utilities with high stranded costs, this claim appears supportable.

The reader is encouraged to closely review the tariffs included in Appendix C to learn how the many minor issues of electricity delivery under a real retail wheeling program are handled.

Public Service Company of New Hampshire.

Appendix C also contains portions of the tariff filed by Public Service Company of New Hampshire (PSNH) in compliance with the New Hampshire Public Utilities Commission's (NHPUC) retail wheeling pilot program requirements. Unlike the CILCO tariff described above, this program requires a "top-down" approach to ratemaking for the purposes of the pilot program. This approach was taken for this program because of the large amount of stranded costs due to the introduction of retail wheeling. A top-down approach is a straight-forward method for dealing with stranded costs without having to specifically quantify them, as is the focus of controversy in California.

In New Hampshire, as in most states, the issue of stranded investment is still unresolved (see Appendix B for a discussion of this issue). PSNH, at the time of this writing, does not want to allow anything less than full recovery of all stranded costs. Meanwhile, the NHPUC and most retail wheeling participants expect some sharing of stranded cost liability by the utility shareholders. Therefore, rather than admit less than 100% recovery, PSNH agreed to give retail wheeling pilot program members a "participation incentive credit" of 10% off the total existing rate. Of course, PSNH has no real desire or need to give customers an incentive to participate in retail wheeling, and this credit is really part of that utility's sharing of its stranded costs.

The next step in the development of the New Hampshire retail wheeling pilot program rate was the determination of the portion of the existing rate that made up the market price of energy and associated capacity. After considerable deliberation, the NHPUC determined that 3.1¢ per kWh of PSNH's existing rate, on average, was energy and associated capacity. Therefore, pilot program participants must pay to PSNH their existing rate, minus the 10% incentive credit, minus 3.1¢. The resulting rate constitutes the distribution charge, ancillary services charge, and stranded cost recovery. This top-down approach, where the rate is determined by subtracting the more readily definable components from the existing rate, was easier in this case than developing from scratch the cost of the remaining components individually, especially the stranded cost component.

The major problem with the top-down approach is that it depends heavily on the agreed-upon forecast of the market price of power to determine the utilities' level of stranded investment. Obviously the utilities have an incentive to under-predict the market price of power and therefore show large stranded investment, which will be rolled into the distribution tariff. The potential impact of this underprediction is vividly illustrated by the current situation in the New Hampshire pilot program where three large nuclear plants are expected to be unavailable just as the pilot program begins. This event, which was unforeseen during the determination of the pilot program market price of power forecast has the potential to drive actual market prices well above those that were forecasted, thus eliminating any profit potential for competitive suppliers. In fact, all suppliers expect to lose money on their power sales, but they have decided that the learning experience of the pilot program more than compensates for this loss.

To illustrate the pricing methodology of the PSNH pilot program tariff, assume a commercial customer pays 12.0¢ per kWh which is about average for New Hampshire commercial customers. Subtracting the participation incentive credit and the assumed cost of energy, the commercial customer will pay PSNH (12.0 - 1.2 - 3.1) = 7.7¢ per kWh for all services except energy and the transmission costs to get it to the utility. Considering that some competing suppliers were offering energy prices as low as 2.5¢ per kWh, this commercial customer may see a rate of 10.2¢ per kWh, which is only a 15% reduction in rates. Clearly, the top-down approach favors utilities while the bottom-up approach favors end-users. Fortunately, the top-down approach should only be used during the transition period to full retail wheeling, since unbundling will necessarily lead to the pricing of each component separately.

Chapter 9

Coordinating Power Supplies

In the retail wheeling purchasing schematic presented in Figure 5-1, the step following the decisions of which services are needed is that of shopping the market for those services and putting them all together. In a vertically integrated industry, the rebundling of the various unbundled products and services was done by the native utility, even if they did not realize it. One thing that can be said about the vertically integrated monopoly, it made buying power easy. Now it will be up to the end-user to perform many of the functions that the utility performs when delivering the final product to the consumer.

The subject of this chapter is the rebundling of the separately purchased energy, capacity, transmission and ancillary services to provide a facility or group of facilities the reliable power supply that end-users are accustomed to. This is not an easy task, although there will be plenty of sources for this service. Some end-users will decide to take more control of their energy purchases and perform much of this rebundling service themselves, especially if the load is such that matching supply with demand is relatively straight-forward. How this can be done will also be discussed, although much of the hardware and software involved has yet to be adapted for the end-user. This chapter will also review who the potential suppliers for all these services might be and where the shopper can go to find out what the prices for those services are. Finally, how the actual transaction takes place and the billing required to settle the accounts at the end of the day are also discussed. Even a sample of what an end-user's electric bill of the future might look like is included.

Rebundling Unbundled Components

Rebundling refers to the purchase of various combinations of energy, capacity, transmission and ancillary services to meet the real-time power needs of a particular facility. This is a four faceted issue. First, the end-user must decide, generally, which types of unbundled products described in Chapter 8 must be purchased. Certainly energy must be purchased, and in most cases, so must some degree of capacity. This is a question directly related to the interruptibility of the load and thus the firmness of the supply, which is discussed later. Unless the energy and capacity are to be purchased from the local distribution company or the native utility, the end-user must also access transmission, which will involve dealing with the transmission company or regional transmission group as well as the local distribution company. If an end-user plans to buy energy and capacity from any entity other than the native utility, distribution services will also be required, unless the end-user is taking service at a transmission level voltage.

The more difficult question is which of the ancillary services will be required:

Energy Imbalances: As described in Chapter 8, the end-user will be required to arrange for energy and capacity supplies to meet and follow the demands of the load. If the mismatch between the amount of energy purchased and that which is taken is within the bandwidth allowed (1.5% per the FERC open access tariffs), the end-user may either set up an energy banking service with the native utility or local distribution company, or the mismatched energy may be purchased from the native utility. The cost for the latter will be a margin above that utility's incremental cost of generation, although in the future most local distribution companies will probably not have their own generation. The better solution is to set up a banking service, which is accommodated in the FERC transmission tariffs, that will absorb and supply meterable mismatch. At the end of some period, such as a month or a year, this account will be zeroed by either purchasing or crediting the deficiency or excess level of energy in the account.

If the mismatch between scheduled purchases and actual demand exceed the bandwidth, a penalty rate will be imposed. This penalty is currently set at the maximum FERC emergency rate of 10¢ per kilowatt-hour, but it may be even higher in the Stage Two tariffs, and justifiably so. Therefore, it is imperative that the end-user ensure that energy nominations fall within the energy balance bandwidth so that this service is never required. In many cases, the 1.5% bandwidth will not be adequate to accommodate expected but unscheduable spikes in demand. In such cases, a broader bandwidth will have to be purchased for a greater price. For example, an arc-furnace load will require the flexibility to subject the system to large swings in demand without notice. Since this load cannot be followed by the off-system supplier, the local distribution company will be forced to accommodate this load. This will require a larger bandwidth and a banking account that is somewhat more active. Nonetheless, the load should still be able to accurately nominate the total energy requirements so that the native utility is not actually supplying or absorbing any energy when the accounts are settled.

Therefore, virtually all users will be required to purchase some energy balancing services from the local interconnected distribution or transmission company. For most loads, the cost of this service will be included in the distribution or transmission charge, unless a greater bandwidth is required to accommodate load swings that cannot be accurately scheduled or nominated.

Transmission losses: All shippers, whether it be the end-user or the supplier, must compensate the transmission or distribution company for real and reactive losses on the system due to the power being shipped. For now, these losses are fixed at 3%. Although this is a required service associated with a specific transmission service, it is considered a separate and unbundled service because it can be procured from various sources.

Scheduling, System control, and dispatch: As discussed in Chapter 8, the scheduling and dispatch of generation or dynamic scheduling are not services ancillary to transmission but are actually part of the coordination service to be discussed in the next section. The operation of the transmission system, which is the function to which FERC is referring, is not an unbundled service in that it must be supplied by the transmission company, and every shipper must pay a share of the costs. Therefore, all end-users must purchase this service, but the cost is included in the basic transmission service rate.

Regulation and frequency response: The instantaneous compensation for the difference between the level of energy used and that scheduled or nominated, like the meterable energy imbalance function, will usually be supplied by the local distribution company and all end-users must purchase it. As with energy imbalances, the cost to provide this service should vary depending on how much a load fluctuates. That is, the greater the load following requirements of a particular load, the greater the share of the costs of providing this service should be. Unfortunately, the cost of providing this service, as differentiated from providing all other services such as voltage support, is very hard to determine. Therefore, the cost has been fixed in the pro forma tariffs. In the future, however, transmission and distribution companies will want to charge separate rates for different levels of fluctuation. This is required to ensure that each end-user pays for its true cost of service. Indeed, it does not make much sense to unbundle this product, since all users must purchase it and it must be supplied by the distribution or transmission utility, unless the amount of load following service varies by end-user. As with energy imbalances, the end-user with the most predictable and constant load will pay the least cost for this service. For now, however, this cost is fixed as is the decision of whether the end-user must buy it.

Operating reserves: Operating reserves are like transmission losses in that all end-users will have to pay for their share, but the service is sold separately because multiple suppliers will be able to provide the service. While the decision of from whom to buy operating reserves is open, and discussed later on, the decision of whether to buy it is not.

Voltage support and reactive power: For now, in the pro forma tariffs, all end-users are required to pay their share of the cost to support the voltage in the local control area, but the end-user has some choice of who will provide the service. In the future, end-users will be able to select varying levels of some service, especially reactive power, since every end-user has differing requirements. For example, an end-user with a self-corrected power factor (e.g., using capacitors installed at the plant) should not have to pay the same for this relatively bundled service as an end-user with a large reactive power draw.

For now, the end-user must pay a fixed rate for these services as part of transmission or distribution service. Voltage support, with respect to the generation resources that the local utility must run to maintain grid voltage, will continue to be a fixed cost service that each end-user will have to pay for. For other voltage support services and for reactive power compensation, the end-user will have more control. If the system that feeds the end-user's load is relatively "stiff," i.e., changes in the end-user's load has minimal effect on grid voltage, that end-user should not have to pay for additional distribution voltage support, and the reactive power charge should be based entirely on the reactive power absorbed by the load. On the other hand, if the system feeding the load is weak, for example the load is at the end of a long distribution radial, the end-user should pay for those devices that are required to support the voltage at the delivery point. In this case, any change in the end-user's load will probably have a significant effect on line voltage.

In summary, with respect to which unbundled services an end-user must buy, the nature of the load is a primary driver. Based on present FERC definitions of ancillary services, every end-user will also have to buy an energy imbalance service and load following from the local transmission or distribution company. The end-user will also be required to buy transmission loss compensation, reactive power and voltage support, and operating reserves (unless the load is interruptible) from some source. In the future, the level of energy imbalance service, load following, voltage support, and reactive power compensation required will depend on how much the particular load requires, where as now those levels are fixed. If not required, the end-user will not have to pay for reactive power compensation, energy imbalance service, or operating reserves if those services are not specifically required.

The second facet to the rebundling issue is the level of firmness. Once the end-user has a full understanding of the interruptibility of the load, it can buy matching quantities of firm and non-firm power. In order to minimize cost, the end-user should not buy power that is more firm than required, and there will eventually be many degrees of firmness. For absolutely critical power needs, firm power should be purchased. For non-firm loads, the level of notice required to interrupt the load can be matched with the notice requirements offered by the supplier, although a perfect match may be difficult to find. For fully interruptible loads, spot market power should be purchased to ensure the lowest cost.

Another option with respect to firmness is to arrange for backup power to complement non-firm power. This is a question of economics. If the combined cost of non-firm and backup power is less than that of firm, spot market power could be purchased for firm loads along with a certain number of hours of backup demand per year. For example, assume an end-user has 10

MW of firm power requirements with a load factor of 70% so that monthly energy purchases are 5.11 million kilowatt-hours per month. The going price for firm power is 3.5¢ per kilowatt-hour (kWh) while the spot market is hovering around 1.8¢ per kWh on average, the price will fluctuate during on-peak and off-peak periods. Backup capacity is available on the open market for $5.00 per kW for 100 hours per year. The end-user performs a transmission capacity study and discovers that spot market power should be available from multiple suppliers during all but peak load times when a certain local generator is out of service. Given the capacity factor of that unit, the end-user determines that this should be no more than 40 hours per year. The average cost for the backup capacity is 0.978¢ per kWh ($5.00 into 730 hours divided by 0.7 for load factor). The total for essentially firm power is then 0.978 + 1.80 = 2.778¢ per kWh, which is substantially less than the 3.5¢ firm rate with the same reliability. In this scenario, the end-user saves almost $37,000 per month using a combination of non-firm power with backup capacity. The end-user has rebundled two separate products to create a bundled, firm product.

The third facet of rebundling is load factor. The end-user should always consider whether buying separate blocks of power at different load factors will be less expensive than buying full requirements power from a single supplier. For this example, assume the same load as above. The load profile study shows that the load evenly fluctuates between 4.0 MW and 10.0 MW every day for an average demand of 7.0 MW. One supplier offers to feed this firm demand at 3.5¢ per kWh, as above, including dynamic scheduling services, i.e., the supplier will track this load with its generator on a real-time basis. The end-user discovers that a large nuclear utility is selling base load capacity at 1.5¢ per kWh at 100% load factor. Shopping the market, the end-user finds a supplier willing to provide dynamic scheduling services for the remaining load, which has a load factor of 50%, for an average of 5.5¢ per kWh. This service costs more because the load is more difficult to feed, but the supplier is also aggregating this with other loads to even out the demand on his generator. Buying 4.0 MW at 100% load factor for 1.5¢ per kWh will cost $43,800 per month, and the remaining 2.19 million kilowatt-hours will cost $120,450. Together, this cost of $164,250 per month will save the end-user $14,600 per month compared to buying the full requirements service at 3.5¢ per kWh.

The final facet of unbundling is the term of the purchases. As discussed above, aggressive end-users will purchase much of their power on the spot market to ensure the lowest price, but others will be encouraged to lock into longer term deals at competitive rates or to ensure a firm supply. As with other aspects of power delivery, terms can also be mixed and matched to optimize costs. In most cases, blocks of low-cost, 100% load factor bulk power will be sold for longer terms to ensure revenue for given capacity, but these blocks may also be available on a short term basis. Spot market power could be used to fill in the load following requirements, although this service could also be arranged for a longer term. Putting the issues discussed above aside, this is obviously a strictly economic issue.

Providing Rebundling Services

Upon learning of the vast array of choices that end-users will face in a competitive power market, many ask: who will do this for me? There is no question that power purchasing will be very complex, more so than gas purchasing and orders of magnitude more so than buying power today. For the purpose of this discussion, the function of rebundling and moving power on the grid will be called supply coordination, based on the label given to this function by PG&E in their direct access proposal. Obviously, this function has been given many other labels, but the concept remains the same. As seen in the discussion of supply coordinators in Chapter 4 and obligations they must perform, most end-users will probably wish to outsource the mechanics of rebundling to suppliers who will offer this service as yet another unbundled service. As we have seen, not everybody will be able to directly access the market and rebundle services, since this will involve arranging transactions on the interconnected transmission grid and thus affecting system reliability and capacity concerns. Transmission companies or grid operators will be allowed to mandate certain performance criteria for supply coordinators to ensure reliability and safety. These grid protocols will mainly ensure that the supply coordinator is able to meet the load requirements of all of its loads on a real-time basis so that the grid is not forced to, and that the supply coordinator has the tools and expertise to receive and understand information relating to generation supplies, transmission, and ancillary services.

As with other services, the end-user will have a range of choices of who will provide supply coordination or rebundling services. A discussion of those options follows.

Native utility or local distribution company.

Chapter 4 included a discussion of the future of the existing vertically integrated electric utilities, which concluded that many utilities will go beyond the functional unbundling required by FERC and divide into separate generation, transmission, distribution, and service companies. While some utilities will stay in the generation business, others will become only regulated transmission and distribution monopolies providing monopoly services and earning a guaranteed rate of return. Beyond this, many utilities will wish to play a greater role in the competitive marketplace and offer some unbundled services to compete with independent suppliers. Note that any competitive service that a transmission or distribution company provides will have to be functionally independent of any monopoly service to ensure that no cross-subsidies exist from the regulated service to the competitive service which might give the utility an unfair edge.

One of the services that local distribution companies will most likely wish to provide is the rebundling or supply coordination service, especially since this is a function that they have essentially been providing for years. These utilities already have much of the needed hardware, software, and expertise needed to perform this function. Therefore, an end-user will be able to receive either bundled electricity service from the local utility, just as is being done now, or the utility could provide the supply coordinator function as a separate, unbundled function. There is little doubt many end-users, especially customers with small loads, will find it easier to continue to purchase power as before and simply continue to take bundled service. While this may be the easiest choice for the end-user, it will also be the most costly. As with just about anything else, the more the end-user puts into taking control of power costs, the greater the return.

There is no reason to believe that a local distribution company could not offer a separate supply coordination service at a price competitive with other suppliers of this service. Companies that were once or still are regulated utilities tend not to do well when suddenly placed in competitive markets, such as was the case in the independent power generation industry. This is unfortunate because the majority of the electrical power systems expertise in this country still resides in the regulated utility industry rather than in the competitive markets, which are largely populated with experts in other competitive markets. While the end-user will probably spend more money to buy bundled electricity service from the native utility, the end-user should consider using that utility for simply the supply coordination service if it is offered and if it is competitively priced.

Power marketers.

The number of power marketers, both independent and affiliated with regulated utilities, has mushroomed since passage of the Energy Policy Act of 1992. While these marketers entered the business to market wholesale power, to and from existing utilities for the most part, there is very little wholesale activity for the marketers to capitalize upon. That is, wholesale buyers and sellers are already good at buying and selling power, and only those utilities that have down-sized to the point where they lost their bulk power sales force are utilizing marketers. The real reason that so many entities have become marketers is to cater to the new and much larger retail power market, which is very inexperienced at buying and selling power.

Power marketers will primarily make money in one of two ways: either they will own actual generation assets and will sell the power from those assets on the market, or they will put together various power products combined with financial products (see Chapter 10) and offer the end-user a rebundled product. That is, the marketer will offer supply coordination services as a key value added service. In fact, when PG&E first defined the role of the supply coordinator, they were thinking of power marketers as the primary entity that would fill this role.

On the positive side, power marketers will be able to offer attractive bundled packages by creating innovative deals for end-users. For example, a power marketer that is also a gas marketer will be able to offer a service where the price of one commodity is based on the other so that the two can be arbitraged. Depending on the financial wherewithal of the marketer, the rate offered to the end-user could be tied to the product that the end-user manufactures so that power does not become tied directly to the bottom line as it is now. These and other financial products will be discussed in the following chapter. The success of many power marketers will depend on their ability to put together creative deals for end-user customers.

On the negative side, power marketers have a product to sell, so they may not be the best choice for a service that involves rebundling products from competitive suppliers. There is no question that power marketers should be considered as suppliers for any or all of the unbundled products described in Chapter 8, but because marketers take title to power and then resell that power to the end-user, they make money only when that power is being sold. Therefore, the end-user that buys a bundled product from a marketer is buying that marketer's power, which may or may not be the lowest cost product on the market. Of course, some marketers will offer the rebundling service as a separate service, but most will be in the business of selling power and should be considered a supplier rather than a coordinator of suppliers.

Power brokers, agents, and consultants.

The latest breed of power coordinators on the scene are independent power brokers, buyers agents, and energy consultants that plan to offer the rebundling and supply coordination service on behalf of the end-user. While power marketers represent the seller of power (which will often be the marketer itself), the power broker will act on behalf of the buyer in shopping the market for low cost power.

On the negative side, power brokers often do not have the required expertise to properly represent the buyer in a complex marketplace. Many of these companies are just starting to develop and are usually staffed with ex-utility operators or commodity brokers from other industries. Seizing on the opportunity, many agents do not have the experience, expertise, or functional capability of properly coordinating multiple suppliers and multiple loads. The end-user is cautioned to carefully screen any potential third party coordinators to ensure that their needs can be met. Also, if the end-user wishes to arbitrage its electricity costs with another commodity or to hedge those prices using financial services, these services will usually have to be supplied outside the structure of the power deal itself.

On the positive side, power brokers, agents, or consultants offer something that no other supply coordinator can: objectivity. Since power brokers do not actually take title to the power, they merely match buyer to seller so they do not have a stake in the sale of any product from any specific supplier. Instead, the agent's only interest is to get the lowest possible price for the end-user. Whereas power marketers will make money in the margin between the price paid for power and price sold, and their rebundling service fee will be in that margin, brokers and agents will charge only for the supply coordination service and pass all other costs directly on to the end-user. This charge will usually be based on the commodity, e.g., a fixed rate per kilowatt-hour, but an hourly or monthly fee structure is also possible.

Another key advantage to using a third party broker or agent is that the end-user can retain as much control of his power purchasing function as he wishes. An end-user may wish to negotiate his own deal with a specific bulk power supplier based on whatever leverage, including arbitrage, he has with that supplier. For example, an aluminum smelter may wish to tie its power rate to the market price of aluminum and pass that risk on directly to the supplier. Or an end-user may have a long-time relationship with a certain supplier that he may wish to maintain. The end-user then uses his supply coordinator to procure transmission and other ancillary services with which the end-user has no familiarity. The supply coordinator will also be responsible for nominating the previously negotiated bilateral contract to the grid operator or transmission company. In this way the end-user can involve himself as much as he wishes in his power supply function and leave the hard part to the experts. While some power marketers may also provide this flexibility, most will want to offer a bundled product and take total control of the rebundling function.

End-user as supply coordinator.

The ultimate in retaining control of power purchases, which is the end-user becoming his own supply coordinator, is an option available to many larger end-users, especially those with multiple facilities. For an end-user to become its own supply coordinator, it must be willing to make the necessary investments in equipment and staffing to operate a 24-hour control center. For those industries where power is an integral part of the processes performed at the facilities, or for those companies that have many large loads, performing the rebundling function in-house may be the most economically favorable option. This may be especially the case considering that the end-user still has the option of farming out some functions while retaining others. The details of operating a control center, whether done by the end-user itself or by a third party, is the subject of the next section of this chapter.

Operating a Control Center

This section will outline some of the factors to consider when setting up a supply coordination or rebundling function by an end-user or by a third party on behalf of an end-user. Because the competitive retail electricity market is still developing, it is impossible to exactly prescribe the type of hardware, software, and personnel which will be required. However, some fundamental services and functions will have to be developed and some infrastructure can be defined at this stage. The reader is cautioned that this is an area where developments in technology occur quickly and where those developments can have a significant impact on how such a service will be created.

The supply coordinator service can be created for a single plant, but it is most efficient if built to serve the needs of multiple loads. These loads can either be a single company's many facilities or they can be diverse loads from various industries, which is favorable since the more diverse the load, the greater the cost-effectiveness of the supply coordinator function. The various loads fed by a singe control center do not have to be in the same geographical region. A single control center, using modern telecommunications technology, can control the minute-by-minute power demands of loads throughout the country. Flexibility, however, is increased for those loads that are close enough to each other to readily wheel power from one to another. Although the wheeling is mostly on paper, retail wheeling does require a physical transmission interconnection, and wheeling charges under any pricing methodology can become prohibitive if distances become great.

The functions that are involved in providing rebundling and supply coordination services are as follows:

Energy management system.

The first function that a power control center operated by or on behalf of a certain end-user should contain is an energy management system, or EMS. This function only applies to those end-users that have more than one self-generation unit, such as a cogenerator. An EMS function is similar to a utility's economic dispatch function in that it determines which generator should run and to what level based on the economics of the unit. The first step is to determine unit commitment, i.e., deciding which units should run at all. In most cases, a generator should run a good percentage of the time in order to recover the fixed costs of the unit. In some cases, a generator must run because the steam output from the generator or its boiler is needed for a process. There are also other technical, economic, and legal reasons for either running or not running a machine. Therefore, it is up to the end-user or operator of the unit to decide how sophisticated to get in deciding how to model the economics of a machine.

If a unit must or should run, which is usually the case, only the incremental cost of operating the unit needs to be considered in an energy management system. The incremental cost of running a unit is almost entirely fuel, and some utilities base unit dispatch ent[illegible] fuel costs. If the other factors that influence when and whether a unit [illegible] down to an economic decision, these factors can be [illegible] to the model. Only when non-economic decisions co[illegible] technical need to operate a unit even when othe[illegible]ces of power and steam are available, does the mode[illegible]

If the end-user can develop an economi[illegible]e *true* incremental cost of running the unit is, taking [illegible] costs, then this number can be compared to other [illegible]ice of power. This requires converting the true cost t[illegible] to the price of power. That is, at what price for electri[illegible] to the entire operation to shut down or throttle dow[illegible] power

Last 2 lines on p. 189: Selections are made based on more than just economic incentives (ratio) of power to be supplied.

off-site? An energy management system can run this model on a continuous basis and send a signal to automatically throttle the units it operates to optimize the entire system's incremental cost based on the total electrical demand of all the plants. Obviously, the more generating units a company has, the more benefit this system can provide to the end-user.

Given a certain total demand of all the end-user's loads and a given level of generation, the EMS will match generation to load selecting the most optimum mix of generation regardless of where that generation is. If the end-user's units are dispersed among plants around the country, this function may still be applicable, although the power from one generator may have to be transmitted over a significant distance to another facility. In this case, the EMS must also take into account transmission costs and capacity. Incorporating transmission information into a supply coordination system is discussed below.

In most cases, an end-user's total generation capacity is less than the total load of all the end-user's facilities. In this case, off-system power must also be purchased. But even if the generation capacity matches the load, the control center should also compare the incremental cost of generation developed by the EMS to the price of power on the open market, which is discussed below. If the amount of generation is greater than the load, the end-user can become a supplier to the open market and submit the incremental price (or greater, as the market will bear) to the open market. If the incremental price to generate power cannot be recovered by selling the power because it is below the market price, the generation should be backed down as far as economically feasible.

This EMS function applies to all supply coordinators that own generation whether it be a utility, which already has this function in the form of economic dispatch, a power marketer, or an end-user. A power broker or agent will not own or control actual generation assets, so this function will not be required.

Market price signals.

Whether a supply coordinator has generation or not, the cornerstone to the rebundling function is the receipt of market signals from various suppliers. The supply coordinator should tie into as many suppliers as possible to increase the number of choices and competitive bids to feed the various loads. The supply coordinator's control center will receive these pricing signals through real-time information networks and communications channels. The suppliers will provide hourly and sub-hourly spot market prices and longer term pricing offers for all the various products that the supplier has to offer, including firm and non-firm energy or capacity and ancillary services. The supply coordinator then analyzes these offers, compares that to the load that must be fed, and matches supplier to load with the most economical combination of products and services (see Figure 9-1).

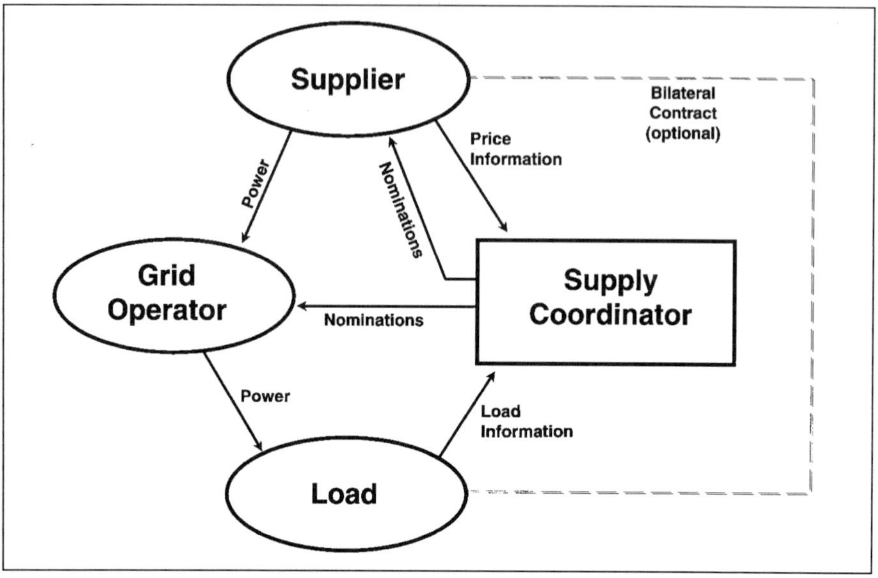

Figure 9-1. The supply coordinator receives pricing signals from the supplier and load information from the end-user, matches them, and then nominates the transaction to the supplier and the grid operator (transmission company).

If the end-user has its own generation, as described above, the incremental price of this generation will be constantly compared to these market pricing signals. Because this incremental price reflects the decision price of whether to generate or not, the supply coordinator can replace self-generated power with system power, even on a very short term basis, if market prices are lower than the generator's incremental cost. This combination of self-generation and spot market pricing will provide many end-users with very low power costs.

The hard part of all this is how to match all the various supply options with constantly changing loads. Additionally, transmission availability must be factored in. Before this is reviewed, some discussion of where the market pricing signals will come from is warranted.

Many utilities and power marketers have been attempting to establish an electricity market price index upon which wholesale purchases could be based and for which the New York Mercantile Exchange contract for electricity futures could be based. Unfortunately, the spot market for wholesale power existed only between dispatchers on the telephone, so there was no centralized market point that developed a transparent price that could be monitored. Some publishing companies calculated indices based on production cost data from FERC Form 714 filings (system lambda data, which reflects a control area's incremental production cost). This was a relatively accurate barometer of market price because most utilities involved in wholesale trades used incremental production costs as the basis for wholesale trades. In other words, there was no market price index because there was really no market price to report.

In late 1994, a group of California utilities and power marketers created a true market index that would track the trading prices of wholesale power between California and the northeast at the California-Oregon border. This index, called the COB index, reports daily firm energy prices, daily non-firm energy prices, and monthly firm energy prices. While a tremendous amount of power flows through the COB, the number of actual transactions (at least on a spot basis) are relatively few, so the value of the COB index as a general market index is limited. However, the creation of this index spawned other true market indices at other locations so that, when combined, a good assessment of the going price of wholesale firm and non-firm, off and on-peak power can be made. Dow Jones publishes a daily price index in the *Wall Street Journal*.

While indices can provide information on the going price for power and can serve as a basis for hedging agreements and the like, it is not a true source of market prices upon which a transaction is proposed. The need for a truly transactional bulletin board, at least for hourly spot market power, led to the development of a service called the Continental Power Exchange, or CPEX. CPEX attempts to address the need for a next-hour energy market to replace the "dialing for deals" method of arranging hourly trades among utilities, i.e., one dispatcher calling another until power is found. With the CPEX bulletin board, hourly spot market prices are posted by sellers for hourly non-firm and firm energy and transmission capacity out of the control area. Although the only type of power that is sold on this service is bulk power at 100% load factor for one or four hour durations, the bulletin board is truly transactional, that is, an interested buyer can make the transaction directly on the computer system that supplies the pricing information. The system is automated so that it also locates the least cost transmission contract path from seller to buyer.

CPEX is only available to wholesale buyers at the time, but there is no reason it cannot be adapted to a retail wheeling environment. CPEX is a spot market in itself, but it is not *the* spot market. On the other hand, there will not be one spot market. Instead, supply coordinators will create their own spot markets, and CPEX will be but one of the supply options. Other suppliers will send in price data as well, and these bids will be communicated through transactional systems that will allow the buyer to make a deal directly with the supplier on the system. The computer systems required to access this data while also monitoring load are available now through an adaptation of similar systems developed for traditional utility functions.

The supply coordinator then takes all these sources of market price signals and feeds them into the control center. In one place, the end-user or his marketer or agent has access to as many supply options as are available from the suppliers. Of course, suppliers will be more than willing to provide these telecommunication links to supply coordinators, whether they be large end-users or agents representing many end-users. Therefore, hundreds of spot markets will develop around the country as suppliers bid prices to the many supply coordinators and the buyers choose the lowest cost bid. Finally, true competition exists because many suppliers compete directly for sales to buyers rather than bidding into a single centralized system.

Transmission.

Once the supply coordinator has tentatively selected the low cost supplier or a combination of them based on the price signals sent to the control center, the next step is to ensure that adequate transmission capacity exists and to arrange for the capacity itself. This can be done one of two basic ways. First, the end-user or supply coordinator can go to the regional transmission group (RTG), or independent system operator (ISO) to both determine where transmission capacity exists and to arrange for short and long term, firm and non-firm transmission capacity. The RTG or ISO will provide these services, once retail wheeling is available, in one place rather than requiring the shipper to separately contact each involved transmission company.

Although the transmission provider could be contacted by the shipper to arrange for transmission services, this process may be too time-consuming for most purchases, and would not be an option for spot market transactions. In most cases, therefore, the supply coordinator will use the newly developed open access same-time information system (OASIS) as required by FERC. OASIS is a bulletin board for transmission (but not energy and capacity) that is developed by the transmission companies, probably in concert with the RTG or ISO. The end-user or supply coordinator will first access OASIS to determine whether there is adequate *incremental* transmission capacity to carry out the transfer of energy or capacity from the supplier to the end-user. The information supplied by the RTG or ISO on OASIS must include transmission capacity between control areas and within the control area in which the load is located (although the latter should rarely be a constraint). OASIS will supply the necessary transmission capacity data for each interface, i.e., the interconnections between control areas, on an hourly basis. Therefore, the determination of whether capacity exists can be carried out in time for a next-hour spot market transaction.

The end-user must next decide the terms of the transmission service that are required. This involves evaluating capacity factors, firmness, and the length of the term. If the energy that is to be transmitted is firm, then the end-user will want to arrange for firm transmission, since non-firm transmission will lessen the reliability of the energy supply. Even if the supply is non-firm, transmission capacity that is non-firm will still reduce the reliability of the power, but that may be an acceptable condition. To make the evaluation of whether to purchase firm or non-firm transmission, the shipper must consider the amount of capacity already reserved on the interface and the terms of interruption set forth in the transmission tariff. As with gas transportation, there is no substitute for understanding the transmission tariffs fully. If OASIS indicates that only a small portion of the line capacity is reserved with firm transmission (OASIS need only show firm commitments), the reliability of non-firm transmission will be very high. If the line is already filled with firm capacity, the risk of non-firm transmission is greater, but it may also be the only type of capacity left.

Finally, the length of the term of the transmission capacity purchase should match that of the energy supply agreement. While transmission can be purchased on an hourly basis, if available, in many cases, the end-user will probably be interested in purchasing a block of transmission capacity for a long-term (more than one hour) period. For example, an end-user finds a very low cost block of 100 MW power from a remote supplier for one month. The end-user or his supply coordinator must then arrange and reserve 100 MW of transmission capacity for one month on each system on the contract path. OASIS will indicate whether there is room, and will probably also indicate the price.

The end-user also has the option of purchasing this 100 MW of transmission capacity on the secondary market. OASIS, like the electronic bulletin boards (EBBs) used for gas transportation, will provide a market for transmission capacity released by other shippers. If the gas market is any indication, the price for this capacity should be well below the price for incremental capacity from the transmission companies.

Now that the type of transmission service is determined, the end-user or supply coordinator purchases or nominates the transmission directly over OASIS. There will be no need to make a separate contract for service with the ISO or RTG because the tariff will specify the terms of the service as purchased on OASIS. The cost of the service will also be available on OASIS or through the ISO/RTG based on the FERC regulated tariff filings. Most likely, payment will be made through the RTG or ISO, which will then allocate the total transmission charge among the involved transmission companies based on either a contract path or megawatt-mile methodology.

Although the majority of the transmission purchase transaction occurs through OASIS and bulletin boards, the RTG and ISO will still serve many roles. For one, the RTG will perform long range transmission loading, reliability, and stability studies to determine where existing bottlenecks are limiting transactions and where new transmission facilities are needed. The RTGs and ISOs will also provide a dispute resolution forum for conflicts between shippers and transmission companies over availability, price, or reliability. These services will be paid for by all shippers as part of the transmission charge assessed by the RTG or ISO for all transmission companies.

Matching load and supply.

The primary function that a supply coordinator's control center must perform is to match the low cost suppliers, based on the market signals received and considering available transmission paths, to the end-user's loads not met with self-generation. This function is the heart of supply coordination, yet it is the most difficult to quantify or qualify. Many of the decisions involved in matching supply to load depend on what the end-user wants. Some end-users are willing to stomach the volatility of the spot market to ensure the lowest cost power supply, while others demand price certainty. Some end-users are willing to buy non-firm energy supplies, back them up with separate capacity, and use non-firm transmission when an interface is not filled with firm commitments. Other end-users will only feel comfortable feeding firm load with firm energy from a utility supplier with multiple resources.

Beyond the ... lies with load to minimize cost is an art form ... tiveness. The supply coordinator must con ... offer, e.g., a month, at a below-market pri ... supplementing that power with other produc ... nts from the spot market. The only knowled ... be aware of all the options and how they ad ... ps an example is the best way to explain.

The end-user has a load profile as shown in Figure 9-2. On a daily basis, the facility's demand peaks at 20 MW but averages 17 MW, and during the night, the load falls to 10 MW. The end-user considers the load firm, although 2 MW constitutes critical load that, if lost, would jeopardize the safety of the workers at the plant. Although this load profile occurs daily, the facility has scheduled a two week shutdown in one month. The end-user's supply coordinator is tied to a number of suppliers and spot market sources and the area's RIN. The price for spot market power has been low, so the spread between on- and off-peak power is smaller than usual.

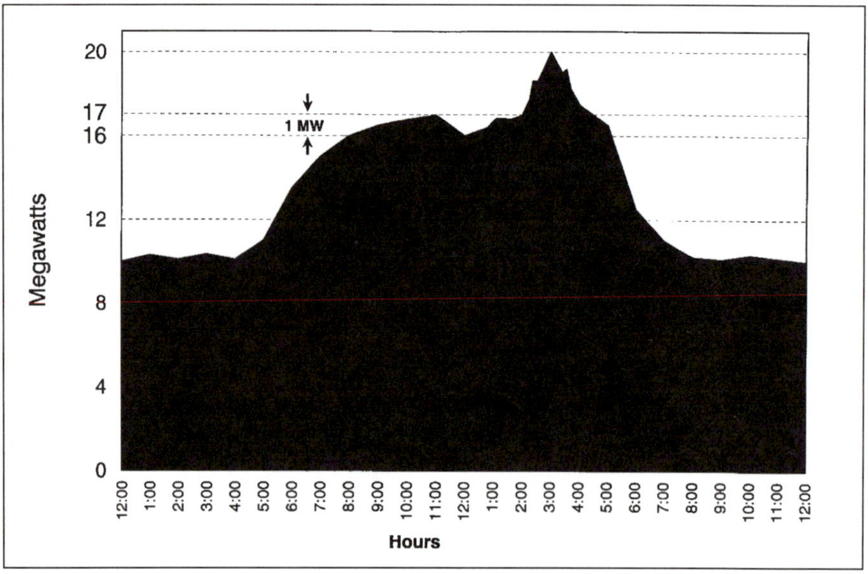

Figure 9-2: Load profile for end-user in example.

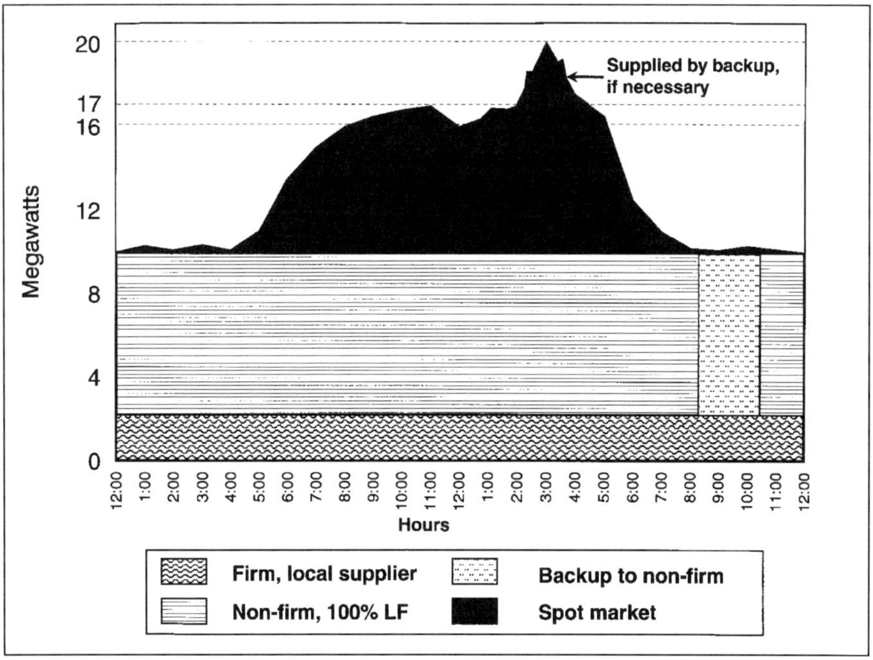

Figure 9-3. Supply options chosen for the example.

First, the supply coordinator arranges for 2 MW of firm supply and transmission from the generation company that was once part of the local transmission company (see Figure 9-3). This is chosen because although the price is higher than other sources, fewer transmission paths reduce the probability of the inability to bring in the firm power due to a physical transmission line outage. Since this load will be running during the plant outage, a one year agreement is negotiated for a rate lower than quoted. Because this power is firm, 100% load factor and local, no transmission, backup, load following, etc. is required.

For the remaining 8 MW demand that is always present, the supply coordinator finds non-firm energy one system away with a one month term; a new supply will be found after the outage. The load factor is 100% and the power is interruptible, so the price is extremely low, almost as low as spot market off-peak power. This block of power should be as low cost as possible because it is the majority of the energy purchased. Spot market power is only slightly cheaper because on- and off-peak differential has been low, so money is saved by buying longer term. Because the risk of curtailment is relatively high, the supply is backed up with capacity that is also one system away. Transmission is arranged through the RIN as firm because capacity on that line is tight, so 8 MW on the interface is reserved for one month. Transmission losses and operating reserves for this 8 MW could be purchased from yet another supplier that specializes in these services if the charges were low enough, but the savings may be minimal with only 8 MW, so losses will be purchased as additional power from the supplier of the 8 MW of energy. Because the load factor is 100%, no load following, energy imbalance, or other ancillary services are required for this block.

The supply coordinator then decides that the remaining power can be best supplied from spot market power because the plant is situated in an area with many interconnections to various suppliers and because the 8 MW of backup capacity reserved for the previous block could be used in a pinch, especially for the 3 MW peak that occurs during the middle of the day. The corresponding transmission must vary as do the sources of the spot power, but non-firm, hourly service is always selected because, if lost, another supplier can be found. Because of the 1 MW load fluctuations during this time (and other times as well), 1 MW of load following and a 1 MW energy imbalance bandwidth is purchased from the local distribution company. Other mandatory ancillary services are purchased from that company as well.

This example illustrates just how complicated rebundling a variety of different services can be, but it also shows how such a scheme is the path to the lowest price power. Also, the services rendered precisely match the services required, so that the end-user is never spending more than necessary by buying more than what is required. This type of purchasing requires a 24-hour staff, the necessary communication and computer equipment, and the required planning, transmission, and accounting software. Suppliers of these systems are available, but all but the largest end-users will probably wish to have these services performed by outside supply coordinators. Some control equipment suppliers are currently developing expert systems that will automate this process. These systems will combine the various supply and transmission parameters in a way to optimize the overall cost. As the market matures and becomes more competitive, such a system will be necessary since the number of suppliers and the variety of options will continue to increase. As the market develops, it will be very hard for a single operator to purchase the optimum combination of services, even if armed with all the information available.

Delivering the power.

The final function that the supply coordinator's control center is to arrange for is the actual delivery of the energy, capacity, transmission, and ancillary services purchased. The actual scheduling and dispatch of both generation and transmission, i.e., the operation of the grid, is performed by the independent system operators (grid operators) or transmission companies. The ISO has the responsibility for ensuring system stability by monitoring voltages and system frequency. For this service, the various reliability standards developed by the utility industry through the North American Electric Reliability Council (NERC) apply. While supply coordinators must be concerned about matching load with supply, providing for backup power during curtailments (or ensuring the curtailment of load), and adequate transmission and generation capacity to meet the demands of their clients, they are not responsible for ensuring overall system integrity.

Once the supply coordinator has made arrangements with the suppliers through bilateral contracts or the spot market and with the transmission companies through OASIS, it must then notify the ISO of the transactions so that they can be scheduled and dispatched. The ISO will use this information to ensure that voltages and frequencies are maintained. The supply coordinator will send this information to the ISO via another communication link. Each transaction will be "nominated" to the ISO (see Figure 9-1). If the ISO determines that a certain transaction cannot be carried out due to system reliability or operational concerns, the supply coordinator will be notified and another transaction will have to be arranged. Of course, enough information should be available to the ISO to avoid getting into these situations.

This example illustrates why the transmission companies and ISOs must be truly functionally independent of any other service supplier. It would be very easy for a ISO with an interest in selling power from its own resources to give those transactions priority over other transactions. This is a case of monopoly power impacting a competitive market. It will be FERC's job to ensure that no single entity retains this level of market power and that all suppliers participate in the market on a level playing field.

Besides nominating each transaction to the ISO, the supply coordinator will also return a nomination to the suppliers selected. The suppliers will take this information and adjust the outputs of their particular generation units to match the nomination received. For generation companies with many facilities, this nomination will be sent to their dispatch center where the nomination will become part of the unit scheduling and dispatch function. Where traditionally the dispatcher of a utility matched generation resources to native load, now those resources will be matched to native load, if any, long term contractual obligations, and outside nominations.

At this point, the process is complete. The suppliers have indicated to the market of available capacity at a given price. Transmission to get that power to the load is arranged because information on capacity is available. And the supply coordinator has selected, purchased, and nominated the supply based on cost and the customer's load. Once nominated, the operators and suppliers can now physically deliver the power to meet the load. The only remaining concern is paying the bills.

Settling the Accounts

The last key function of a supply coordinator or rebundler in the power procurement process is the settling of accounts. Settling accounts refers to both ensuring that the total number of kilowatt-hours used equals the number of kilowatt-hours purchased and ensuring that everyone gets paid for the services provided to deliver those kilowatt-hours. These are both accounting functions, and software has been developed to track accounts automatically as power is purchased, nominated, and delivered on the grid.

Both of these functions are driven by metering. The supply coordinator will monitor on a real-time basis all of the facilities for which it buys power. This information will be provided to the supply coordinator via telemetering from the plant to the control center. The supply coordinator will then know exactly how much power was consumed, including peak demand levels, total energy consumed, and power factor. At the same time, the supply coordinator will receive either directly metered quantities from the suppliers or billing information. In either case, the number of kilowatt-hours must match.

Because of constantly fluctuating loads, however, differences between actual consumption and the ability of a meter to follow the load will result in some mismatch between metered quantities. Most of this mismatch will be absorbed in the energy imbalance function described in Chapter 8. Therefore, the end-user will have to settle the energy imbalance account on a periodic basis by paying for energy supplied in addition to what was nominated or receive a credit for power not taken. In either case, the supplier of the energy imbalance or banking function will charge a fee since the ability to both deliver and absorb energy is a service that it is being provided.

After the energy imbalance account is settled and zeroed, the number of kilowatt-hours purchased and supplied must match the level transmitted. This imbalance will usually not be an issue because transmission pricing will be based almost entirely on capacity rather than energy. There are no variable costs to transmission except for losses. Since losses are fixed at 3%, the imbalances in energy supplied to the transmission company versus that delivered to the end-user must be accounted for in the loss compensation function. All transmission companies realize that actual kilowatt-hour losses cannot be realistically metered and allocated among shippers, so no settling of accounts will be required for this stage.

Once everyone is clear as to how many kilowatt-hours were bought and sold, based on meterable quantities versus scheduled amounts, the remaining task is to settle the billing accounts. Most likely, the supply coordinator will handle all billing, although some suppliers will directly bill the end-user. If an end-user negotiates a power service agreement directly with a supplier, the terms of the agreement may call for the end-user to directly compensate the supplier. These types of direct bilateral contract arrangements must be allowed because it may not always be just money that changes hands. For example, an end-user with gas reserves may "sell" that gas to a generation company in exchange for power. It would be very difficult for the supply coordinator to handle this billing arrangement.

The supply coordinator will have to handle all the billing for all the services that it arranges, however, and for some end-users, that may be the entire bill. Power marketers and utilities that are also acting as supply coordinators may charge the end-user a negotiated amount for the bundled product, much like utilities do today, and then make their profit on the margin between the

MUP Monopoly Utility Power Co.

Billing statement for **WIDGET MANUFACTURING**
MAY, 1995

Metered quantities:	Hours: 744	
Demand:	Previous reading:	001310
	Current reading:	001330
	Multiplier:	x 1000
	Peak Demand:	20,000 kW
Energy:	Previous reading:	00235566
	Current reading:	00245972
	Energy use:	10,416,000 kWh
Billing amounts:		
Demand:	Metered peak demand:	20,000 kW
	x Demand:	$12.50 / kW
	= Demand charge:	$250,000.00
Energy:	Metered energy use:	10,416,000 kWh
	x Energy rate:	$0.0313 / kWh
	Energy charge:	$326,020.00
Other charges:	Basic service charge:	$1,000.00
	Nuclear decommissioning charge:	$0.00012 / kWh = $1,249.92
	Retail taxes:	@ $0.0005 / kWh $5,208.00
Sub-total:		***$7,457.92***
TOTAL BILL:		**$583,477.92**
		Thank you!

Figure 9-4. Typical bill from a traditional utility supplier.

billed amount and the moneys paid to all the various other suppliers. Power brokers, agents, and third party supply coordinators will probably send the end-user an itemized bill with a line item for each unbundled product, including a per-kilowatt-hour charge for the rebundling services. Once the supply coordinator receives payment from the end-user for the billed amount, the supply coordinator will be responsible for ensuring that each supplier gets compensated in turn.

Under traditional ratemaking and utility billing practices, an end-user's bill comprises only four basic components:

- Fixed customer charge: A fixed monthly charge is often assessed to pay for equipment not related to the level of service provided, e.g., metering equipment. For industrial customers, this is usually a very small component of the total bill.
- Demand charge: In theory, the demand charge should cover the utility's fixed costs for equipment required to meet the demand of the load, i.e., the *ability* to feed the load when demanded. Since

this is a function of the peak demand recorded during the billing period (and often for an entire year using a ratchet mechanism), the demand charge is based on metered peak kilowatts (kW).

- Energy charge: Under traditional ratemaking theory, the energy charge should recover the variable costs required to generate the energy used, which is almost entirely the cost of the fuel to generate the electricity. Often times, however, utilities transfer costs to and from energy rates to either encourage or discourage use at certain times. Because the energy charge is based on actual energy usage, it is based on metered kilowatt-hours (kWh).
- Other charges: Public utilities have often been used to collect revenues for costs beyond energy and demand, such as low-income bill assistance, demand-side management programs, etc. This type of social ratemaking is inconsistent with a competitive market place, and those costs will have to be funded from general tax revenues in the future. Many states tax retail electricity sales, however, which can still apply in a competitive market.

Figure 9-4 shows a typical electric bill for an industrial customer fed from a traditional investor-owned, monopoly utility. This sample bill is simplistic in that many utilities used tiered demand and energy rates to encourage high load factors and on- and off-peak rates to encourage off-peak usage. The point is that the series of unbundled products that go into the delivery of electricity are buried in the demand and energy charges because all functions are supplied by a single, vertically integrated company. If the end-user in a retail wheeling world buys bundled power from either the local distribution company or from some power marketers, the electric bill will look the same.

If the end-user utilizes a supply coordinator, the bill may look something like Figure 9-5. Like the sample traditional bill, this one is also simplistic; the list of unbundled services that could go into a month of service to a single customer could get very long. In the unbundled gas industry today, which is less complex than power, some monthly reconciliation reports are small books by themselves. The sample bill of Figure 9-5 is based on the example given earlier in this chapter for a 20 MW customer with a 70% load factor. Each supplier is listed separately, including the monopoly services provided by the local utility. Note that the rebundling fee is added on as a per kilowatt-hour charge, i.e., it is another unbundled service that is part of the overall cost of energy and should be paid from the end-user's energy budget.

Note also that the average price of power dropped from 5.6¢ per kWh to 2.9¢ per kWh. Admittedly these numbers are entirely conjectural, but they are similar to the rates that would be available if retail wheeling were here at the time of this writing. These rates also ignore the potential for significant transition costs due to stranded investment, which is discussed in Appendix B, but these costs will only be temporary and are still unsettled.

Benevolent Supply Coordinator Services Co.

Billing statement for **WIDGET MANUFACTURING**
MAY, 1995

1. Supplier:	Monopoly Utility Generating Co.
Service:	2.0 MW, 100% LF, firm capacity + energy
Rate:	$7.50 / kW-month $0.030 / kWh
Charge:	(2000 x 7.50) + (2000)(744)(0.030) = $59,640.00
2. Supplier:	Jim-Bob's Cheapo Power Co.
Service:	8.0 MW, 100% LF, non-firm energy, plus 3% (0.24 MW) transmission losses
Rate:	$0.016 / kWh
Charge:	(8240)(744)(0.016) = $98,088.90
3. Supplier:	Monopoly Utility Transmission Co.
Service:	8.0 MW, firm transmission (without losses), 100% LF
Rate:	$0.0025 / kWh
Charge:	(8000)(744)(0.0025) = $14,880.00
4. Supplier:	New-pex Spot Services
Service:	Spot market energy + ancillary services
Metered Energy:	2,976,000 kWh (all on-peak)
Rate:	$0.0180 / kWh (Average on-peak)
Charge:	(2,976,000)(0.0180) = $53,568.00
5. Supplier:	Gibraltar Power Inc.
Service:	8.0 MW Backup capacity (No metered energy)
Rate:	$5.00 / kW
Charge:	(8000)(5.00) = $40,000.00
6. Supplier:	Monopoly Utility Distribution Co.
Service:	Load following, voltage support, reactive power, operating reserves
Metered Energy:	10,416,000 kWh
Rate:	$0.001 / kWh
Charge:	(10,416,000)(0.001) = $10,416.00
7. Supplier:	Benevolent Supply Coordinator Services Co.
Service:	Rebundling
Rate:	$0.0015 / kWh
Charge:	(10,416,000)(0.0015) = $15,624.00
8. *Other Charges:*	
Metered Energy: Nuclear Decommissioning Charge:	10,416,000 kWh @ $0.00012 / kWh = $1249.92
Retail Taxes:	@ $0.0005 / kWh = $5208.00
Sub-total:	*$7,457.92*
TOTAL BILL:	**$299,674.82** Thank you!

Figure 9-5. Sample electric bill from a supply coordinator.

Chapter 10

Using Financial Tools

End-users for the first time will have the opportunity to purchase electricity on an open, spot market that is subject to tremendous price fluctuation based on continually varying supply and demand for power. Some end-users will choose to ride the roller coaster of widely variable spot market prices since this is usually the best way to ensure the lowest cost for power. On the other hand, most end-users will want either price certainty or the ability to hedge the risk of an unexpected rise in the cost of spot market power. As with other products newly available to the retail end-user as a result of competition, the necessary financial tools to hedge electricity prices and to manage risk are now available as yet another unbundled product. Like other products, financial services must be considered in the mix of products that make up the total power delivery package.

As competition is introduced into the electricity industry, the electricity itself has become transformed from a product or a service into, for the first time, a commodity. Like any other commodity, such as oil, natural gas, or even pork bellies, electricity can be traded on futures exchanges, sold on option, hedged, resold, arbitraged and otherwise be treated like any other product with liquidity. In fact, electricity may be the ultimate in a liquid commodity because it is entirely fungible and instantly deliverable. On the other hand, it is difficult to trade a product that must be manufactured, transported, and retailed the very instant that it is demanded, but the various market forces and services that drive other commodity markets have reached the electricity industry, and an entirely new set of financial tools are available to its users.

This chapter is intended to introduce the reader to some of the financial products and services that have become available for electricity sellers and buyers as electricity has become commoditized. The focus of this book, however, is on the technical, economic, and regulatory aspects of retail wheeling, and the intricacies of the financial derivatives market could justify a book by itself. Therefore, this chapter should be considered only an introduction to some of these concepts rather than a complete review of the issues.

Managing Risk

Financial products and services should be considered by the end-user to be yet another unbundled service that can be procured from an independent supplier. The general reason for using some of these services is to manage the risk of purchasing an actively traded commodity and to calm the volatility of the spot market for power. In a way, monopoly utilities provide this service as part of their traditional bundled product in that they sell the product at a fixed rate with slow and relatively minor adjustments for fuel costs. The risk of the volatility of actual production costs and wholesale market prices is spread among all the utility's customers. The sheer size of the utility's group of purchasers is by itself a hedge against price volatility. Now, as with all other aspects of electricity service, the end-user can remove this by-product of bundled electricity service and either buy power without it, which will still be the lowest cost option, or to seek risk management services from outside sources.

The intense interest shown by the financial services community in the electricity market and the rapidly increasing number of various financial products provides an indication of the potential size of these markets. It seems that everyone is interested in assuming the risks associated with electricity prices on behalf of the purchasers. As with power marketers, the number of industry entrants is not due to the opening of the wholesale power market, but instead is geared for the prospect of an open retail market. At this point, most financial services companies are marketing those services to power suppliers, such as IPPs, marketers, and utilities. But there is little doubt that, when possible, retail end-users will be inundated with financial service companies looking for clients. For example, many power marketers are hoping to use financial services as the principal value added service that they can offer to retail end-users.

There are two primary financial market tools used to limit risk: the futures market and over the counter cash derivatives. Both tools perform the same function of managing the risk of price volatility by hedging the buyer's position in the market, but while futures are based on standardized contracts, over the counter derivatives are negotiated instruments customized to meet the end-user's needs. This chapter will introduce futures and some financial derivative products that are applicable to the electricity industry, such as forward contracts, options, and swaps. Other alternative buying mechanisms will also be introduced.

The market function of all derivative products, including futures, is to provide the following:

- Price transparency: The ability of market players, i.e., buyers and sellers of the commodity and the futures and options, to know the changes in spot prices of the commodity and the changes in expectations of the *future* price performance of the commodity.
- Risk transfer: The futures market and the over the counter derivatives market is primarily in place to transfer risk from the buyer or seller of the commodity that desires price certainty to an entity willing to take risk for the opportunity to make money on the changes in market prices of the commodity.

- Speculation: While not a goal of the end-user, the derivatives markets provide an opportunity for some to make money on the pure speculation of changing commodity prices.
- Delivery: Although rare, some suppliers or marketers may actually use the derivatives market to sell the commodity, and some end-users or marketers may use the market to buy the commodity.

Usually the buyers and sellers of the derivatives "cash out," or settle derivative contracts rather than deliver or take delivery of the commodity. That is, they either continue to assign the right or obligation to deliver or take the commodity or they offset rights and obligations at a common price.

Derivatives

The financial tools that suppliers, marketers, and end-users use to manage risk, hedge prices, and provide market price transparency can all be classified as derivative products, i.e., financial products derived from the sale of the commodity itself. These financial products, like other unbundled power services, will either be purchased independently from suppliers that specialize in these services, or bundled with the power products themselves. Many power marketers are depending on the creative use of many derivative financial products to provide the value added service that will separate their power from other suppliers. The need to differentiate suppliers of a completely fungible product such as electricity, plus the need for end-users to control price volatility, is the driving force behind the creation of these diverse financial products.

While the number of different financial products continues to grow, the basic derivative products are as follows:

Forward contracts.

A forward contract is the simplest of the derivative products in that it is merely a contract for the obligation to deliver power at some point in the future, depending on the term of the agreement. It is like an option contract, which is detailed below, except that the right to purchase the product at a later date is replaced with the obligation to do so. For example, during the summer, an end-user anticipates a rising market price for power in the winter due to capacity shortages in some northern regions. The end-user purchases a forward contract to buy power at above market rates for the upcoming winter anticipating that this price will be below the market price at the time. While this may result in a windfall for either party, it is little more than speculation and can be very risky. The end-user is better advised to invest that money on options contracts.

Options.

An option is a device that gives the buyer of the option the *right*, but not the obligation, to purchase or sell a certain product or commodity at a future date at a fixed price. For example, a home buyer finds a house that he likes but is unsure if he can sell his current house. To prevent the sale of the new house to another buyer while he puts the old house on the market, he pays the owner a fee or premium to hold the house until the buyer knows whether he can sell his existing house. So the buyer purchases an option to purchase the new house in the next 90 days, say, for $5,000. This price is consideration for the seller to promise not to sell the house during the 90 days. If the buyer can sell his old house, he exercises the option and buys the new house for some previously agreed upon price. If he cannot, the time period lapses, the seller can sell to someone else, and the potential buyer is out $5,000.

This function can apply to the purchase of power as well as houses. The use of options in the commodity market can get rather complex, well beyond the scope of this chapter, but the general purpose is to limit the exposure to price fluctuations by placing floors and caps on the commodity price. Two basic types of option contracts are "puts" and "calls." A call is a type of option that sets a cap to the price paid for power by a purchaser. The end-user (or his marketer) purchases the right to buy power from a generator that is idled because the price for that power is above the current market price. The end-user pays the generator a premium for the option to "call" on that capacity if the market price rises to the price for that capacity. The owner of the generator receives some money even though no power is produced, and the marketer has a source of power at a fixed price if the market rises to a certain price. Although the end-user may never call on the capacity, the cost of the option is like an insurance policy against a high market price for power. In fact, if the option is never exercised, the end-user will be saving money because the market price for power has remained low.

The opposite of a call is a put, in which the end-user agrees to purchase power from a certain supplier if the market price for power drops below a certain value. In this case, the end-user is receiving the premium, which may be in the form of a credit from a power marketer or supplier, in exchange for accepting a floor price for power. If the market price never drops below the floor, the end-user has saved money. However, the end-user takes a risk that prices could go lower. A put and call together form a "collar" around the current market price for power. As long as power never rises above or below the collar, no options are exercised. If power prices on the spot market are volatile, the exercising of the puts and calls will provide a comfortable hedge against fluctuating power prices.

There are many variations on this theme, such as tying the "strike" prices, i.e., the rates that trigger the exercise of the option, to other commodities and indices. To provide the reader with an indication of how many variations exist, below is a partial list of derivative products related to option contracts:

- As-you-like options
- Compound options
- Equity lookback options
- Guaranteed exchange rate options
- Risk reversals
- Deferred strikes
- Average rate options
- Downs and ins/outs
- Exploding options
- Outperformance options
- Synthetic forwards
- Yield spread options

Obviously, it is beyond the scope of this chapter to explain each of these "option options."

Rate swaps.

A rate swap is a device successfully used in the natural gas market as a means to indirectly provide the function of an option collar without requiring the potential for an actual delivery of power. Rather than transferring the risk of price volatility to the supplier, a rate swap transfers the risk to another end-user. This is entirely a financial device in that no supplier is involved directly, so no actual transmission path or means to deliver the power is necessary. Therefore, rate swaps could be created between two end-users in different interconnection regions.

A rate swap requires one end-user that has some sort of fixed price delivery contract and another that has a power supply arrangement subject to price volatility. The former desires lower prices, while the latter enjoys low cost power but desires price certainty and risk hedging. The end-user with the low cost variable priced power pays a premium to the end-user with high cost power to help offset the latter's electricity costs. In return, the end-user with high rates assumes the risk of the other end-user's variable price power and pays any difference from a fixed rate.

This concept is best explained with an example. Figure 10-1 shows two end-users. End-user A has a long-term, high-cost, full requirements contract for firm power from which he cannot get out. Although the price for power is fixed, the rates are high and he needs lower cost power. End-user B has a short term, variable cost contract for non-firm power which is subject to wide price fluctuations. While the cost is low on average, the company's management needs price certainty for budgeting reasons, even at the expense of a higher average cost. Assuming that each party cannot just switch suppliers, the two could agree to a rate swap. End-user A agrees to pay end-user B's electric bill and absorb the risk of price fluctuation. To do this, end-user B agrees to pay end-user A 4.0¢ per kilowatt-hour (kWh). Although this is higher than the 3.0¢ per kWh average, it is a fixed rate. End-user A gets 4.0¢ per kWh to pay a bill that averages 3.0¢ and uses the difference to reduce his 5.0¢ per kWh electric bill to 4.0¢ as well. End-user B is effectively paying end-user A 1.0¢ per kWh to absorb the risk of the variable rate.

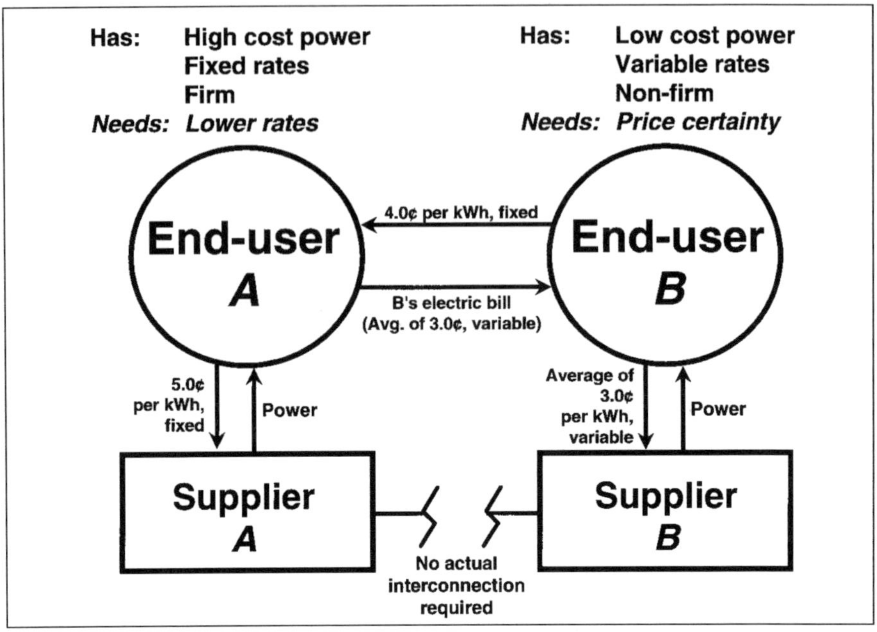

Figure 10-1. A rate swap arrangement between an end-user with a low-cost variable rate and an end-user with a high cost fixed rate.

Of course, end-user B could get almost anyone else to absorb the risk of the variable rate contract for the price paid to end-user A. On the other hand, this same methodology could be used to hedge any type of variable rate contract, including those that vary according to some other commodity. In effect, this is very similar to an option collar in that it transfers risk to another party for a price. Note that swaps are also called contracts for differences, which are used in the British poolco system to hedge price risk.

When reviewing the myriad of financial derivatives, such as options or swaps, the end-user must remember the reason for buying these services is to manage risk. Effectively, the consumer uses financial derivatives to transfer the risk of changing spot market prices to his suppliers or the purchaser of the option contracts, such as a power marketer. As mentioned above, many financial houses and power marketers are eager to assume this risk at no or low cost because where there is risk there is opportunity. Many power marketers hope to be very profitable by correctly assessing and applying risk in the power market. Of course, hedging risk is never free to the end-user. In high risk times, price caps and hedging contracts will exact high premiums, and during low risk and high opportunity times, the end-user could lose much of the benefits of a low market price for power. As said often before, the end-user with the stomach to face a volatile spot market for power will usually end up with lower overall power costs. For end-users that desire or demand price certainty, transferring and managing risk involves a service that costs money.

Electricity Futures

On March 29, 1996, the New York Mercantile Exchange (NYMEX) began the trading of electricity futures at the California-Oregon border (COB) and the Palo Verde nuclear station switchyard in Arizona. The purpose of a futures contract is to provide risk management and price transparency for a tradable commodity. Once electricity could be traded openly, at least on a wholesale basis, a perceived need for a price hedge and a market price index led NYMEX to follow its successes in developing and offering similar contracts in oil products and natural gas. The electricity futures contract is a deliverable contract, at least for exchanges in the Western Interconnect, although most transactions are expected to be for a cash settlement, as is the case with the natural gas futures market.

A futures contract is nothing more than a standardized contract for the purchase and sale of the commodity for delivery at some point in the future. It is similar to a forward contract except for the obligation to deliver at the term of the agreement. Because the price for that commodity in the future is based on interaction between buyer and seller, the price for the contract sets a market price for the commodity. The futures market for electricity will enable suppliers or even end-users to reduce the volatility of the spot market for power by basing the price of the commodity on the market price at the delivery point. Even if the power itself does not actually get delivered to the COB delivery point, the market index that has been created at the COB can be used as a basis for fluctuating prices at other points. If a supplier or end-user wishes to hedge the price for power on the open market, the supplier or end-user can purchase the power on the futures contract, which in affect is buying the power for future delivery. If the price of power increases over the futures value, the buyer of the contract will receive the difference, and if the price is less, the buyer of the future must pay the difference. This way, the buyer of the futures contract, whether it is the buyer or the seller of the power, can be assured of a constant electricity price during the term of the futures contract. This is a means for hedging the risk of volatile prices for power on the open market. In most cases, the futures market is not used as a means to buy the actual commodity, but is only used as a means to hedge the price for an actual sale held somewhere else. That is, the contract for the future delivery of power is rarely exercised to force that delivery, instead the contract is sold, so as to provide the price hedge, and thus relieving the obligation to deliver the actual power.

Besides offering this hedging function, a futures contract also provides the marketplace with price transparency, i.e., a discoverable market price index. The NYMEX futures contract trades electricity on a daily basis, although delivery will be done on an hourly basis (see below). The futures contracts will be purchased and sold by both buyers and sellers of electricity. For every purchase of a future delivery of power, there must be a seller. If the market is flush with excess power, the greater supply (i.e., more sellers than buyers) will force prices down. During capacity shortages, the greater demand (i.e., more buyers than sellers) will force prices up. This direct interaction between buyers and sellers, accommodated by NYMEX, will create a true competitive market for electrical energy as an hourly commodity sold at a price fixed on a daily basis. Thus, a true daily market price for power in the Western Interconnect will develop.

Unlike other commodities, the nature of electricity will probably require the creation of many regional futures contract delivery points in addition to the COB. At a minimum, separate delivery points are required in the three isolated interconnection regions since there is no physical way that power could be delivered to a point in another interconnection region. Even beyond this, multiple delivery points are likely because electricity market prices are much more dependant on regional factors such as local fuel prices and weather than are other commodities. This is simply due to the fact that electricity is consumed in relative proximity to where it is produced. For the price indices developed by the futures contracts to have much validity, the basis for the futures transactions cannot be in an area where there is no correlation to the local price. That is, regional electricity prices fluctuate somewhat independently of each other, so each region will probably have separate contract delivery points.

Futures are a widely used pricing hedge for many other commodities, and NYMEX expects similar success with the electricity futures contract. The contract approved in 1995 for the COB delivery point is for 736 megawatt-hours of power delivered over a monthly period. The delivery rate (if the power is delivered, which most likely will not be the case in 95% of the contracts) will be two megawatts per hour for sixteen on-peak hours, five days per week. This leaves three days per month in which no deliveries will take place, which are scheduled for the third business day prior to the first day of the month. The delivery period can be modified by mutual consent of the buyer and the seller. Prices are quoted in dollars per megawatt-hour, and no further division beyond a penny per megawatt-hour will be allowed. The maximum fluctuation allowable is three dollars per megawatt-hour above or below the previous day's price. Actual power delivery will be subject to reliability and transmission constraints set by the Western Systems Coordination Council, which is the NERC region for the entire Western Interconnect.

Futures contracts are also financial derivatives and are effectively combinations of options contracts. The buyer of a futures contract is purchasing the obligation to exchange dollars for the commodity at a predetermined price, or "strike" price, at some point in the future. The seller has the obligation to either deliver or take delivery of the commodity at the strike price. This is creating a hedge against price volatility by buying a call and buying a put. Instead of resulting in the future obligation to deliver or take delivery, most futures contracts are settled by assigning the contract or offsetting puts and calls. Futures contracts are basically standardized options contracts, as described above, and options contracts are considered the over-the-counter market for futures trading using non-standardized or negotiated contracts.

Alternative Purchasing Mechanisms

In addition to purchasing futures, derivatives, or the power directly, the end-user has other alternatives with respect to purchasing electricity on the open market. Besides providing creative ways to purchase power, these mechanisms can also be used to control risk and to limit exposure to fluctuating power prices. More so than futures or derivatives, these alternatives are very much based on the particular nature of the end-user's business and thus are, by nature, customized for each end-user.

Arbitrage.

An arbitrage is the simultaneous purchase of two commodities so as to profit from the difference in price. With respect to purchasing energy, an end-user that requires multiple forms of energy is in a position to optimize all energy purchases by arbitraging the various energy products. Therefore, the end-user is actually purchasing energy in a more raw form, i.e., by the BTU rather than in the different forms of electricity, natural gas, etc. The arbitrage function is usually set up by an energy marketer or broker that markets both products.

The end-user can take advantage of an arbitrage opportunity in two ways. First, if the end-user has some flexibility with respect to fuel usage, such as using more gas when that commodity is cheaper, then that end-user is taking advantage of the difference in price between energy commodities. Second, the end-user can purchase options or futures in one commodity if he thinks the difference in price is increasing or decreasing. The first function is sensible fuel management while the second is more speculation and should be approached carefully. Most end-users will leave speculative arbitraging to marketers who will use such arbitrage opportunities to increase profits at their own risk.

Indexing.

End-users who manufacture or use other openly traded commodities can tie electricity prices to the price of that other commodity. Aluminum manufacturers have commonly tied the price they pay for electricity to the market price of aluminum because the manufacture of aluminum is extremely electricity intensive. In this case, the price of power increases as the price the manufacturer gets for their aluminum increases. This is a means of transferring some of the risk of changing prices in both commodities to the electricity supplier. Another way to index prices is to do the opposite, that is tie the price of electricity inversely to the price of a commodity used to manufacture a product. For example, a refinery may wish to tie their price of power to the commodity price of crude oil so that if the price of crude oil goes up, the price of electricity will drop. This will benefit the refiner by holding total supply costs even while again transferring the risk of another commodity to the supplier. In both of these instances, the supplier must be willing to take the risks of price volatility in other commodities. As mentioned above, many power marketers are willing and able to take such risks, at a premium, for the opportunity to sell power.

Secondary market.

Finally, an end-user may be able to purchase energy, capacity, transmission and ancillary services, to some degree, on the secondary market. FERC has suggested the creation of secondary markets in transmission capacity, similar to capacity release in gas, and in those ancillary services to which a secondary market can technically apply. The success of the secondary market in gas transportation demonstrates the interest in this type of market and purchasing opportunity. This market will be available to the end-user through both official transmission bulletin boards, such as the open access same-time information systems mandated by FERC, and through informal communication networks.

Most end-users will use the secondary market to release unused capacity during scheduled and unscheduled plant outages. Many others will purchase this released capacity during the loss of a primary supplier or to meet an unusual increase in demand. Some end-users will actively and constantly approach the secondary market to purchase energy and transmission so as to minimize costs. Experience in the gas industry has shown that the cost to purchase secondary capacity can be a fraction of the original cost. Of course, there is risk in relying on the secondary market, but it is a reasonable supplement to the spot market for many services, and end-users should consider the secondary market as one more supplier from which to choose.

Chapter 11

The Future

The focus of this book is on the future: an unbundled and competitive electricity marketplace where the ultimate consumer has choices and the suppliers face competitive pressures. But that future is practically here. Utilities already face competitive pressures from the alternatives that end-users have now, such as cogeneration and municipalization, and many states are quickly developing retail wheeling programs. The unbundled electricity market described in the past few chapters is being formed as market participants are asking not whether retail wheeling is necessary but rather how will retail wheeling work. Although true retail competition has not yet fully developed, it is a readily discernable future that is imminently poised on the horizon.

This chapter looks another step further and asks what new technologies are being developed and what other issues will continue to shape the evolving power industry. One of the primary benefits of competition is technical innovation, even in the power industry where significant technological developments have historically been few and far between. Already the prospect of a competitive market has led to the development of exciting new technologies that were never necessary in the monopoly industry. As with the telephone industry, a technological explosion is predictable and will lead to better service and reliability at lower costs.

It would be presumptuous to forecast every development in the electricity industry and discuss its impact, so this chapter will only look at a few that are currently outstanding.

Storage

Electricity has always been a product that has been characterized as one that must be manufactured, transported, and retailed in the very instant that it is demanded. Electricity cannot be placed into a container and inventoried for later use. The lack of storage facilities for electricity means that extra product cannot be made during low demand times for use during high demand times. As a result, more so than any other commodity or product, the price of electricity can increase by orders of magnitude during peak use periods.

The willingness of consumers to pay very high prices during peak use times for electricity has led to the reevaluation of the presumption that electricity cannot be stored on a utility scale. Electricity storage could play a very important role in an unbundled electricity market, just as natural gas storage has in that industry. Grid operators have long sought to use storage technology to instantaneously correct for instability situations caused by the unanticipated loss of major generation or transmission facilities. Storage could also be used for frequency regulation, load following, and peak shaving. Likewise, an end-user could use storage technology to level a fluctuating load curve so that the supplier need only provide low cost, 100% load factor power. The big advantage to storage, however, is for providing a source of power during peak demand times when the spot market price for power is high enough to justify the use of even expensive generation. In this way, as with gas, the end-user can resort to storage rather than be forced to buy high cost power or face an interruption. Storage then becomes one more option for sourcing power that the supply coordinator would consider in its everyday economic rebundling analysis.

To some degree, electricity can be stored in the form of water behind a hydroelectric dam. Unless constrained by minimum and maximum river flows, which has increasingly become the case, a hydroelectric dam operator can "pond" water in the reservoir above the dam during the night time when electrical demand is low and drain the reservoir through the turbines during the day. This concept has been taken to its logical extreme in the development of hydro pumped storage technology, which is specifically designed to level the capacity factors on a system wide basis. A pumped storage facility involves two reservoirs, one each at the top and bottom of a mountain. Inside the mountain are enormous motors that pump water from the lower to the upper reservoir at night using low cost dump energy, usually from the utility's underutilized nuclear plant. During the day, the water flows back down through the mountain and the motors are operated as generators. These facilities have enormous outputs, as high as 2,400 MW, but they cannot provide the true storage function for an end-user that can instantaneously supply a needed quantity of power on demand. While they serve as a source of spinning reserve or quick start reserve capacity, the lack of a meaningful response time limits the effectiveness of hydroelectric or pumped storage options for end-users.

To provide ready access to storage, compressed air energy storage has been developed. Combustion turbines are used to pressurize large air storage chambers, such as salt caverns or depleted natural gas fields. When power is required, the compressed air is fed back through the turbine. Compressed air storage, however, is relatively inefficient because the compression turbines must be continually run to maintain the air pressure. Also, response time is quicker than for pumped storage but still too slow to be used as a true storage option for the end-user.

Instantaneous response times are achievable with battery storage, which is certainly not new technology, although technical advancements have made batteries a real option for bulk power storage in recent years. Battery storage is expensive, in part due to the fact that AC/DC converters are required to store the energy in the battery, and many battery technologies create serious environmental concerns. Recently, however, a series of five 20 MW batteries were installed on a 115-kV transmission system in Puerto Rico to provide spinning reserve capability. As with other small and isolated systems, the Puerto Rican power supply cannot depend on hundreds of generation facilities to provide system security. Instead, instantaneous reserves are necessary, either in the form of excess capacity on spinning generators, which have become scarce due to load growth, or the instantaneous response provided by battery storage. The large battery installations in Puerto Rico demonstrate that battery technology is a feasible storage option. While expensive, the batteries are 95% efficient and can deliver 20 MW each for 40 minutes. While these batteries may provide enough time for the Puerto Rico Electric Power Authority to black start other generation facilities, this capacity is not enough to provide a true alternative source to large loads during peak hours.

The latest development in electrical storage is superconducting magnetic energy storage, or SMES technology. A superconducting coil, inexpensively cooled with nitrogen, stores energy in the form of direct current circulating in the coil. The current is generated by creating a magnetic field within the coil, and the energy continues to flow in the coil as direct current because the coil has no resistance. Since the current always flows, the response time of SMES is instantaneous. On the negative side, there is some concern over the environmental effects of the large magnetic field that is created, and the amount of energy that has been stored in demonstration units has been only on the order of hundreds of kilowatts for only seconds. However, the goal is to develop a system that could deliver up to 1000 MW for five hours so that a true energy storage service could be offered. At the time, the development cost of an SMES system of this size is reportedly over $1 billion, so this option may be a few years off. But one developer has already designed a unit that can deliver 100 MW for up to three minutes. It may not sound like much, but the need for storage services could quickly drive this technology to commercial application.

In summary, storage technologies are presently only useful for providing uninterruptible backup supplies for highly sensitive loads such as computers and controllers. Development continues, however, towards a storage technology that would allow an end-user to buy and store cheap power during off-peak periods and use that power that has already been purchased during on-peak periods.

Flexible AC Transmission System

Another oft-repeated truism of power delivery technology is that the flow of power cannot be controlled. That is, there are no valves to tell the electrons which transmission line to use so that the physical world can correspond to the contract paths that the lawyers have developed. This is not entirely true. Existing technology allows for blocking flows on high voltage transmission lines with the use of large transformers with variable taps called phase shifters. These in-line devices cause slight voltage angle changes that add a large effective impedance to the line thus causing power to flow down other lines. These were used on a widespread basis in the 1970s in the northeast as a means to block inadvertent parallel path flows caused by large wheeling transactions between Ontario Hydro and the New York Power Pool. The use of phase shifters has been widely curtailed because they tend to have a high failure rate caused by moving coil taps under high voltage, and those failures caused line interruptions since they were in-line or series devices. Also, being electro-mechanical devices, phase shifters are too slow to respond quickly to changing system conditions.

The Electric Power Research Institute (EPRI), a utility-sponsored research organization, recently developed a solid state device that performs basically the same function as a phase shifter in that it changes the effective impedance of a high voltage transmission line. The device, called a thyristor-controlled series capacitor (TCSC), is part of EPRI's research program to increase the flexibility and efficiency of the nation's transmission grid. This program, called the Flexible AC Transmission System or (FACTS), is attempting to develop efficient devices and methodologies to increase the control of load flows on transmission lines and to increase transmission capacity on existing lines.

Unlike a phase shifter, the TCSC device is a solid state device with no moving parts, which can respond instantaneously to changing system parameters using computer controls. Like the phase shifter, it can be used to add series impedance to a transmission line in order to redirect power flow. Although some may wish to use this device to control power flows to more closely match contract path flows for wheeling transactions, its better use is to increase system reliability and transmission capacity. When a large generator or transmission line inadvertently trips, perhaps due to a lightning stroke, the integrated transmission grid attempts to instantaneously redirect power flows to feed the load that was once fed by the lost generator. Other generators on the system cannot instantaneously increase output due to the inertia of the generator's rotational mass. Instead, massive and instantaneous load flow changes are seen across the system. System planners always design and operate the transmission grid to accommodate a single contingency, such as the loss of a large generator or transmission line, so they run studies to determine these changes in load flow. To allow such flows until the other generators can get up to speed, the transmission lines must be able to handle the increased loads. As a result, transmission companies often reserve capacity on some transmission lines to accommodate these occurrences.

The FACTS project will eliminate the need for these system stability margins by instantaneously responding to the contingency with the TCSC device. Flows can be redirected to meet the needs of the system during such an occurrence without overflowing any lines. This will result in the increase in capacity of some lines by up to 50%, according to EPRI. More significantly, it will increase the reliability of the transmission grid and the system in general. It should probably not be used to control power flows to accommodate wheeling transactions, since adding impedance to a line will usually, but not always, decrease the overall efficiency and capacity of the system.

The recent development of the FACTS technologies is a significant indication of the effect of competition on the industry. Improvements in gas-fired combustion turbine technology are bringing generator heat rates down to record lows, i.e., record high efficiency due to the development of the independent power industry. However, few expected transmission technology to also be affected by the changing electricity market. Nonetheless, it too will increase system reliability, stability, and capacity to everyone's benefit.

Fuel Cells

Fuel cells are devices that convert natural gas or other fuels directly into electricity using a chemical process rather than combustion. Fuel cells were originally developed for the space program as a clean and compact source of electricity and have long been considered as a potential alternative to conventional electrical generation. Unfortunately for fuel cell developers, the increasing efficiency of combustion turbine generation has delayed the day when fuel cell technology could catch up. Fuel cell researchers have recently demonstrated commercially viable fuel cells in public, and claims have been made that fuel cells will be priced within the cost of an expensive conventional generator by the year 2000. The advantage of fuel cells is that because they having no moving parts, they can respond instantly to load changes so that load factor is not an issue with respect to price. If an end-user's load was fed with a fuel cell, no load following service would be required because the fuel cell will precisely match the load, even on a minute-to-minute basis. Because the natural gas is oxidized chemically rather than burned, the byproducts are only carbon dioxide and water. Furthermore, fuel cells are compact and can be compartmentalized so that maintenance could be as easy as replacing one small part of the fuel cell while the remaining cells continue to operate. The only apparent disadvantage appears to remain the price.

While fuel cells will certainly be an option for utilities, suppliers, and industrial end-users, the possibility exists that they may revolutionize the residential retail power industry instead. Imagine in every basement, along side the gas-fired furnace and water heater, is a gas-fired fuel cell sized to meet the total electrical demand of the household. No backup or load following service is required, so no interconnection with the centralized utility is necessary. Of course this could only happen when the capitalized cost of a residential-size fuel cell is less than the cost of local distribution service. With retail wheeling, most consumers will see a small reduction in electricity costs as all suppliers become more efficient. This will push off the advent of the residential fuel cell industry. However, retail wheeling will also force all end-users to pay for their actual cost of service. Those residential and small commercial customers that are in rural areas or at the end of a long service line may see the cost of power on a per kilowatt-hour basis actually climb significantly in some cases. These customers might provide a broad, new market for fuel cell developers as a result of the advent of retail wheeling.

Generation Capacity Forecasts

Although it has little to do with emerging technologies, considerable discussion has taken place concerning the availability of generation and the need for new resources in the future. Most of this concern has been raised in response to the lack of interest by most investor-owned utilities in building new, large, base load units. As discussed in Chapter 2, most utilities are getting out of the generation business since they can no longer compete with independent developers. More significantly, most utilities are no longer building generation because there are large amounts of excess capacity in most regions. Indeed, this excess supply is one of the high cost results of existing ratemaking principles and one of the driving forces behind the need for industry restructuring.

Nonetheless, many analysts are noting that many utility-owned base load units are quickly aging and that very little new capacity is planned on the horizon to replace it. One report noted that 306,000 megawatts of installed capacity in the U.S. is 25 years old. Furthermore, environmental forces may shut down older and dirtier coal-fired plants, some nuclear units face early retirement, and many high cost oil-fired plants will be shut down in a competitive market. Compounding this perceived problem is the difficulty in building new base load capacity because of high installation costs compared to smaller gas-fired turbines, environmental concerns, and the NIMBY (not in my backyard) syndrome. Estimates for new capacity requirements through the year 2013 range as high as 210,000 megawatts (see Figure 11-1) with almost half of this needed capacity unplanned by any supplier.

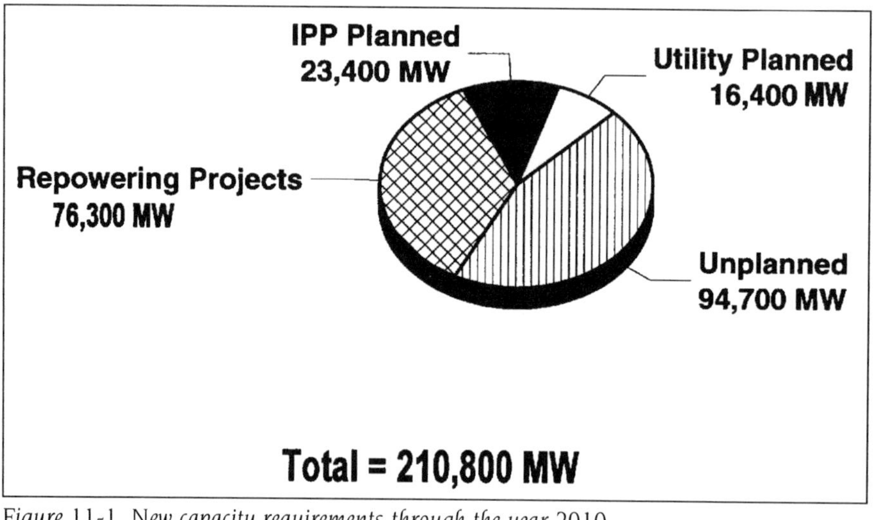

Figure 11-1. New capacity requirements through the year 2010.

These estimates, usually supplied by the investor-owned utilities, fail to take into account two significant factors. First, when electricity becomes commoditized, the price an end-user will pay for power will be based on real-time market prices, and the cost of power during peak demand times will be substantially higher than that during off-peak times. There will be very strong incentives for many end-users to curtail use during these times. Since peaking resources comprise the bulk of the need for generation installed since 1975, much of this needed capacity will not materialize. The forces of market pricing will dwarf the most ambitious and successful demand side management program implemented by any regulatory agency or utility. While total energy use may increase due to lower prices, the level of system demand requirements will most likely decrease substantially.

Second, the market forces will be equally strong on the supply side as they are on the demand side. If enough capacity is required to raise prices above the market-clearing prices seen today, the market will not take long to supply that demand. As with demand side management, market pricing signals will put to shame integrated resource plans and least cost planning programs mandated by regulators or implemented by utilities. The market can be trusted to respond quickly and efficiently to any need for capacity in the future.

Appendix A

Discussion of Federal and State Jurisdiction

FERC Order *888 and the giga-*NOPR *that preceded it directly addressed the issue of jurisdiction for both retail and wholesale wheeling and stranded cost recovery. Like many* FERC NOPRs *and* Notices *of* Inquiry, *the giga-*NOPR *on open access transmission tariffs included a well-written and complete summary and background of the jurisdiction issue. Rather than repeat that summary here, the reader is encouraged to read the discussion on jurisdiction in the giga-*NOPR *for a more detailed analysis of the issue.*

A fundamental legal issue facing the re-regulation of the electricity industry is that of jurisdiction, i.e., what aspects of the newly structured industry is regulated by federal agencies and which are regulated by the states. This issue is entirely shaped by historical factors (with some politics thrown in) and has little to do with common sense or efficiency. Because the issue boils down to a conflict between the federal government and the individual states, jurisdiction over electricity industry regulation becomes a question of federalism and states' rights, i.e., the very stuff of which civil wars are made. And as with all battles, the outcome is uncertain, and victory is never complete.

The federal government is granted jurisdiction over all activity in interstate commerce by the U.S. Constitution. Because all powers not specifically enumerated in the constitution are reserved to the states, according to the tenth amendment, all aspects of commerce that are not interstate fall within state jurisdiction. The Federal Power Act of 1935 granted jurisdiction over the interstate transmission of electrical energy to the Federal Power Authority, which later became FERC, based on the commerce clause of the U.S. Constitution. The federal government also claimed jurisdiction over wholesale transactions, defined as sales of electricity for resale.

The Supreme Court in 1982 ruled that *all* transmission is in interstate commerce. In a case involving a wheeling transaction between two wholesale entities in southern Florida, the court determined that because the electric grid is so highly interconnected, some current will flow across state lines regardless of how intrastate the contract path is. While this may be true from a mathematical and engineering viewpoint, it is still somewhat of a legal fiction. But it raises two interesting issues. First, is there no federal jurisdiction over the electricity industry in Texas, since ERCOT is electrically isolated from the rest of the U.S.? Apparently not, according to recent FERC decisions that found jurisdiction regardless of a true lack of interstate commerce.

Second, and more importantly, what is transmission? According to the recent FERC Order 888 and the giga-NOPR that preceded it on open access transmission tariffs, jurisdictional boundaries will be determined by whether certain facilities are for transmission or distribution. FERC has claimed that this is a question of fact for FERC to decide, but there are bound to be enumerable conflicts that cannot be settled technically. For example, Public Service Company of New Hampshire has a highly developed, 34.5 kV distribution system that grew out of an existing 34.5 kV sub-transmission system. In that utility, 34.5 kV lines are used both to move power within the PSNH system and for distribution. In fact, engineers at PSNH call the 34.5 kV their "transbution" system. It is probably safe to say that for every looped 34.5 kV line with distribution taps, there is a radial 115 kV line feeding a single customer, which can only be described as distribution.

FERC has described seven factors that they will consider when deciding whether a facility is transmission or distribution, and thus regulated by FERC or by the state, respectively. Note that, in addition to these factors, FERC said that they expect *all* retail transactions to involve some distribution facilities. FERC must be aware that many industrial end-users take service directly from what is normally considered transmission voltages. Even the supplying utilities label this service as transmission service and charge a lower price since the cost of fewer facilities must be allocated to that customer. With this in mind, those seven factors are:

- The proximity of the retail customer to the facilities. The FERC reasons that distribution facilities are normally in close proximity to retail customers, but does this apply to customers fed at high voltages?
- Whether the circuit is radial or looped. Radial circuits are usually for distribution, but not always.
- The direction of power flow. If power flows into the circuit, it is probably a distribution circuit, but power flows into many transmission systems as well.
- Whether power flows through the circuit. Distribution systems are not used to transport power while transmission systems are.
- Whether the power into a circuit is consumed nearby. Again, it is unclear as to what is meant by "nearby," i.e., whether this means nearby electrically or geographically.
- The location of meters. If a circuit is metered, it is probably used for distribution, although transmission systems are metered at control center interfaces and for wholesale customers.
- Voltage levels. Distribution circuits are usually lower voltage systems.

FERC clearly is willing to make the distribution/transmission distinction differ very much from the distinction most utility engineers would make. These factors could be readily used to find that a 200-megawatt steel mill taking service at 115 kV off multiple taps a few miles from a transmission substation is a distribution service. It seems that, except for the last factor, virtually all retail service could be found to involve some distribution facilities, just as FERC predicted. Unfortunately, this could lead to a high number or improbable findings and seemingly arbitrary lines drawn for state and federal jurisdiction.

FERC has admittedly left the bright line between state and federal jurisdiction remain somewhat dim. These factors are loose enough to accommodate many varying political factors. Unfortunately, this determination of federal versus state jurisdiction will be fertile ground for energy lawyers. The above analysis applies only to retail wheeling, since FERC claims jurisdiction over all aspects of wholesale transactions, even if they involve what are later determined to be distribution facilities.

As we have seen, FERC claims, and rightly so, jurisdiction over interstate transmission, but it cannot issue any order that is contingent on providing retail wheeling. However, if all transmission is in interstate commerce, as the Supreme Court believes (and probably rightly so), then all retail wheeling transactions will involve interstate transmission and invoke FERC jurisdiction. There is, in other words, an inherent jurisdictional conflict with retail wheeling. It seems inevitable that this conflict will have to be litigated and settled by the Supreme Court. Efforts towards this judicial resolution of the jurisdictional issue are underway.

Appendix B

Discussion of the Stranded Investment Issue

The recently issued FERC *Order* 888 *addresses stranded investment on a wholesale basis and leaves the issue of costs stranded by retail wheeling to the states (although it claims concurrent jurisdiction). The so-called "giga-*NOPR*" that preceded* Order 888 *supplemented an initial* NOPR *on stranded investment issued in July of* 1994. *These* NOPRs *included a thorough discussion of the regulatory history and background to the stranded investment issue. The purpose of this discussion is not to replicate that work, but only to provide some discussion of the issue from an end-user perspective. The reader is strongly encouraged to read the giga-*NOPR *for a well-written and thorough review of this and other issues.*

As part of the regulatory bargain, electric utilities had a duty to serve all customers that will not exist in a completely open market with direct access for all customer classes. To meet this duty, utilities installed facilities that cannot now operate at competitive prices. Before being thrown into a competitive market, utilities claim that they are entitled to compensation for these uneconomic assets so that they too can effectively compete. The recovery of this so-called "stranded investment" is considered to be the primary obstacle to a swift and smooth transition to a fully competitive electric energy marketplace.

The issue is driven by the fact that the market value of certain utility assets is below the book value. Economists and commentators have estimated the magnitude of so-called electric utility stranded investment from tens of billions of dollars to over $200 billion (although this latter value is nearly equal to the total revenues from all retail electricity sales in the U.S.!). The question is: who will pay for these sunk costs? Should it be the exiting utility customer, the utility shareholder, the native ratepayer, or a combination of all three?

Considering that total U.S. utility assets have a book value of about $600 billion with equity investment close to $175 billion, many utilities see the resolution of the stranded investment issue as a struggle for survival. Others point to the magnitude of the problem as a clear indication of the inefficiency of maintaining a monopoly generation supplier. Economists indicate that if the cost of stranded investment were removed and market prices prevailed, retail prices would decline, on average, 15% for all customer classes. Even more savings will be realized as market forces act to increase operational efficiencies and spur new technological innovations.

The Energy Policy Act of 1992 created new opportunities for wholesale buyers to access competitive generation, but it also created the attendant stranded investment problem as wholesale customers considered ceasing purchases of power from their native utilities. For example, when certain municipal power purchasers terminated service from Entergy and sought to purchase power from alternative sources while wheeling power through the utility, FERC allowed Entergy to include wholesale stranded investment charges in Entergy's wholesale transmission rates. FERC stated that if Entergy made investment decisions based on a "reasonable expectation at that time that it would continue to serve theses customers, it should be able to recover from them the legitimate and verifiable costs invested on their behalf."

Rather than continue to address the stranded investment issue on a case-by-case basis, FERC issued a Notice of Proposed Rulemaking (NOPR) on *wholesale* stranded investment in July of 1994. In this initial proposed rule, FERC stated that for new wholesale contracts (executed after the date the rule would have become final), any stranded cost recovery would be limited to the terms of the contract, and no recovery could be obtained through transmission rates. For existing wholesale contracts, if stranded investment is explicitly addressed, then recovery is limited to the terms of the contract. If not, within the following three years from the date of the final rule, the parties must make a good faith attempt to negotiate and file a contract amendment that resolves the stranded investment issue. If negotiations fail within the three year period, the utility can unilaterally file a contract amendment with FERC that addressed the issue, and the customer can file an alternate amendment as well.

With regard to stranded investment caused by departing retail customers, either through retail wheeling or through the formation of a new municipal electric utility, this initial NOPR stated that "while we believe the Commission has the authority to address retail stranded costs through its jurisdiction over the rates, terms, and conditions of interstate transmission services used by retail or newly-created wholesale customers, we also believe that the recovery of the costs of transition to competition at the retail level is a matter that should be addressed by State authorities."

In conjunction with the giga-NOPR on open access transmission tariffs, FERC issued a supplemental NOPR on stranded investment that made some modifications to the rule proposed in the initial NOPR. The rules on standard cost recovery suggested in the giga-NOPR were adopted in FERC Order 888. One such change is that now FERC does indeed claim jurisdiction over the stranded investment costs resulting from a retail customer leaving due to municipalization. Furthermore, that retail customer can ask the native utility to estimate those costs as part of its evaluation of the municipalization option! Most significantly, however, FERC proposed that all wholesale stranded investment costs, once determined as "legitimate and verifiable" and minimized through an as yet undefined mitigation program, would be *entirely* borne by those wholesale customers leaving the native utility system. Unlike similar transition costs in the natural gas industry caused by abandoned take-or-pay contracts, no sharing of those costs with utility shareholders or other ratepayers is proposed. The reader is reminded that this rule only applies to wholesale stranded investment, which is a fraction of the potential stranded investment costs that will result from retail wheeling, and that states are still responsible for developing their own policies with respect to the stranded investment issue. Nonetheless, this federal policy will likely carry significant weight with state policymakers when deciding how to handle the same problem on the retail side.

Resolution of the stranded investment problem has been complicated by *Cajun Electric Power Coop v. FERC*, in which the U.S. Court of Appeals (D.C. Circuit) ruled that Entergy's transmission rates could not be used as a vehicle to recover stranded investment costs. The court noted that by coupling stranded investment (a cost tied to generation) to transmission (a product over which Entergy has market control), Entergy is creating a classic "tying" arrangement, which is illegal under anti-trust laws. If this logic is upheld, regulators may have to resort to some form of exit fee to recover stranded investment, which is arguably nothing more than a disguised transmission adder itself.

Given the magnitude of the economics of stranded investment, it is a hotly contested issue on both the federal and state level. Utilities argue that all investments were made in response to their obligation to serve and that the costs were forced on the utilities by regulators, such as high priced QF contracts under PURPA, demand side management programs, and inclusion of environmental externalities in decision making. Industrial consumers contend that most of the utility investment decisions were independently made by utility management and that the utility business must prosper or fail in the marketplace like other U.S. industries. Residential and commercial customers are concerned that stranded investment costs will be shifted to them as large industrial customers begin to leave the system through retail wheeling or municipalization.

The stranded investment debate boils down to two issues. The first and most difficult is how to determine what those costs are. This issue involves determining whether any investments are truly stranded or just revalued in a competitive market. Utilities want the entire difference between the existing revenues that an asset is earning now and the revenues that would be earned in the market price. Industrials argue that this provides no incentive to mitigate stranded costs and that only those investments that were truly forced, such as QF contracts, should be recovered. All other investments are the result of business decisions that are now stranded due to a change in regulation. The utilities have no argument that this justifies recovery of those investments because other industries face stranded investments due to regulatory changes every day. For example, the owner of a refinery built for $800 million that has to be rebuilt for another $600 million due to new reformulated gasoline requirements cannot recover those lost costs from its customers, even though the decision to build was not erroneous at the time. The utilities and their shareholders should face the same risk, since the change from the regulatory bargain to a competitive market is also nothing more than a change in governmental regulation.

The second basic issue with respect to stranded investment is the allocation of those costs once they are determined and mitigated. While the FERC NOPR proposed allocating all costs to the exiting customers, one FERC staffer explained that this was seen as a necessary bone to throw to the utilities in order to get them to agree to the open access tariffs. The FERC staffer explained that FERC fully expects the states to develop methodologies to share those costs among exiting customers, utility shareholders, and perhaps even remaining ratepayers. One such methodology that may result in a fair allocation is an extension of an idea introduced by the New York Public Service Commission (NYPSC) in a Niagara Mohawk rate case. In this case, the NYPSC was trying to find a way to get Niagara Mohawk to reduce over a ten-year period its investment in high cost generation that was resulting in its high rates. Applying the methodology from this case to removing stranded investment costs over a five-year period would work this way: Stranded investment costs are determined for the entire system and allocated to each end-user in proportion to the end-user's demand compared to the total system demand. If the end-user wishes to leave the native utility during the first year of the program and purchase power on the open market, it must pay 80% of the stranded cost allocated to that load, and the utility shareholders absorb the remaining 20%. The next year, the end-user would only have to pay 60% of its allocated share of stranded investment costs, while the shareholders absorb 40%. This continues until the fifth year when all end-users can leave the utility without any stranded investment cost assessment. The utility meanwhile has five years to write down its remaining stranded investment. This methodology would provide an incentive to the utility to mitigate its stranded investments while also providing an economic signal to end-users upon which they can base their decision of when to leave the system. Additionally, this method will phase in retail wheeling as some end-users will pay the stranded cost allocation early on in order to quickly realize the benefits of retail wheeling, while for others, the cost of leaving the system will not be justified until later years in the transition.

Momentum towards competition in the electric industry is growing, however, before a smooth transition can be made to an open market, the stranded investment issued must be resolved. Some equitable sharing of pain will be worked out by FERC and the state regulators that will give utilities the necessary incentive to embrace competition and allow utilities, as well as other industry players and consumers to reap the benefits of competition. This was done in the natural gas industry where all industry participants and consumers shared in absorbing the transition costs that were attributed primarily to high cost take-or-pay gas supply contracts. Most will agree that competition has served to create a more efficient and cost effective natural gas supply system. In electricity, a joint resolution of the stranded investment issue will speed the transition to a competitive marketplace.

Appendix C

Retail Wheeling Pilot Program Tariffs

This Appendix contains portions of retail wheeling tariffs from two utilities involved in retail wheeling pilot programs at the time of this writing. The first two, from Central Illinois Lighting Company (CILCO), *is the result of a voluntary experiment in which no stranded cost recovery was sought.* CILCO *submitted two tariffs:* Rate 33 *for industrial end-users and* Rate 34 *for residential and commercial end-users. Both are provided in this Appendix. The second,* Public Service Company of New Hampshire (PSNH), *is the result of a mandated retail wheeling experiment. The material provided below from* PSNH *is only part of a larger filing submitted to comply with retail wheeling pilot program mandate.*

The reader is encouraged to compare the two filings. Note *that the* CILCO *tariffs are "bottom-up" tariffs (the overall rate is determined from the sum of the various components) and that the* PSNH *tariff is a "top-down" tariff (the overall rate is determined from reductions from the existing rate). These differences are clearly tied to the fact that one is voluntary and the other mandated. The value for the reader in reviewing these tariffs is in gaining an understanding of how retail wheeling tariffs will look, and how much they will differ, in the future.*

Central Illinois Light Company

Ill. C. C. No. 9 - Electric
Original Sheet No. 62

RATE 33 - PILOT ELECTRIC TRANSMISSION SERVICE

Availability:

Service under this rate is available for a period of two years after the rate's initial effective date, to customers that experienced peak electric demands of ten megawatts or greater on the Company's electric system at any time during the twelve months ending July 31, 1995.

Definitions:

As used in this rate, the following terms shall have the meanings specified:

"Available receipt point" means a receipt point that the Company has determined has adequate capacity under normal operating conditions to accept delivery of scheduled off-system purchases without impairing the reliability of the Company's electric system or the quality of service to other customers.

"Capacity deficient period" means a period when the Company anticipates that its available generating capacity may not be sufficient to meet all demands of the Company's native load plus required reserves plus off-system commitments without interrupting customers or purchasing wholesale power at prices the Company determines to be uneconomical.

"Company" means Central Illinois Light Company.

"Customer" means one premises for which all electric usage, as of July 31, 1995, was integrated for purposes of billing.

"Delivery day" means the 24-hour period from midnight to midnight, local time, when off-system purchases may be scheduled for delivery to available receipt points.

"Delivery point" means a point where the Company's electric system is connected to a Rate 33 customer.

"Distribution capacity" means electric lines and related facilities at nominal system voltage levels less than 138 kv.

"MAIN" means the Mid-America Interconnected Network.

"NERC" means the North American Electric Reliability Council.

Issued - March 29, 1996, Pursuant to Order of the Illinois Commerce Commission entered March 13, 1996 Docket No. 95-0435

Effective - The later of April 30, 1996, or the date CILCO has an approved retail transmission in tariff in effect at FERC

Issued by - S. A. Cisel, Vice President
Peoria, Illinois

Central Illinois Light Company

Ill. C. C. No. 9 - Electric
Original Sheet No. 63

RATE 33 - PILOT ELECTRIC TRANSMISSION SERVICE

"Off-system purchases" means electric power purchased by Rate 33 customers from electric suppliers other than the Company.

"Person" means an individual, corporation, partnership, governmental body or agency, or other recognized entity.

"Receipt point" means a point or points where the Company is interconnected with another public utility or with any other supplier of electric energy.

"Supplier" means any person that contracts with a customer to furnish off-system purchases or any other service that customers are permitted by this rate to purchase off-system.

"Transmission capacity" means electric lines and related facilities operating at nominal system voltage levels of 138 kv or higher.

Nature of Service:

The Company will contract to deliver to Rate 33 customers, during the time this rate is available, up to an aggregate maximum of fifty megawatts (50 MW) of off-system purchases.

The services provided by the Company under this rate will include firm delivery of off-system purchases from an available receipt point to the customer's delivery point. In addition, the Company will provide administrative service, and, to the extent not otherwise provided, load following service, system protection service, reactive power/voltage control service, and system loss service.

Except as hereinafter set forth, Rate 33 customers shall be entitled to service under and shall continue to be subject to the charges in the respective rates and contracts under which the customers were served immediately prior to electing service under this Rate 33, including any changes in those rates that may be approved by the Commission from time to time. If a Rate 33 customer purchases no power or energy under such prior rate during any month, the customer shall be billed the minimum applicable charge under the prior rate and under any applicable service contract, plus any separate facilities charges, plus the charges applicable under this Rate 33.

Off-system purchases delivered to the customer shall be deemed to be the first power and energy delivered to the customer, except when the customer is purchasing full requirements or load following service off-system, in which event the off-system purchases delivered to

Issued - March 29, 1996, Pursuant to Order of the Illinois Commerce Commission entered March 13, 1996 Docket No. 95-0435

Effective - The later of April 30, 1996, or the date CILCO has an approved retail transmission in tariff in effect at FERC

Issued by - S. A. Cisel, Vice President
Peoria, Illinois

Central Illinois Light Company

Ill. C. C. No. 9 - Electric
Original Sheet No. 64

RATE 33 - PILOT ELECTRIC TRANSMISSION SERVICE

the customer shall be deemed to be the last power and energy through the customer's meter.

Special Terms and Conditions:

(a) Service under this rate is offered on a limited basis for the purpose of allowing the Company and its customers to gain knowledge and experience in the purchase by customers of some or all of their electric requirements from suppliers other than the Company. The Company reserves the right to petition the Illinois Commerce Commission at any time or times during the availability of this rate for approval of changes in the terms and conditions under which service is offered under this rate, and, if the Company believes appropriate, to terminate this rate. The Company may elect to terminate this rate if a regulatory agency or court having jurisdiction determines that the Company, by reason of this rate or any rate of the Company on file at the Federal Energy Regulatory Commission, is obligated to provide retail open access to any customer not included within the availability provision of this rate and not located within an open access site designated by the Company pursuant to the Company's retail Rate 34. Such election shall be exercised by the Company by filing notice of the termination with the Illinois Commerce Commission, and this rate shall terminate seven days after such filing. The Company shall promptly mail notice of such election to all customers then receiving service under this rate, but failure to give such notice to customers shall not prevent the termination of this rate as specified herein. In the event this rate is terminated prior to two years after its initial effective date, and a Rate 33 customer is thereby precluded from receiving off-system purchases for which the customer has contracted under a contract which the customer has no option to terminate, the Company will, at the Company's option, either continue to transport the customer's off-system purchases pursuant to the provisions of this rate and the contract with the customer under this rate, or buy out the customer's contracted off-system supply, provided, however, the Company's obligation under this provision will be limited to that portion of off-system purchases contracted through the earliest of the following dates: (i) the expiration date of the contract between the customer and the Company under this rate; (ii) the expiration date of the contract between the customer and the off-system supplier; and (iii) the second anniversary of the initial effective date of this rate.

(b) The fifty megawatts of capacity available under this rate will be allocated by the Company in full megawatts to the customers that are eligible for service under this rate in proportion to the customers' respective peak demands during the twelve months ended July 31, 1995. The Company will communicate the respective allocations to the eligible customers not less than thirty days before this rate becomes effective. If, at the time this rate becomes effective, any eligible customer has not elected in writing to reserve

Issued - March 29, 1996, Pursuant
to Order of the Illinois Commerce
Commission entered March 13, 1996
Docket No. 95-0435

Effective - The later of April 30,
1996, or the date CILCO has an
approved retail transmission in
tariff in effect at FERC

Issued by - S. A. Cisel, Vice President
Peoria, Illinois

Central Illinois Light Company

Ill. C. C. No. 9 - Electric
Original Sheet No. 65

RATE 33 - PILOT ELECTRIC TRANSMISSION SERVICE

the customer's full allocated capacity, the unsubscribed capacity will be made available for a period of ten days to the other eligible customers in proportion to their respective peak demands during the twelve months ended July 31, 1995. Any unsubscribed capacity at the end of that ten days will be made available to the eligible customers on a first-come, first-served basis.

(c) Within thirty days after reserving capacity under this rate, and before receiving service under this rate, a customer must enter into a contract with the Company for such service, in a form determined by the Company. At a minimum, the contract shall specify the annual capacity to be reserved on the Company's transmission and distribution systems for delivery of off-system purchases, the primary receipt points for the customer's off-system purchases, the services that are to be furnished by off-system suppliers, and the services that are to be furnished by the Company. The primary receipt points designated in an executed contract shall be deemed available receipt points with respect to that contract.

(d) The Company shall have no responsibility for delivery of off-system purchases until the power has been received into the Company's system. The Company shall not be liable for an inability to receive off-system purchases into the Company's system because of any lack of available capacity at a receipt point or any cause beyond the Company's reasonable control. In the event of a lack of capacity to handle all electric flows at an available receipt point, the Company will comply with the rules, regulations, and guidelines of MAIN and NERC applicable to such situations. In the event the Company is unable, for any reason, to deliver to a Rate 33 customer any scheduled off-system purchases that the Company is otherwise able to receive into its system for the account of such customer, the customer shall either interrupt the delivery to the Company of such off-system purchases during the period the Company is unable to deliver to the customer, or shall sell the off-system purchases to the Company during such period at the Company's avoided energy cost specified in Rate 28.

(e) Before the Company commences delivery of off-system purchases to a customer, the customer shall furnish to the Company, at a minimum, the following information: the name and address of the suppliers of the customer's off-system purchases, the locations of the generating equipment from which the customer's off-system purchases will be supplied, the transmission path from the generating equipment to the receipt point, a detailed statement of the services to be furnished to the customer by such off-system suppliers, a specification of the available receipt points where the off-system purchases are to be delivered to the Company, and a representation that each such supplier is obligated to notify the Company by telephone within ten minutes if, for any reason, the supplier ceases to furnish all or any part of the power scheduled to be furnished for the

Issued - March 29, 1996, Pursuant to Order of the Illinois Commerce Commission entered March 13, 1996 Docket No. 95-0435

Effective - The later of April 30, 1996, or the date CILCO has an approved retail transmission in tariff in effect at FERC

Issued by - S. A. Cisel, Vice President
Peoria, Illinois

Central Illinois Light Company

Ill. C. C. No. 9 - Electric
Original Sheet No. 66

RATE 33 - PILOT ELECTRIC TRANSMISSION SERVICE

customer's account and is obligated to notify the Company immediately after supply is resumed. Updated information shall be furnished to the Company promptly after it is available to the customer.

(f) A customer electing service under this rate shall be obligated to contract and pay for transmission and distribution capacity on the Company's system for a minimum term of one year, but not beyond the termination date of this rate. By written requests to the Company, the customer may from time to time increase the amount of contracted capacity and the related payment obligation during the balance of the contract term to the extent additional capacity is available within the 50 MW aggregate maximum. A customer shall be permitted, upon 24 hours' advance written notice, to reduce the amount of contracted capacity and the related payment obligation, provided, however, the customer may not thereafter increase the amount of contracted capacity under this rate except upon ninety days' advance written notice. Any capacity released under this provision shall be available for reservation by Rate 33 customers on a first-come, first-served basis, subject to the limitations set forth above.

(g) Not later than noon of the twentieth day of each calendar month, each Rate 33 customer shall furnish the Company, in writing, a schedule of the off-system purchases to be delivered to the Company for the account of the customer during the immediately succeeding calendar month. Scheduling shall be done in full megawatt increments. The schedule may provide for delivery to the Company of off-system purchases on an hourly, daily, weekly or monthly basis, in total amounts ranging from zero to the customer's maximum contracted capacity, and shall specify the receipt points for the off-system purchases. Not later than 10:00 a.m. of the day preceding the delivery day, the customer may amend the delivery schedule for the delivery day, and shall amend delivery schedules at such intervals, not more frequently than daily, as deemed necessary by the Company to reflect expected changes in usage resulting from weather changes or any other cause. All amended schedules shall be furnished to the Company in writing. Schedules for full requirements service or load following service may be rejected by the Company if the Company determines, in its sole judgment, that the schedules do not reasonably reflect the customers' expected requirements for electricity. If the Company determines it is unable for any reason to accept off-system purchases at any receipt point scheduled by a customer, the Company will notify the customer promptly after such determination is made, and work with the customer to schedule delivery of the customer's off-system purchases so that the reliability of the Company's electric system is not impaired and the quality of service to other customers is not diminished. If the Company notifies the customer no later than 9:00 a.m. of the preceding day that the delivery day is, in whole or in part, a capacity deficient period, then during such capacity

Issued - March 29, 1996, Pursuant
to Order of the Illinois Commerce
Commission entered March 13, 1996
Docket No. 95-0435

Effective - The later of April 30, 1996, or the date CILCO has an approved retail transmission in tariff in effect at FERC

Issued by - S. A. Cisel, Vice President
Peoria, Illinois

Central Illinois Light Company

Ill. C. C. No. 9 - Electric
Original Sheet No. 67

RATE 33 - PILOT ELECTRIC TRANSMISSION SERVICE

deficient period the customer shall cause off-system purchases to be delivered to available receipt points in amounts totaling the customer's full contracted capacity.

(h) Schedules shall be furnished to the Company's Energy Control Center by messenger, by certified or registered mail, return receipt requested, or by telephone facsimile, provided, however, that facsimile delivery will not be accepted by the Company unless the customer confirms by telephone, within thirty minutes after sending the facsimile message, that the message has been received at the Company's Energy Control Center. otice by the Company to customers of a capacity deficient period may be given by telephone or by telephone facsimile, at the customer's option. Rate 33 customers shall provide the Company with customer telephone numbers to receive notice. The customer shall be deemed to have received notice if the telephone is not answered when called by the Company, or in the event of a mechanical breakdown or interruption of service which prevents the call or facsimile message from being received.

(i) At the request of any eligible customer that has elected service under this rate, and subject to receipt of all necessary regulatory approvals, the Company will enlarge existing interconnections and will add an interconnection with any adjacent supplier of energy, subject to the Facilities Charge specified in this rate.

(j) A Rate 33 customer may schedule delivery of off-system purchases to the Company's system through any available receipt point for re-delivery of off-system purchases by the Company to the customer's delivery point.

(k) No customer receiving service under this rate may elect to have load following service provided by any supplier other than the Company unless that customer, at the customer's sole expense, installs the necessary telemetry to allow the Company, the supplier providing the load following service, and the control area where the supplier's generation is located to ascertain instantly all changes in the customer's usage of power.

(l) In addition to the foregoing Special Terms and Conditions, service under this pilot rate shall be subject to the Company's General Terms and Conditions applicable to electric service. In the event of any conflict between the Company's General Terms and Conditions and the Special Terms and Conditions contained in this rate, the Special Terms and Conditions shall control with respect to service under this rate, and the General Terms and Conditions shall control with respect to service under any other applicable rate.

Issued - March 29, 1996, Pursuant to Order of the Illinois Commerce Commission entered March 13, 1996 Docket No. 95-0435

Effective - The later of April 30, 1996, or the date CILCO has an approved retail transmission in tariff in effect at FERC

Issued by - S. A. ‿isel, Vice President
Peoria, Illinois

Central Illinois Light Company

Ill. C. C. No. 9 - Electric
Original Sheet No. 68

RATE 33 - PILOT ELECTRIC TRANSMISSION SERVICE

Monthly Charges:

Customers receiving service under this pilot rate shall be subject to the following monthly charges:

Delivery Service:

Transmission Component: \$.96 per kilowatt of contracted transmission capacity per month.

Distribution Component: \$.50 per kilowatt of contracted distribution capacity per month.

Load Following Service: One-third (1/3) mill per kilowatthour for all energy delivered to the customer under this rate. Any customer may elect to purchase this service from an off-system supplier.

System Protection Service: One-third (1/3) mill per kilowatthour for all energy delivered to the customer under this rate. Any customer may elect to purchase this service from an off-system supplier.

Reactive Power/Voltage Control Service: One-third (1/3) mill per kilowatthour for all energy delivered to the customer under this rate. Any customer may elect to purchase this service from an off-system supplier.

Administrative Service Charge: One-third (1/3) mill per kilowatthour for all off-system purchases delivered to the customer under this rate.

Other Charges:

In addition to the monthly charges described above, the customers receiving service under this rate shall be subject to the following charges:

Facilities Charge: In the event the customer requests the construction of an interconnection or other facilities to receive service under this rate, or in the event the Company determines, in its sole judgment, that additional metering or other facilities are reasonably required in order to provide service under this rate without degrading or impairing the service provided to any other customer, the customer

Issued - March 29, 1996, Pursuant
to Order of the Illinois Commerce
Commission entered March 13, 1996
Docket No. 95-0435

Effective - The later of April 30, 1996, or the date CILCO has an approved retail transmission in tariff in effect at FERC

Issued by - S. A. Cisel, Vice President
Peoria, Illinois

Central Illinois Light Company

Ill. C. C. No. 9 - Electric
Original Sheet No. 69

RATE 33 - PILOT ELECTRIC TRANSMISSION SERVICE

under this rate shall pay the Company the cost of such interconnection, metering and other facilities, plus ten percent.

Company-supplied Power: Except for power billed under Imbalance Charge, Supplier Shortfall Charge or System Loss Service, the charge for any power, other than off-system purchases by the customer, delivered by the Company to a delivery point serving the customer shall be billed under the Company's prior electric service rate applicable to the customer, as such rate may be changed from time to time.

Imbalance Charge: In the event the actual deliveries of off-system purchases to a receipt point for the account of any customer purchasing load following service from an off-system supplier deviates during any hour by more than 1.5 percent of the scheduled deliveries, the customer shall be charged ten cents per kilowatthour for that part of the deviation that is more than 1.5 percent above or below the scheduled amount.

Supplier Shortfall Charge: In addition to the Company-supplied Power charge, a charge of ten cents per kilowatthour shall be applied on an hourly basis to all usage of a Rate 33 customer during a capacity deficient period up to the customer's contracted capacity less scheduled deliveries. Notwithstanding the provisions of the charge for Company-supplied Power, any demand placed upon the Company's system by the customer during a capacity deficient period that is in excess of the customer's scheduled deliveries of off-system purchases shall be included in the determination of the customer's monthly billing demand under any other rate or contract. The Supplier Shortfall Charge shall not be applicable when an Imbalance Charge is applicable.

System Loss Service: The energy losses incurred during the delivery of off-system power shall be calculated based on the type of electric service provided by the Company to the customer's delivery point. The sum of hourly off-system purchases scheduled to be delivered to delivery points for the account of the customer shall be divided by an Energy Loss Factor based on the table below:

Type of Electrical Service Provided to the Customer's Delivery Point	Energy Loss Factor
Delivery at nominal system voltage of 138 KV	0.99368

Issued - March 29, 1996, Pursuant to Order of the Illinois Commerce Commission entered March 13, 1996 Docket No. 95-0435

Effective - The later of April 30, 1996, or the date CILCO has an approved retail transmission in tariff in effect at FERC

Issued by - S. A. Cisel, Vice President
Peoria, Illinois

Central Illinois Light Company

Ill. C. C. No. 9 - Electric
Original Sheet No. 70

RATE 33 - PILOT ELECTRIC TRANSMISSION SERVICE

Delivery at nominal system voltage of 69 KV or 34.5 KV	0.98306
Supply voltage at nominal system voltage of 138 KV, 69 KV or 34.5 KV with delivery through dedicated transformation facilities to the customer's delivery point	0.97797

Only one Energy Loss Factor will be applicable. Any customer taking service under this rate may elect to purchase system loss service from the Company, in which event the Company will make up the difference between the off-system purchases delivered to receipt points for the account of the customer and the lesser amounts that would otherwise be delivered to delivery points after system losses. The charge for this service will be at a rate equal to the Company's average production cost per kilowatthour during the most recent completed calendar year, plus 10%, applied to the losses made up by the Company.

Minimum Monthly Charge:

The minimum monthly charge under this rate shall be the sum of the charges for Delivery Service plus the Administrative Service Charge, plus any separate facilities charges and any minimum charges under any other rate and any service contracts applicable to the customer.

Payments:

Unless otherwise provided in Section 280.90 of Title 83 of the Illinois Administrative Code, bills will be considered past due if not paid by the due date, which will not be less than fourteen (14) days after the postmark date of the bill. An amount equal to 1½% per month will be applied to any unpaid balance existing at the immediate subsequent regular billing date.

Issued - March 29, 1996, Pursuant to Order of the Illinois Commerce Commission entered March 13, 1996 Docket No. 95-0435

Effective - The later of April 30, 1996, or the date CILCO has an approved retail transmission in tariff in effect at FERC

Issued by - S. A. Cisel, Vice President
Peoria, Illinois

Central Illinois Light Company

Ill. C. C. No. 9 - Electric
Original Sheet No. 71

RATE 34 - PILOT SERVICE TO OPEN ACCESS SITES

Availability:

Service under this rate is available for a period of five years after the rate's initial effective date, to all customers located within specified geographical areas designated by the Company and known as "open access sites."

Definitions:

As used in this rate, the following terms shall have the meanings specified:

"Available receipt point" means a receipt point that the Company has determined has adequate capacity under normal operating conditions to accept delivery of scheduled off-system purchases without impairing the reliability of the Company's electric system or the quality of service to other customers.

"Capacity deficient period" means a period when the Company anticipates that its available generating capacity may not be sufficient to meet all demands of the Company's native load plus required reserves plus off-system commitments without interrupting customers or purchasing wholesale power at prices the Company determines to be uneconomical.

"Company" means Central Illinois Light Company.

"Customer" means a single premises for which the electric service is aggregated for purposes of billing.

"Delivery day" means the 24-hour period from midnight to midnight, local time, when off-system purchases may be scheduled for delivery to available receipt points.

"Delivery point" means a point where the Company's electric system is connected to a Rate 34 customer.

"Distribution capacity" means electric lines and related facilities at nominal system voltage levels less than 138 kv.

"MAIN" means the Mid-America Interconnected Network.

"NERC" means the North American Electric Reliability Council.

Issued - March 29, 1996, Pursuant to Order of the Illinois Commerce Commission entered March 13, 1996 Docket No. 95-0435

Effective - The later of April 30, 1996, or the date CILCO has an approved retail transmission in tariff in effect at FERC

Issued by - S. A. Cisel, Vice President
Peoria, Illinois

Central Illinois Light Company

Ill. C. C. No. 9 - Electric
Original Sheet No. 72

RATE 34 - PILOT SERVICE TO OPEN ACCESS SITES

"Off-system purchases" means electric power purchased by Rate 34 customers from electric suppliers other than the Company.

"Person" means an individual, corporation, partnership, governmental body or agency, or other recognized entity.

"Receipt point" means a point or points where the Company is interconnected with another public utility or with any other supplier of electric energy.

"Supplier" means any person that contracts with a customer to furnish off-system purchases or any other service or facility which customers are permitted by this rate to purchase off-system.

"Transmission capacity" means electric lines and related facilities operating at nominal system voltage levels of 138 kv or higher.

Nature of Service:

The Company will contract to deliver during the time this rate is available, to eligible customers that elect service under this rate (Rate 34 customers), the off-system purchases of such customers.

The services provided by the Company under this rate will include firm delivery of off-system purchases from an available receipt point to the customer's delivery point. In addition, the Company will provide administrative service, and, to the extent not otherwise provided, load following service, system protection service, reactive power/voltage control service, and system loss service. Any Rate 34 customer may elect to purchase his meter, meter maintenance, meter reading and billing service from alternate suppliers, provided they conform with the Company's standards of accuracy and safety, and the Company has reasonable access to the meter to test and read the same. Customers electing all such services from alternate suppliers shall receive a credit equal to the monthly customer charge under any other applicable rate.

Except as hereinafter set forth, Rate 34 customers shall be entitled to service under and shall be subject to the charges in the respective rates and contracts under which the customers would be served if they were not receiving service under this Rate 34. If a Rate 34 customer purchases no power or energy under such other rate during any month, the customer shall be billed the minimum applicable charge under such other rate and under any applicable service contract, plus any separate facilities charges, plus the charges applicable under this Rate 34.

Issued - March 29, 1996, Pursuant to Order of the Illinois Commerce Commission entered March 13, 1996 Docket No. 95-0435

Effective - The later of April 30, 1996, or the date CILCO has an approved retail transmission in tariff in effect at FERC

Issued by - S. A. Cisel, Vice President
Peoria Illinois

Central Illinois Light Company

Ill. C. C. No. 9 - Electric
Original Sheet No. 73

RATE 34 - PILOT SERVICE TO OPEN ACCESS SITES

Off-system purchases delivered to the customer shall be deemed to be the first power and energy delivered to the customer, except when the customer is purchasing full requirements or load following service off-system, in which event the off-system purchases delivered to the customer shall be deemed to be the last power and energy through the customer's meter.

Special Terms and Conditions:

(a) Service under this rate is offered on a limited basis for the purpose of allowing the Company and its customers to gain knowledge and experience in the purchase by customers of some or all of their electric requirements from suppliers other than the Company. The Company reserves the right to petition the Illinois Commerce Commission at any time or times during the availability of this rate for approval of changes in the terms and conditions under which service is offered under this rate, and, if the Company believes appropriate, to terminate this rate. The Company may elect to terminate this rate if a regulatory agency or court having jurisdiction determines that the Company, by reason of this rate or any rate of the Company on file at the Federal Energy Regulatory Commission, is obligated to provide retail open access to any customer not included within an open access site designated by the Company and not included within the availability provision of the Company's retail Rate 33. Such election shall be exercised by the Company by filing notice of the termination with the Illinois Commerce Commission, and this rate shall terminate seven days after such filing. The Company shall promptly mail notice of such election to all customers then receiving service under this rate, but failure to give such notice to customers shall not prevent the termination of this rate as specified herein. In the event this rate is terminated prior to five years after its initial effective date, and a Rate 34 customer is thereby precluded from receiving off-system purchases for which the customer has contracted under a contract which the customer has no option to terminate, the Company will, at the Company's option, either continue to transport the customer's off-system purchases pursuant to the provisions of this rate and the contract with the customer under this rate, or buy out the customer's contracted off-system supply, provided, however, the Company's obligation under this provision will be limited to that portion of off-system purchases contracted through the earliest of the following dates: (i) the expiration date of the contract between the customer and the Company under this rate; (ii) the expiration date of the contract between the customer and the off-system supplier; and (iii) the fifth anniversary of the initial effective date of this rate.

(b) Before receiving service under this rate, a customer or the customer's agent must enter into a contract with the Company for such service, in a form determined by the Company. A single contract may be executed on behalf of customers whose off-system

Issued - March 29, 1996, Pursuant to Order of the Illinois Commerce Commission entered March 13, 1996 Docket No. 95-0435

Effective - The later of April 30, 1996, or the date CILCO has an approved retail transmission in tariff in effect at FERC

Issued by - S. A. Cisel, Vice President
Peoria, Illinois

Central Illinois Light Company

Ill. C. C. No. 9 - Electric
Original Sheet No. 74

RATE 34 - PILOT SERVICE TO OPEN ACCESS SITES

purchases are to be aggregated. At a minimum, the contract shall specify the level of off-system purchases by each customer, the primary receipt points for each customer's off-system purchases, the services that are to be furnished by off-system suppliers, the name of any person that is to aggregate the customer's off-system purchases with those of other Rate 34 customers, and the services that are to be furnished by the Company. The primary receipt points designated in an executed contract shall be deemed to be available receipt points with respect to that contract.

(c) Rate 34 customers that are eligible for service under residential Rate 1, Rate 2, or Rate 3 must elect to purchase their entire electric requirements off-system. Other Rate 34 customers may elect to purchase their entire electric requirements or a specific daily level of electricity off-system. Any Rate 34 customer may aggregate his off-system purchases with those of other Rate 34 customers of the same customer class. For purposes of this provision, customer classes are residential and non-residential. The aggregation may be arranged through a marketer, a broker, a supplier or any other person. The customer shall be obligated to contract with the Company for service under this rate for a minimum term of one year, but not beyond the termination date of this rate. A non-residential customer shall contract and pay for transmission and distribution capacity for the term of the contract, provided, however, a non-residential customer may, by written request to the Company, from time to time increase the amount of contracted capacity and the related payment obligation during the balance of the contract term, and shall be permitted, upon 24 hours' advance written notice to the Company, to reduce the amount of contracted capacity and the related payment obligation, provided further, the customer may not thereafter increase the amount of contracted capacity under this rate except upon ninety days' advance written notice. Residential customers shall have the option to elect or terminate service under this rate upon the same conditions and limitations applicable to changes by non-residential customers.

(d) The Company shall have no responsibility for delivery of off-system purchases until the power has been received into the Company's system. The Company shall not be liable for an inability to receive off-system purchases into the Company's system because of any lack of available capacity at a receipt point or any cause beyond the Company's reasonable control. In the event of a lack of capacity to handle all electric flows at an available receipt point, the Company will comply with the rules, regulations, and guidelines of MAIN and NERC applicable to such situations. In the event the Company is unable, for any reason, to deliver to a Rate 34 customer any scheduled off-system purchases that the Company is otherwise able to receive into its system for the account of such customer, the customer shall either interrupt the delivery to the Company of such off-system purchases during the period the Company is unable to deliver to the

Issued - March 29, 1996, Pursuant to Order of the Illinois Commerce Commission entered March 13, 1996 Docket No. 95-0435

Effective - The later of April 30, 1996, or the date CILCO has an approved retail transmission in tariff in effect at FERC

Issued by - S. A. Cisel, Vice President
Peoria, Illinois

Central Illinois Light Company

Ill. C. C. No. 9 - Electric
Original Sheet No. 75

RATE 34 - PILOT SERVICE TO OPEN ACCESS SITES

customer, or shall sell the off-system purchases to the Company during such period at the Company's avoided energy cost specified in Rate 28.

(e) Before the Company commences delivery of off-system purchases to a customer, the customer shall furnish to the Company, at a minimum, the following information: the name and address of the suppliers of the customer's off-system purchases, the location of the generating equipment from which the customer's off-system purchases will be supplied, the transmission path from the generating equipment to the receipt point, a detailed statement of the services to be furnished to the customer by such off-system supplier, a specification of the available receipt points where the off-system purchases are to be delivered to the Company, and a representation that the supplier is obligated to notify the Company by telephone within ten minutes if, for any reason, the supplier ceases to furnish all or any part of the power scheduled to be furnished for the customer's account and is obligated to notify the Company immediately after the supply is resumed. Updated information shall be furnished to the Company promptly after it is available to the customer.

(f) Not later than noon of the twentieth day of each calendar month, each Rate 34 customer shall furnish the Company, in writinq, a schedule of the off-system purchases to be delivered to the Company for the account of the customer during the immediately succeeding calendar month. Scheduling shall be done in full megawatt increments. The schedule may provide for delivery to the Company of off-system purchases on an hourly, daily, weekly or monthly basis, in total amounts ranging from zero to the customer's maximum contracted capacity, and shall specify the receipt points for the off-system purchases. Not later than 10:00 a.m. of the day preceding the delivery day, the customer may amend the delivery schedule for the delivery day, and shall amend delivery schedules at such intervals, not more frequently than daily, as deemed necessary by the Company to reflect expected changes in usage resulting from weather changes or any other cause. All amended schedules shall be furnished to the Company in writing. Schedules for full requirements service or load following service may be rejected by the Company if the Company determines, in its sole judgment, that the schedules do not reasonably reflect the customers' expected requirements for electricity. If the Company determines it is unable for any reason to accept off-system purchases at any receipt point scheduled by a customer, the Company will notify the customer promptly after such determination is made, and work with the customer to schedule delivery of the customer's off-system purchases so that the reliability of the Company's electric system is not impaired and the quality of service to other customers is not diminished. If the Company notifies a non-residential customer no later than 9:00 a.m. of the preceding day that the delivery day is, in whole or in part, a capacity deficient period, then during such

Issued - March 29, 1996, Pursuant
to Order of the Illinois Commerce
Commission entered March 13, 1996
Docket No. 95-0435

Effective - The later of April 30, 1996, or the date CILCO has an approved retail transmission in tariff in effect at FERC

Issued by - S. A. Cisel, Vice President
Peoria, Illinois

Central Illinois Light Company

Ill. C. C. No. 9 - Electric
Original Sheet No. 76

RATE 34 - PILOT SERVICE TO OPEN ACCESS SITES

capacity deficient period the customer shall cause off-system purchases to be delivered to available receipt points in amounts totaling the customer's full contracted capacity.

(g) Schedules shall be furnished to the Company's Energy Control Center by messenger, by certified or registered mail, return receipt requested, or by telephone facsimile, provided, however, that facsimile delivery will not be accepted by the Company unless the customer confirms by telephone, within thirty minutes after sending the facsimile message, that the message has been received at the Company's Energy Control Center. Notice by the Company to customers of a capacity deficient period may be given by telephone or by telephone facsimile, at the customer's option. Rate 34 customers shall provide the Company with customer telephone numbers to receive notice. The customer shall be deemed to have received notice if the telephone is not answered when called by the Company, or in the event of a mechanical breakdown or interruption of service which prevents the call or facsimile message from being received.

(h) At the request of any eligible customer that has elected service under this rate, and subject to receipt of all necessary regulatory approvals, the Company will enlarge existing interconnections and will add an interconnection with any adjacent supplier of electric energy, subject to the Facilities Charge specified in this rate.

(i) A Rate 33 customer may schedule delivery of off-system purchases to the Company's system through any available receipt point for re-delivery of off-system purchases by the Company to the customer's delivery point.

(j) No customer with peak demand of ten megawatts or greater that is receiving service under this rate, may elect to have load following service provided by any supplier other than the Company unless that customer, at the customer's sole expense, installs the necessary telemetry to allow the Company, the supplier providing the load following service, and the control area where the supplier's generation is located to ascertain instantly all changes in the customer's usage of power.

(k) For Rate 34 customers that qualify for service under Rate 1, 2, or 3, and for non-residential Rate 34 customers that have elected to purchase their full requirements from off-system suppliers, and are not required by this rate to install and have not actually installed telemetry equipment, within ten days after the end of each billing month, the Company will reconcile each such customer's actual usage during that month with the off-system deliveries for the account of that customer during that month. The difference between the actual usage and the off-system purchases shall be billed or paid for in accordance with the Imbalance Charge in this rate.

Issued - March 29, 1996, Pursuant
to Order of the Illinois Commerce
Commission entered March 13, 1996
Docket No. 95-0435

Effective - The later of April 30, 1996, or the date CILCO has an approved retail transmission in tariff in effect at FERC

Issued by - S. A. Cisel, Vice President
Peoria, Illinois

Central Illinois Light Company

Ill. C. C. No. 9 - Electric
Original Sheet No. 77

RATE 34 - PILOT SERVICE TO OPEN ACCESS SITES

(l) In addition to the foregoing Special Terms and Conditions, service under this pilot rate shall be subject to the Company's General Terms and Conditions applicable to electric service. In the event of any conflict between the Company's General Terms and Conditions and the Special Terms and Conditions contained in this rate, the Special Terms and Conditions shall control with respect to service under this rate, and the General Terms and Conditions shall control with respect to service under any other applicable rate.

Monthly Charges:

Rate 34 customers that qualify for service under Rate 1, 2, or 3 shall be subject to the following monthly charges for service under this rate:

Transmission/Distribution Charge: 2.28 cents per kilowatthour for all off-system purchases delivered to the customer.

Load Following Service: One-third (1/3) mill per kilowatthour for all off-system purchases delivered to the customer. Any customer may elect to purchase this service from an off-system supplier.

System Protection Service: One-third (1/3) mill per kilowatthour for all off-system purchases delivered to the customer. Any customer may elect to purchase this service from an off-system supplier.

Reactive Power/Voltage Control Service: One-third (1/3) mill per kilowatthour for all off-system purchases delivered to the customer. Any customer may elect to purchase this service from an off-system supplier.

Administrative Service Charge: One-third (1/3) mill per kilowatthour for all off-system purchases delivered to the customer.

Rate 34 customers that do not qualify for service under Rate 1, 2, or 3 shall be subject to the following monthly charges for service under this rate:

Delivery Service:

Transmission Component: $.96 per kilowatt of contracted transmission capacity per month.

Issued - March 29, 1996, Pursuant to Order of the Illinois Commerce Commission entered March 13, 1996 Docket No. 95-0435

Effective - The later of April 30, 1996, or the date CILCO has an approved retail transmission in tariff in effect at FERC

Issued by - S. A. Cisel, Vice President
Peoria, Illinois

Central Illinois Light Company

Ill. C. C. No. 9 - Electric
Original Sheet No. 78

RATE 34 - PILOT SERVICE TO OPEN ACCESS SITES

Distribution Components:

Subtransmission: $.50 per kilowatt of contracted subtransmission distribution capacity per month for customers served at the subtransmission level.

Primary: $3.77 per kilowatt of contracted primary distribution capacity per month for customers served at the primary level.

Secondary: $5.63 per kilowatt of contracted secondary distribution capacity per month for customers served at the secondary level.

Only one distribution component will be applicable.

Load Following Service: One-third (1/3) mill per kilowatthour for all energy delivered to the customer under this rate. Any customer may elect to purchase this service from an off-system supplier.

System Protection Service: One-third (1/3) mill per kilowatthour for all energy delivered to the customer under this rate. Any customer may elect to purchase this service from an off-system supplier.

Reactive Power/Voltage Control Service: One-third (1/3) mill per kilowatthour for all energy delivered to the customer under this rate. Any customer may elect to purchase this service from an off-system supplier.

Administrative Service Charge: One-third (1/3) mill per kilowatthour for all off-system purchases delivered to the customer.

Other Charges:

In addition to the monthly charges described above, the customers receiving service under this rate shall be subject to the following charges:

Facilities Charge: In the event the customer requests the construction of an interconnection or other facilities to receive service under this rate, or in the event the Company determines, in its sole judgment, that additional metering or other facilities are reasonably required in order to provide service under this rate without degrading or impairing the service provided to any other customer, the customer under this rate shall pay the Company the cost of such interconnection, metering and other facilities, plus ten percent. Non-residential Rate 34 customers shall be required to install, or have the

Issued - March 29, 1996, Pursuant to Order of the Illinois Commerce Commission entered March 13, 1996 Docket No. 95-0435

Effective - The later of April 30, 1996, or the date CILCO has an approved retail transmission in tariff in effect at FERC

Issued by - S. A. Cisel, Vice President
Peoria, Illinois

RATE 34 - PILOT SERVICE TO OPEN ACCESS SITES

Company install at the customer's expe.ıse, meters that measure and record demand and energy usage at hourly intervals.

Company-supplied Power: Except for power billed under Imbalance Charge, Supplier Shortfall Charge or System Loss Service, the charge for any power, other than off-system purchases by the customer, delivered by the Company to a delivery point serving the customer shall be billed under the Company's electric service rate that would be applicable to the customer if service were not supplied under this rate.

Imbalance Charge: Rate 34 customers that qualify for service under Rate 1, 2, or 3 shall be charged ten cents for each kilowatthour of actual monthly usage in excess of off-system purchases in that month. The Company will pay its avoided energy cost, as specified in Rate 28, for each kilowatthour of off-system purchases by any such customer in excess of the actual usage of such customer during any billing month. Any other Rate 34 customer that purchases full requirements service from off-system suppliers and is not required by this rate to install and has not actually installed telemetry equipment, shall be charged ten cents for each kilowatthour of actual monthly usage in excess of off-system purchases during that month. The Company will pay its avoided e· ergy cost, as specified in Rate 28, for each kilowatthour of off-system purchases by any such customer in excess of the actual usage of such customer during any billing month. In the event the actual deliveries of off-system purchases to a receipt point for the account of any non-residential customer purchasing load following service, but not full requirements service, from off-system suppliers deviates during any hour by more than 1.5 percent of the scheduled deliveries, the customer shall be charged ten cents per kilowatthour for that part of the deviation that is more than 1.5 percent above or below the scheduled amount.

Supplier Shortfall Charge: In addition to the Company-supplied Power charge, a charge of ten cents per kilowatthour shall be applied on an hourly basis to all usage of each non-residential Rate 34 customer dur.ng a capacity deficient period up to the customer's contracted capacity less scheduled deliveries. Notwithstanding the provisions of the charge for Company-supplied Power, any demand placed upon the Company's system by the customer during a capacity deficient period that is in excess of the customer's scheduled deliveries of off-system purchases shall be included in the determination of the customer's monthly billing demand under any other rate or contract. The Supplier Shortfall Charge shall not be applicable when an Imbalance Charge is applicable.

System Loss Service: The energy losses incurred during the delivery of off-system power shall be calculated based on the tvoe of electric service provided by the

Issued - March 29, 1996, Pursuant to Order of the Illinois Commerce Commission entered March 13, 1996 Docket No. 95-0435

Effective - The later of April 30, 1996, or the date CILCO has an approved retail transmission in tariff in effect at FERC

Issued by - S. A. Cisel, Vice President
Peoria, Illinois

Central Illinois Light Company

Ill. C. C. No. 9 - Electric
Original Sheet No. 80

RATE 34 - PILOT SERVICE TO OPEN ACCESS SITES

Company to the customer's delivery point. The sum of hourly off-system purchases scheduled to be delivered to delivery points for the account of the customer shall be divided by an Energy loss factor based on the table below:

Type of Electrical Service Provided to the Customer's <u>Delivery Point</u>	Energy Loss <u>Factor</u>
Delivery at nominal system voltage of 138 KV	0.99368
Delivery at nominal system voltage of 69 KV or 34.5 KV	0.98306
Supply voltage at nominal system voltage of 138 KV, 69 KV or 34.5 KV with delivery through dedicated transformation facilities to the customer's delivery point	0.97797
Delivery at nominal system voltage of 4 to 15 KV	0.96814
Delivery at nominal system voltage of 0 to 1 KV	0.93872

Only one Energy Loss Factor will be applicable. Any customer taking service under this rate may elect to purchase system loss service from the Company, in which event the Company will make up the difference between the off-system purchases delivered to receipt points for the account of the customer and the lesser amounts that would otherwise be delivered to delivery points after system losses. The charge for this service will be at a rate equal to the Company's average production cost per kilowatthour during the most recently completed calendar year, plus 10%, applied to the losses made up by the Company.

Issued - March 29, 1996, Pursuant
to Order of the Illinois Commerce
Commission entered March 13, 1996
Docket No. 95-0435

Effective - The later of April 30, 1996, or the date CILCO has an approved retail transmission in tariff in effect at FERC

Issued by - S. A. Cisel, Vice President
Peoria, Illinois

Central Illinois Light Company

Ill. C. C. No. 9 - Electric
Original Sheet No. 81

RATE 34 - PILOT SERVICE TO OPEN ACCESS SITES

Minimum Monthly Charge:

The minimum monthly charge for a residential customer under this rate shall be the Administrative Service Charge plus any separate facilities charges and any minimum charges under any other rate and any service contracts applicable to the customer. The minimum monthly charge for a non-residential customer under this rate shall be the sum of the charges for Delivery Service plus the Administrative Service Charge, plus any separate facilities charges and any minimum charges under any other rate and any service contracts applicable to the customer.

Payments:

Unless otherwise provided in Section 280.90 of Title 83 of the Illinois Administrative Code, bills will be considered past due if not paid by the due date. The due date will not be less than twenty-one (21) days for Residential Customers and fourteen (14) days for Non-Residential Customers after the postmark date of the bill. An amount equal to 1½% per month will be applied to any unpaid balance existing at the immediate subsequent regular billing date. The Company will waive the assessment of a late payment charge for residential customers one time in a twelve-month period.

Issued - March 29, 1996, Pursuant to Order of the Illinois Commerce Commission entered March 13, 1996 Docket No. 95-0435

Effective - The later of April 30, 1996, or the date CILCO has an approved retail transmission in tariff in effect at FERC

Issued by - S. A. Cisel, Vice President
Peoria, Illinois

FERC NO. __ & NHPUC NO. 1 - ELECTRICITY DELIVERY
PUBLIC SERVICE COMPANY OF NEW HAMPSHIRE

Original Page 24
Rate DS1

PILOT PROGRAM
RESIDENTIAL DELIVERY SERVICE RATE DS1

AVAILABILITY

Subject to the Terms and Conditions of the Tariff of which it is a part, this rate is for Delivery Service to Eligible Customers in individual urban, rural and farm residences and apartments located in the Company's Service Area. Delivery Service under this rate is not available in conjunction with electric service rendered under the Company's Tariff for Electric Service.

This rate is not applicable to commercial purposes except as specified hereafter. Multiple use of Delivery Service within the residence through one meter shall be billed in accordance with the predominant use of the demand. When wired for connection to the same meter, Delivery Service under this rate shall include the residence and connecting and adjacent buildings used exclusively for noncommercial purposes.

The use of single-phase motors of 5 H.P. rating or less is permitted under this rate provided such use does not interfere with the quality of service rendered to other customers. Upon written application to the Company, the use of larger motors may be authorized where existing distribution facilities permit.

CHARACTER OF SERVICE

Delivery Service supplied under this rate will be single-phase, 60 hertz, alternating current, normally three-wire at a nominal voltage of 120/240 volts.

RATE PER MONTH

Meter Charge . . . . $9.16 per month

Energy Charges:

	Per Kilowatt-Hour
Distribution Service	1.900¢
Transmission Service	0.420¢
Acquisition Premium	2.970¢

Issued: May 1, 1996

Effective: Per Section 2.1(e) Issued by: Gary A. Long

Expires: Per Section 2.1(c) Title: Vice President Customer Service and Economic Development

FERC NO. __ & NHPUC NO. 1 - ELECTRICITY DELIVERY
PUBLIC SERVICE COMPANY OF NEW HAMPSHIRE

Original Page 25
Rate DS1

Stranded Cost:

First 250 kilowatt-hours	2.759¢
Next 550 kilowatt-hours	6.942¢
All additional kilowatt-hours	5.288¢
Participation Incentive Credit	(1.550¢)

TRANSMISSION SERVICE CREDIT

In all cases where an Eligible Customer has acquired power from one or more resources that have been transmitted to the Point of Receipt pursuant to the NU System Companies' Point-to-Point Transmission Service Tariff for the New Hampshire Retail Competition Pilot Program ("Point-to-Point Tariff"), such Eligible Customer shall be entitled to a credit against its charges under this Tariff. Such credit shall be calculated by allocating the revenues received under the Point-to-Point Tariff in connection with the delivery of such Eligible Customer's resource(s) among the NU System Companies in accordance with the Sharing Agreement and crediting the Eligible Customer for the portion of such revenues allocated to the Company thereunder. In circumstances where a third party has acquired resources on behalf of one or more Eligible Customer taking service hereunder, such third party shall provide information to the Company showing the portion of each Eligible Customer's total resources that has been transmitted under the Point-to-Point Tariff so that the credit can be calculated.

LOSSES

For reporting purposes under the NEPOOL Agreement, the Eligible Customer's energy and capacity delivered under this Rate Schedule shall be adjusted for losses. The kilowatt-hour energy shall be increased by an average loss factor of 6.37 percent in each hour except that during the hour of system peak, the loss adjustment shall be 7.83 percent.

Issued: May 1, 1996

Effective: Per Section 2.1(e) Issued by: Gary A. Long

Expires: Per Section 2.1(c) Title: Vice President Customer Service and Economic Development

FERC NO. __ & NHPUC NO. 1 - ELECTRICITY DELIVERY
PUBLIC SERVICE COMPANY OF NEW HAMPSHIRE

Original Page 26
Rate DS1

SERVICE CHARGE

When the Company establishes or re-establishes a Delivery Service account for an Eligible Customer at a meter location, the Company will be entitled to make a service charge in addition to all other charges under this rate. The service charge will be $8.00 if the Company does not have to send an employee to the meter location to establish or re-establish Delivery Service. When it is necessary for the Company to send an employee to the meter location to establish or re-establish Delivery Service, the service charge will be $16.00. When it is necessary for the Company to send an employee to the meter location outside of normal working hours to establish or re-establish Delivery Service, the service charge will be $32.00.

TERMS

The charges for Delivery Service under this rate are net, billed monthly and payable upon presentation of bill. Eligible Customers may elect to pay for all service rendered under this rate on a Level Payment Plan Available on application to the Company.

Issued: May 1, 1996

Effective: Per Section 2.1(e) Issued by: Gary A. Long

Expires: Per Section 2.1(c) Title: Vice President Customer Service and Economic Development

FERC NO. __ & NHPUC NO. 1 - ELECTRICITY DELIVERY
PUBLIC SERVICE COMPANY OF NEW HAMPSHIRE

Original Page 27
Rate DS2

PILOT PROGRAM
SMALL GENERAL DELIVERY SERVICE RATE DS2

AVAILABILITY

Subject to the Terms and Conditions of the Tariff of which it is a part, this rate is for Delivery Service to Eligible Customers whose loads as defined for billing purposes do not exceed 100 kilowatts. Delivery Service under this rate is not available in conjunction with electric service rendered under the Company's Tariff for Electric Service.

Eligible Customers taking Delivery Service under this rate shall provide any necessary transforming and regulating devices on the Eligible Customer's side of the meter.

CHARACTER OF SERVICE

Delivery Service supplied under this rate will be 60 hertz, alternating current, either (a) single-phase, normally three-wire at a nominal voltage of 120/240 volts, or (b) three-phase, normally at a nominal voltage of 120/208 or 277/480 volts. In underground secondary network areas, Delivery Service will be supplied only at a nominal voltage of 120/208 volts.

RATE PER MONTH

	Single-Phase Service	Three-Phase Service
Meter Charge	$9.80 per month	$19.61 per month

Customer's Load Charge:

	Per Kilowatt of Customer Load in Excess of 5.0 Kilowatts
Distribution Service	$4.00
Transmission Service	$1.50
Stranded Cost	$3.66

Issued: May 1, 1996

Effective: Per Section 2.1(e) Issued by: Gary A. Long

Expires: Per Section 2.1(c) Title: Vice President Customer Service and Economic Development

FERC NO. __ & NHPUC NO. 1 - ELECTRICITY DELIVERY
PUBLIC SERVICE COMPANY OF NEW HAMPSHIRE

Original Page 28
Rate DS2

Energy Charges:

	Per Kilowatt-Hour
Distribution Service	
First 500 kilowatt-hours	1.900¢
All additional kilowatt-hours	0.000¢
Transmission Service	
First 500 kilowatt-hours	0.420¢
All additional kilowatt-hours	0.000¢
Acquisition Premium	2.970¢
Stranded Cost:	
First 500 kilowatt-hours	6.406¢
Next 1,000 kilowatt-hours	4.399¢
All additional kilowatt-hours	3.203¢
Participation Incentive Credit:	
First 500 kilowatt-hours	(1.550¢)
All additional kilowatt-hours	(1.350¢)

TRANSMISSION SERVICE CREDIT

In all cases where an Eligible Customer has acquired power from one or more resources that have been transmitted to the Point of Receipt pursuant to the NU System Companies' Point-to-Point Transmission Service Tariff for the New Hampshire Retail Competition Pilot Program ("Point-to-Point

Issued: May 1, 1996

Effective: Per Section 2.1(e) Issued by: Gary A. Long

Expires: Per Section 2.1(c) Title: Vice President Customer Service and Economic Development

FERC NO. __ & NHPUC NO. 1 - ELECTRICITY DELIVERY
PUBLIC SERVICE COMPANY OF NEW HAMPSHIRE

Original Page 29
Rate DS2

Tariff"), such Eligible Customer shall be entitled to a credit against its charges under this Tariff. Such credit shall be calculated by allocating the revenues received under the Point-to-Point Tariff in connection with the delivery of such Eligible Customer's resource(s) among the NU System Companies in accordance with the Sharing Agreement and crediting the Eligible Customer for the portion of such revenues allocated to the Company thereunder. In circumstances where a third party has acquired resources on behalf of one or more Eligible Customer taking service hereunder, such third party shall provide information to the Company showing the portion of each Eligible Customer's total resources that has been transmitted under the Point-to-Point Tariff so that the credit can be calculated.

LOSSES

For reporting purposes under the NEPOOL Agreement, the Eligible Customer's energy and capacity delivered under this Rate Schedule shall be adjusted for losses. The kilowatt-hour energy shall be increased by an average loss factor of 6.37 percent in each hour except that during the hour of system peak, the loss adjustment shall be 7.83 percent.

ELIGIBLE CUSTOMER'S LOAD

Eligible Customer's load is defined as the greatest rate of taking Delivery Service in kilowatts for any thirty (30) minute interval during the current monthly billing period.

Eligible Customer's load shall be measured whenever (a) such load is known or estimated to be 5.0 kilowatts or more, or (b) the Eligible Customer's use of service is 750 kilowatt-hours or more per month for three (3) consecutive months. However, any Eligible Customer's load may be measured at the Company's option. When measured, Eligible Customer's load shall be determined to the nearest one-tenth (0.1) kilowatt for billing purposes.

SERVICE CHARGE

When the Company establishes or re-establishes a Delivery Service account for a Eligible Customer at a meter location, the Company will be entitled to make a service charge in addition to all other charges under this rate. The service charge will be $8.00 if the Company does not have to send an employee

Issued:	May 1, 1996		
Effective:	Per Section 2.1(e)	Issued by:	Gary A. Long
Expires:	Per Section 2.1(c)	Title:	Vice President Customer Service and Economic Development

FERC NO. __ & NHPUC NO. 1 - ELECTRICITY DELIVERY
PUBLIC SERVICE COMPANY OF NEW HAMPSHIRE

Original Page 30
Rate DS2

to the meter location to establish or re-establish Delivery Service. When it is necessary for the Company to send an employee to the meter location to establish or re-establish Delivery Service, the service charge will be $16.00. When it is necessary for the Company to send an employee to the meter location outside of normal working hours to establish or re-establish Delivery Service, the service charge will be $32.00.

Issued: May 1, 1996

Effective: Per Section 2.1(e) Issued by: Gary A. Long

Expires: Per Section 2.1(c) Title: Vice President Customer Service and Economic Development

PILOT PROGRAM
PRIMARY GENERAL DELIVERY SERVICE RATE DS3

AVAILABILITY

Subject to the Terms and Conditions of the Tariff of which it is a part, this rate is for Delivery Service associated with high voltage electric service. It is available to those Eligible Customers whose maximum demands as defined for billing purposes shall not exceed 1,000 kilowatts. Delivery Service under this rate is not available in conjunction with electric service rendered under the Company's Tariff for Electric Service.

Suitable transforming, controlling and regulating apparatus, acceptable to and approved by the Company, shall be provided at the expense of the Eligible Customer. In locations in which space limitations or other factors make it impossible or inadvisable, in the opinion of the Company, for the Eligible Customer to have transforming apparatus devoted to his exclusive use, and in secondary network areas in which primary service is not made available by the Company at its option, Delivery Service shall be supplied from Company-owned transforming apparatus which also supplies other customers. In such cases, this rate is available provided the Eligible Customer pays an annual rental charge equal to eighteen percent (18.0%) of the cost of the equivalent transformer capacity he would furnish or rent to serve his load if exclusive use of a transformer bank by him were possible or if primary, three-phase service were available and provided the Eligible Customer pays in full the estimated cost of installing such equivalent transformer capacity at the time Delivery Service is initiated.

CHARACTER OF SERVICE

Delivery Service supplied under this rate will be three-phase, 60 hertz, alternating current, at a nominal voltage determined by the Company, generally 2,400/4,160, 4,800/8,320, 7,200/12,470, or 19,920/34,500 volts. A reasonably balanced load between phases shall be maintained by the Eligible Customer.

Issued:	May 1, 1996		
Effective:	Per Section 2.1(e)	Issued by:	Gary A. Long
Expires:	Per Section 2.1(c)	Title:	Vice President Customer Service and Economic Development

FERC NO. __ & NHPUC NO. 1 - ELECTRICITY DELIVERY
PUBLIC SERVICE COMPANY OF NEW HAMPSHIRE

Original Page 32
Rate DS3

RATE PER MONTH

Meter Charge . . . . $130.69 per month

Demand Charges:

	Per Kilowatt of Maximum Demand
Distribution Service	$1.90
Transmission Service	$1.30
Stranded Cost:	
First 100 kilowatts	$5.56
Excess Over 100 kilowatts	$4.96
Participation Incentive Credit	($0.85)

Energy Charges:

	Per Kilowatt-Hour
Acquisition Premium	2.970¢
Stranded Cost:	
First 200,000 kilowatt-hours	3.176¢
All additional kilowatt-hours	2.393¢
Participation Incentive Credit	(0.920¢)

TRANSMISSION SERVICE CREDIT

In all cases where an Eligible Customer has acquired power from one or more resources that have been transmitted to the Point of Receipt pursuant to the NU System Companies' Point-to-Point Transmission Service Tariff for the

Issued: May 1, 1996

Effective: Per Section 2.1(e) Issued by: Gary A. Long

Expires: Per Section 2.1(c) Title: Vice President Customer Service and Economic Development

FERC NO. __ & NHPUC NO. 1 - ELECTRICITY DELIVERY   Original Page 33
PUBLIC SERVICE COMPANY OF NEW HAMPSHIRE   Rate DS3

New Hampshire Retail Competition Pilot Program ("Point-to-Point Tariff"), such Eligible Customer shall be entitled to a credit against its charges under this Tariff. Such credit shall be calculated by allocating the revenues received under the Point-to-Point Tariff in connection with the delivery of such Eligible Customer's resource(s) among the NU System Companies in accordance with the Sharing Agreement and crediting the Eligible Customer for the portion of such revenues allocated to the Company thereunder. In circumstances where a third party has acquired resources on behalf of one or more Eligible Customer taking service hereunder, such third party shall provide information to the Company showing the portion of each Eligible Customer's total resources that has been transmitted under the Point-to-Point Tariff so that the credit can be calculated.

DISCOUNT FOR LONG HOURS' USE

A discount of seven hundred and four thousandths cents (0.704¢) per kilowatt-hour will be allowed on all energy in excess of 300 hours' use per month of the maximum demand.

PRIMARY METERING LOSS ADJUSTMENT

When at the Company's option Delivery Service is metered at delivery voltage (2,400 volts nominal and above), all demand and energy meter readings shall be reduced by one and three-quarters percent (1.75%). Where feasible and at the Company's option, a value other than one and three-quarters percent (1.75%) may be used when specific data is available and this value is a more accurate representation of electrical losses.

LOSSES

For reporting purposes under the NEPOOL Agreement, the Eligible Customer's energy and capacity delivered under this Rate Schedule shall be adjusted for losses. The kilowatt-hour energy shall be increased by an average loss factor of 6.22 percent in each hour except that during the hour of system peak, the loss adjustment shall be 7.52 percent.

Issued: May 1, 1996

Effective: Per Section 2.1(e)   Issued by: Gary A. Long

Expires: Per Section 2.1(c)   Title: Vice President Customer Service and Economic Development

FERC NO. __ & NHPUC NO. 1 - ELECTRICITY DELIVERY
PUBLIC SERVICE COMPANY OF NEW HAMPSHIRE

Original Page 34
Rate DS3

MAXIMUM DEMAND

The kilowatt (KW) demand and, at the Company's option, the kilovolt-ampere (KVA) demand during each thirty-minute interval of the current monthly billing period shall be determined by measurement. Maximum demand shall be defined as the highest kilowatt (KW) demand during said period or, if kilovolt-ampere (KVA) demand is measured, the greater of (a) the highest kilowatt (KW) demand during said period or (b) 80 percent of the highest kilovolt-ampere (KVA) demand during said period. Maximum demand shall be determined to the nearest whole (1.0) kilowatt (KW) or kilovolt-ampere (KVA) for billing purposes.

Off-peak service is available under this rate (1) to all customers who were receiving off-peak service hereunder on January 31, 1984 and who have off-peak metering in accordance with the "Metering" section herein, and (2) to all other customers who create a registered off-peak demand in excess of 300 kilowatts (KW). For such customers, the maximum demand for billing purposes shall be the maximum demand, as defined above, occurring during on-peak hours, or one-half (1/2) of the maximum demand, as defined above, occurring during off-peak hours, whichever is greater. The off-peak period shall be the period including the hours after 8:00 p.m. and before 7:00 a.m., Monday through Friday, and the entire day on Saturdays, Sundays, and holidays. Holidays shall be as defined in Section 16.0 of the Terms and Conditions of this Tariff. The on-peak period shall be all hours not included in the off-peak period.

GUARANTEES

Except as provided by the Terms and Conditions and exclusive of any charges made under the provisions of the section in this rate entitled "Apparatus", the minimum monthly charge shall be $603.70 per month.

APPARATUS

Substation foundations, structures, and all necessary controlling, regulating, and transforming apparatus shall be furnished, owned, and maintained by the Eligible Customer at his expense. However, controlling, regulating, and transforming apparatus may be rented from the Company at a charge of eighteen percent (18.0%) per year of the equipment cost. The cost of installing such equipment shall be paid in full at the time delivery service is initiated. In no event shall the Company be required to rent apparatus to the Eligible Customer the total cost of which shall exceed $10,000. In case the

Issued: May 1, 1996

Effective: Per Section 2.1(e) Issued by: Gary A. Long

Expires: Per Section 2.1(c) Title: Vice President Customer Service and Economic Development

FERC NO. __ & NHPUC NO. 1 - ELECTRICITY DELIVERY
PUBLIC SERVICE COMPANY OF NEW HAMPSHIRE

Original Page 35
Rate DS3

Eligible Customer elects to rent apparatus from the Company, he shall guarantee, in addition to any other guarantees, to continue to pay rental therefor for a period of not less than four (4) years. Should the Eligible Customer discontinue delivery service before four (4) years shall have elapsed and such Delivery Service is not replaced by electric service under PSNH's Tariff for Electric Service for the remaining period, the guaranteed rental then unpaid shall immediately become due and payable.

METERING

The Company may install one or more meters at its option. Metering shall be located on the low voltage side of the Eligible Customer's transforming apparatus provided, however, that metering may be at delivery voltage at the option of the Company.

TERMS

The charges for Delivery Service under this rate are net, billed monthly and payable upon presentation of bill. All amounts previously billed but remaining unpaid at any meter reading date (normally 30 days from the prior meter reading date) shall be subject to a late payment charge of one and one-half percent (1 1/2%) thereof, such amounts to include any prior unpaid late payment charges.

Issued: May 1, 1996

Effective: Per Section 2.1(e) Issued by: Gary A. Long

Expires: Per Section 2.1(c) Title: Vice President Customer Service and Economic Development

FERC NO. __ & NHPUC NO. 1 - ELECTRICITY DELIVERY
PUBLIC SERVICE COMPANY OF NEW HAMPSHIRE

Original Page 36
Rate DS4

PILOT PROGRAM
LARGE GENERAL DELIVERY SERVICE RATE DS4

AVAILABILITY

Subject to the Terms and Conditions of the Tariff of which it is a part, this rate is for Delivery Service associated with high voltage electric service. It is available to those Eligible Customer whose loads are larger than those that would be permitted under Primary General Delivery Service Rate DS3 of this Tariff. Delivery Service under this rate is not available in conjunction with electric service rendered under the Company's Tariff for Electric Service.

Substation foundations and structures, and suitable controlling, regulating, and transforming apparatus, all of which shall be acceptable to and approved by the Company, together with such protective equipment as the Company shall deem necessary for the protection and safe operation of its system, shall be provided at the expense of the Eligible Customer.

CHARACTER OF SERVICE

Delivery Service supplied under this rate will be three-phase, 60 hertz, alternating current, at a nominal delivery voltage determined by the Company, generally 34,500 volts or higher. A reasonably balanced load between phases shall be maintained by the Eligible Customer.

RATE PER MONTH

Meter . . . . $392.10 per month

Demand Charges:

Per Kilovolt-Ampere of Maximum Demand

Distribution Service $1.70

Transmission Service $1.15

Stranded Cost $5.65

Participation Incentive Credit . . . . ($0.85)

Issued: May 1, 1996

Effective: Per Section 2.1(e) Issued by: Gary A. Long

Expires: Per Section 2.1(c) Title: Vice President Customer Service and Economic Development

FERC NO. __ & NHPUC NO. 1 - ELECTRICITY DELIVERY
PUBLIC SERVICE COMPANY OF NEW HAMPSHIRE

Original Page 37
Rate DS4

Energy Charges:

	Per Kilowatt-Hour
Stranded Cost:	
On-Peak Hours (7:00 a.m. to 8:00 p.m. weekdays excluding Holidays as defined in this rate)	
First 150 hours' use of the maximum demand . . .	3.874¢
All additional kilowatt-hours	2.307¢
Off-Peak Hours (all other hours)	
All kilowatt-hours	1.654¢
Acquisition Premium	2.970¢
Participation Incentive Credit	(0.850¢)

MAXIMUM DEMAND

The kilovolt-ampere (KVA) demand during each thirty-minute interval of the current monthly billing period shall be determined by measurement. Maximum demand shall be determined for billing purposes to the nearest whole (1.0) kilovolt-ampere and shall be defined as the greater of

(1) the highest kilovolt-ampere demand registered during the on-peak hours of said period, or

(2) fifty percent (50%) of the highest kilovolt-ampere demand registered during the off-peak hours of said period, except that for any portion of the customer's highest off-peak kilovolt-ampere demand in excess of 30,000 kilovolt-amperes the multiplier applicable to the amount of such demand within each successive 10,000 kilovolt-ampere block of such excess portion shall be increased from fifty percent (50%) by successive ten percent (10%) increments, up to a maximum multiplier of one hundred percent (100%) for that portion of demands in excess of 70,000 kilovolt amperes, or

Issued: May 1, 1996

Effective: Per Section 2.1(e) Issued by: Gary A. Long

Expires: Per Section 2.1(c) Title: Vice President Customer Service and Economic Development

FERC NO. __ & NHPUC NO. 1 - ELECTRICITY DELIVERY
PUBLIC SERVICE COMPANY OF NEW HAMPSHIRE

Original Page 38
Rate DS4

(3) eighty percent (80%) of the amount by which the greatest amount defined in (1) and (2) above during the eleven (11) preceding months exceeds 1,000 kilovolt-amperes.

The off-peak period shall be the period including the hours after 8:00 p.m. and before 7:00 a.m., Monday through Friday, and the entire day on Saturdays, Sundays, and holidays. Holidays shall be as defined in Section 16.0 of the Terms and Conditions of this Tariff. The on-peak period shall be all hours not included in the off-peak period.

TRANSMISSION SERVICE CREDIT

In all cases where an Eligible Customer has acquired power from one or more resources that have been transmitted to the Point of Receipt pursuant to the NU System Companies' Point-to-Point Transmission Service Tariff for the New Hampshire Retail Competition Pilot Program ("Point-to-Point Tariff"), such Eligible Customer shall be entitled to a credit against its charges under this Tariff. Such credit shall be calculated by allocating the revenues received under the Point-to-Point Tariff in connection with the delivery of such Eligible Customer's resource(s) among the NU System Companies in accordance with the Sharing Agreement and crediting the Eligible Customer for the portion of such revenues allocated to the Company thereunder. In circumstances where a third party has acquired resources on behalf of one or more Eligible Customer taking service hereunder, such third party shall provide information to the Company showing the portion of each Eligible Customer's total resources that has been transmitted under the Point-to-Point Tariff so that the credit can be calculated.

LOSSES

For reporting purposes under the NEPOOL Agreement, the Eligible Customer's energy and capacity delivered under this Rate Schedule shall be adjusted for losses. The kilowatt-hour energy shall be increased by an average loss factor of 2.37 percent in each hour except that during the hour of system peak, the loss adjustment shall be 3.95 percent.

Issued:	May 1, 1996		
Effective:	Per Section 2.1(e)	Issued by:	Gary A. Long
Expires:	Per Section 2.1(c)	Title:	Vice President Customer Service and Economic Development

FERC NO. __ & NHPUC NO. 1 - ELECTRICITY DELIVERY
PUBLIC SERVICE COMPANY OF NEW HAMPSHIRE

Original Page 39
Rate DS4

DISCOUNT FOR SERVICE AT 115,000 VOLTS

A monthly discount of forty-three cents ($0.43) per kilovolt-ampere (KVA) of maximum demand shall be given to Eligible Customers who contract to take Delivery Service under this rate at a delivery voltage of 115,000 volts and to pay charges based on a monthly maximum demand of at least 10,000 kilovolt-amperes. Except as provided in the last sentence of this paragraph, this discount is available only at specified delivery points on the 115,000 volt transmission system of the Company as it exists from time to time where, in the opinion of the Company, there is sufficient capacity in facilities to supply the Eligible Customer's requirement and where system integrity and operating flexibility will not be impaired by the addition of the Eligible Customer's load. The discount is available also at other delivery points, provided the Eligible Customer satisfies the Company's requirements under this Tariff.

In the event that any Eligible Customer qualifying for and receiving the discount provided in this section shall require a substantially larger or substantially smaller amount of capacity, the Eligible Customer shall so notify the Company in writing at least two (2) years prior to the date when such larger or smaller amount shall be required.

GUARANTEES

Except as provided by the Terms and Conditions and exclusive of any charges made under the provisions of the section in this rate entitled "Apparatus", the minimum monthly charge shall be the sum of the demand charges but not less than $610.96 per month.

APPARATUS

Substation foundations and structures, and all necessary controlling, regulating, transforming, and protective apparatus shall be furnished, owned, and maintained by the Eligible Customer at his expense. However, controlling, regulating, and transforming apparatus may be rented from the Company at a charge of eighteen percent (18.0%) per year of the equipment cost. The cost of installing such equipment shall be paid in full at the time Delivery Service is initiated. In no event shall the Company be required to rent apparatus to the Eligible Customer the total cost of which shall exceed $10,000. In case the

Issued:	May 1, 1996		
Effective:	Per Section 2.1(e)	Issued by:	Gary A. Long
Expires:	Per Section 2.1(c)	Title:	Vice President Customer Service and Economic Development

FERC NO. __ & NHPUC NO. 1 - ELECTRICITY DELIVERY
PUBLIC SERVICE COMPANY OF NEW HAMPSHIRE

Original Page 40
Rate DS4

Eligible Customer elects to rent apparatus from the Company, he shall guarantee, in addition to any other guarantees, to continue to pay rental therefor for a period of not less than four (4) years. Should the Eligible Customer discontinue service before four (4) years shall have elapsed and such Delivery Service is not replaced by electric service under PSNH's Tariff for Electric Service for the remaining period.

METERING

The Company may install one or more meters at its option. Metering shall be at delivery voltage, provided, however, that metering may be at a lower voltage at the option of the Company, in which case the maximum demand and kilowatt-hour energy use shall include the losses imposed by transformers between the delivery and metering points. In the latter case, the Company may at its option correct for the transformer losses by compensated metering or estimate such losses by another suitable method.

TERMS

The charges for Delivery Service under this rate are net, billed monthly and payable upon presentation of bill. All amounts previously billed but remaining unpaid at any meter reading date (normally 30 days from the prior meter reading date) shall be subject to a late payment charge of one and one-half percent (1 1/2%) thereof, such amounts to include any prior unpaid late payment charges.

Issued: May 1, 1996

Effective: Per Section 2.1(e) Issued by: Gary A. Long

Expires: Per Section 2.1(c) Title: Vice President Customer Service and Economic Development

Appendix D

System Lambda Data for Major Utilities

The following is a summary of all average system lambda information filed by the major investor-owned utilities in the U.S. based on data filed under FERC *Form* 714. *For a description of this information and its value, see Chapter* 3. *The information provided here is based on the latest data provided to* FERC *as of this writing.*

This system lambda data is grouped by NERC *reliability region and includes the minimum, maximum, and average hourly system lambda value for each utility. The values below are in dollars per megawatt-hour. "Not CA" indicates that the utility is not an independent control area so no dispatch function requiring a system lambda calculation is provided. Some utilities failed to provide the required data to* FERC *for the time period indicated and are so indicated with "Not Avail."*

Except where noted, the following information is based on 1994 *System Lambda data submitted to* FERC *on June* 1, 1995.

ECAR

Utility	Utility Acronym	Notes	SYSTEM LAMBDA $ per MWh AVERAGE	MAXIMUM	MINIMUM
Allegheny Power Service	APS		20.85	102.49	12.65
American Electric Power	AEP		14.95	31.82	9.21
AMP-Ohio	AMPO	Not CA	-	-	-
Big Rivers Electric Corp	BREC		14.97	88.36	2.49
Buckeye Power, Inc.	BUCK	Not CA	-	-	-
Cleveland Electric Illum.	CEI		21.82	136.00	12.00
Cincinnati Gas & Electric	CGE		19.73	110.00	11.54
Consumers Power Co.	CPC	Not CA	-	-	-
Dayton Power & Light	DPL		13.92	27.38	10.50
Detroit Edison Co.	DECO	Not CA	-	-	-
Duquesne Light Company	DLCO		17.92	77.08	11.94
East Kentucky Power Coop	EKPC		13.63	26.73	11.70
Hoosier Energy	HE		16.53	18.44	14.56
Indianapolis Power & Light	IPL		10.48	33.72	8.22
Kentucky Utilities Company	KUC		15.12	77.50	11.10
Lansing Board of Water & Light	LANS	Not CA	-	-	-
Louisville Gas & Electric	LGE		10.45	41.50	8.30
Michigan Electric Coordinated System	MECS		20.57	142.00	11.69
Northern Indiana Public Service Co.	NIPS		14.49	18.64	10.94
Ohio Edison Company	OE		14.40	60.63	9.04
Ohio Valley Electric Corp.	OVEC	Not Avail.	-	-	-
PSI Energy, Inc.	PSI		12.23	18.52	8.90
Southern Indiana Gas & Electric	SIGE		16.35	62.80	7.00
Toledo Edison Co.	TE		18.38	264.00	8.00
Wabash Valley Power Assn.	WVPA	Not CA	-	-	-
Wolverine Power Supply Coop.	WPSC	Not CA	-	-	-

ERCOT

Utility	Utility Acronym	Notes	SYSTEM LAMBDA $ per MWh AVERAGE	MAXIMUM	MINIMUM
Central Power & Light Co.	CPL		18.06	26.33	15.22
City of Austin	AUST		14.53	23.89	10.18
Houston Lighting & Power	HLP		16.96	35.85	8.79
Lower Colorado River Authority	LCRA		13.88	25.83	1.50
Northeast Texas Elec. Coop	NTEC	Not CA	-	-	-
Sam Rayburn G&T, Inc.	SRGT	Not CA	-	-	-
San Antonio Public Serv. Board	SANT		16.10	32.72	9.03
South Texas Electric Coop	STEC		15.79	42.18	10.10
Texas Utilities Electric	TU		16.77	35.10	4.70
Texas Municipal Power Pool	TMPP		18.42	35.27	12.16
Texas-New Mexico Power Co.	TNMP	Not CA	-	-	-
Texla Electric Cooperative	TEXLA	Not CA	-	-	-
West Texas Utilities Co.	WTU		17.44	26.89	9.83

MAAC

Utility	Utility Acronym	Notes	SYSTEM LAMBDA $ per MWh AVERAGE	MAXIMUM	MINIMUM
Atlantic City Electric Co.	ACE	See PJM	-	-	-
Baltimore Gas & Electric	BGE	See PJM	-	-	-
Delmarva Power & Light Co.	DPL	See PJM	-	-	-
General Public Utilities	GPU	See PJM	-	-	-
PA-NJ-MD Interconnection	PJM		22.60	87.18	0.42
Pennsylvania Power & Light	PPL	See PJM	-	-	-
Philadelphia Electric Co.	PECO	See PJM	-	-	-
Potomac Electric Power Co.	PEPC	See PJM	-	-	-
Public Service Electric & Gas	PSEG	See PJM	-	-	-

MAIN

Utility	Utility Acronym	Notes	SYSTEM LAMBDA $ per MWh AVERAGE	MAXIMUM	MINIMUM
Central Illinois Light Co.	CILC	1993	10.52	19.25	3.56
Central Illinois Public Serv.	CIPS		14.67	44.15	11.38
Commonwealth Edison Co.	CECO		14.12	81.59	4.57
Electric Energy, Inc.	ELEN		11.01	12.89	9.21
Illinois Power Company	IPC		18.48	100.00	11.27
Madison Gas & Electric	MGE		15.07	61.84	6.40
Southern Illinois Power Coop	SIPC	Not Avail.	-	-	-
Springfield (Illinois) City Water, L&P	SPIL	1993	11.87	75.75	7.26
Union Electric Company	UE		18.14	98.16	10.50
Wisconsin Electric Power	WEPC		12.58	35.20	4.20
Wisconsin Power & Light Co.	WPL		13.84	29.36	8.44
Wisconsin Public Service	WPS		12.20	51.97	4.58

MAPP

Utility	Utility Acronym	Notes	SYSTEM LAMBDA $ per MWh AVERAGE	MAXIMUM	MINIMUM
Basin Electric Power Coop	BEPC	Not CA	-	-	-
Central Iowa Power Coop	CIPC	Not CA	-	-	-
Cooperative Power Assoc.	CP	Not CA	-	-	-
Corn Belt Power Coop	CBPC	Not CA	-	-	-
Dairyland Power Coop	DPC		15.24	39.13	10.11
Heartland Consumers Power	HCPD	Not CA	-	-	-
Hutchinson Utilities Comm.	HUC	Not CA	-	-	-
IES Industries Inc.	IES		15.30	49.88	6.10
Interstate Power Company	IPC		18.60	30.72	1.80
Iowa-Illinois Gas & Electric	IIGE		11.17	15.02	6.27
Lincoln Electric System	LES		11.49	66.00	6.21
Midwest Power Systems Inc.	MWPS		15.30	49.88	6.10
Minnesota Power & Light Co.	MPL		11.71	16.00	9.00
Minnkota Power Coop. Inc.	MPC	Not CA	-	-	-
Missouri Basin Mun Power	MBMP	Not CA	-	-	-
Montana-Dakota Utilities	MDU	Not CA	-	-	-
Municipal Energy Agency	MEAN	Not CA	-	-	-
Muscatine Power & Water	MPW		10.49	86.10	4.90
Nebraska Public Power District	NPPD	Not Avail.	-	-	-
Northern States Power Co.	NSP		10.79	49.80	8.40
Northwest Iowa Power Coop.	NIPC	Not CA	-	-	-
Northwestern Public Serv.	NWPS	Not CA	-	-	-
Omaha Public Power Dist.	OPPD		7.78	36.60	6.14
Otter Tail Power Co.	OTP		11.47	99.00	5.37
Rochester Public Utilities	RPU	Not CA	-	-	-
Southern Minnesota Mun.	SMMP		11.41	31.70	9.80
Square Butte Electric Coop	SBEC	Not CA	-	-	-
United Power Association	UPA		11.59	90.00	7.18
WAPA-Billings	WAPA	Not Avail.	-	-	-
Wisconsin Public Power Inc.	WPPI	Not CA	-	-	-

NPCC

Utility	Utility Acronym	Notes	SYSTEM LAMBDA $ per MWh AVERAGE	MAXIMUM	MINIMUM
Bangor Hydro-Electric Co.	BHE	Not CA	-	-	-
Boston Edison Co.	BECO	Not CA	-	-	-
Central Hudson Gas & Electric	CHGE	Not CA	-	-	-
Central Maine Power Co.	CMP	Not CA	-	-	-
Central Vermont Public Serv.	CVPS	Not CA	-	-	-
Commonwealth Electric Co.	COEL	Not CA	-	-	-
Consolidated Edison Co. - NY	COED	Not CA	-	-	-
Eastern Utilities Assoc.	EUA	Not CA	-	-	-
Green Mountain Power Corp.	GMP	Not CA	-	-	-
Long Island Lighting Co.	LILC	Not CA	-	-	-
Mass. Muni Wholesale Electric	MMWE	Not CA	-	-	-
New York Power Pool	NYPP		16.61	160.98	3.02
New England Power Pool	NEPOOL		19.56	59.26	6.69
New York Power Authority	NYPA	Not CA	-	-	-
New York State Electric	NYS	Not CA	-	-	-
New England Power Co.	NEES	Not CA	-	-	-
Niagara Mohawk Power Corp.	NMPC	Not CA	-	-	-
Northeast Utilities	NU	Not CA	-	-	-
Orange & Rockland Utilities	OR	Not CA	-	-	-
Rochester Gas & Electric	RGE	Not CA	-	-	-
United Illuminating Co.	UI	Not CA	-	-	-
Vermont Electric Power Co.	VEPC	Not CA	-	-	-

SERC

Utility	Utility Acronym	Notes	SYSTEM LAMBDA $ per MWh AVERAGE	MAXIMUM	MINIMUM
Alabama Electric Coop Inc.	AEC		15.69	90.68	14.43
Carolina Power & Light	CPL	Not Avail.	-	-	-
Central Electric Power Coop	CEPC	Not CA	-	-	-
City of Chattanooga	CEPB	Not CA	-	-	-
City of Gainesville	GAIN	Not Avail.	-	-	-
City of Lakeland	LAKE	Not CA	-	-	-
City of Lake Worth	LALW	Not CA	-	-	-
City of Memphis	MEMP	Not CA	-	-	-
City of Tallahassee	TAL		18.79	31.44	13.98
City of St. Cloud	STC	Not CA	-	-	-
Duke Power Company	DUKE		15.61	78.01	4.00
Greenville Utility Comm.	GUC	Not CA	-	-	-
Fayetteville Public Works	FPWC	Not CA	-	-	-
Flint Electric Membership Coop	FLINT	Not CA	-	-	-
Florida Power Corporation	FPC		19.18	47.80	12.70
Florida Power & Light	FPL		20.49	89.99	7.79
Florida Municipal Power Agency	FMP	Not CA	-	-	-
Greenville Utilities Comm.	GUC	Not CA	-	-	-
Jacksonville Electric Authority	JEA		17.49	55.50	10.50
Kissimmee Utility Authority	KUA	Not Avail.	27.49	83.50	16.40
Lee County Electric Coop	LCEC	Not CA	-	-	-
Nantahala Power & Light	NPL	Not CA	-	-	-
Oglethorpe Power Corp.	OPC	Not CA	-	-	-
Old Dominion Electric Coop	ODEC	Not CA	-	-	-
Orlando Utilities Comm.	OUC		23.41	72.80	14.50
Seminole Electric Coop	SEC		16.39	17.54	13.33
South Carolina Electric & Gas	SCEG	Not Avail.	-	-	-
South Carolina Public Service Authority	SCPS		14.25	16.89	12.79
Southern Company Services	SOCO	1993	25.84	100.14	13.42
South Mississippi Electric Power	SME	Not Avail.	-	-	-
Tampa Electric Company	TECO		15.28	44.94	10.38
Tennessee Valley Authority	TVA		15.44	76.18	10.00
Virginia Electric & Power	VIEP		16.45	45.69	7.40
Vero Beach Municipal	VERO	Not Avail.	-	-	-
Walton Electric Member Coop	WEMC	Not CA	-	-	-

SPP

Utility	Utility Acronym	Notes	SYSTEM LAMBDA $ per MWh AVERAGE	MAXIMUM	MINIMUM
Associated Electric Coop	AEC	Not Avail.	-	-	-
Arkansas Electric Coop	AECC	Not CA	-	-	-
Cajun Electric Power Coop	CAJN	1993	15.18	24.39	14.05
Central Louisiana Electric Co.	CLEC		22.15	33.74	6.51
City of Columbia	COL	Not Avail.	-	-	-
City of Independence, MO	INDE		16.18	18.07	4.00
Empire District Electric	EMDE		20.00	100.00	13.00
Entergy System Power Pool	ENTR		16.47	34.12	8.86
City of Goodland	GOOD	1993	32.82	42.00	28.00
Lafayette Utility System	LUS	Not Avail.	-	-	-
Gulf States Utilities	GSU	1993	35.85	56.12	25.91
City of Kansas City	KCPU	Not Avail.	-	-	-
Kansas City Power & Light	KCPL		12.35	107.00	7.11
LA Energy & Power	LEPA	Not CA	-	-	-
Missouri Public Service Co.	MPS	Not Avail.	-	-	-
Oklahoma Gas & Electric Co.	OKGE	1993	28.48	42.79	10.20
Oklahoma Muni Power Auth.	OMPA	Not CA	-	-	-
Public Service Co. of OK	PSOK		16.57	29.93	8.29
Southwest Power Pool	SPP	Not CA	-	-	-
Southwestern Electric Power	SWEP		16.57	84.77	10.94
Southwestern Power Administration	SWPA	Not Avail.	-	-	-
Southwestern Public Service	SWPS		15.52	25.76	7.55
Springfield City of	SPRM	Not CA	-	-	-
St. Joseph Light & Power	STJ	Not Avail.	-	-	-
Sunflower Electric Power Corp.	SEPC		10.37	15.87	9.40
Western Farmers Electric Coop	WFEC	1993	13.41	20.58	10.42
WestPlains Energy, Kansas	WPEK	Not CA	-	-	-
Western Resources Inc.	WR		13.06	109.57	3.35

WSCC

Utility	Utility Acronym	Notes	SYSTEM LAMBDA $ per MWh AVERAGE	MAXIMUM	MINIMUM
Arizona Electric Power Coop	AEPC	Not CA	-	-	-
Arizona Public Service Co.	APS		12.85	35.20	5.20
Black Hills Power & Light	BHPL	Not CA	-	-	-
Bonneville Power Admin.	BPA	Not Avail.	-	-	-
California Dept. Water Resources	CDWR	Not CA	-	-	-
Central Lincoln People's Utility Dist.	CLPU	Not CA	-	-	-
City of Anaheim	ANAH	Not CA	-	-	-
City of Glendale	GLEN	Not CA	-	-	-
City of Los Angeles	LADWP	1993	21.37	30.60	14.57
City of Pasadena	PASA	1993	25.43	34.07	22.06
City of Santa Clara	SANT	Not CA	-	-	-
City of Seattle	SCL	Not Avail.	-	-	-
Colorado Springs, City of	COSP	Not CA	-	-	-
Deseret Generation & Transmission	DGTC	Not CA	-	-	-
El Paso Electric Co.	EPE	1993	21.43	32.60	14.41
Eugene, City of	EWEB	Not Avail.	-	-	-
Idaho Power Company	IPC	Not Avail.	-	-	-
Imperial Irrigation District	IID	Not Avail.	-	-	-
Metropolitan Water District	MWD	Not CA	-	-	-
Modesto Irrigation District	MID	Not CA	-	-	-
Montana Power Company	MPC	Not Avail.	-	-	-
Nevada Power Company	NEVP	1993	26.90	75.00	11.00
Northern California Power Agency	NCPA	Not CA	-	-	-
Pacific Gas & Electric Co.	PG&E		20.27	67.93	12.00
PacifiCorp	PACC	Not Avail.	-	-	-
Placer County Water Agency	PCWA	Not CA	-	-	-
Plains Electric Gen.&Trans. Coop.	PEGT	Not CA	-	-	-
Platte River Power Authority	PRPA	Not CA	-	-	-
Portland General Electric	PGE	Not Avail.	-	-	-
Public Service Co. of Colorado	PSCO		12.58	32.48	9.91
Public Service Co of New Mexico	PSNM	Not Avail.	-	-	-
PUD of # 1 Chelan	CHEL	Not Avail.	-	-	-
PUD # 1 of Douglas County	DPUD	Not Avail.	-	-	-
PUD # 2 of Grant County	GPUD	Not Avail.	-	-	-
Puget Sound Power	PSPL	Not Avail.	-	-	-
Sacramento Municipal Utility District	SMUD	Not CA	-	-	-
Salt River Project	SRP		14.79	41.39	9.70
San Diego Gas & Electric	SDGE		20.75	73.60	10.30
Sierra Pacific Power Co.	SPP	1993	20.05	34.80	16.90
Southern California Edison	SCE		18.20	24.92	12.66
Tacoma City Light	TCL	Not Avail.	-	-	-
Tucson Electric Power Co.	TEPC		16.56	37.00	3.54
Turlock Irrigation District	TID	Not CA	-	-	-
WAPA - Upper Missouri	WALC	Not Avail.	-	-	-
WAPA - Colorado/Missouri	WACM	Not Avail.	-	-	-
Washington Water Power Co.	WWP	Not Avail.	-	-	-
Western Systems Coord. Council	WSCC	Not Avail.	-	-	-
Westplains Energy	WPE	Not CA	-	-	-

Appendix E

State-by-State Status of Retail Wheeling Initiatives

The following is a summary of retail wheeling initiatives in the U.S. and Canada on a state-by-state basis. These summaries are based on the latest news reports as of date this book went to press. More so than any other part of this book, the following information is subject to frequent changes, so there is no claim of accuracy or timeliness with the following information. For the latest update to this information, please contact the author at the following address:

Strategic Energy Ltd.
Two Gateway Center
Pittsburgh, PA 15222
(412) 394-5600

Retail Wheeling Initiatives: A State-by-State Update

Alabama

On May 6, 1996, Governor Fob James signed into law a bill supported by Alabama Power and other utilities that grants the state's utilities full stranded cost recovery through exit fees. The bill, introduced on February 21, protects the state's investor-owned and public power utilities from any stranded investments that may result from industry restructuring or from special contracts negotiated between utilities and end-users. The original bill provided this protection indefinitely, but it was revised to expire five years after retail wheeling is introduced in Alabama or a neighboring state. Industrial end-users unsuccessfully fought the law claiming that it so well protects the utilities from any effects of competition that it basically prevents the introduction of electricity competition to the state.

Only six days after this stranded cost recovery bill was introduced to the Alabama legislature, a retail wheeling bill was introduced that places the burden on the existing utility to show why a retail wheeling transaction could not be done. The proposed bill allows end-users or alternative suppliers to petition the Alabama Public Service Commission (PSC) for the right to wheel power if the supplying utility has reciprocal rights to access the supplier's customers. While stranded cost recovery may be guaranteed, the proposed bill prohibits the state's utilities from imposing any penalty or undue cost that would otherwise frustrate the ability to wheel power. The outlook on this bill appears to be greatly dimmed given the passage of the stranded cost recovery bill.

Jim Sullivan, President of the Alabama Corporation Commission, expects that the move toward retail wheeling in Alabama will be slow due to the low operating costs of the state's utilities and unique jurisdictional issues. The Commission has said that it "does not foresee any benefits to the state from retail wheeling."

A 1984 law gives municipal electric companies and rural electric cooperatives the right to negotiate among themselves to allocate new industrial customers. Any such agreement must be approved by the legislature; it is unknown if any such agreements are in place. This law survived a legal challenge in the U.S. Court of Appeals.

Alaska

A bill that would prohibit the introduction of retail wheeling by establishing exclusive service areas has passed the committee stage and is scheduled for hearings. No further detail on this proposal was available at the time of this writing.

The Alaska Public Utilities Commission is currently considering the implementation of integrated resource plans and economic dispatch within the state as a means to a more efficient electricity industry. While this may seem years behind the development in other states, one commissioner has said that if these methods do not achieve the lowest cost power, "retail wheeling may warrant attention."

Arizona

A bill has been introduced to the state legislature that would create a 10-member legislative committee to study retail wheeling and the effects of competition on the industry. If the bill is passed, as is expected, a report would be due by the end of 1997 so that implementation of competition could begin no later than December 31, 1999.

On December 5, 1995, Arizona Public Service Company, the state's largest investor-owned utility, and the Arizona Corporation Commission (ACC) issued a negotiated settlement agreement which identified issues to be resolved in order to implement retail wheeling in the state by the year 2000. Among the key issues identified were the necessary changes to state and federal law that would be required to support direct access. The settlement proposes hearings to begin in 1996 to develop recommendations that could be presented to state and federal legislatures in 1997. Given the existing ACC investigation into retail wheeling (see below), this agreement is an initial step toward building a statewide consensus on key direct access issues.

On January 25, 1995, the ACC convened a "Working Group on Retail Electric Competition" that is charged with assisting the ACC in developing a retail wheeling policy. A final report of this working group was released that listed options and issues related to restructuring but contained no specific recommendations. From this report, ACC staff will prepare questions raised by the report that will be answered in phase two of the investigation. This next step should result in the development of general restructuring principles and perhaps specific recommendations, a rulemaking, or legislative suggestions by the summer of 1996. Forty-six stakeholders are taking part in this working group.

Meanwhile, a retail wheeling bill was introduced into the state legislature that would have ordered the ACC to allow retail wheeling even sooner. The bill died when the legislature adjourned in April 1995. The Arizona Association of Industries (AAI), however, did not support the bill because it believed the power to mandate retail wheeling resides with the ACC. The AAI has formed a committee to investigate retail wheeling and whether changes in state law are required before it can be proposed.

The ACC held a workshop on retail wheeling on September 7, 1994, in which Chuck Bayless, chief executive officer of Tucson Electric (and former PSNH VP), was an unexpected proponent of competition. Bayless suggested allowing access to competitive power to the state's top 50 customers, but the Commission said it would not do anything "right away." The Commission is facing pressure from the state legislature, but the Commission said that, "the legislature doesn't understand it."

The Chairman of the ACC, Renz Jennings, filed comments on the California restructuring plan that reflected considerable concern about the implementation of a "poolco" model. Those concerns centered on the influence that existing utilities could wield over transactions throughout the region. The Chairman said, "Any pooling arrangement is best left voluntary." On the other hand, another commissioner wrote that "retail wheeling is probably not in the public interest. It promotes chaos where there is stability."

On October 13, 1994, the ACC approved an arrangement for North Star Steel (see Nevada) that allows wheeling through the Western Area Power Administration. ACC Chair Marcia Weeks said that this brings retail wheeling to the state "in an indirect fashion." North Star Steel claims that this is a true retail wheeling program since it will be acting as its own dispatcher and directly accessing suppliers, although it is unwilling to supply specific details. While there are many transactions like this in the West, the ACC seems to be treating this deal like an experimental retail wheeling program.

Arkansas

In early 1995, a bill was introduced to the state legislature to allow direct access in a limited form, but the bill was withdrawn soon after. The Arkansas Public Service Commission indicated that it may begin a restructuring investigation in 1996, but no action has been taken to date.

California

On April 29, 1996, pursuant to the restructuring roadmap recently issued by the California Public Utilities Commission (CPUC), the state's three major utilities filed to FERC their proposals for a statewide power exchange (PX) and an independent system operator (ISO). The PX filing will create a spot-market exchange mechanism (formerly called "Poolco") through which generators can bid supply and consumers can bid demand on an hourly basis. The ISO filing requires Pacific Gas & Electric, San Diego Gas & Electric, and Southern California Edison to turn control of their transmission systems over to an independent operator to assure open access to the transmission system. These filings were made to the FERC, which has jurisdiction over ISOs, power pools, and the transmission component of a retail wheeling transaction, only five days after it issued its landmark Order 888 on open access transmission tariffs. FERC has yet to issue any rules on ISOs or power exchanges, although Order 888 includes a set of guidelines and principles for their formation.

On March 13, 1996, the CPUC issued its final "roadmap" outlining a schedule for electricity restructuring in the state. Among the dates listed in the new schedule:

- The state's three major utilities must file state and federal applications to form a power exchange and an ISO by April 29, 1996 (see above).
- Unbundled rates must be filed by July 15, 1996.
- Direct access proposals must be filed by August 30, 1996.

Also, a number of key issues were identified to be resolved before the first retail wheeling occurs in 1998. The CPUC then divided itself into teams to oversee the major groups of issues as follows:

- Fessler (Chairman): ISO and power exchange development.
- Conlon: market power and the competition transition charge;
- Knight: direct access and customer protection;
- Neeper: public benefit programs and renewable resources; and
- Duque: rate unbundling and performance–based ratemaking.

Finally, the Commission requested that stakeholders form working groups to develop agreements on the major issues. The first such group, dealing with the development of the ISO and the power exchange, has already begun meeting, while a working group dealing with direct access issues was defined in the order.

Furthering and hindering the movement toward retail competition, a slew of bills has been proposed to the California legislature relating to the electricity industry. While many deal with relatively minor issues, some would have a significant impact on the manner in which the CPUC is conducting the restructuring effort. While one bill facilitates aggregation of small loads in order to allow participation by smaller customers, others would prohibit further development unless certain special interests are preserved. On January 3, 1996, a bill to pass transition costs only to large end-users was introduced to the legislature. At least one bill has been developed to provide the necessary statutory infrastructure to allow the CPUC to restructure the industry as proposed in its December decision (see following).

While retail electricity competition appears to be moving soon to California, Pacific Gas & Electric (PG&E) filed a legal action to block a retail customer from moving to another supplier. The Modesto Irrigation District (MID) has plans to feed a Praxair facility in Pittsburg, California, under an existing provision in its charter that lets irrigation districts feed retail loads outside its service territory under certain circumstances. MID will use the transmission agreement signed between Destec and PG&E to move the power to the Praxair facility. In its attempt to block the deal, PG&E successfully obtained permission from the CPUC to charge these customers an interim competition transition charge (to recover stranded costs from the loss of the load). The charge would be high enough to remove any economic benefit from leaving PG&E at this time.

On December 20, 1995, the California Public Utilities Commission (CPUC) issued its final electric industry restructuring decision based on a 3-2 decision by the commissioners. The decision implements direct access for 1,800 MW of load (in all customer classes) no later than January 1, 1998. Direct access for all customers must be phased in within five years, if not sooner. The decision mostly reflects the agreement discussed in the September 11, 1995, memorandum of understanding (MoU) that attempted to resolve the poolco vs. direct-access debate. The decision creates an ISO under FERC jurisdiction that will provide transmission services on a nondiscriminatory basis. The ISO will be responsible for maintaining system integrity and preserving reliability across the grid. A separate power exchange will provide a spot market for power. The state's utilities must sell all power generated into the exchange during the five-year transition period, and all power to feed regulatory customers must come from the exchange. The power exchange is voluntary for direct-access customers, non-utility generators, and out-of-state suppliers.

With respect to direct access, the decision allows smaller customers to participate through aggregation, and all transactions must be nominated to the ISO. Utilities will be able to recover 100% of their stranded generation assets through a nonbypassable competition transition charge (CTC). The decision provides the utilities with incentives to divest their generation assets and requires them to submit a plan to divest 50% of those assets in the next five years. All social programs will be funded through the CTC as well.

The decision identifies a number of issues relating to direct access that must be resolved by involved stakeholders, especially the utilities. The most significant of these is development of a selection process for determining which end-users can participate in the first 1,800 MW of direct access. The decision originally called for these issues to be resolved by January of 1996, but an agreement among all parties was to extend the deadline until August.

The next step is for the legislature to respond by passing the appropriate legislation needed to implement the new structure. While a comment period is planned, the decision is final, so the comments are really geared for the legislature. A key issue to be resolved is the jurisdictional bright line between the CPUC and FERC, especially given the decisions reliance on a FERC-regulated ISO and its transmission pricing proposals.

This decision is the culmination of the debate over the restructuring of the electricity industry in California triggered by the CPUC's landmark "Blue Book" issued in April of 1994. On May 24, 1995, the CPUC issued an initial proposal for how a competitive industry will be structured. It was considered a significant retreat from the "Blue Book" proposal to implement retail wheeling as early as 1996 because it called for implementation of a wholesale power pool (the "poolco" model). An alternative proposal, issued by Commissioner Knight, called for state-wide retail wheeling (the "direct access" model) based on voluntary bilateral contracts.

The MoU on which the decision is based was the result of an effort by Governor Pete Wilson to get those campaign contributors that are on opposite sides of the debate to agree to an electricity industry restructuring solution. The five parties involved include: Southern California Edison, a strong Poolco proponent, the California Manufacturers Association, the California Large Electric Consumers Association, Californians for Competitive Electricity, and the Independent Energy Producers. This proposal was much closer to the original blue book than either of the May 24 proposals, and it gained substantial support among various parties.

Colorado

On February 20, 1996, a draft retail wheeling bill that was introduced in 1995 was removed from consideration after the bill's sponsor failed to develop enough support to get the bill out of the committee stage. Another bill that would have only directed a retail wheeling study was also removed. This preliminary rejection of competition is primarily due to the work of a coalition of retail wheeling opponents, which is primarily supported by the state's electric cooperatives. The coalition was specifically formed to block this bill and other retail wheeling proposals.

Connecticut

In contrast to other New England states, Connecticut has shifted to a "go slow" approach to retail electricity competition. In a preliminary report, a legislative task force failed to specify a comprehensive approach to restructuring, instead focusing on the need to protect residential ratepayers and demand-side management programs. The lack of enthusiasm for retail wheeling at the legislative level has been attributed to Northeast Utilities' (NU) influence there and the number of special contracts negotiated with large end-users in the state. On June 2, 1995, the Connecticut legislature passed a bill creating a task force to study electric industry restructuring although retail wheeling was not specifically mentioned. This task force consists of representatives from all stakeholder groups, including industrial users, in an effort to craft some sort of coalition. This study has been done in parallel with the Connecticut Department of Public Utility Control (DPUC) proceeding on retail wheeling. A final report, which may include suggested changes in legislation, is due by January 1, 1997.

On July 14, 1995, the DPUC issued its final report to the legislature on industry restructuring following its second round proceeding to investigate retail wheeling that began in January. On the wholesale side, the DPUC did not even go as far as to suggest a mandatory poolco model. The DPUC instead claimed that the New England Power Pool should continue to dispatch generation in the region. As for retail wheeling, the DPUC said only that full access will benefit customers under "certain circumstances," but that wholesale restructuring must precede retail wheeling. No timetable for implementation of retail competition nor any type of pilot program was proposed. As for stranded investment, the order suggested compensating the utilities for the full difference between retail prices and market prices. Not surprisingly, NU hailed the order as "thoughtful and constructive."

In comments to the DPUC filed March 22, 1995, NU said that it would consider a pilot open access plan sometime after the year 2000. NU, however, would only consider the plan once all stranded investment costs were recovered under some sort of universal service charge. Also, NU proposes only buy/sell arrangements rather than true direct access. In these comments, filed in response to the inquiry described below, NU also asked for performance–based ratemaking (by 1997, of course). Nonetheless, an NU spokesman said, "Given the right circumstances, we would be able to support retail wheeling."

A state court removed an injunction against a cogenerator that has plans to sell power to two industrial end-users. The native utility, Connecticut Light & Power, (CL&P) a Northeast Utilities' subsidiary, claimed that the transaction is retail wheeling and had taken legal actions to stop it. An injunction was granted based on technical issues, but the same court has now found that those problems are not a barrier. Of course, CL&P is continuing its legal challenge. A positive development for retail wheeling, on November 7, 1995, the DPUC upheld the legality of the retail sale, so the issue now goes back to the state courts.

The Connecticut Office of Policy and Management issued a state energy plan that recommends consideration of alternative electricity options, including retail wheeling, as a means to attract industrial growth to the state.

Connecticut law allows the DPUC to order wheeling from a QF to a retail customer, but it has declined to do so due to possible harm to the utilities. CL&P wheels power to Aetna Insurance from a QF it partially owns, but there does not appear to be any general wheeling policy in place.

Delaware

Delmarva Power & Light has presented its own plan for dealing with the move toward retail competition. Under the plan, called "Collaborative for Change and Customer Choice," retail wheeling would be phased in over six to eight years starting in 1997. After the phase-in period, no further stranded costs would be recovered. Understanding that many parties may want no stranded costs and a shorter phase-in period, Delmarva suggested preliminary discussions at this point.

A bill was passed by the State Legislature that allows the Delaware Public Service Commission (PSC) to "deregulate services provided by electric utilities" when found to be in the public interest. The purpose of the bill is to allow the PSC to approve special power supply contracts as a means to retain industry in the state, and it does not specifically address or allow retail wheeling.

District of Columbia

The District of Columbia was one of only a few regulatory regions that, in a recent survey, said that it does not allow negotiated rates between utilities and end-users. Hawaii, Washington, and the District of Columbia were the only states that claim that they do not allow special contracts.

The District of Columbia Public Service Commission (PSC) has initiated an investigation into electricity restructuring in response to the FERC NOPR on open access transmission. In investigating competition, PSC Chair Howard Davenport has said that they, as regulators, must consider retail wheeling and compare it to other means toward competition. He also said, however, that he failed to see how he could ensure just and reasonable rates when increased competition would only benefit some ratepayers, and therefore "retail wheeling may not be as attractive here."

Florida

A legislative committee recently killed an effort to at least get the Florida Public Service Commission (PSC) to study retail wheeling. This rejection of competition follows other recent defeats of measures to introduce direct access in a limited form earlier in 1996. Responding to intense lobbying by Florida utilities, the committee stated that studying retail wheeling is tantamount to implementing it, leaving the PSC one of the few in the nation that has not investigated retail competition.

Enron, the gas and power marketer, attempted a public effort to introduce retail wheeling to Florida by capitalizing on the strong anti-tax sentiment in the state. Enron proposed to allow retail wheeling for state buildings as a means to lower state expenses enough, according to Enron, to balance the state's budget. Responding to a letter from Enron outlining the proposal, the director of electric and gas for the PSC said he threw the letter away.

A member of the PSC said, "In this state, in my opinion, the threat of retail competition is minimal." The PSC member feels that retail wheeling will not exist in Florida for at least five to ten years.

An effort to force retail wheeling in Florida through the use of an antitrust claim was rejected by the U.S. Court of Appeals, 11th Circuit, based on the state action defense.

Georgia

On December 20, 1995, a bill was introduced to the state legislature that would mandate direct access for all retail customers. The bill, actively opposed by the state's utilities, would give the Georgia Public Service Commission (PSC) a year to issue rules for implementing retail wheeling. No stranded investment recovery is allowed, and no exit fees would be assessed. While admitting that stranded investment would have to be discussed, the sponsor of the bill wanted to act quickly to beat neighboring states to retail competition.

On December 8, 1995, the PSC announced that it will be reviewing existing electricity regulations given the recent movement toward competition. Existing state laws give new industrial customers with more than 900 kW of load a one–time choice among state suppliers of electricity. There are, however, relatively few suppliers in Georgia to choose from. This review will determine if additional competitive measures are required.

Idaho

Spokane-based Washington Water Power (WWP) announced a plan on May 6, 1996, to allow its 30 largest customers in Washington and Idaho to access competitive power supplies for up to one–third of the existing load. In its filing to the Idaho Public Utilites commission (PUC), WWP proposes a two-year program in which a specific tariff rate is used to cover all costs besides energy and transmission. The program is scheduled to start in September of 1996 if approved by state regulators.

The PUC announced on January 31, 1996, that it plans to begin a formal investigation into retail wheeling and electricity industry restructuring. Workshops were held in February and March of 1996.

Illinois

After a delay in getting the applicable transmission tariffs approved by FERC, Illinois became the first state in which end-users could openly shop the competitive electricity marketplace, albeit on a limited basis. Under separate filings approved by the Illinois Commerce Commission (ICC), retail wheeling experimental programs proposed by Illinois Power (IP) and Central Illinois Lighting Co. (CILCO) began operation on April 25, 1996. While approval of these proposals was expected, the aggressive starting date of these programs suddenly placed Illinois in front of the state race to retail electricity competition.

The IP plan allows its 21 largest industrial end-users to purchase 100% load factor blocks of power from 2 to 10 MW from off-system suppliers. The program utilizes IP's open access transmission rate filed with FERC and includes no stranded cost recovery (although IP reserves the right to collect stranded costs due to the experiment at a later date). This experiment was part of IP's overall retail wheeling implementation program developed in 1995 (see below) and is largely in response to pressure exerted by the utility's industrial end-users. Aggressive responses to the experimental program have resulted in delivered, bundled electricity rates reportedly as low as two cents per kilowatt-hour for some of the participants.

CILCO developed two retail wheeling pilot program tariffs, one for industrial customers and the other for commercial and residential customers, that implement the experiment. Under Rate 33, industrial loads of more than 10 MW (CILCO's eight largest customers) will have access to off-system suppliers for up to a total of 50 MW of load. Under Rate 34, commercial and residential customers in three designated "open access sites" will also be able to purchase power from alternative suppliers. Unlike the IP plan, this experiment may involve a customer's full requirements, and like the IP plan, no stranded costs are recovered. The three open access sites were identified as the towns of Heyworth, Manito, and Williamsville, Illinois. Early results show prices delivered to the CILCO control area as low as 1.6¢ per kilowatt-hour (distribution charges would then be added to that), but these numbers are somewhat skewed by the participation of QST Energy, CILCO's affiliate power marketer. QST was reportedly offering deals for below-market priced power early on in the process, and thus locked in the vast majority of participants.

Learning how to succeed in retail wheeling, even if it helps to be the utility that offers access, CILCO has begun developing a plan to bring full competition to all retail customers in Illinois by January 1, 1998. The key to the program is dealing with stranded cost recovery by placing the burden on those utilities with stranded costs to show that recovery is required to keep the company financially viable. Therefore, under the plan, stranded cost recovery would be based on need and mitigation rather than on lost revenues. The plan is similar to one proposed recently by the state Citizens Utility Board (see below), and favors utilities, like CILCO, with few stranded investments.

The momentum of retail wheeling in Illinois has claimed the most unlikely of utilities, Commonwealth Edison (CE). On December 13, 1995, CE issued a legislative proposal to phase in direct access from 1998 through 2003, although specific details were somewhat lacking. CE is calling for full recovery of stranded costs and a finding that retail competition is in the public interest, which some see as a means to delay the restructuring process.

In response to CE's high rates and potentially high stranded costs, an Illinois consumer group, the Citizens Utility Board, has issued its own statewide restructuring plan. Under this proposal, full bilateral agreements would be allowed and stranded cost recovery would be limited only to that necessary for financial viability. Hoping for the required legislative changes by 1997, the Board would expect full retail wheeling for all customer classes by 1999.

The Illinois legislature created a Joint Committee on Electric Utility Reform, which will hold hearings on electric industry restructuring and submit specific legislative proposals by November of 1996.

The Central Illinois Public Service Co. (CIPS) retail wheeling program proposes to recover 50% of the "largest" stranded investment of each utility through a direct–access fee over three years beginning in 1999, which is when the CIPS plan would begin. This fee would apply to all utilities in the state, even those with no stranded costs. Under this proposal, new load would be eligible for direct access by 1999, and by 2002 existing customers with more than 5 MW of load will become direct-access customers. This threshold would allow 24 CIPS customers to retail wheel, which involves 16% of the utility's total load.

Beyond the plans submitted by the utilities, the ICC itself has expressed interest in retail wheeling development. In a plan released on March 7, 1996, ICC Chair Dan Miller addresses stranded investment recovery by suggesting a five year "safe zone" in which utilities could mitigate and recover stranded costs. After the five-year period, no further recovery would be allowed.

Indiana

In November of 1995, Indianapolis Power & Light Co. (IPALCO) released an outline of its plan for restructuring the electricity industry throughout the nation. The focus of the proposal was to rely on federal legislation to lead the restructuring effort, even with respect to retail wheeling. Citing the need for common rules on independent system operators and stranded investment, IPALCO does not believe that direct access can be implemented on a state-by-state basis. The plan calls for three transmission regions in the U.S., the removal of all cost-based ratemaking and contract path transmission, and the rejection of stranded costs based on lost revenue. IPALCO believes it could be a competitive, low-cost provider in an open market, but that competition must be implemented for all customer classes on a nationwide basis.

American Electric Power (AEP), which has retail customer load in Indiana, issued a position statement on October 26, 1995, favoring retail competition and direct access in the region it serves. Full discussion of this proposal is in the Ohio section of this report.

PSI Energy, now part of newly formed CINergy, filed on June 15, 1995, a tariff revision that will allow new industrial customers in the state to choose suppliers for new capacity. To avoid retail competition issues, PSI will buy the power on a wholesale basis and pass through the power to the customer. Industrial groups praise the offer as a step toward competition, "be it ever so humble." This tariff follows an unsuccessful attempt to introduce competition by offering its 20 largest customers open access to off-system suppliers if those suppliers (presumably other utilities) would offer open access to their customers. Both of these programs are based on PSI's well known and respected agreement with Nucor Steel, now called Rider 19.

On April 26, 1995, a bill was signed into law that allows the Indiana Utility Regulatory Commission (URC) to approve "alternative regulation proposals upon a showing that traditional regulation in a particular service sector is no longer required." Unfortunately, these proposals can only come from the state's utilities. The URC has also undertaken an inquiry into electricity competition, but a staff report is not expected until November of 1997. Roundtable discussions continue to be held, but no schedule has been set.

Iowa

On May 14, 1996, the Iowa Utilities Board (IUB) issued a list of ten principles upon which any proposed restructuring proposal must be based. The principles are generally similar to those seen in other states, i.e., great pains are taken to keep all stakeholders happy. These principles are the product of the first task of a 22-member Electric Competition Advisory Group that will "provide comment and analysis" to the IUB as it evaluates retail competition in the state. The group consists of members from all stakeholder groups (although only one industrial end-user representative is named). A final IUB order is expected to be issued by October 1996.

On February 24, 1995, the IUB issued a Notice of Inquiry concerning the restructuring of the state's electric industry. The IUB held a roundtable discussion on April 19, 1995, in which six working groups addressed specific questions relating to retail competition, such as jurisdiction, stranded investment, technical considerations, etc. Following this roundtable meeting, written comments were filed on June 30, 1995. In its comments, the Iowa Industrial Energy Group proposed a pilot retail wheeling program in collaboration with Iowa utilities that would place all parties on the learning curve with respect to the benefits and technical issues involved in retail competition.

Kansas

The Kansas State Corporation Commission (SCC) has indicated its reluctance to acknowledge competitive forces in the state's electricity industry. In one case, the Commission rejected a proposal by Western Resources to offer industrial customers discounts in exchange for a long-term (seven-year) commitment. The rejection was based on the Commission's refusal to consider any deviation from a traditional full rate case. In a response to Western Resource's concerns about competition, the Commission said that because there are "no means by which retail wheeling transactions could occur" in the state, any threat of competition is "highly speculative."

Along the lines of the SCC, a legislative committee voted in October 1995 to recommend a moratorium on retail wheeling initiatives for three years while certain issues are studied by a 17-member task force of various stakeholders. These recommendations would be implemented in a proposed bill that would give the task force until 1998 to report its findings and would block competition until 1999. Another bill was introduced in January 1996 that would allow competition in "blocks" that could retail wheel, but the bill will probably not leave the committee stage.

Kentucky

American Electric Power, which has retail customer load in Kentucky, issued a position statement on October 26, 1995, favoring retail competition and direct access in the region it serves. Full discussion of this proposal is in the Ohio section of this report.

Led by Southwire Company, a large aluminum manufacturer, Kentucky industrial customers are preparing a proposed retail wheeling bill for introduction to the state legislature when it reconvenes in January of 1996. Southwire claims that it is time for retail wheeling in Kentucky.

The Kentucky Public Service Commission sponsored a conference on retail wheeling and other changing electricity market issues in October and December of 1995.

Louisiana

In a reversal of a previous decision, the New Orleans City Council has agreed to initiate a full-scale investigation of retail competition for electricity service in the city. The order was issued on January 18, 1996, and interested parties had 60 days to file comments. Besides the usual issues of stranded costs, benefits to smaller customers, and implementation, the investigation will focus on how the city could implement retail wheeling in only its jurisdiction. This investigation reverses a prior rejection of a proposal from the New Orleans Business Energy Council, a group of industrial end-users, to implement retail wheeling in the city through a local ordinance. The proposal had a poor response from the city council and action was postponed. New Orleans is unique in that the city has its own utility regulatory agency separate from state regulators.

Two bills were introduced into the state legislature in 1995 that would allow limited retail wheeling in the state, but both died in committee. One bill would allow retail wheeling for nonutility generation and the other for generation from agricultural wastes.

The Louisiana Public Service Commission has been studying electricity competition since 1992, but finally voted to open an investigation into retail wheeling on June 22, 1995.

Maine

A compromise electricity industry restructuring bill has been passed by the Maine legislature that will require the Maine Public Utilities Commission (PUC) to investigate how retail wheeling can be implemented. The bill assumes that retail competition is required and charges the PUC with the responsibility of finding a way to achieve it by 2000. The bill does not require divestiture of utility assets (which some proposed bills did), and it requires a determination of the stranded investment transition costs that will be incurred. The law will require the PUC to create an 18-member working group, representing all interested parties. The PUC must then provide the state legislature with a draft restructuring plan by July 1996. According to the new law, any proposal garnering support of two-thirds of the working group must be included in the PUC's plan.

On December 11, 1995, the PUC issued an order requesting all interested parties to submit their own detailed restructuring plans by January 31, 1996. This step was required because no consensus was formed within the 18-member working group to get the two-thirds support necessary to float a plan. This leaves it to the PUC to submit its own plan by July 1996.

On January 31, 1996, Central Maine Power (CMP), the state's largest investor-owned utility, submitted its own restructuring plan that calls for corporate separation of generation and transmission functions. CMP is the only party to file a plan to the PUC (see above), although other parties have filed comments to the CMP plan and the original plan developed by the working group, which was supported by the industrial end-users in the state but not by CMP. While the CMP plan is unique in that it calls for complete divestiture of generation assets, it still calls for full stranded cost recovery and predicts rate and reliability exposure for smaller customers. As a result, some customers would have open access by 2000, but others would have to be phased in after that. Critics of the plan say that the need for full stranded cost recovery and the longer phase-in period puts Maine behind other New England states in electricity industry restructuring.

The Maine PUC allows an industrial customer to wheel power to an "affiliated" facility, e.g., self-service wheeling, or from a QF to a noninterconnected utility. It is unknown if any such wheeling has been done.

Maryland

Delmarva Power & Light, a Delaware utility with customers in Maryland, has presented its own plan for dealing with the move toward retail competition. Under the plan, called "Collaborative for Change and Customer Choice," retail wheeling would be phased in over six to eight years starting in 1997. After the phase-in period, no further stranded costs would be recovered. Understanding that many parties may want no stranded costs and a shorter phase-in period, Delmarva suggested preliminary discussions at this point.

In a surprising about-face, the Maryland Public Service Commission (PSC) agreed to reconsider its previous decision that found retail wheeling not to be in the public interest (see below). No details on the renewed investigation are available as of this writing.

In September of 1995, following its inquiry into retail wheeling initiated a year before, the PSC ruled that retail wheeling was not in the public interest. Based on a proceeding, dominated by investor-owned utilities and other parties adverse to retail wheeling, the Commission determined that the problems and complexities of retail wheeling outweigh the benefits and that wholesale open access would provide most of the competitive benefits. The primary issues in this decision were reciprocity with other states, recovery of stranded costs, cost shifting to captive customers, system reliability, continued support of environmental and social programs, the impact on municipal utilities and cooperatives, and jurisdictional complexities.

The PSC did agree to allow utilities to offer special contracts with customers that: recover more than variable costs, respond to viable competitive alternatives, and do not result in "excessive rate increases for other customers." This should provide some opportunity for rate reduction for industrial customers in Maryland.

Massachusetts

Details on Massachusetts Electric's unilateral retail wheeling pilot are starting to become more clear. The first phase of the pilot will start July 1, 1996, for thirteen of the utility's industrial customers that belong to an industrial end-users group that will act as the group's aggregator and buyer's agent. The group has issued an Request-for-proposal to find a mix of suppliers for the pilot. The second phase will begin on January 1, 1997, and will include about 10,000 of the utility's residential and small commercial customers. Contrary to the open market that retail wheeling participants in New Hampshire have, Massachusetts Electric has chosen a consulting firm called Environmental Futures that will select "three or four" suppliers from which the participants can chose. Environmental Futures will also issue an RFP to find those suppliers.

On May 1, 1996, the Massachusetts Department of Public Utilities (DPU) issued a draft rule outlining the restructuring of the electricity industry in the state in order to introduce full retail wheeling by January 1, 1998. In an order similar to that issued by California in December 1995, the DPU called for the creation of an ISO and a separate power exchange. Unlike California, however, the ISO would replace an existing regional transmission operator, i.e., the New England Power Pool, which may evolve into the ISO and power exchange. The proposal also calls for stranded cost recovery through incentives for divestiture of generation and functional unbundling consistent with FERC's recently issued Order 888. The draft rules have been generally supported by industrial end-users and power marketers, although a final rule is not due until October 4, 1996.

In developing this draft rule, the DPU required the state's major investor-owned utilities to file their own restructuring proposals. The real competition appears to have been in coming with a name for the respective plans. Although the DPU plan issued in May will become the focus of further debate, below is a summary of the plans that were filed:

Governor William Weld (February 13, 1996): In a plan called "Power Choice," the governor proposed to begin retail wheeling pilot programs in 1997 and give all customers direct access by January 1, 1998. The plan would only apply to investor-owned utilities, and corporate unbundling would be voluntary; however, to receive stranded cost recovery, the utilities would have to spin off or sell generation assets to determine the market value. This plan was filed by the Division of Energy Resources on behalf of the governor and appears to be the most thorough of all the plans filed. The DPU plan that was approved is most closely related to this plan.

Boston Edison (February 14, 1996): Boston Edison's "E-Plan" would also begin full retail wheeling in 1998, but the 1997 pilot program would consist of a retail wheeling simulation program that would determine the savings from direct access without true off-system purchases. The purpose of doing "virtual" retail wheeling first, according to the plan, is to let end-users determine if direct access works in their favor. Stranded costs would be fully recovered over a ten-year transition period.

Massachusetts Electric (February 16, 1996): The subsidiary of New England Electric System refiled its "Choice: New England" proposal originally filed in October of 1995. The revised plan, which is considered the most progressive of all, also calls for full retail wheeling by 1998 and stranded cost recovery over ten years. In the plan, Massachusetts Electric said that it would implement a unilateral retail wheeling pilot program (see above). The plan also calls for a New England-wide restructuring plan for an independent system operator since many transmission and access issues involve the entire region.

COM/Electric (February 15, 1996): The sister companies of Cambridge Electric and Commonwealth Electric filed a plan called "Competitive Challenge" that calls for auctioning off all of their utility and non-utility supply contracts in a procedure to be worked out in the next few months. Note that this is the only plan filed that is consistent with the Governor's views on full generation divestiture. COM/Electric's formal restructuring plan is not due until August of 1996.

Western Massachusetts Electric (February 16, 1996): The Northeast Utilities (NU) subsidiary filed the least aggressive of the restructuring plans. Rather than specifying a timetable for the introduction of retail wheeling, NU suggests introducing change slowly through price caps and pilot programs. While this may not meet the DPU's requirement for a restructuring plan, the utility was considering ignoring the mandate and filing nothing as a protest.

Eastern Utilities Associates (January 1996): Under Eastern Utilities Associates' (EUA) plan, stranded investment recovery would be limited to only nuclear plants and independent power producers contracts and would not include uneconomic fossil fuel or hydro-electric plants. Stranded costs and social programs would be paid for through a non-bypassable transition charge that would apply to all customers over a ten-year period. The plan also calls for EUA to act as an aggregator or marketer for those customers that choose to stay with the company.

On August 16, 1995, the Massachusetts Department of Public Utilities issued an order that outlines seven principles for restructuring the electricity industry in that state. Similar to those developed in Rhode Island and copied in other New England states, these principles include nonspecific concepts such as competitive generation markets, customer choice, stranded cost recovery, unbundled services, etc. These proposals were developed by a coalition that included industrial customers, environmentalists, utilities and independent power producers, the Attorney General, and power marketers. The order directs the state's largest utilities to include in their plans direct access for all customer classes, stranded cost recovery, unbundling, and incentive ratemaking for monopoly services such as transmission.

A proposed retail wheeling bill that addresses small customer concerns was introduced to the state senate and appears to be garnering significant support. This bill would allow small users to take advantage of competition through aggregation and rate protection mechanisms. A timetable for implementation and stranded cost recovery was not addressed, but further revisions were expected.

On December 4, 1995, the Senate Committee on Post Audit and Oversight issued its recommendation for restructuring the state's electricity industry and joined many other entities supporting retail competition. Finding that the state cannot "turn its backs on the benefits of competition," the report finds that end-users will accept the risks and responsibilities that come with direct access and recommends that end-users have the option of purchasing power directly or through an aggregator (for smaller customers). The report also proposes the creation of a "default pool" that will supply power to customers who chose neither direct access nor aggregation. The report also addresses transition charges, which would be assessed through a "wires charge" for all customers, even those that remain with existing utilities.

Raytheon Company, the state's largest employer, has publicly threatened to leave the state unless it can negotiate a 40% decrease in its rates charged by Massachusetts utilities. Raytheon turned down an offer by its utilities for a 20% discount to keep the company in the state. Instead, Raytheon wants direct access and is pushing for retail wheeling legislation. Raytheon has approached the state legislature with an intensive lobbying effort for retail wheeling as an alternative if it cannot achieve its desired cost savings. Several bills have been introduced to the legislature to achieve these objectives. One allows retail wheeling in the state, while another provides economic retention rate discounts of 40% below existing rates for defense contractors (e.g., Raytheon). Since the threat of Raytheon leaving the system was announced, virtually all Massachusetts investor-owned utilities have offered or proposed plans to reduce industrial rates in the state by up to 20%.

On January 6, 1995, the Massachusetts Division of Energy Resources (DOER) proposed retail wheeling as part of an integrated resource planning process (IRP) in a plan commonly referred to as the "wire charges plan." The DOER claims that suggesting retail wheeling as a form of IRP is the first such proposal in the country. As with some other retail wheeling initiatives, however, this plan proposes to give transmission and distribution access only to customers with incremental load. The DOER thus sees retail wheeling only as an alternative to new generation facilities. The plan has been criticized as being too restrictive and incomplete, but the DOER claims it is only an interim policy until a comprehensive restructuring plan is developed.

Michigan

In response to an April 12, 1996, order from the Michigan Public Service Commission (MPSC), Consumers Power and Detroit Edison submitted retail competition plans on May 15, 1996. Unfortunately, the plans fall well short of implementation plans and merely address recommendations by the state's Jobs Commission to allow direct access for new load, rather than existing load. Consumers proposes to allow retail wheeling for new commercial or industrial customers and for new load from existing customers greater than 3 MW. However, the supplying utility would have to allow reciprocal access to its system. Detroit Edison also agreed to allow access to new load by January, 1, 1997, but only if certain issues, like stranded investment, are resolved by then. Obviously, the reciprocity and stranded cost requirements are essentially deal killers, and the plans have drawn sharp criticism from all sides.

A steel forging facility has petitioned the MPSC for the right to competitively source new and existing load despite other retail wheeling proposals in the state. Simply claiming that its rates are too high, MascoTech Forming Technologies Incorporated, a Detroit Edison customer, has demanded the right to access other suppliers. While many end-users also want retail wheeling, the MPSC will consider this request because it involves new load as well as existing load.

The MPSC approved an agreement between Wisconsin Electric Power Company (WEPCO) and Upper Peninsula Power Company (UPPCO) that allows each utility to feed retail load in each other's service territory. While the MPSC hails the agreement as another step toward retail wheeling, the agreement itself goes out of its way to avoid the label. Lacking the ability to feed an expanding mining load in the Upper Peninsula, UPPCO agreed to allow WEPCO to feed the load in exchange for similar rights with some of WEPCO's load in the Upper Peninsula, although the contract is somewhat ambiguous as to the circumstances that would allow UPPCO to feed WEPCO load. WEPCO will pay UPPCO $180,000 per year in transmission charges, but no reciprocal transmission arrangement was included. The agreement also notes that no stranded costs will be incurred as a result of the arrangement.

As evidence of the political nature of the retail wheeling debate in Michigan, Governor John Englar issued his own industry restructuring proposal that would allow retail wheeling for new industrial customers within a year. The governor's plan would require the MPSC to develop unbundled transmission and distribution tariffs and to create a plan to buy down stranded costs. While new load gets direct access in a year, all customers would have direct access by 2001. As an intermediary step, a wholesale power pool with an ISO would be operating in 1998.

American Electric Power (AEP), which has retail customer load in Michigan, issued a position statement on October 26, 1995, favoring retail competition and direct access in the region it serves. Full discussion of this proposal is in the Ohio section of this report.

On September 11, 1995, Consumers Power reached an agreement with the staff of the MPSC to implement a "limited direct access" program. Along with other special tariff and contract provisions, the agreement would allow a Consumers Power customer with more than 3 MW of load to purchase power from an independent power producer within its service territory (which is an admittedly small group of suppliers). The quid pro quo for Consumers Power is that it can recover investment in 330 MW of the Midland Cogeneration Venture that has until now been unrecoverable in conventional rates. The limited access program would only allow in-state suppliers to compete for the participating load, which may make the program meaningless. The program would use the wheeling rates issued for the experimental retail wheeling program (see below).

On June 19, 1995, the MPSC issued its final order on the experimental retail wheeling program announced in its April 11, 1994, interim order (see below). The final order primarily addresses the retail delivery rates that Consumers Power and Detroit Edison (DECO) can charge in the experiment; these rates were remanded in the interim order. Contrary to the transmission rates of more than 3.5¢ per kilowatt–hour suggested by the utilities, the MPSC set transmission rates, based on embedded costs, at 0.8¢ and 1.2¢ per kilowatt–hour for Consumers Power and DECO, respectively. A key issue that remains open is whether the MPSC has the authority to set the rates, terms, and conditions of transmission service given FERC's recently issued Order 888 on open access transmission tariffs. The final order also addressed other issues raised by various parties in response to the interim order.

On April 11, 1994, the MPSC ordered a five-year experimental retail wheeling program for 150 MW of industrial load on Consumers Power and DECO. The plan is contingent upon the utilities filing resource plans that call for new capacity. The PSC based its authority on the Commission's general powers rather than on any specific legislative mandate. This may pave the way for other state programs; however, it also required any third-party supplier to get a certificate of public convenience and necessity and to get franchise approval from the local municipality. On April 12, 1996, an MPSC administrative law judge recommended that that DECO be required to add more than 1200 MW of new capacity by the year 2004. This would potentially trigger the retail wheeling experiment.

On August 26, 1994, DECO filed a formal challenge to the Michigan plan in federal court. The challenge is based on a claimed lack of jurisdiction by the MPSC, or any other state for that matter, to order retail wheeling. This is a key legal issue that has been expected to be raised at some point. Most analysts agree, however, that the Energy Policy Act of 1992 clearly gives states the right to implement such a plan. On May 5, 1995, the court rejected DECO's petition on the grounds that the federal court does not have jurisdiction over the MPSC because of eleventh amendment immunity. On July 19, 1995, DECO filed an appeal based on the final decision of the MPSC.

In the early 1980's, Dow Chemical wheeled power from its QF in Ontario to a Michigan facility through Ontario Hydro, DECO and Consumers Power. However, there is no general provision for self-service wheeling.

Minnesota

On December 7, 1995, the Minnesota Public Utilities Commission (MPUC) issued a set of 15 draft principles of restructuring in response to its investigation into electricity initiated in May. While supporting competition, the guidelines encourage a slow pace of change, contrary to a proposal from Northern States Power to implement retail wheeling in the near future. The MPUC suggested that all parties will share in transition costs and that unbundling is the path toward competition, but no specific order to unbundle rates was included. A final written order is due in December 1996. The ruling generally favored that of a coalition of other state utilities and environmentalists that formed for the express purpose of delaying the introduction of retail wheeling into the state.

In July 1995, the Department of Public Service announced that it investigated retail wheeling in parallel with the MPUC inquiry, given that it generally favors retail competition.

A legislative committee responsible for jobs and business development in the state has begun holding hearings on retail wheeling and electricity competition as it relates to the economic health of the state. A retail wheeling bill may result.

Mississippi

The Mississippi Public Service Commission has reportedly begun an informal study of retail wheeling for certain areas of the state. No details are available.

Missouri

The University of Missouri in Columbia has an agreement with its local municipal electric utility to independently procure electricity on the open market. This retail wheeling agreement is made possible because the utility is regulated by neither the FERC nor state regulators.

Missouri Public Service Commission Chair Allan Mueller claims that retail wheeling will be addressed differently in the "heartland" than on the coasts where recent development has been more active. This is due to less pressure from industrial end-users to lower rates and more efficiently run utilities. Missouri hopes to learn from the mistakes of those states leading the way.

Montana

Montana Public Service Commission (PSC) Chair Bob Anderson said that retail wheeling is a "natural response" of industrial end-users who believe that electricity costs are too high. As a result, the Commission has opened a restructuring inquiry by requesting input on issues to address. The PSC issued a set of principles and guidelines in February upon which further discussion will be based.

In its comments to this inquiry, Montana Power Company encouraged transition to a competitive market taking five to ten years. As with other plans, unbundling generation from other services would be required and social programs would be funded through a non-bypassable service charge to all customers.

Nebraska

Because the entire state of Nebraska is fed by publicly owned utilities, the state has shown little interest in retail wheeling.

Nevada

A bill was passed by the Nevada Legislature that will create a legislative committee to study retail wheeling and electricity industry competition. The law requires a report to be filed with the full legislature by the 1997 session, although recommendations are expected to be filed by August 1996. It also requires the committee to investigate the stranded investment issue and to create a methodology for implementing retail wheeling in the state. Although the recent demise of a full retail wheeling implementation bill (as opposed to only ordering a study) was heralded by utility lobbyists, the Nevada Senate Committee on Commerce and Labor held hearings on retail wheeling on April 25 and 26, 1995, since there are "other legislators still interested in studying the issue."

At the same time, the Nevada Public Service Commission (PSC) continues to study retail wheeling as part of an inquiry opened in December 1994. The docket remains active while the legislature begins its investigation, and a final report is expected in June 1996.

Nevada has enacted the country's first retail wheeling statute, but it applies only to new load so as to attract industry to the state. Additional restrictions are that the end-user must invest $50 million into the state, the products must be 50% recyclable, the utility must show that it does not raise rates for residential customers, and the PSC must approve every contract. Some say this renders the bill meaningless. The steel company (North Star Steel) for which this statute was designed decided to build in Arizona, not Nevada. Retail wheeling opponents saw this as a victory because it proved that retail wheeling is not very important for industrials.

New Hampshire

Late News

On May 22, 1996, New Hampshire became the first state to pass legislation to mandate the implementation of full retail competition for all customer classes by a certain date, in this case mid-1998. Bill 1392 was signed by Governor Steve Merrill just as competition to feed participants in the state's retail wheeling pilot program (see below) was heating up. The bill is based on the principles developed by a legislative committee in December of 1995, but the issue of stranded investment recovery is still unresolved. Public Service Company of New Hampshire (PSNH), the state's largest utility, has threatened litigation unless it recovers 100% of its stranded costs, while the New Hampshire Public Utilities Commission (PUC) wants to tie stranded cost recovery to a utility's cooperation during the transition to competition. Under the new legislation, PSNH has until July of 1996 to submit a detailed restructuring plan which must be approved by the PUC by mid-1997 to avoid having a plan imposed on the utility. Just before the bill was passed, PSNH offered to roll back prices in the state if retail competition was delayed until the year 2000. The governor, however, said it was "too little, too late" and ignored the offer.

In the nation's first mandated retail wheeling pilot program, the forces of competition are bringing out the best and worst of the free market. As hot air balloons advertising a "green" power alternative fly overhead, suppliers are offering everything from saplings to first-aid kits to $50 checks to sign up customers. The fight for the few larger commercial and industrial loads is so fierce that most participants are receiving price quotes well below the market cost of power. The market created in New Hampshire is somewhat skewed in that so many suppliers are chasing after so little load, as only 3% of the state's load, divided among randomly selected customers of all classes, is subject to the experiment. More details on this experiment are given below.

On yet another front, New Hampshire again made retail competition history when the state's Supreme Court upheld a PUC finding that there are no exclusive utility franchise territories in the state. Although full retail wheeling may make the point somewhat moot, the ruling was hailed as a victory for end-users, especially in other states where the ruling could be used to set a precedent. The case was heard in the context of the Freedom Electric case, which is described fully below.

Retail Wheeling Legislation

On February 1, 1996, the New Hampshire House of Representatives passed, without debate, legislation that would implement full retail wheeling for all customer classes by mid-1998. In April, however, the state senate modified the bill by requiring the PUC to develop a statewide plan rather than using the plans submitted by the utilities. The house then approved those changes, and the governor has signed it. Key provisions of this bill include:

- All rate classes must benefit from competition, and electricity service must be functionally unbundled. Details on how existing services will be unbundled will be left to the detailed utility plans.
- The implementation will be coordinated with the retail wheeling experiment (see below).
- A legislative oversight committee will be created to monitor the restructuring effort and report to the legislature.
- Stranded investment recovery is allowed, but full recovery is not guaranteed. The PUC, which will determine the level of recovery for each utility, will base its decisions on reasonableness and the degree to which the utilities cooperate in the transition process.

Retail Wheeling Pilot Program

On February 28, 1996, the PUC issued its final guidelines for the retail wheeling pilot program. The program is the result of a law signed by New Hampshire Governor Steve Merrill that also created the Retail Wheeling and Restructuring Study Committee. Governor Merrill, who finds himself in a political battle against PSNH, said he wants his state "to be among the first states to begin the deregulation of electric utilities and open the doors for competition."

In a deal that removed the last main barrier to New Hampshire's retail wheeling pilot program, PSNH and the New Hampshire PUC agreed on some key elements to the retail wheeling pilot. While refusing to accept anything less than 100% stranded cost recovery, the Northeast Utilities' subsidiary agreed to a minimum 10% discount for pilot program participants, which works out to be approximately the same as recovering 70% of the utility's stranded costs. During the first week in April, the PUC held hearings on the "compliance filings" submitted by each utility subject to the experiment in which particulars of the experiment were discussed (see below). New England Electric System agreed to participate in the pilot program on January 5, 1996. This agreement allows Granite State Electric to recover 75% of its stranded costs during the experiment, rather than the 50% proposed by the original guidelines and the 100% demanded by PSNH.

Features of the pilot program guidelines include:

- The program will begin May 28, 1996, and extend for two years.
- Each utility in the state must allow 3% of its load to be served by competitive suppliers. This amounts to about 50 MW in the state with 35 MW allocated to PSNH.
- This load will be allocated among all customer classes, and the participating customers will be chosen at random from a pool of volunteers.
- The PUC also agreed to divide participation evenly between a group of randomly selected end-users and some chosen from certain "geographic regions of choice."

- Real-time metering will not be required (but may be optional), so approximate load profiles will be developed for each ratepayer class for the purposes of the pilot.
- The PUC will require all state utilities to submit transmission tariffs to both the PUC and to FERC, and these tariffs will apply to transmission under the retail wheeling experiment. PSNH has challenged the authority of the PUC to order it to file a FERC tariff.
- No exit or reentry fees may be assessed.
- Stranded investment costs are to be determined over the course of the experiment. Once established, they will be shared 50/50 between the utilities and the participating customer.
- A separate docket will be opened to address this issue after the first year of the experiment.
- All competitive suppliers must belong to or be associated with a member of the New England Power Pool (NEPOOL). While this may be a barrier to entry, it resolves many technical issues for purposes of the pilot.

Freedom Electric Case

A New Hampshire attorney (and ex-PSNH officer) is proposing the formation of a new public utility that would serve industrial customers with low-cost power available on the wholesale market. The PUC could approve the utility, called Freedom Electric Power Company, under a New Hampshire law that allows competition when it is in the "public good." Ironically, Freedom Electric has already arranged to purchase 20 MW of capacity from Seabrook, the nuclear power plant that caused the demise of PSNH.

On May 31, 1995, the PUC ruled that franchise areas in the state are not exclusive so that Freedom Electric could serve loads presently served by PSNH. The state Supreme Court upheld this finding in May of 1996 (see above). Before this can happen, however, the plan would still have to be found to be in the public good, and the new utility must obtain a certificate of public convenience and necessity, as does every utility. According to the PUC, Freedom Electric is a utility and not a marketer because it owns some generation and transmission assets.

The Freedom Electric plan may also provide the first test case for the "sham wholesale transaction" clause of the Energy Policy Act. PSNH is claiming that Freedom Electric does not qualify as a wholesale entity since it has no distribution assets, so the utility cannot be forced to provide transmission services. To cover all its bases, Freedom Electric is also applying for a power marketing license with FERC.

New Hampshire law also allows a QF to sell power directly to up to three retail customers and forces the utility to wheel this power. The PUC recently upheld this law.

New Jersey

On May 23, 1996, the New Jersey Board of Public Utilities (BPU) issued Phase II of its "Energy Master Plan," which calls for the implementation of wholesale wheeling by 1997 and the development of a timeline for retail wheeling. The plan calls for the creation of a negotiating team, consisting of representatives of all stakeholders, which will hold hearings and issue a report by October of 1996 and the retail wheeling timeline by the end of the year. The team will consider issues such as divestiture of generation assets, introduction of retail wheeling, stranded investment, and low-income ratepayer protection.

Phase I of the Energy Master Plan implemented a flexible rate program through legislation. This legislation was passed, thus ordering the BPU to develop procedures for approving flexible contracts. This legislation was also revised to make it very difficult for utilities to recover the discounts given up in the special contracts from remaining customers.

New Mexico

A state legislative committee investigating electricity restructuring found that neither retail wheeling nor industry restructuring was in the best interest of the state and recommended no legislative action. While supporters of retail competition claim the issue is not dead, the issue cannot be revived until the next legislative session in 1998. The Public Utilities Commission (PUC) investigation (described below) will continue. The demise of the legislative front was reportedly due to intense lobbying by the major investor-owned utilities in the state.

On November 28, 1995, the New Mexico PUC issued a notice of inquiry into retail wheeling and sought comment on how the state's electricity industry should be restructured. As evidence of the PUC's outlook, Lawrence Ingram, Chair of the New Mexico Public Utility Commission, said, "I doubt we will see retail wheeling in the near future in New Mexico."

A series of retail wheeling bills were introduced in the 1995 New Mexico legislature, but were killed early on by utility opposition. The most aggressive bill, similar to that initially proposed by Tom Wray in 1993, provided for phased-in retail wheeling over six years and has been endorsed by the New Mexico Industrial Energy Consumers Group. Other bills include a variety of piecemeal measures that deal with industry competition, such as self-wheeling and mandatory rate comparisons on customers' bills. A legislative committee approved proposed legislation to direct the Public Service Commission (PSC) to monitor and evaluate retail wheeling developments in other states, but the resolution did not promote retail wheeling legislation at this time.

The U.S. Army and Air Force have notified El Paso Electric that they intend to seek competitive bids for retail service to bases in New Mexico. El Paso is fighting it in the State PSC, and the Army has responded that the PSC cannot prevent it on jurisdictional grounds. An industrial group has intervened with an argument that this is an ideal opportunity for an experimental retail wheeling program. A Commission ruling is pending.

New York

On May 16, 1996, the New York State Public Service Commission (PSC) issued is long-awaited plan to introduce retail competition to the state, and it surprised a few stakeholders by suggesting that retail wheeling be offered to all customers in all classes by 1998. The ruling requires all of the state's utilities to file restructuring plans (except Niagara Mohawk, which already did so, see below) which must state how retail wheeling will be implemented in this timeframe, show how they will restructure their companies, provide a rate plan, and address certain social issues. The plan requires the establishment of an ISO by 1997 and the implementation of a "wires charge" to recover stranded costs and social program costs. Other than that, however, details of implementing retail wheeling were left to the utility plans rather than included in the PSC order. Given that the order mostly includes general principles, many criticized the plan for lacking the details to address implementation and stranded cost issues.

New York will suddenly join the bandwagon of retail wheeling pilot programs on June 1, 1996, as the New York PSC approved Orange and Rockland (O&R) Utilities' "PowerPick" program. Under this pilot program, O&R's largest industrial customers will be able to shop the market for energy while capacity and delivery services are provided by the utility (although the energy is actually bought and resold by the utility). On January 1, 1997, some 1,500 commercial and residential customers will also be able to participate. Because the utility buys most of its power anyway, it does not plan to recover any stranded costs, although participants must share half of their savings with the utility to recover stranded regulatory assets.

Noting that legislative support for retail wheeling is still required, several New York legislators have proposed their own electricity restructuring plan that would not allow full direct access until 2000. The plan, called "Competition Plus," would require full generation divestiture by 2002 and would not guarantee stranded investment recovery for utilities. Bipartisan support is expected, and a companion bill for the Senate will also be introduced. The proposed bills will leave the details of a competitive market to the regulators. As an alternative to this legislation, an industrial end-user group has introduced a bill which would allow full retail wheeling for all customers by mid-1997 and minimal stranded cost recovery. This proposal preceded the PSC plan described above and is somewhat eclipsed by it.

As part of the PSC's investigation into retail wheeling, various coalitions of utilities, end-users, and other interested parties submitted proposals to the PSC. Sithe Energy, the state's largest independent power producer (IPP), suggests delaying retail access until the state's seven large investor-owned utilities (IOUS) are merged into one or two companies. The state's utilities, except for Niagara Mohawk (see below), have formed a group that argues that a wholesale poolco model is a necessary first step. The Energy Association of New York, the utility group, favors full recovery of stranded cost and a delay in implementation of direct access. More aggressive restructuring proposals are described below.

The New York Power Authority (NYPA) is also a retail wheeling advocate in New York, joining an ever-increasing list in the state. In its contribution to the PSC's proceeding on competition, NYPA proposed a model in which it would be the sole transmission company in the state and become an ISO for a voluntary generation pool. The plan would allow direct access for retail customers through bilateral contracts and would leave distribution services to the existing utilities. As for stranded costs, NYPA proposes to purchase the utility's transmission system above its embedded cost as a means to compensate the utilities (including nonutility generation agreements). This would result in passing off stranded costs through the transmission charge, which may have some legal problems. NYPA has come on the record in firm opposition to both the Sithe plan and the PUC's Administrative Law Judge decision described above.

On October 6, 1995, Niagara Mohawk (NiMo) announced a proposal to restructure the ailing utility so as to allow retail wheeling within three years. This restructuring includes splitting the company into separate generation, transmission, distribution, and marketing companies. NiMo's plan calls for a voluntary poolco and bilateral contracts that would allow direct retail access to competitive generation. If the company is unable to separate its expensive generation costs from its other services, it claims that it might be forced into a Chapter 11 bankruptcy. Part of NiMo's "PowerChoice" plan is to renegotiate its non-utility generation contracts, and it has threatened to use its power of eminent domain to take over the plants if renegotiation is unsuccessful.

Three towns in New York have petitioned the PSC to allow retail wheeling as pilot programs. In all three cases, Wheeled Electric Power, an aggregator and marketer, has been the driving force behind the petitions, but any supplier would be eligible to feed the loads. Reportedly these petitions are in response to PSC encouragement to towns to "test the benefit of the market."

The state legislature has stepped up its involvement in the retail wheeling debate by holding a series of roundtable discussions on restructuring. Claiming that the PSC does not have adequate jurisdiction to introduce retail wheeling, legislation may be forthcoming. A bill has been circulated through the New York legislature that will allow end-users to purchase power directly from IPPs as part of an economic development program. Qualified end-users must have at least 2 MW of load or own 20% or more of the power project.

In early June 1995, the PSC issued a final version of its set of regulatory "principles" that it will use to "guide the transition to a more competitive industry." The PSC stated that it is "committed to encouraging more competition" and will accept comments on retail wheeling. The final version modifies the original proposal by deleting references to wholesale wheeling as the only means to electricity competition. Among the nine listed principles is one that states that the present vertically integrated monopoly structure is "incompatible with effective wholesale or retail competition." The other principles attempt to balance price fairness, system reliability, and economic development.

The State Energy Planning Board (EPB), which consists of the State Energy Office, the PSC, and other state agencies, issued a "State Energy Plan," which is "required guidance" for all state agency decisions affecting energy. In the plan, the EPB promises to address the future of the state's electricity industry over the next two years through a series of public issue forums. The report found the following:

- Genuine retail competition could reduce costs; however, retail wheeling may not necessarily be the best means to that end.
- It is unclear whether retail wheeling is in the best overall interest of the state, and greater reliance on retail competition will raise difficult transition issues.
- The PSC has been encouraging the development of alternative ratemaking approaches, including special contracts.
- The PSC should encourage the utilities to develop "expanded options" for their customers.
- A New York State-based Regional Transmission Group should be seriously considered.

A group of Long Island schools has filed a petition to purchase power on the wholesale market to replace LILCO as a retail supplier. The Education/Electric Buying Group would be a wholesale buyer that would then deliver power to LILCO for retail sale back to the schools.

The PSC previously issued rules on implementing flexible rates as a means to keep industrial customers on the system and to avoid retail wheeling. The crux of the rules is that both ratepayers and shareholders should bear the cost of the program. Peter Bradford, Chairperson of the PSC said, "Electric utilities need to behave as if retail wheeling is going to happen."

The PSC approved two arrangements that approach retail wheeling. Grumman Aerospace was allowed to sell power from one of its cogeneration facilities to Forest Laboratories, Incorporated as part of a real estate deal. Another cogenerator, Sithe Energies, was allowed to sell power to two industrials (Alcan Rolled Products and Liberty Paperboard) which are neighboring facilities. The PSC will grant the Sithe facility a certificate of public necessity and convenience so that it can sell retail power.

There are numerous contractual arrangements for wheeling NYPA hydro power to various private and public end-users via state IOU-owned lines. This is based on specific legislative authority dating back to the early 1960s.

A New York Public Utilities Commission Commissioner (O'Neill) says that the commission studied retail wheeling in 1988 and found the cost to residential customers too high, but that the Commission could legally order it without legislation.

In August 1993, Consolidated Edison submitted to FERC a wheeling agreement with the JFK Airport to transmit power from a cogeneration project to the airport. The leverage? JFK was previously taking retail-wheeled NYPA power.

North Carolina

On July 21, 1995, the North Carolina Utilities Commission decided not to initiate a formal investigation into retail wheeling due to stalls at the time in California, Connecticut, and Michigan. This ruling was in response to a retail wheeling petition filed by a group of industrial customers in the state. The Commission was not enthusiastic about retail wheeling, and one commissioner said that retail competition "is a long way off." The petition filed by the Carolina Utility Customers Association would allow all customers, including residential, to have access to transmission. Duke Power and North Carolina Power have taken a neutral stand on retail access, recognizing that competition is inevitable. Carolina Power & Light, which has the highest industrial rates in the Southeast, has said that even an investigation into retail wheeling would be unnecessary and costly.

Moody's Investor Services has said that the important role played by the industrial sectors in North and South Carolina makes it "likely that retail wheeling will ultimately occur" in those states.

North Dakota

On February 20, 1996, the North Dakota Public Service Commission (PSC) opened a formal investigation into the "economic, technological, institutional, and legal" issues of retail competition. The initial inquiry and request for comments was patterned after a similar effort in Minnesota. Hearings will begin in May 1996.

Ohio

In what the Public Utility Commission of Ohio (PUCO) termed a "baby step" toward retail wheeling, it recently reaffirmed a pilot program to introduce interruptible "buy-through" contracts to the state. Under the program, approved in April 1996, interruptible customers would be able to search for and purchase off-system supplies during capacity shortages. If an alternative source is found, the native utility must purchase the power and resell it to the customer. Apparently, actual wheeling of the power is not involved. The pilot program will last two years.

In another baby step toward retail wheeling taken in May 1996, the PUCO issued guidelines on conjunctive billing, which would allow smaller customers or end-users with multiple facilities to aggregate their load and take advantage of load diversity and greater power purchasing power. The Conjunctive Electric Services tariff would be mandatory for all Ohio utilities, once approval for the program is given, and would be implemented as a two-year experimental program.

State Representative Ron Amstutz, sponsor of a failed full retail wheeling bill introduced in 1994, introduced another retail wheeling bill in March 1996. The draft proposal includes direct access for all customers by January 1, 1998, and includes a provision for the sharing of stranded investment costs. The 1994 bill was somewhat unexpected and was introduced without support; so for the 1996 bill support is being collected before it is introduced. Amstutz claims that the bill will probably not pass the legislature in 1996, but that it will set the stage for passage in 1997 for implementation in 1998. The bill has the backing of many end-user groups and, surprisingly, American Municipal Power — Ohio, Incorporated, the state's municipal utility joint action agency. (Municipal electric companies in many states oppose retail competition.) The new Amstutz bill also reportedly has bipartisan support.

The 500-pound gorilla of transmission in mid-America is the latest advocate of retail wheeling. American Electric Power (AEP), which is the parent company for seven utilities feeding load in seven states, issued on October 26, 1995, a series of principles favoring retail competition. Although rather broad, these principles favor direct access for all customer classes throughout the region it serves, but also maintains that stranded cost recovery through an access fee is required and should be handled on a utility-by-utility basis. AEP's proposal includes a regional power exchange which would be a voluntary poolco that would operate in conjunction with an ISO. Interestingly, this is the first poolco proposal that suggests creating a half-hour energy market.

On December 6, 1995, the Ohio Office of Consumer's Counsel issued a set of principles regarding customer choice in electricity. The ratepayer advocacy group acknowledges that retail competition is beneficial for Ohio if all customer classes get a chance to participate fairly.

Oklahoma

A legislative bill that would have introduced retail competition on a limited basis was killed by intense utility lobbying. The bill was introduced as a "shell bill" that would serve to hold a place in line while the legislative committee established in 1995 (see below) worked out the details. Since no details were included in the bill, there was little substance to the opposition except that "the IOUs are adamantly opposed to retail wheeling," according to a staffer on the committee. In classic legislative style, the committee is setting up a commission to do a two-year study of retail wheeling before taking further action.

In June 1995, a 14-member task force was created by the state legislature to investigate a broad variety of electricity regulation issues, including retail wheeling, the state's existing franchise law, and the effect of FERC's NOPR on open access transmission. During one of these task force meetings, the chairman, state Senator Kevin Easley, stated that he wanted to see a retail wheeling pilot program in the state given the success of introducing competition into the natural gas industry. No specific proposal has been reported.

The Oklahoma Commerce Commission (OCC) has sponsored workshops on electric industry restructuring and is reportedly interested in opening a docket on competition. The chairman of the OCC has said that it is "time to consider opening up certain elements of the electric market to competition."

Existing law allows new load of more than 1 MW to be fed from a choice of suppliers. Details of this provision and whether it has ever been exercised was not available.

Oregon

While continuing to observe development of retail wheeling in other states, the Oregon Public Utility Commission (PUC) will support market-based rates through special contracts for industrial customers with "viable supply alternatives." Joan Smith, Chair of the PUC, has stated that she believes that the benefits of competition could be achieved without retail wheeling.

The legislature passed a bill that gives the PUC the authority to allow "alternative regulation," although no formal retail wheeling investigation is under way beyond information gathering.

Pennsylvania

Interest in retail wheeling was suddenly sparked in Western Pennsylvania by Pittsburgh Mayor Tom Murphy, who claimed publicly that retail competition was the answer to Duquesne Light's relatively high rates. In response, Duquesne Light ran a two-page newspaper ad over three consecutive days explaining that it supports competition but at a slow pace and with full stranded cost recovery. The Pennsylvania Public Utility Commission (PUC) held a public hearing on retail competition on March 5, 1996, in Pittsburgh. The Commission plans to participate in a number of hearings and mini-seminars throughout the state to ensure that the public is aware of the issue and is able to participate in the restructuring debate.

At least three full retail wheeling bills have been introduced by Pennsylvania legislators. On January 2, 1996, legislation was introduced to the Pennsylvania General Assembly to require the PUC to adopt a plan within six months for implementing retail wheeling and customer choice in electricity services. The bill would require full retail competition for all customer classes and unbundling within five years. While many details are left to the PUC, the bill would place most of the burden of stranded investment on the utilities and limit recovery to the five-year transition period.

While this bill was sponsored by the minority party in the state (Democrat Mike Veon), the other two bills were introduced by Republicans (Senator David Brightbill and Representative Frank Tulli). In both bills, all customers would have access to competitive markets after a five-year transition period and utilities would recover less than their full stranded costs. In Tulli's bill, the PUC would have until 1997 to develop a customer choice plan, including the development of an ISO and a separate power pool. The sponsors of both bills have expressed a need for rate relief in the state and the concern that Pennsylvania appears to be falling behind the curve in the movement toward retail competition.

While the legislature seems to favor retail competition on both sides of the aisle, the PUC remains split on the issue. One Commissioner (John Hangar) is speaking around the country in favor of competition, another (Lisa Crutchfield) remains opposed. Commissioner Hangar has repeatedly warned the commission that the state will be disadvantaged by failing to keep up as the industry changes around it. A report from the commission, following the staff report discussed below, is expected in June 1996 following a renewed year-long investigation.

In comments to the renewed inquiry on retail wheeling by the PUC, four of the state's six large investor-owned utilities endorsed retail wheeling, although only after a transition period under a mandatory wholesale poolco model. The state's industrial end-user group promoted a six-year phased-in approach with some end-users getting access to competitive generation by 1997.

On August 8, 1995, the staff of the PUC issued a 268-page report summarizing its investigation into competition in the electricity industry. Unfortunately, the report found that the risk of deregulation to residential consumers outweighs the potential benefits of competition. The report also cited many legal, regulatory, and technical uncertainties as reasons for not recommending changing the existing regulatory structure. The report was the result of the PUC's investigation into retail wheeling and competition that was initiated on April 14, 1994.

Equitable Gas Company, a Pittsburgh-based local gas distribution company, proposed a pilot program to allow full competition for both gas and electricity. Equitable is proposed to perform the pilot program in the borough of Pleasant Hills, an affluent Pittsburgh suburb, that happens to be presently served by four gas companies and two electric utilities. The program would allow all six companies to compete with each other to supply all energy services to the borough's residents. The plan was rejected by the PUC as premature given other developments on industry restructuring.

In response to the April 14 inquiry, the Pennsylvania Consumer Advocacy Council recently issued a strong condemnation of retail wheeling to the PUC. The Chair of the group called retail wheeling "an unmitigated disaster."

Rhode Island

Narragansett Electric Company and the Rhode Island legislature reached an agreement on a proposed bill to restructure the electricity industry in the state to allow full retail competition beginning in 1998 and to be fully implemented by 2001. The new law, entitled the "Utility Restructuring Act of 1996," would require each state utility to file a restructuring plan by 1997 that would include functional unbundling and a twelve-year transition charge. Once each plan is in place, retail wheeling would be phased in over four years by customer class. While the bill reportedly has gubernatorial and bipartisan support, it has been criticized for allowing too much stranded cost recovery over a very long transition period. However, passage of the measure is expected. Narragansett Electric, a wholly owned subsidiary of New England Electric System, serves 80% of the retail load in Rhode Island.

In its restructuring proposal, Eastern Utilities Associates (EUA), parent company for Blackstone Valley Electric Company and Newport Electric Corporation, suggests full retail access for all customer classes by January 1998. Most interesting is EUA's proposal to include no stranded cost recovery for stranded fossil generation assets. Like other proposals from New England utilities, this plan includes a regional power exchange and ISO.

In a surprisingly quick series of developments, retail wheeling almost came to Rhode Island in a limited form. On July 3, 1995, both houses of the state legislature passed bill amendments that would allow the Rhode Island Port Authority to not only develop a generation facility in a state-owned industrial park but also to sell that power to any end-user in the state. Very soon afterward, the governor vetoed the bill in response to intense opposition. This special arrangement might jeopardize the discussions surrounding the consortium that has put Rhode Island near the front of the pack of states heading toward a competitive electricity market.

On July 21, 1995, the Rhode Island Division of Public Utilities and Carriers (PUC) adopted the restructuring proposal developed by the diverse coalition of stakeholders that has served as an example for other New England states investigating retail wheeling. In May, the PUC established an Electric Industry Restructuring Task Force that issued a statement endorsing a direct-access proposal that would include residential customers. The task force, which includes a coalition of investor-owned utilities, independent producers, industrial customers, environmental groups, and low-income advocates, issued a list of 17 principles designed to guide the transition to a competitive marketplace.

South Carolina

The South Carolina Public Service Commission (PSC) rejected a proposal to create a formal panel to investigate retail wheeling, but it did direct its staff to solicit input on retail wheeling from interested parties. The request for a more formal investigation was filed by a group of large industrial end-users and vigorously opposed by Carolina Power & Light. Duke Power, which is active in the power marketing arena, said that it could support retail wheeling but encouraged the type of informal investigation that was adopted.

The PSC has stated that it is unclear whether state law gives the Commission authority to order retail wheeling, although state law does not specifically prohibit it. One commissioner has said that he would oppose any retail wheeling scheme that did not make a contribution to residential consumers.

Moody's Investor Services said that the important role being played by the industrial sectors in North and South Carolina makes it "likely that retail wheeling will ultimately occur" in those states.

A top executive at South Carolina Electric & Gas said he expects retail wheeling in his state in "the next few years," at least for industrials. He claimed that this is the logical start to a competitive industry and that there are no technical hurdles, even for residential retail wheeling.

South Dakota

South Dakota law allows new customers with usage of two or more megawatts to petition the Public Utilities Commission (PUC) to select their electrical supplier. Smaller users must contract with their assigned utility.

The PUC has taken a pro-competition position as a favorable alternative to regulation. It supports retail wheeling as long as captive customers are protected and "true" competition exists.

Tennessee

American Electric Power, which has retail customer load in Tennessee, issued a position statement on October 26, 1995, favoring retail competition and direct access in the region it serves. Full discussion of this proposal is in the Ohio section of this report.

Texas

In a surprising move for a Texas utility, Texas-New Mexico Power Company (TNP) released a retail wheeling proposal that would grant all customers direct access by 2002. In a plan called "Community Choice," submitted to the Texas Public Utility Commission (PUC) for approval, TNP would allow its larger customers to participate in the program as early as January 1997 and allow smaller customers to aggregate their loads as the program is phased in.

A new coalition of industrial, commercial, and residential end-users is being formed by a state industrial users group to renew legislative efforts toward retail wheeling. Noting that retail wheeling proponents were "trounced" in the last legislative session, the new coalition will have until January 1997 to make its case for direct retail access for all customers in the state.

On November 3, 1995, the PUC announced its intention to investigate retail competition issues even though the legislature refused to go beyond wholesale wheeling in its recent restructuring law (see below). Rather than wait for the legislature, the PUC decided to accept comments on unbundling and stranded investment in order to develop recommendations for the 1997 legislative session. However, sources indicate that the PUC is reluctant to spend too much time on retail wheeling inquiries given the mandate from the legislature to focus, for now, on wholesale market issues.

The Texas legislature has passed a bill that substantially deregulates the Texas wholesale market and makes other changes in the state's utility code, but does not address or otherwise change the status of retail wheeling. Last-minute compromises eliminated all references to retail wheeling including a utility-sponsored ban as well as a self-service wheeling provision. A primary impact of the bill is to authorize exempt wholesale generators (EWG) in Texas (ERCOT is not subject to the EWG provisions of the Energy Policy Act), and allow power marketers to operate in the state for the first time. It also specifies procedures to govern utility affiliate transactions, provides for flexible pricing to retain customers, and substantially deregulates electric cooperatives.

A PUC Commissioner was quoted as saying, "Our mission is to exterminate the old regulated monopoly and to replace it with competition." A report issued by the PUC suggests that competition may be introduced through a new integrated resource planning process that would include flexible ratemaking.

Utah

On January 24, 1996, the Utah Public Service Commission issued a notice of inquiry on electric industry restructuring thus opening a formal investigation into retail competition. While the usual issues will be reviewed, no word on a proposed timetable was available.

Utah State University in Logan, which buys electricity from a local municipal electric company, is considering seeking alternative suppliers due to high rates. The issue is whether the university is a wholesale entity that could force utilities to wheel power under the Energy Policy Act. Although one university official says the officials are only trying to understand changes in the electricity market, some sources indicate that this initiative may trigger a retail wheeling investigation in the state.

Vermont

As scheduled, the Vermont Public Service Board (PSB) staff has issued a report that was intended to resolve the differences in principles on retail wheeling between the major stakeholders in the state. On November 21, 1995, the PSB issued a specific schedule under which state utilities, end-user groups, and other interested parties were to submit a collaborative restructuring proposal. After a series of scheduled negotiation sessions, the PSB was to issue a report that would rule on those issues to which the parties could not agree so that by May 15 specific plans can be submitted by each state utility. However, the April report still leaves open the key issue that Vermonters were unable to resolve: stranded cost recovery. The PSB wants to achieve a restructured industry in place by the end of 1997 so as to coincide with similar restructuring efforts in other New England states.

In its comments on industry restructuring, Green Mountain Power endorsed retail competition and proposed a unique method for evaluating stranded costs. In addition to the usual provisions for direct access for all customer classes, the proposal suggests an "auction" for all generation facilities and power supply contracts as a means for setting the difference between market and book value. The proposal agrees with the restructuring principles created by the PSB working group discussed below.

On September 17, 1995, Vermont Governor Howard Dean announced new initiatives to bring competition to the state's electricity industry by the end of 1997. First, the legislature will be asked to approve a set of principles outlining the restructuring and to address the stranded investment issue. Second, the PSB has opened a formal docket to investigate retail wheeling and competition. Under this proposal, each utility will have to file a plan to the PSB by May 1996 that outlines how competition will be introduced to its company. Much of this action was spurred by the inability of the PSB's working group (see below) to agree on a set of restructuring principles.

On July 17, 1995, a working group created by the PSB in December 1994 issued a list of 14 principles for restructuring the electricity industry. The principles were very similar to those developed in Connecticut, Massachusetts, and Rhode Island. Unlike those states, however, not all stakeholders have agreed to all the principles. A group of end-users has opposed the use of a non-bypassable service charge to recover stranded investment and renewable resource charges during the transition period. Therefore, the group issued two reports that will be identical except for this provision.

While the PSB is now aggressively pursuing retail access, it once had a markedly opposite approach to competition. In 1994, a Vermont utility was fined by the PSB for arranging a voluntary transaction between a customer and another supplier without prior approval. The PSB claimed that the transaction bore "some resemblance" to retail wheeling, with which it found numerous dangers.

Virginia

American Electric Power, which has retail customer load in Virginia, issued a position statement on October 26, 1995, favoring retail competition and direct access in the region it serves. Full discussion of this proposal is in the Ohio section of this report.

On September 18, 1995, the Virginia State Corporation Commission initiated a formal investigation into retail wheeling and competition in general. As with similar efforts in other states, the investigation will look at all facets of restructuring, including stranded investment.

Washington

On May 24, 1996, Puget Sound Power & Light joined Washington Water Power (see below) in the sudden rush to embrace retail wheeling in the state. In a filing to the Washington Utilities and Transportation Commission (UTC),

Puget offered to allow customers with more than 2.4 MW of load to access competitive suppliers if the UTC approves its proposed merger with Washington Energy Company All other customers would be phased into the program over five years, but stranded cost recovery would be spread over 10 years. Once the merger is consummated, the utility plans to convene a users group that will develop a retail wheeling implementation plan, and the utility plans to support legislative changes necessary to accommodate the proposal.

Spokane-based Washington Water Power (WWP) announced a plan on May 6, 1996, to allow its 30 largest customers in Washington and Idaho to access competitive power supplies for up to one-third of the existing load. In its filing to the UTC, WWP proposes a two-year program in which a specific tariff rate is used to cover all costs besides energy and transmission. The program is scheduled to start in September 1996 if approved.

On December 13, 1995, the UTC issued a set of guiding principles in response to a year-long inquiry into competition in electricity. While the UTC supports customer choice and unbundling in principle, it adopted a "go-slow" approach to retail competition citing risks to small customers and social programs. Therefore, rather than lead the drive toward competition, it will watch developments in other states. In 1996, the UTC will begin investigating the steps required to implement its principles, including gradual movement toward retail wheeling and stranded cost recovery.

The state of Washington was one of only a few regulatory regions that, in a survey, said it does not allow negotiated rates between utilities and end-users. Hawaii, Washington, and the District of Columbia were the only states that claim that they do not allow special contracts.

West Virginia

American Electric Power (AEP), which has retail customer load in West Virginia, issued a position statement on October 26, 1995, favoring retail competition and direct access in the region it serves. Full discussion of this proposal is in the Ohio section of this report.

The Public Service Commission (PSC) threatened retail wheeling as a "radical" alternative to Wheeling Power's refusal to offer industrial customers a reasonable interruptible rate. The PSC staff thinks this is a credible threat to AEP, the parent company.

PSC Chair Boyce Griffith likened retail wheeling to death and taxes, with respect to inevitability, of course. He also said, however, that retail wheeling's approach will be at glacial speeds unless the state legislature takes action or allows the PSC to do so.

Wisconsin

Sensing a slowdown in retail wheeling developments in a state that lead the pack for a brief time, a coalition of industrial and commercial end-users, utilities, and independent power producers has formed to put Wisconsin back on track. The Coalition for Competition in Electricity has developed a list of basic competition principles and plans to accelerate the proceedings at the Wisconsin Public Service Commission (PSC).

On December 19, 1995, the PSC approved a plan to introduce retail competition by the year 2000, if certain market conditions are set. The plan, which was developed by PSC Chairman Scott Neitzel, implements a 32-step process that phases in competition over five years. The plan is seen as a compromise between one group of stakeholders wanting rapid reregulation [mostly the large investor-owned utilities (IOUs) and industrial users groups] and those wanting to go slow (one utility and public power groups). The plan calls for resolution of key issues such as open access transmission, creation of an ISO, the risk of exporting low-cost power generated in Wisconsin, reliability, affiliate dealing, and social programs. A final report is being prepared for the legislature.

The state legislature announced that it would not consider any retail wheeling proposal from the PSC until early 1997 to ensure that both sides of the debate take the time to "get it right." While the retail wheeling opponents claimed victory, so did the proponents noting that this timeframe matches theirs for developing an overall package. Development on the retail wheeling proposal will continue at the Commission, but direct access opponents claim that this move indicates a lack of public support for retail competition in Wisconsin.

A draft environmental impact statement prepared by the PSC as part of its inquiry claims that while overall retail prices under a competitive structure may be lower initially, eventually prices will rise due to a shortage of low-cost generation.

The Ho Chunk Indian nation, located near Madison, claims that it has the right to retail wheel because it is a sovereign nation not subject to the laws of the state. As a result, it chose Wisconsin Power & Light to feed its new 900-kW casino, but Madison Gas & Electric, the native supplier, is challenging the action.

Emotions are running high in Wisconsin as numerous issues are dividing the state's IOUs. Besides arguments over the timing of retail wheeling and the Ho Chunk situation (see above), merger proposals involving most of the state's major utilities are keeping utility spokespersons busy. Recently, the utilities have involved the public through a series of advertisements making their claim. A typical ad is one run by Madison Gas & Electric, an opponent of reregulation, with a picture of a large pig (industrials and the other utilities) that says, "under 'customer choice' we big guys get all the electricity at prices we want and you get what's left over."

Wyoming

The Wyoming Public Service Commission held a retail wheeling video teleconference seminar and collaborative workshop on October 11, 1994.

A strong interest in the economic benefits of retail wheeling and exporting power has been demonstrated by state legislators. Retail wheeling may be on the next legislative agenda.

Federal Programs

While retail wheeling has been a state issue since the passage of the Energy Policy Act of 1992, federal interest continues to heat up. The Senate Energy and Natural Resources Committee opened a series of hearings on electric industry restructuring in March 1996. The focus of the hearings appears to be jurisdiction, although the committee will also review recently proposed federal legislation (see below).

The executive branch has also entered the discussion on federal retail wheeling legislation. Deputy Energy Secretary Charles Curtis has indicated that the Clinton administration is working on a comprehensive electricity industry restructuring bill that would bring full retail competition to all states. Unfortunately, Curtis refused to divulge any details.

At least three Congressional representatives have introduced restructuring legislation recently, and the interest in retail wheeling exists on both sides of the aisle. While reaction to these bills has followed expected stakeholder lines, serious Congressional consideration is not expected this year given the range of other issues facing Congress during an election year.

Senator J. Bennett Johnston (D-La.) introduced a comprehensive electricity industry restructuring bill on January 25, 1996, that would implement retail wheeling nation-wide by 2010. In addition to repealing the Public Utility Holding Company Act and the Public Utility Regulatory Policies Act, the law would give explicit state authority for implementing retail wheeling. The proposed bill also allows the states to developed their own stranded cost recovery rules; however, if necessary, the federal government would step in to force direct access and address stranded investment in the absence of a state program.

Representative Dan Schaefer (R-Colo.) and Chairman of the House Commerce energy and power subcommittee, has announced that he plans to introduce legislation that will address retail wheeling and stranded costs. While details are not available, Schaefer has said that he is strongly in favor of competition down to the retail level. Schaefer is unclear as to whether federally mandated retail wheeling is necessary or if federal law is only required to remove the barriers to programs implemented on a state level. In any case, such legislation would be a comprehensive package that would address PUHCA and PURPA as well.

Representative Ed Markey (D-Mass.) has introduced legislation that claims to have bipartisan support, including that from Schaefer. While leaving restructuring details to the states, Markey's "Electric Power Competition Act of 1996" would create federal standards for generation divestiture, unbundling, open-access transmission, and retail direct access. Stranded investment recovery would be allowed under a non-bypassable wires charge that would also fund social programs. Once the states and FERC certify that competition exists, then PUHCA and PURPA would be repealed.

Recently passed federal defense legislation includes language that will allow Department of Defense (DOD) loads to competitively procure electricity. Intense lobbying efforts by utility groups to oppose this measure are under way, but the language merely removes a special exception to a 1984 law that requires all Pentagon expenditures to be based on competitive sourcing. The new bill notes that the DOD spends $2 billion per year on electricity and that competitive sourcing may reduce these expenditures by 20%. Many of the DOD's supplier utilities have now expressed an interest in negotiating special supply contracts for these facilities rather than face precedent-setting enabling legislation. As a result, the provision will probably be dropped in favor of working with FERC to find ways for military facilities to wheel power as wholesale buyers under existing law.

As part of a settlement agreement between the Bonneville Power Administration (BPA) and some of its industrial end-user customers, those customers are now free to leave the BPA and shop for power from outside suppliers. The end-users, known as Direct Service Industrials, have specific statutory authority to purchase power from the BPA even though it is a form of retail wheeling, because they are often interconnected to local distribution companies. Although they are now free to purchase power elsewhere, only one company has attempted to do so given the low cost power provided by BPA.

The Chair of the Tennessee Valley Authority (TVA) has unveiled a surprisingly bold initiative to "bring down the fence" that surrounds the TVA's service territory. An investigation has been undertaken that will consider allowing the TVA to serve customers outside its federally mandated service area and similarly allow other suppliers to compete for existing TVA load. The investigation should result in proposed legislation to enable the plan. A parallel issue that is receiving considerable attention is whether the TVA should be privatized, especially considering this proposed open-access plan.

The Western Area Power which sells its hydro power to 148 end-users (all federal, state, or local governmental agencies, e.g., hospitals, universities, military bases, irrigation and water districts, etc.), wheeled more than 48 transmission companies in 12 western states. The authority for this action is in the federal statutes that created this agency and is apparently outside FERC or state Public Utilities Commission jurisdiction. These statutes require utilities to wheel to "preferred" users, which is intended to be government-related loads; however, there have been disputes over what that term includes, e.g., a public transit system.

Canada

A municipal electric company in *New Brunswick* has begun a search for a new wholesale supplier for bulk power as an alternative to New Brunswick Power. Unlike in the U.S., however, this type of wholesale wheeling may not yet be legal. Nonetheless, the municipal utility says that Canada must begin to restructure its industry along the lines of its southern neighbor.

Ontario Hydro introduced a new proposal to phase in full retail competition from 1997 through 2000. In a report entitled "Competition, Convergence, and Customer Choice," or the "4C" report, Ontario Hydro suggests full unbundling and direct access for all customer classes by 2000 without the privatization of the utility, which is a crown corporation. The plan includes breaking up Ontario Hydro into separate generation, transmission, and retail distribution companies following the privatization of the utility. This proposal follows previous statements supporting retail wheeling in principle.

In *Alberta*, the Department of Energy has adopted a four-part electricity industry restructuring plan that includes wholesale wheeling, creation of a spot market, disintegration of the provincial utilities, and incentive ratemaking. Retail wheeling, however, was pushed out into the future but was not ruled out. The mandatory wholesale "poolco" began operation on January 1, 1996, and all suppliers are required to sell into the pool while all distributors must buy from it. The plan includes a "side market for bilateral hedging contracts" that will supposedly replace the need for direct access.

The government of *British Columbia*, (B.C.) has asked the B.C. Utilities Commission to examine the potential for retail wheeling and unbundled services. This inquiry is in response to pressure from both industrials and B.C. Hydro, which stands to benefit from open access due to its low rates.

Even *Quebec* is beginning to think about change, although competition still seems far off. A recently issued report that followed a year-long roundtable discussion opposes any change but has sparked the debate over issues such as privatization and the economic health of Hydro Quebec, the province's crown corporation. The furthest that the roundtable would recommend is the implementation of integrated resource planning.

Bibliography

102d Congress 2d Session, *Energy Policy Act of 1992, Conference Report: Title VII-Electricity*. Washington, D.C.: House of Representatives, 1992.

Bayless, Charles E., "The Market Transition: Is FERC Pricing Policy on the Wrong Side of the Road?" *Public Utilities Fortnightly*, February 15, 1995, pp. 21-25.

Destec Power Services, Inc. and Pacific Gas and Electric Company, "Control Area and Transmission Service Agreement." December 5, 1994.

Dudley, William M., *Electric Power Purchasing*. New York: Reid & Priest, 1993.

Edison Electric Institute, *Services Associated with the Provision of Transmission Services*, June 1993.

Federal Energy Regulatory Commission, "Inquiry Concerning Alternative Power Pooling Institutions Under the Federal Power Act." *Federal Register*, Vol. 58, No. 194, October 8, 1993, pp. 52420-52438.

Federal Energy Regulatory Commission, "Subchapter K-Regulations Under the Public Utility Regulatory Policies Act of 1978." 18 C.F.R. § 290 et seq. (1993).

Gale, Roger W., *The 1995 Electric Industry Outlook*. Washington, D.C.: Washington International Energy Group, 1995.

Harty, Fred R., Jr., "Options in Energy Storage." *Electricity Journal*, July/August 1994, pp. 21-26.

Hyman, Leonard S., *America's Electric Utilities: Past, Present and Future, Fifth Edition*. Arlington: Public Utilities Reports, Inc., 1994.

Illinois Power Company and Illinois Municipal Electric Agency, "Coordination and Interchange Agreement." January 10, 1994.

Leach, Bradford G. et al, "Letter Regarding Outstanding Electricity Futures Contract Issues." January 20, 1995.

Makovich, Larry, "1993 Forecast: The Electric Power Industry 2010." *Electrical World*, November 1993, pp. 17-24.

Maize, Kennedy P., "The Alberta Approach to Electric Utility Restructuring Embraces Real Grid Access." *Electricity Journal*, March 1995.

Merrill, Hyde M., *Transmission Access and Power Wheeling*. Schenectady: Power Technologies, Inc., 1989.

Miller, Robert H., *Power System Operation*. New York: McGraw-Hill, 1994.

Moody, Diane, "U.S. Electric Utility Generating Capacity Is Aging." *Public Power*, January/February 1994, pp. 24-25.

Moore, Taylor, "Storing Megawatthours with SMES." EPRI *Journal*, July/August 1994, pp. 24-33.

North American Electric Reliability Counsel, "Reliability Assessment 1994-2003: The Reliability of Bulk Electric Systems in North America," September 1994.

North American Electric Reliability Counsel, "1995 Summer Assessment: Reliability of Bulk Electricity Supply June-September 1995," May 1995.

Penn, David W., *Change: The Old and New World of Competition*. Washington, D.C.: American Public Power Association, 1994.

Rustebakke, Homer M., *Electric Utility Systems and Practices*. New York: Wiley-Interscience, 1983.

Sammut, A., "Ancillary Services: An Overview." *Detroit Edison*, January 28, 1994.

Santa, Donald F., Jr., *Lessons from the Natural Gas Restructuring: Are They Applicable to Electric Policy?* Oklahoma: Federal Energy Regulatory Commission, 1994.

Scarfone, Allen, "Short-Circuit Simulations Help Quantify Wheeling Flow." IEEE *Computer Applications in Power*, Vol. 8, No. 2, April 1995, 44-47.

Spiewak, Scott, "Electricity Rate Swaps." Cogen, September/October 1993, pp. 6-11.

Spiewak, Scott, "Uses of Options in Electric Power Marketing." *Cogen*, Spring 1994, pp. 6-16.

Stojka, John P., "Automating the Next-Hour Energy Market." *Public Utilities Fortnightly*, November 1, 1994, pp. 22-25.

Taylor, Loren L., "Pricing of Unbundled Services." *Northern States Power Company*, December 2-3, 1993.

Taylor, Paula, "Spinning Reserve in Puerto Rico Doesn't Spin—It's a Battery."

Electrical World, April 1995, pp. 42-44.

Tessmer, Raymond G., *Project Considerations and Design of Systems for Wheeling Cogenerated Power*. Chattanooga: TBFM Enterprises, 1994.

Weiss, Larry, *The Wheeling and Transmission Manual*. Lilburn: Prentice-Hall, Inc., 1991.

Index

O

P

Q

R

S